Georgia in Black and White

Georgia in Black and White

Explorations in the Race Relations
of a Southern State,
1865–1950

Edited by John C. Inscoe

The University of Georgia Press
Athens & London

Designed by Kathi L. Dailey
Set in Ehrhardt by Tseng Information Systems, Inc.
Printed and bound by Princeton Academic Press, Inc.
The paper in this book meets the guidelines for permanence
and durability of the Committee on Production Guidelines
for Book Longevity of the Council on Library Resources.

Printed in the United States of America

98   97   96   95   94   C   5   4   3   2   1

Library of Congress Cataloging in Publication Data

Georgia in Black and white : explorations in the race
relations of a southern state, 1865–1950 / edited by
John C. Inscoe.
p.   cm.
Includes bibliographical references and index.
ISBN 0-8203-1620-2 (alk. paper)
1. Afro-Americans—Georgia—History.   2. Georgia—Race
relations.   I. Inscoe, John C., 1951–
E185.93.G4G46   1994
975.8′00496073—dc20   93-29650

British Library Cataloging in Publication Data available

Russell Duncan's essay is drawn from *Entrepreneur for Equality:
Governor Rufus Bullock, Commerce, and Race in Post–Civil
War Georgia* (Athens: University of Georgia Press, 1994) and
appears here with permission of the press.

Glenn T. Eskew's essay first appeared in the *Journal of Southern
History* 58 (November 1992): 637–66 and is reprinted here with
the journal's permission.

Andrew S. Chancey's essay is a revised version of an article that
appeared in the *Georgia Historical Quarterly* 75 (Summer 1991):
321–53 and appears here with the permission of the journal.

Contents

Foreword

Numan V. Bartley

In his classic study published in 1944, Gunnar Myrdal described race relations as the "American Dilemma." No other issue so clearly portrayed the contradiction between rhetoric and practice. Although Americans proclaimed their commitment to such national ideals as liberty, justice, and equality of opportunity, they rarely practiced such precepts in the field of race relations. The conflict between what Myrdal termed the "American Creed" and the "Negro problem" stirred among some whites guilt and anxiety and among many blacks disillusionment and despair.

Myrdal was certainly not alone in noting the centrality of race relations. In the early years of the Republic, Thomas Jefferson anguished over the conundrums embedded in the nation's racial institutions and practices. European visitors to the United States frequently agreed with Alexis de Tocqueville that the "danger of a conflict between the white and the black inhabitants perpetually haunts the imagination of the Americans, like a painful dream." From Frederick Douglass to Martin Luther King, Jr., black Americans searched for solutions to the nation's "dilemma." In the late 1960s the National Advisory Commission on Civil Disorders lamented that trends in American race relations threatened the nation's core democratic values.

Nowhere else of course were such matters so relevant than in the United States South. Huge numbers of historians and social commentators have explicitly or implicitly agreed with Ulrich B. Phillips that race relations was "the central theme of Southern history." Visiting Atlanta in the early twentieth century, journalist Ray Stannard Baker observed that among whites "the Negro in the South is both the labour problem and the servant question; he is preeminently the political issue, and his place, socially, is of daily and hourly discussion." Among black southerners the issue was "sort of life and death with us." Throughout regional society, Baker discerned, "the South is overwhelmingly concerned in this one thing."

To be sure it is easy to oversimplify the issue of race. Racial matters have often served as a substitute for class conflict, deflecting legitimate economic grievances into ethnic hostilities. Race has not infrequently acted as a focal point for broader popular concern with cultural change. Race has been deeply intertwined with gender, and it is hardly surprising that changes in race relations have often resulted in social changes relating to gender. The endlessly reiterated argument by white racists that social equality would lead to intermarriage was only the most obvious example of the close association between sex and race. Clearly, relations between blacks and whites have varied as a result of time, place, and social and economic circumstance.

The essays in this volume demonstrate an acute consciousness of the varieties of race relations. The authors were at the time they composed the essays graduate students at the University of Georgia. They would probably not describe themselves as specialists in Georgia history, but all have an abiding interest in race relations and southern society. Georgia proved to be an extremely fertile ground for exploring basic issues in southern race relations. Why people have been treated so differently because of the color of their skin remains highly debatable, but as Thomas Jefferson once observed, the difference "is as real as if its seat and cause were better known to us." These essays examine the complexities of the issue and offer perceptive insights on race relations and southern and Georgia history.

The excellence of the essays provides more than an adequate explanation for the appearance of this volume, but Professor John C. Inscoe, a faculty member in the department of history at the University of Georgia and the editor of the *Georgia Historical Quarterly,* provided its inspiration. The only contribution I can claim is that I had the opportunity to work with the authors while they were students, and for that I am appreciative.

Georgia in Black and White

Introduction

John C. Inscoe

"Georgia is beautiful," wrote W. E. B. Du Bois in *The Nation* in 1925. "Yet on its beauty rests something disturbing and strange. . . . There lies a certain brooding on the land—there is something furtive, uncanny, at times almost a horror." Racial hatred was at the core of this rather ominous description of Georgia's "spiritual gloom" by the man who was then America's most prominent black spokesman. Returning to the state and the South a decade and a half after completing a thirteen-year stint at Atlanta University, Du Bois sought to explain the racial realities of the southern state he had come to know most intimately to a predominantly white, nonsouthern readership. Such realities were not as obvious as many observers assumed, however, and Du Bois acknowledged the inscrutability of much about how southern whites and blacks interacted. "There is a certain secrecy about this world," he wrote. "Nobody seems wholy frank—neither white nor black; neither child, woman, nor man . . . behind all are the grim bars and barriers; subjects that must not be touched, opinions that must not be questioned." [1]

Yet what makes that 1925 essay so intriguing is that, far more than most of his contemporary chroniclers of the American South, Du Bois seemed to penetrate many of those inscrutable barriers he described, and in so doing, provided an unusually insightful, and even dispassionate, analysis of the complexities of southern race relations. Although it remained first and foremost a forceful indictment of the evils inherent in the state's white supremacist regime (he titled the piece "Georgia: Invisible Empire State"), Du Bois's assessment moved beyond the obvious injustices of what he had earlier labeled "the color line" to examine the variations, contradictions, and exceptions that made that line far less rigid or absolute than he had earlier implied.[2] He confronted a wide range of topics: the exploitation of white labor; the machinations of political demagoguery; new signs of racial tolerance in certain urban and college campus settings; even the liberal guilt, though much sup-pressed, of certain "forward-thinking" white Georgians—all demonstrated the variables that made southern race relations so complex and multifaceted. In effect, he suggested, with cautious optimism, that there were cracks in the armor of Jim Crow.

Few of Du Bois's contemporaries acknowledged this sort of fluidity in dealing with matters of race in the South. The most influential of southern commentators failed to recognize, or chose to ignore, the subtle shadings that permeated the biracial society in which they lived. From Thomas Dixon and U. B. Phillips to W. J. Cash and Lillian Smith, southern voices, as both de-fenders and critics of the racist regime in which they were raised, conveyed to nonsouthern readerships its distinctive nature in far more monolithic and rigidly defined terms, which gave little credence to evidence of deviation, ambiguity, or exception in the racial status quo to which Du Bois was so sensitized. To Smith, who condemned that social order more eloquently and unequivocally than any other white native of the region, the idea of segrega-tion had "become so hypnotic a thing that it binds a whole people together, good, bad, strong, weak, ignorant and learned, sensitive, obtuse, psychotic and sane, making them one as only a common worship or a deeply shared fear can do." [3]

Nor did Cash, so perceptive about so much concerning the southern past, ever acknowledge any variation in its Jim Crow mindset. A recent assess-ment of the North Carolina journalist's depiction of race in *The Mind of the South* suggested that he "could only grope searchingly, dragging a rigid white supremacy awkwardly up through time, bumping and jerking it across the hard places of history like some stiff mannequin, toward historical realities his society had chosen to forget and moreover, worked diligently to prevent his recalling." [4] That myopic vision in regard to race is equally characteristic of earlier—and even of later—generations of regional observers.

But historians are at long last expanding that field of vision in dealing with southern race relations, and in so doing are discovering, as Du Bois did, far more intricate and nuanced interactions that operated within, or in spite of, the all-too-readily apparent "color line." Joel Williamson, one of the most insightful of these revisionists, noted in 1984 that while historians have been providing a vast array of work on slavery and the Old South for well over sixty years, it has only been in the last generation or so that post-Reconstruction race relations have begun to attract the same sort of scholarly scrutiny. Yet Williamson claimed that, with the exception of C. Vann Wood-ward's *The Strange Career of Jim Crow*, "the printed literature springing from that movement remains relatively thin, both in narrow factual studies and in broad interpretative works." [5]

Indeed, the 1960s and 1970s did see an outpouring of scholarship on slavery, the depth and breadth of which are only recently being matched in treatments of post-emancipation race relations. In the decade since William-son's assessment, any perceived void has been rapidly filled with work that has effectively challenged the earlier assumptions of Cash, Smith, and others as to the rigidity and perpetuity of the racial order of the pre–Civil Rights South.[6] At the same time, historians are looking beyond the more obvious issues of segregation, disfranchisement, lynchings, and race riots to dis-cover—as did Du Bois—less conspicuous, but no less significant, manifes-tations of how southerners of both races interacted with each other in the age of Jim Crow.

This volume is itself a reflection of that trend. By juxtaposing a variety of depictions of how black and white Georgians challenged the social, politi-cal, and legal system of white supremacy, the vast spectrum over which the dynamics of race have been played out within the bounds of a single state becomes apparent. Despite the perception of a regime of deeply entrenched and rigidly enforced racial repression, we can still be struck by the range of individuals and groups that defied the regime and the diversity of venues through which such challenges were posed. Those are the stories told here. If the circumstances and settings are often familiar, these essays provide fresh twists, new insights, and alternative interpretations of the actions and re-actions of the men and women involved in these struggles for racial justice and reform.

Before the implementation of Jim Crow, such variation was of course less surprising; indeed it was the very crux of the Reconstruction process, when unprecedented change and opportunity redefined the very essence of the South's social, economic, and political structure. Several essays deal with that volatile period and offer new perspectives on the degree of empowerment of both African Americans in the wake of emancipation and of the white men in positions of political and religious authority who championed their cause.

Jonathan Bryant discovers unusual militance and surprising resilience among politicized freedmen in postbellum Greene County. Focusing on the efforts of Abram Colby, the county's most influential black leader, Bryant ar-gues that the legal system, always central to the freedmen's hopes for political equality and economic justice, ultimately worked in conjunction with vio-lence and other forms of white intimidation to render most of their efforts futile.

Colby was among the thirty-one African Americans expelled from the Georgia state legislature in the infamous act of defiance by that body's con-servative majority in 1868. Russell Duncan offers another perspective on that incident by examining the role of perhaps its most central player, the state's only Republican governor, Rufus Bullock. In a revisionist portrait of Bullock that refutes his reputation as a corrupt opportunist whose interest in the rights of black Georgians was superficial and vacillating, Duncan characterizes the governor's successful, if extreme, campaign to reinstate the ousted legislators as a courageous act of principle over political expediency.

Daniel Stowell provides a very different picture of interracial interaction in Reconstruction Georgia in his study of Methodist Episcopal ministers and laymen in the state and their struggle for nearly a decade after the Civil War to unite black and white Methodists. Despite initial success in their organizational efforts, their vision of a biracial denomination was ultimately doomed. While Stowell fully analyzes the multiple factors that contributed to the breakdown of a united organization, his focus is on the extraordinary extent to which, for the first few postwar years, ministers and congregations of both races worked and worshipped together.

As a radically reformulated era in southern race relations, Reconstruction in Georgia, as elsewhere in the former Confederacy, was characterized by experimentation, opportunism, and idealism. It was exceptional both in the variety and the intensity of activity and optimism among newly freed African Americans as they sought to carve their niches in the new southern order imposed and presided over by a victorious North. Yet, as other essays reveal, the raised consciousness and assertiveness of those black men and women, both individually and as groups, did not end with Reconstruction and the collapse of federal protection and authority. Jennifer Lund Smith and Glenn Eskew deal in very different ways with the beneficiaries of one of the more enduring legacies of Reconstruction—the higher education of blacks. As college graduates and college educators, Georgia's freed men and women impacted race relations in the state long after Redeemers blunted the great promise of the postwar years.

Smith documents one of the unheralded success stories among late nineteenth-century African Americans: the achievements of Atlanta University's female graduates as teachers and social activists in Atlanta and elsewhere in the state. She documents the ways in which their own college experiences instilled in these women a sense of mission to their black communities inspired both by the northern, bourgeois values derived from their American Missionary Association training and by self-generated racial pride.

Eskew examines the extraordinary career of Lucius Henry Holsey, a Methodist Episcopal bishop and founder of Paine College in Augusta, whose racial philosophy underwent some dramatic and unorthodox shifts. Holsey, the protégé of one of Stowell's "religious scalawags," Bishop George F. Pierce, adhered to an elitist stance that embraced the white planter hegemony and accepted the subservience of most blacks to a privileged few. Only with the new intensity of racist repression in the 1890s did Holsey discard his assumptions of intraracial hierarchy and advocate instead black nationalist ideals of racial solidarity and separatism.

Although Holsey ultimately retreated from his extremist views, black nationalism emerged again in the state soon after his death in 1920. Mary Rolinson reveals the astonishing extent to which Marcus Garvey's "Back to Africa" movement infiltrated rural Georgia during the 1920s. The broad appeal that poor southern African Americans found in this militant, Harlem-based Jamaican and his separatist message and their remarkable loyalty to both provide a striking indication of their economic and racial desperation, Rolinson concludes. That despair triggered what was in the end a short-lived sense of racial consciousness and collective identity that by the mid 1920s proved more threatening to rival black organizations, particularly the NAACP, than to southern white conservatives.

Two entries stand apart in the unique angles from which they approach issues of racial interaction and attitudes. Mark Schultz examines a far more private and thus historically elusive aspect of southern race relations—the long-term economic effects of miscegenation. In particular, Schultz traces the ancestry of black land-holding families in Hancock County (a county whose history is already among the state's most scrutinized) and documents the extent to which a white planter ancestry proved a key determinant to their middle-class status. Through a variety of individuals and families, Schultz reconstructs the means by which multigenerational interracial kinship ties served as conduits of wealth across the color line.

Elizabeth Hale places the issue of gender and generational distinctions at the center of her exploration of white racial attitudes through contrasting portraits of two accomplished Athens women who expounded very different ideas about their region, their society, and the defining role of race in both. Hale offers astute analyses of Mildred Rutherford, the visible and vocal historian-general of the United Daughters of the Confederacy, and of artist Lucy Stanton, whose portraits of black and white Athenians reflected far more sensitivity to racial issues and doubts about the legitimacy of white supremacy.

Finally, three essays approach the mid twentieth century with graphic indications that neither the vehemence of racist repression nor the idealism and vision of its opponents were lacking during the waning days of Jim Crow. From both of these extremes, the actions in the 1940s described in these pieces echoed the legacy of the first Reconstruction and at the same time foreshadowed the second Reconstruction less than a decade ahead.

Randall Patton examines the internal dynamics and external pressures that made the decade-long existence of the Southern Conference on Human Welfare such a turbulent one, noting that its demise was in effect a reflection of the fragmentation of southern liberalism during and after the Second World War. Focusing on the leadership of the organization's last president, Atlantan Clark Foreman, Patton reveals how his efforts toward achieving social and economic justice for black and white workers were all but lost amid the divisiveness and competing priorities of other SCHW factions.

Andrew Chancey demonstrates how the similar but more single-minded goals of two Baptist ministers, Clarence Jordan and Martin England, came to fruition in a very different form. Their vision of a social gospel mission applied to agricultural reform led to the creation of a communal farm in the heart of south Georgia's black belt, the interracial makeup of which posed unique challenges to Sumter County residents and to the participants of this "demonstration plot for the Kingdom of God."

The collection concludes with the only essay that focuses on the perpetrators of racial violence. Wallace Warren assesses one of the state's last and most unusual lynchings—the brutal murder of two black couples in Walton County in 1946. Warren sees in this crime significant deviations from the well-established patterns of southern lynching, and he argues that such deviation reflected the uncertainty of social and economic changes underway throughout the post–World War II South, in this case the first political primary in which black voters participated. The variety of responses to the lynching by different classes and both races offers insights into the collective mood of the South on the eve of far greater regional transformation and racial upheaval.

Barbara Fields has warned us of the dangers of according race "a transhistorical, almost metaphysical, status," noting that "ideas about color, like ideas about anything else, derive their importance, indeed their very definition, from their context."[7] The sheer variety of ways in which the racial struggles depicted here manifested themselves reminds us that neither racial ideology nor the racial interaction based on that ideology existed in a vacuum but were subject to the exigencies of locale, of community, of time period, and of human nature. These essayists have been sensitive to these particularities, setting their subjects firmly within the context of specific situations and addressing their attitudes, beliefs, motives, goals, methods, and ultimate achievements as functions of those specifics.

These essays also highlight the extent to which personal variables were often vital to the directions taken by individuals, black and white. Booker T.

Washington once commented after a tour of South Carolina that he always encountered "at least one white man who believed implicitly in one Negro and one Negro who believed implicitly in one white man; and so it goes all through the South."[8] Such relationships and personalities cannot be discounted in evaluating the solidarity of the Jim Crow South. More often than not, those contacts were crucial in shaping the direction taken by the activists portrayed here. Abram Colby's postwar leadership was very much a function of the pre-emancipation opportunities made available to him by both his white father and a later owner. Lucius Holsey's ministerial career and racial philosophy owed much to his white mentor and benefactor, George Pierce. Lucy Stanton's black acquaintances and servants provided a very tangible means for conveying her own racial sentiments through her art. And the long-term and intensely private kinship linkages between Hancock County whites and blacks account for the relative prosperity and social status achieved by the latter over several generations.

Such contacts suggest other variables as well. Southern white liberals, by their very exceptionalism, have formed one very visible end of a vast ideological and moral spectrum, the opposite end of which consisted of equally conspicuous racist extremism. A number of the essays here suggest that southern blacks also demonstrated a broader and more subtle ideological range than that suggested by the familiar Washington–Du Bois polarity. Black conservative voices—from the younger Holsey to the Atlanta University community—were as significant in the state as the more radical African-American activists from Reconstruction to Garveyism. Such variations raise the question of how much of the public rhetoric of both blacks and whites was mere posturing or role-playing: that is, to what extent did certain individuals conform to societal expectations without betraying their true (and sometimes quite different) convictions? Only through a full appreciation of the times and the situations in which these men and women acted can we measure, as the authors here often attempt to do, the depth and sincerity of their motives and principles.

These essays, when viewed as a whole, also suggest the importance of chronological context. On the assumption that black life in the Jim Crow South was static and unchanging, North Carolina black novelist Mary Mebane once commented that "stasis becomes a problem for the writer" documenting the southern black experience "when change, no matter how slight, is introduced into the picture. . . . How much significance does it have in the way [a writer] sees black folk and in the way black folk see themselves, the world, and their role in it?"[9] These essayists have been sensitive to the impact of change, however minor, and in case after case have demonstrated

the degree to which subtle shifts—in either political realities, community
dynamics, or personal relationships—triggered race-related responses, both
positive and negative.

Yet in the midst of these almost infinite variables, certain continuities also
emerge across the eighty-odd years explored here. Though working through
different forums and against different sorts of odds, the commitment of Clark
Foreman to biracial economic justice in the 1940s was very much in the spirit
of Rufus Bullock's fight for freedmen's rights in the late 1860s. Likewise,
the ostensible goals of Foreman's Southern Conference on Human Welfare
resembled in many ways those of Abram Colby's Equal Rights Association.
The racial separatism espoused by the elderly Bishop Holsey at the turn of
the century and by rural Garveyists in the 1920s reemerged in yet another
form and with new meaning in its experimental realization at Koinonia farm
during and after the Second World War. By the same token, the biracial religious vision of Koinonia's Clarence Jordan and Martin England echoed that
of the Methodist Episcopal "scalawags" of Reconstruction. The racial violence that erupted in 1872 in Greene County and in 1946 in Walton County
was spurred in both cases, at least in part, by resentment over recent political
gains by local blacks, although those incidents could hardly have been more
different in almost every other respect.

Such parallels and comparisons seem almost endless; yet taken together,
these essays convey a continuum of struggle and resistance that extended
throughout the long, dark years of Jim Crow, and suggest that such activism
in the fight for racial justice was not merely an ongoing legacy of Reconstruction but a precursor of the Civil Rights movement as well.

The existence of such diversity of racial attitudes and behavior should
come as little surprise in the state that claimed spokesmen and activists as
varied as Joel Chandler Harris and Jean Toomer, Tom Watson and Rebecca
Felton, U. B. Phillips and Walter White, Lillian Smith and Lester Maddox,
Martin Luther King, Jr., and Jimmy Carter. This is not to underestimate the
formidable impact of racist dogma, ritual, and mores so deeply ingrained in
generation after generation of southern whites and blacks. The individuals
named above who were staunch defenders of that status quo were often the
loudest and most popular messengers among their fellow Georgians. To cite
again the eminently quotable (and in her own state, largely unheard) Lillian
Smith, she spoke of nearly all white southerners at mid century when she
stated that "we learned the intricate system of taboos, of renunciations and
compensations, of manners, voice modulations, words, feelings, along with
our prayers, our toilet habits, our games." [10]

Numerically, the challengers of so entrenched a system were insignificant,
and many of their challenges proved futile. Indeed, one must resist the urge

to equate the achievements of the various men and women portrayed in this volume as victories over that system. As admirable as their intentions, their spirits, and even their accomplishments were, few can ultimately be viewed as success stories.

It is sobering to realize that perhaps the most successful protagonists portrayed in this collection were the Walton County lynch mob and those who abetted them in the cover-up of their crime. In the wake of that atrocity, Lillian Smith wrote an extraordinary letter to the parents of the girls at her Laurel Hills summer camp in Rabun County. The campers were extremely upset about the lynching, she wrote, and "asked questions that are hard for a grown-up to answer." Among them were whether or not the two women victims had children; if so, who was caring for those orphans; how did they feel about living in America; and did they hate white people for what a few had done to their parents. Finally, these teenage white girls asked what they could do to help. This, Smith found, was the most challenging question of all. "I think the most heartbreaking and frustrating thing for all of us who feel decent inside ourselves is to know what to do." [11]

This was the challenge that faced most of those individuals and groups portrayed here who felt "decent inside themselves." After Reconstruction and before the Civil Rights movement, the opportunities and outlets for challenging racial injustice in the South were few and the effectiveness of their efforts often minimal. To varying degrees many, if not most, must have felt the helplessness that so tore at Lillian Smith and her campers, or that of Bishop Holsey, who toward the end of his career, admitted with despair: "I have always been impressed and understood from boyhood, that no matter . . . what social or political changes or upheavals might appear, the white man of the South would be on top." [12]

Almost all of these essays demonstrate the intensity and strength that those white men determined to keep themselves on top brought to their cause and the considerable resources they had at their disposal to do so. Yet more importantly, these essays testify to the myriad chinks in the armor of Jim Crow that allowed for challenges on a number of fronts, some of more significance than others. An artist in Athens, a Republican governor, Hancock County planters and their mulatto offspring, a black bishop and college president, a Greene County freedman and legislator, Garveyites throughout rural Georgia, two Baptist agrarian utopians, and an Atlanta economist—all defied those rituals, taboos, and norms in order to confront southern racism and oppression head on.

Du Bois concluded his 1925 assessment of Georgia's racial situation by describing the train trip that carried him north, out of Georgia, back home. "I am in the hot, crowded, and dirty Jim Crow car, where I belong," he wrote. In passing through the state's northern hills, he looked out the train window at the log cabins of poor mountain residents who peered back at him from their doors, "dead white faces and drawn, thin forms." Despite the bleak and still violent racial climate he was leaving behind him and would soon document so graphically for a national readership, he claimed that he departed the state rather optimistically: "Somehow it seems to me that here in the Jim Crow car and there in the mountain cabin lies the future of Georgia—in the intelligence and union of these laborers, white and black. . . . They hate and despise each other today. They lynch and murder body and soul. They are separated by the width of a world. And yet—and yet, stranger things have happened under the sun than understanding between those who are born blind." [13]

Such expectations by a black man coming out of the Deep South in the mid 1920s is remarkable and, at that stage in Jim Crow's tenure, perhaps unrealistic. The means through which such hopes were ultimately fulfilled belong largely to an era beyond the scope of this volume. Yet they were the very sort of challenges, exceptions, and variables documented in these essays that Du Bois himself seemed to have noticed as he toured the state and that inspired him to venture even so tentative a prediction of eventual biracial harmony in the South. Few of his contemporaries—including the very men and women generating the challenges Du Bois observed—were as optimistic as he about the future course of race relations. And it is only in recent years that we as historians are slowly coming to acknowledge and to assess the complexities and contradictions that allowed him to entertain the hopes he did.

This volume represents the work of graduate students in the history department at the University of Georgia produced over a three-year period. Drawn from dissertations, theses, and seminar papers, these essays are in large measure reflections of the training and guidance of two professors who have long wrestled, though in very different ways, with the complexities of southern and American race relations: Bud Bartley and Bill McFeely. Either one or the other, and in most cases both, of these scholars have had much to do with the questions these students have raised and with how they have gone about answering them. Emory Thomas, Jean Friedman, Eugene Genovese, Will Holmes, Lester Stephens, Bob Pratt, Peter Hoffer, and that most inimitable of emerti, Ben Wall, can also claim considerable input into the shaping of the ideas, the interests, and the output of many of the volume's contributors.

I can claim no credit for any of them or their work. It is only as editor of the *Georgia Historical Quarterly* that I have come to know and to appreciate the innovative work produced by so many of our graduate students and to encourage them to submit articles drawn from their work to the *Quarterly.* Four of the essays that appear here had already been accepted for future publication in the *Quarterly,* and I was in the process of recruiting several more when the inspiration for this volume hit in the form of an essay collection on nineteenth-century Virginia made up of the work of Edward Ayers's graduate students at the University of Virginia.[14] That impressive volume (on which this one is perhaps too blatantly modeled) posed a variety of challenges to the conventional wisdom about southern and Virginian society before and after the Civil War. As such, it reflected the new questions and fresh perspectives that are indicative of the best graduate student research and writing. We hope that these qualities are evident in this exploration of Georgia race relations as well.

The contributors and I are grateful to Jacqueline Jones and Edmund Drago, who assessed the volume for the press. Both gave the entire manuscript thorough and careful readings and provided each of us with substantive advice and valuable suggestions that we agree have much improved the final product. Our colleagues in the history department—both faculty and graduate students—were tremendously supportive of this project. Two departmental chairmen, John Morrow and David Roberts, both non-southern historians, provided more tangible support in the form of departmental funding for the book's production. The wit and wisdom of Tom Dyer enhanced this project, as they do so much of what I try to do.

I appreciate Malcolm Call's initial enthusiasm for the project, and as usual, found it a genuine pleasure to work with the University of Georgia Press editors and staff. Kim Cretors handled us and our work with tender, loving, and efficient care. Mark Pentecost proved a painstaking copyeditor and caught much that had slipped by the volume's nominal, and not always painstaking, editor. Finally, Sheree Dendy, the assistant editor of the *Quarterly,* lent the same editorial talents, organizational skills, and creative input to this project that she does to every issue of the *Quarterly,* for which we are all most grateful.

Notes

1. W. E. Burghardt Du Bois, "Georgia: Invisible Empire State," *The Nation* 120 (June 21, 1925): 63–67. The full text of Du Bois's essay is included in William F. Holmes, ed., *Struggling to Break the Chains of Tradition: Twentieth Century Georgia: A Documentary Collection* (Savannah, Ga.: Beehive Press, 1994). On Du Bois's years in Atlanta, see David Levering Lewis, *W. E. B. Du Bois: Biography of a Race, 1868–1919* (New York: Henry Holt, 1993), 211–387.

2. Du Bois's often-quoted statement, "The problem of the twentieth century is

the problem of the color-line . . ." opens the second chapter of *The Soul of Black Folk: Essays and Sketches* Chicago, 1903; reprint ed., New York: Signet, 1969), 54.

3. Lillian Smith, *Killers of the Dream*, rev. ed. (New York: W. W. Norton, 1961), 79.

4. Joel Williamson, *The Crucible of Race: Black-White Relations in the American South since Emancipation* (New York: Oxford University Press, 1984), 2. For other recent treatments of Cash and southern race relations, see C. Eric Lincoln, "Mind and Countermind: A Personal Perspective on W. J. Cash's *Mind of the South*"; and Nell Irvin Painter, "Race, Gender, and Class in *The Mind of the South:* Cash's Maps of Sexuality and Power," both in Paul D. Escott, ed., *W. J. Cash and the Minds of the South* (Baton Rouge: Louisiana State University Press, 1992), 226–42, 88–111; Bruce Clayton, "No Ordinary History: W. J. Cash's *The Mind of the South*," in Charles W. Eagles, ed., *The Mind of the South: Fifty Years Later* (Jackson: University of Mississippi Press, 1992), 16–21; and Clayton, "The Proto-Dorian Convention: W. J. Cash and the Race Question," in Jeffrey J. Crow, Paul D. Escott, and Charles L. Flynn, eds., *Race, Class, and Politics in Southern History: Essays in Honor of Robert F. Durden* (Baton Rouge: Louisiana State University Press, 1989), 287–313.

5. Williamson, *Crucible of Race*, viii.

6. Although it is now over half a decade out of date, the most comprehensive historiographic treatment of this scholarship remains Dan T. Carter, "From Segregation to Integration," in John B. Boles and Evelyn Thomas Nolen, eds., *Interpreting Southern History: Historiographical Essays in Honor of Sanford W. Higginbotham* (Baton Rouge: Louisiana State University Press, 1987), 408–33.

7. Barbara J. Fields, "Ideology and Race in American History," in J. Morgan Kousser and James M. McPherson, eds., *Region, Race, and Reconstruction: Essays in Honor of C. Vann Woodward* (New York: Oxford University Press, 1982), 144, 146.

8. Quoted in Thomas J. Woofter, Jr., *Negro Migration: Changes in Rural Organization and Population in the Cotton Belt* (New York: W. D. Gray, 1920), 53.

9. Mary E. Mebane, "Black Folk of the American South: Two Portraits," in Louis D. Rubin, Jr., ed., *The American South: Portrait of a Culture* (Baton Rouge: Louisiana State University Press, 1980), 87.

10. Smith, *Killers of the Dream*, 27–28.

11. Lillian Smith to parents of campers, mid summer 1946, in Margaret Rose Gladney, ed., *How Am I To Be Heard? Letters of Lillian Smith* (Chapel Hill: University of North Carolina Press, 1993), 106.

12. Quoted in Glenn T. Eskew's essay in this volume, p. 125.

13. Du Bois, "Georgia: Invisible Empire State," 67.

14. Edward L. Ayers and John C. Willis, eds., *The Edge of the South: Life in Nineteenth-Century Virginia* (Charlottesville: University Press of Virginia, 1991).

"We Have No Chance of Justice before the Courts"

The Freedmen's Struggle for Power in Greene County, Georgia, 1865–1874

Jonathan M. Bryant

At eleven o'clock on the night of October 29, 1869, two freedmen demanding help woke a detachment of federal soldiers in Greenesboro, Georgia. The Ku Kluxers, they said, had broken into Abram Colby's house, and they feared for his life. George Hoyt, commanding the troops, dressed and let the freedmen into his tent. At first he did not believe their story. Hoyt and his men had orders to protect the local freedmen's school teacher, who had been attacked by the Ku Klux Klan. He had heard nothing about threats to Abram Colby, a black leader and a member of the Georgia legislature. But, as Hoyt questioned the freedmen, he decided that they told the truth. Leaving three men to guard the camp, Hoyt and seven soldiers set out with the informants to rescue Abram Colby.[1]

When the Klansmen broke open the door of Abram Colby's house they found him in bed, asleep. A robed and masked Klansman put a pistol to Colby's head and demanded that he surrender. "Of course I surrender," he replied. After terrorizing Colby's family with their guns, the Klansmen took him deep into some nearby woods, stripped him, and began beating him systematically. Twenty-three men took turns whipping him until Dr. John E. Walker, one of the Klansmen, pronounced Abram Colby dead. Two men complained to Tom Robinson, their leader, "Captain, we have not struck him a lick." "Go on and lick him; he is a dead man," replied Robinson. After the two men beat Colby some more, the Klansmen mounted and rode away.[2]

Meanwhile, Hoyt's patrol had marched about half the distance to Abram Colby's house when they met Colby's brother. He told them that "it was all over." He had followed the Klansmen to the edge of the woods, heard the beating, his brother's screams, and then a gunshot. Abram Colby was dead, said the brother. Lieutenant Hoyt convinced the brother to show him the place, and the soldiers searched the woods for over an hour, finding no sign of Colby or the Klansmen. Exhausted, the soldiers finally returned to Greenesboro.[3]

But Abram Colby did not die that night. He later recalled lying on the ground, semiconscious, the beating having continued so long that he could no longer feel the blows. "Doctor Walker came up to feel my pulse," remembered Colby, "finding my wrist all wet and bloody, he did not feel my pulse, but said 'he is dead.'" After the Klansmen left, Colby managed to drag himself to a nearby cabin, whose inhabitants helped him. The next day Colby's brother took word to Lieutenant Hoyt that Abram survived the attack, and Hoyt visited Colby's hideout that afternoon. He found Colby in bed, unable to move, his back cut to shreds. "He was in very bad condition," reported Hoyt.[4]

The beating left Abram Colby with internal injuries and constant pain. It so injured his spine that he lost the use of his left hand and had difficulty rising from a bed. Despite these injuries, additional threats, and more attacks, Abram Colby continued to fight for justice as a leader of a militant and well organized black constituency. In December 1870, following an attempt to shoot him just days before the election, Colby won a second term in the Georgia House where he worked for legislation to help protect Georgia's freedpeople.[5]

Like Abram Colby, the African Americans of Greene County demonstrated enormous political durability in the face of great odds. Struggling against economic pressures, cultural impediments, threats, violence, and an oppressive legal system, Greene's freedpeople battled for justice and on occasion struck back at their oppressors. Though several recent works trace the extent and the impact of black people's politics during Reconstruction, few works adequately explore the role of the law and the legal system in those politics. In Greene County, and in much of Georgia, the development of political consciousness among the freedpeople grew out of their experience with the law and the legal process. Their later disillusionment and political defeat was also in large part due to the legal system. The freedpeople's inability to win justice through the courts at first galvanized them to political action, but ultimately undermined their political success and helped reduce them to economic dependency.[6]

Greene County lies in Georgia's eastern piedmont, part of the so-called plantation belt or black belt that sweeps in an inverted crescent south from Virginia through middle Georgia and west to Texas. Occupying four hundred square miles between the Oconee and Ogeechee rivers, Greene County offered farmers a variety of soils: rich alluvial bottoms along the streams and rivers, rolling oak and hickory uplands where a thin layer of rich brown soil covered brick red piedmont clay, and the southeast quarter of the county where less fertile white sandy soil predominated. The county seat of Greensboro, a town of about one thousand people in 1860, occupied the geographic center of the county. Seven miles north of Greensboro, in the heart of a plantation district known as Prosperity Ridge, stood the town of Penfield and Mercer University. Five miles east of Greensboro lay Union Point, a creation of the railroad during the 1830s that grew into a good-sized town. These towns served as depots and market centers for the plantations and farms that dominated Greene County.

Abram Colby's white father, John Colby, settled in Greene County about 1800. His timing proved fortunate, for over the next few decades growing world demand for cotton precipitated an agricultural revolution that swept across the deep South, creating the "Cotton Kingdom." John Colby rode the cotton boom to prosperity, accumulating land and slaves, eventually becoming one of Greene County's wealthiest planters. Sometime after his wife Abigail's death in 1808, Colby began a sexual relationship with a teenage slave named Mary. Mary ultimately bore him several children, including Abram, who was born about 1820. John Colby raised Abram himself, and the boy grew to be a large, powerful man, though illiterate like his father.[7]

In June 1850, John Colby died. He left all of his real property, 2,665 acres of farmland, to his legitimate daughter by his white wife. He also left her most of his 106 slaves. But his will continued: "knowing the laws of Georgia are opposed to and entirely forbid any wish I might indulge toward liberating a fraction of my slaves, I do here give to William L. Strain the following negroes, requesting and trusting that he will treat them with kindness and humanity." Those designated for this special guardianship were Mary and her seven children, including Abram. Strain, a lawyer and the postmaster of Greensboro, took his friend John Colby's charge to heart. From that day on Mary and her children lived as free people in their own home, working at their own trades, though they remained slaves at law.[8]

Between 1850 and 1865, Abram Colby lived a relatively independent life,

working in Greenesboro as a barber. He married and became the father of
several children, the oldest a son named William born in October 1850. Beyond this, as with most slaves, little information about his life exists. Slavery
functioned largely on a private and personal level, and usually information
about an individual slave's life was not recorded. Even census enumera-
tors merely noted the age and sex of each slave, not the names. One can
only speculate that as a barber Abram Colby held elite status among Greene
County's slaves and lived well compared to his peers. More interestingly,
barbering probably acquainted him with several leading men of the county
and at the least allowed him to listen in on discussions of business and politics. This, then, constituted Abram Colby's education.[9]

Like John Colby, Greene County grew wealthy from the cotton boom.
By 1860 more than twelve thousand people lived in Greene, two-thirds of
whom were black slaves. Of the almost nine million dollars worth of property
reported in 1860, approximately five and one-half million represented the
value of slaves, over 60 percent of all wealth in the county. Of the 798 households recorded in the 1860 census, 56 percent owned one or more slaves.
More than 18 percent of households owned twenty or more slaves, and about
4 percent owned more than fifty. The per capita wealth of free individuals exceeded $2,200, more than six times the average wealth nationally. The
schools, churches, homes, and plantations of Greene County exemplified the
sort of economic success southerners used to counter outsiders' criticisms of
slavery.[10]

The Civil War destroyed Greene County's slave society. In November
1864, William T. Sherman's forces swept through Georgia on their way to
the sea. Union troops raided Greenesboro as part of a feint toward Augusta,
while other troops destroyed the railroad, the bridges, the ferry, and the community of Park's Mill along the Oconee River. Worse were the stragglers and
bummers, Confederate and Union, large numbers of whom passed through
Greene stealing livestock and provisions. Day after day groups of armed men
roamed the county, but finally they too were gone, and Greene's inhabitants
began to ponder what war had wrought.[11]

Although only a few of Greene's eight thousand slaves followed Sherman's
troops to Savannah, those that remained knew that their world had irrevo-
cably changed. As part of that change, in 1864 black slaves organized their
first completely independent church in Greenesboro, the Springfield Baptist
Church. Created, led, and paid for by people still ostensibly slaves, Springfield symbolized their determination to build new lives. During the last six
months of war more and more slaves began to live apart from their masters,
and beginning in May 1865 hundreds of Greene County's newly freed slaves

relocated. These freedpeople moved to join families, escape oppressive masters, or merely to exercise their new freedom. Around Springfield Church a black squatter community called Canaan sprang up, attracting a growing population of both former town servants and freedpeople from the country. Living in town offered the former slaves more personal liberty than the countryside and let blacks experience for the first time life in an independent, supportive community.[12]

When Sidney Andrews, a New Englander touring the defeated South, visited Canaan in November 1865, he found it hard to understand why so many freedpeople chose to live together in squalor when they could have remained with their former masters and enjoyed a better standard of living. He asked an elderly freedwoman about this, trying to understand her reasons for living in Canaan.

"What did you leave the old place for, Auntie?" asked the confused Andrews.

"What fur? [En]*Joy my freedom!*" replied the old woman.

For all his empathy, Andrews still could not understand the meaning of personal autonomy and community independence to people who had been slaves, nor could he understand valuing this autonomy above one's comfort and standard of living. Pondering the slaves' choices, which did not seem rational to a white New Englander, Andrews asked a crucial question, "What is the 'freedom' that war has brought this dusky race?"[13]

Others asked the same question, including many black people who were struggling to define and shape their new freedom in conflict with their former masters. In late 1865 the Augusta *Colored American* called for a convention of Georgia's freedmen to meet in Augusta and consider the problems facing freed slaves. Even before the Freedmen's Convention assembled on January 10, 1866, the *Colored American* called for the delegates to demand equal rights. This should be done aggressively, argued the paper: "we counsel no fawning nor bowing because of former associations."[14]

Delegates from all Georgia's major cities and several rural counties went to Augusta. Greene County sent three delegates to the convention: Valentine Thomas, Charles Martin, and Abram Colby. The convention met for four days. During this time Gen. Davis Tillson, the head of the Freedmen's Bureau in Georgia, explained his conception of liberty within the new free labor system. The former slaves aggressively questioned Tillson for several hours and, unsatisfied with his understanding of the freedpeople's problems, they proceeded to elaborate their own concept of freedom. They heard reports concerning the legal, political, and educational problems facing Georgia's freed slaves, and in response passed resolutions that called for

personal independence, citizenship, and equal civil rights. To pursue these
goals the freedmen organized the Georgia Equal Rights Association. As Reverend Ulysses Houston of Savannah explained, "We have met to ask for free
laws, we mean to seek justice for all men, irrespective of color or condition.
The laws which now govern us, [are] oppressive and cruel, we want them
changed." [15]

While the freedmen met in Augusta, the all-white Georgia legislature met
for its first postwar session. As part of their attempt to define the nature of
freedom, the Freedmen's Convention drew up an address to the legislators,
hoping to influence them with an eloquent plea for justice. "As we are willing to bury the past and forget the ills of slavery," argued the address, "we
expect your encouragement by the creation of such laws as are equitable and
progressive." The delegates knew that the legislature's decisions concerning
the legal status of Georgia freedmen could shape their future, and they argued that freedmen were entitled to the same legal rights as white men. The
freedmen explained that as equal citizens they looked forward to the duty and
the right to sit on juries, to practice law, and to vote. Clearly, the delegates
expected any definition of their freedom to include complete equality at law. [16]

If the Georgia legislators noticed the freedmen's plea for equal justice,
their actions did not show it. Meeting from December 1865 through March
1866, the legislature ratified the Thirteenth Amendment to the U.S. Constitution, then turned to questions about the social and political role of freed
blacks in Georgia. The Georgia legislature avoided creating a "black code"
of direct legal prohibitions and restrictions based upon race. In light of the
anger other states' black codes caused in the North, the Georgia legislature
attempted to be more subtle. Instead of a code of restrictions, they created
a system of positive rights organized by categories of persons. "Persons of
color," which included everyone with "one-eighth or more of negro or African blood," had the rights to marry, to divorce, to make and enforce contracts, to sue or be sued, to own property, even to be witnesses in legal cases
involving a person of color as a party. Other categories of persons given positive rights included corporations, aliens, residents not aliens, and citizens.
Citizens included "all white persons born in this state." Male citizens had
the rights to vote, to serve on juries, and to hold public office. Just in case
someone missed the point, the law emphasized that "persons having one-eighth or more negro or African blood are not white persons" and therefore
not citizens. [17]

Meanwhile, in Greene County, whites struggled to make sense of their
changed world, to order some recognizable society despite emancipation.
They elected prewar leaders to local offices and tried to rebuild the antebel-

lum factorage financial system, but they could not escape the reality of defeat and emancipation. In March 1866 the grand jury lamented that "we cannot congratulate ourselves as in other days on a bright and hopeful future. We have just emerged from a mighty revolution the consequences of which cannot even be imagined. We began the War in good faith, we were honest, and upon its result we stayed our future and our sacred honor. But we have been beaten, by our defeat we have lost millions in Confederate issue, millions in the emancipation of our slaves, we have virtually lost [everything]." [18]

One of the unimagined consequences continued even as the grand jury met. Abram Colby and the Equal Rights Association organized the freedmen of Greene County for political action. Though the ultimate goal of the Equal Rights Association was political equality, local organizations had more immediate issues to deal with. The most pressing local issue for Greene County's freedpeople, and for freedpeople in many parts of Georgia, was the unresponsive legal system and unfair treatment by employers. Black laborers who contracted to work during 1865 or 1866 often suffered blatant economic exploitation and abuse. This resulted in part from the freedmen's own ignorance of the workings of a contract system, or perhaps merely from their ignorance of the cost of a year's subsistence for a family. Thus, some individuals contracted for absurdly low wages or tiny fractions of the final crop. Other freedmen were victims of outright fraud by employers. Especially common was the practice of driving black laborers working on share-wages off the land before the completion of the contract, then insisting that the freedmen had breached the agreement.[19]

Seeking justice in the courts, however, only confronted blacks with their own powerlessness. During its first postwar session, the Georgia legislature created county courts to handle minor criminal cases and civil suits of less than two hundred dollars. The newly created county court became the venue for the vast majority of cases involving Greene County's freedpeople. Columbus Heard sat as judge and Thomas W. Robinson served as solicitor of the court. Both men came from prominent planter families, and they administered justice to the freedpeople in a manner reminiscent of plantation slave discipline, merely moving those principles from the private sphere to the public courtroom.

From the beginning Judge Heard revealed his determination to deal strictly with the freedpeople. Henry Brook, "a person of color," was found guilty of stealing one-half bushel of corn. Judge Heard sentenced him to thirty-nine lashes. Henry Allen took two watermelons from his employer's garden. Judge Heard gave him three months at hard labor on the county chain gang. Lousia Park used obscene language in the presence of Mary Simmons, a white woman. For her crime Lousia received thirty lashes, though they were administered inside the jail to preserve her modesty. Major Jackson pled guilty to stealing nine pieces of bacon from John Wright's smokehouse. Judge Heard ordered thirty-nine lashes and a fine of one hundred dollars. In lieu of the fine Major Jackson could serve on the chain gang for twelve months. These cases typified the harsh punishments given for petty crimes before the county court. The results of civil suits were much the same. During 1866 nine freedpeople sued their employers for unpaid wages or breach of contract. In all but one case the black plaintiffs lost and had to pay costs, an expensive lesson for people who were desperately poor. In this way the county court attempted to impose strict order, and allowed men who had been members of the planter class another chance to define the outlines of blacks' freedom.[20]

Like most Americans, Abram Colby and other black leaders in Greene County believed in the law's abstract promise of equal justice. The law claimed to stand apart from the social structure, above it and autonomous, and so could arbitrate between the various interest groups in society. This positivistic conception of law led the freedpeople to hope that they could secure legal rights and justice through the legal system. But, as Abram Colby exclaimed in the spring of 1866, "I do most solemnly declare in the presence of God and man—that I do not see the most distant shadow of right or equal justice here in Greenesboro." The county court had demonstrated the sort of justice African Americans could expect at the hands of their former masters, so the freedpeople began to organize a concerted effort to effect change.[21]

In the summer of 1866, Abram Colby and three other freedmen appealed to Gen. Tillson for help with the legal system. "We humbly ask you to give us the right of tribunal to settle business between colored and others without going to court," the freedmen's petition read. "We know from what we have seen that we have no chance of justice before the courts. We ask of you, sir, some right to defend ourselves and make those who contract with us stick to the contract. Our former masters are determined to oppress us." Colby's message closed with a plaintive postscript: "If there is nothing else can be done, can't we have an attorney, if we have to support him, so that we may have fairplay." Colby signed the letter, apparently believing that the fault lay in the men administering the legal system, not in the system itself. If blacks could gain equal access to the legal system, if only through an attorney to represent them, Colby and the others believed that the legal system would fulfill its promises and afford them justice. Tillson never responded to Colby's letter, and the problems faced by Greene County's freedpeople continued to grow.[22]

The black people of Greene County were not compliant victims. Instead, the oppressive contract system, the unequal laws passed by the state legislature, and the "justice" meted out by the courts only accelerated the growth of an active political consciousness among a people who by virtue of racial ideology and the experience of slavery already had a shared identity. Greene County's freedpeople quickly learned that they could not depend upon the federal government to bring lasting change to their lives, nor could they rely upon their former masters. If there was to be meaningful change in Greene County, the freedpeople themselves would have to make it happen.

Through the local branch of the Equal Rights Association, the freedpeople of Greene County built a powerful political organization. An American Missionary Association schoolteacher praised Abram Colby as the leader of this organization, "one of the largest and most enthusiastic branches" in the state. Henry McNeal Turner, a black leader and minister from Macon, Georgia, spoke to the Greensboro association in the summer of 1866. He encouraged the freedmen to protect themselves actively and in particular to drive the white men who exploited black women out of society. His remarks angered a group of whites listening to the meeting, but when they attempted to attack Turner they were faced down by armed freedmen who were part of Colby's organization. "I never saw more firearms among one set of people in my life," Turner marveled later. "I have not seen so determined a set of colored people as they are at Greensboro." [23]

At meetings members of the association read newspapers aloud, discussed political issues, planned strategies for dealing with the justice system, and demanded suffrage for black men. But the freedmen's participation in state politics remained hypothetical until the spring of 1867. In March 1867, responding to southern recalcitrance over the issues of Reconstruction, the U.S. Congress passed the First Reconstruction Act over a presidential veto. This act established military government in Georgia with specific preconditions for the resumption of civilian rule. These conditions included the elimination of the Georgia legislature's carefully constructed categories of persons, and required that African Americans be accorded the rights of citizenship and be allowed to vote. [24]

These demands astonished most whites. Not only had they lived within a culture that justified slavery as a benefit to an inferior race, but the larger world market system of which they were a part used a complex "scientific" racial hierarchy to explain the relations between groups in the world economy. In the summer of 1867 a front page article in the *Greensboro Herald* quoted Louis Agassiz's recent study of the races conducted at Harvard University. "The whole physical organization of the negro differs quite as much from the white man as it does from that of the chimpanzee," explained Agassiz, "the chimpanzee has not much further to progress to become a negro than the negro has to become a white man." In light of such "scientific" truth, the newspaper commented upon the insanity of considering blacks equal to whites and then lamented, "We poor Southerners have fallen into the hands of a strange people."[25]

Voter registration in the late summer of 1867 only emphasized the strangeness of the new situation: 1,002 white men and 1,528 freedmen registered to vote. By sheer numbers, blacks could control Greene County politics. This threat spurred white Democrats to action, and they called a mass meeting of all white voters at the courthouse, "to take counsel together to direct black suffrage in the right channel." The organizers emphasized the importance of the meeting by pointing out that *"Inaction is political death."* The meeting itself, however, revealed that white leaders did not fear an indigenous, self-directed black political movement, for they believed that blacks were incapable of such action. Instead, the Democrats feared that Republicans would manipulate the blacks, using them as the basis of political power. The mass meeting resolved that because someone had to control the black voters, the Democrats should attempt to gain that control.[26]

Black voters, however, were not as easily controlled as the whites imagined. Abram Colby's Equal Rights Association combined with the much weaker local Union League to build a solid base for black political activity. The freedmen in Greenesboro also organized a militia company, and though they apparently never received any arms, the mere existence of the company suggested increasing black solidarity. Rebuffed in their attempts to approach black voters, Democratic leaders devised another response to the requirements of military Reconstruction. They adopted a strategy of noncooperation, a sort of nonviolent resistance that attempted to deny the Reconstruction government legitimacy by refusing to participate in it. The largest noncooperative movement was a statewide boycott of the election of delegates to a new state constitutional convention required by the Reconstruction Act. In Greene the radical candidate ran unopposed and spoke grandly about restructuring Georgia's constitution to insure legal justice for the freedpeople. On November 2, 1867, the *Herald* proudly announced that only "One White Man Voted!!" One thousand white men boycotted the polls, reported the paper, and the only white man who voted was J. W. Tom Catching, the candidate, who voted for himself.[27]

During the celebration of Tom Catching's victory, tragedy struck. While parading through the streets of Greenesboro, hurrahing and firing guns into the air, Catching's pistol accidentally discharged, killing a black child. The following week brought more tragedy. A black Republican named Allen Jackson argued with William Curry, a poor white artisan. Enraged, Curry drew his gun and killed Jackson. A mob of freedmen grabbed Curry and began to beat him but were stopped by the town marshall, who arrested Curry and took him to jail. More than two hundred angry blacks gathered outside the jail demanding Curry be hung immediately, threatening to do it themselves. The marshall and his men armed themselves and took up positions to defend the fortress-like building. Seeing assault would be futile, the frustrated crowd soon dispersed. A month later Curry mysteriously escaped the jail's two-foot thick walls and disappeared.[28]

The last few months of 1867 had frightened many of Greene County's white residents. Organized black militia drilling in Greensboro, an election controlled by black voters, unrestrained freedmen reveling in the streets, and a black lynch mob convinced Greene's white leaders to change their tactics. Apparently, Greene County's black population intended to participate fully in the body politic. "From the demonstrations made by the colored population we think it high time that some precautionary measures be adopted by the citizens," commented the *Herald.* The county Democratic party put it more bluntly: "The time for inactivity is gone, the time for action is at hand."[29]

The new strategy of action by white conservatives began early in 1868. Democrats began to organize their voters in order to contest the upcoming April election of state officers. "The ball is now in motion," argued Greene County Democrats, "let every man bestir himself and see what can be done to defeat the wicked designs of the negro Radical party." Some Democrats did more than merely bestir themselves. On February 27, 1868, a simple, one-line comment in the *Herald* announced that "Gen. N. B. Forrest was in Atlanta on the 24th." Gen. Nathan Bedford Forrest, among his many accomplishments, led the Ku Klux Klan. Apparently, he visited Atlanta in February 1868 to finalize the organization of the Klan in Georgia.[30]

Dudley M. DuBose of nearby Wilkes County, Robert Toombs's son-in-law and law partner, became Grand Titan of the Klan for Georgia's Fifth Congressional District, which included Greene County. Each Georgia county contained several militia districts, and the Klan found this organization convenient for its purposes. DuBose established dens consisting of five to ten Confederate veterans in each militia district. Since most Georgia counties had eight to twelve militia districts, any county Klan organization could on a few hours notice raise fifty to a hundred armed and mounted men. The leadership of the Klan included many of each county's prominent men, usually reflecting the leadership of the local Democratic party. In Greene County the leaders of the Ku Klux Klan included James R. Sanders, a wealthy and influential planter; John E. Walker, the county's leading physician; and Thomas Robinson, brother of the County's Superior Court Judge and solicitor of the county court.[31]

While the Democrats and the Ku Klux Klan organized, some ambitious whites concluded that greater opportunity lay with Greene's new Republican party. Less than a dozen white men openly cooperated with the Republicans, but all were from prominent families or were well known themselves. Most had also been slaveowners. Tom Catching owned twenty-nine slaves in 1860, while David A. Newsom and Greene Thompson came from prosperous slaveowning families. The most successful of the white Republicans, however, claimed to be a self-made man. Born into modest circumstances, Robert L. McWhorter began work at age nineteen clerking in a Penfield mercantile firm. In three years he became a partner in the firm, and through marriage he tied himself to some of Georgia's leading planter families. By 1860 McWhorter owned a large plantation, mercantile interests, fifty-five slaves, and had served two terms in the Georgia House. In 1861 he led a company of soldiers from Penfield to war and eventually rose to the rank of major. After surrendering at Appomattox, he returned to Greene County determined to rebuild his fortunes as a planter and politician. McWhorter represented Greene in Georgia's first postwar legislature, but in early 1868 he shocked the county by joining the Republican party. In March the Republicans nominated Abram Colby and Robert L. McWhorter for Greene's two seats in the Georgia House of Representatives.[32]

A week after Colby and McWhorter's nominations a brief notice appeared in the *Herald.* Headlines in bold capitals read "K-K-K" and told its readers that "Bob McWhorter will take pleasure in explaining the meaning of the above letters. Give him a call." As the targets of Klan harassment, both men also received Klan threats that promised "to kill or drive every damn Radical out of the county." Warnings to the freedmen appeared in the paper as well, telling blacks that "when voting time comes you had best go to your old master and . . . he will tell you what to do." But these threats and suggestions had little effect on Greene County's black voters. Colby and McWhorter trounced their opponents in the April 1868 election, and white Republicans won all local offices as well.[33]

On July 4, 1868, when the legislature assembled in the new capital of Atlanta, 29 of the 172 members of the House were black, and 3 of the Senate's 44 members were black. On the first day of business Robert L. McWhorter won election as Speaker of the House. As time passed, he came to be known as a moderate Republican, one of a group of white legislators who held a swing-vote position between the conservative Democrats and the radical

Republicans and their black allies. Abram Colby became a member of the Committee on Agriculture and Internal Improvements, but he spent most of his time learning his new job. Colby could still barely read, so his teenage son William accompanied him constantly, acting as his secretary. On July 21, 1868, Colby joined a majority in the House in ratifying the Fourteenth Amendment, an act that ended military reconstruction in Georgia, but after that things began to go sour.[34]

Abram Colby and the other black legislators had high hopes when they began the legislative session of 1868, but their hopes did not last long. The Georgia constitution of 1868 failed to specifically grant black men the right to hold public office in Georgia, and conservatives argued that blacks were thus ineligible to sit in the legislature. By August the Democrats managed to convince many "moderate" Republicans of their position. The *Greenesboro Herald* observed, "there are Republicans [who] are acting with the Democratic wing . . . we can safely say to the people of Greene that their representative has resolved to shape his course with the Democratic party." Robert L. McWhorter, Colby's fellow Republican from Greene, would cooperate with the Democrats on the issue of eligibility. In September, Speaker McWhorter managed to be absent when the matter came to a vote, and the speaker *pro tem* who took his place ruled that black legislators could not vote on the issue of eligibility. Thirty white Republicans voted with the Democrats or abstained. By a vote of eighty-three to twenty-three the legislature expelled its black members and replaced them with their Democratic opponents from the April elections.[35]

This reversal of fortune stunned the black legislators. Like Abram Colby, most had trusted their white Republican allies. Henry McNeal Turner, speaking for Colby and several other black assemblymen, addressed the House on the expulsion issue. "The Anglo-Saxon race, sir, is a most surprising one," said Turner, directing his remarks to Speaker McWhorter. "No man has ever been more deceived than I have been for the last three weeks. The treachery exhibited by gentlemen belonging to that race has shaken my confidence more than anything that has come under my observation from the day of my birth." Turner threatened, pleaded, and reasoned, but under it all lay his enormous outrage. "How dare you make laws by which to try me and my wife and children, and deny me a voice in the making of those laws." Finished, Turner asked for permission to leave the chamber, approached the Speaker's chair, brushed the dust from his feet, and walked out the door.[36]

The *Greenesboro Herald* crowed that "the people of Georgia have reason to rejoice . . . they now have a legislature composed of white men." More importantly, argued the paper, the Republicans would split, for the freedmen

knew they could not trust the white radicals. Abram Colby and the other expelled legislators, however, did not give up. In October 1868 they assembled
at Henry M. Turner's request in Macon to form the Civil and Political Rights
Association, a new organization comprised only of black members. Together,
they began to campaign for federal help in regaining their seats in the Georgia
General Assembly.[37]

But even as the freedmen struggled to regain their political positions, a
wave of Ku Klux Klan-inspired violence swept across Georgia. Democrats
were determined to win the November general elections, and from August
through October the Freedmen's Bureau reported 142 attacks on blacks,
including thirty-one murders. In Greene County twelve beatings and two
murders occurred during the same period, the perpetrators going unpunished. Klan activity in Greene became so open that on October 24, 1868, the
Mercer University baseball team played at Penfield against the Ku Klux club
of Covington. Mercer won, 65 to 32. In the weeks before the election the
Klan rode nightly, beating and terrorizing freedmen. As Robert McWhorter's
brother Joe explained, "The K K Democracy . . . are determined to prevent
the negro from voting. A great many negroes are hid out in the woods every
night for fear of losing their lives." Outside Penfield a disguised group of
twenty mounted men beat a black man to death for complaining about his
employer to the Freedmen's Bureau, and for the same crime they beat a black
woman until she miscarried. One week before the election, the editor of the
Herald reminded the "colored voters of Greene" of the violence, telling them
"to remember the fate of poor Tray, may the Lord have mercy on his soul,"
when deciding whether to vote.[38]

Despite the threats and violence, Abram Colby and the black voters stood
together for the November 1868 election. Perhaps on the advice of John
Sullivan, the Freedmen's Bureau agent, black voters organized themselves
into companies. On election day company after company marched to the
polls, their numbers and unity forestalling white attempts at intimidation.
About twelve hundred of Greene's fifteen hundred eligible black voters dared
to cast ballots. Republican candidates, including Ulysses Grant, won ma-
jorities in Greene, while in most neighboring counties white intimidation of
black voters facilitated Democratic victories.[39]

Ku Klux Klan violence continued in Greene County, and John Sullivan,
the Freedmen's Bureau agent, asked the grand jury to investigate. On November 30, after months of open Klan activity, the grand jury announced
"we have made a diligent inquiry and can learn nothing to satisfy us as to the
existence of any such bands." Even if the leading citizens that sat on the grand
jury were not themselves Klan members, they obviously did not want to limit

its activities. During 1869 Klan violence continued, committed both by local groups and by Klansmen from neighboring counties. Houses were burned, dozens of freedmen beaten, and several blacks murdered. In August Abram Colby wrote Republican governor Rufus Bullock begging for help. "I don't know what course to pursue," he confessed, "on saturday last they taken out 20 men, and they shot an innocent person on last thursday night. . . . Governor, the Clu Clux [sic] is found riding in our county every night." On the nights of September 17, 18, and 19 the Klan organized a large-scale attempt to eliminate the radical leadership in the county, trying to capture the American Missionary Association teacher as well as local black leaders, including Abram Colby. Wagonloads of students from Mercer University were brought to Greenesboro from Penfield to assist in this all out effort. The Klansmen found the white AMA teacher and frightened him into leaving the county, but the black community successfully hid their leaders from the mob.[40]

As violence grew, federal authorities sent a company of sixty-five soldiers to Greene County to keep order. Apparently, the troops spent their time chasing back and forth across the county, neither catching any Klansman nor finding many witnesses who would testify against the Klan. Meanwhile, blacks themselves fought back against the violence. When the Klan murdered a freedman in the southern part of Greene, twenty-five armed blacks launched an attack upon the home of a Klan leader, wounding him in the gunfight that followed. Local authorities arrested most of the blacks involved in this "insurrection," but Jordan Williams, a black resident of the area, explained that there had been no insurrection. The attackers acted "believing it to be indispensable for their own safety and liberty in the county of Greene," argued Williams, asserting the freedpeople's right to respond to "crimes committed upon their people when the civil authorities permitted those who committed outrages upon the colored people to go at large."[41]

Unable to defeat Colby politically and unable to frighten blacks into submission, Democratic leaders in Greene decided to try another approach. On October 27, 1869, a group of Greensboro merchants offered Colby $5,000 to join the Democratic party, or $2,500 to resign his seat in the legislature. Colby told them he would not do it for all the wealth in Greene County. Two nights later he was attacked and beaten.[42]

The *Herald* never reported the attack upon Colby, just as it never reported other such attacks in the county, but the military investigation that followed as well as a $5,000 reward offered by Governor Bullock for the arrest of the attackers certainly meant the event was well known. In December 1869 Congress reimposed military rule in Georgia, and the military governor reseated Abram Colby and the other expelled black legislators in January 1870. There they tried to pass a bill creating a black militia to protect the freedpeople, but they failed. In fact, though Republicans dominated the legislature throughout 1870, they accomplished little to help the freedmen in their ongoing struggle for justice. Explaining later the failure to take effective action in the legislature, Colby complained that "the white Republicans were too weak for us."[43]

As the December 1870 election for the General Assembly approached, Greene's Democrats hoped that the split between Robert L. McWhorter and Abram Colby would divide black voters, allowing Democrats to control the election. Their chances seemed good, for many blacks harbored great anger against McWhorter. A black politician from neighboring Clarke County called McWhorter "no friend of the colored people," and the *Herald* predicted the split would destroy the Republicans. In November Henry McNeal Turner visited Greensboro and spoke to a mass meeting of black voters in Canaan. He called for Republican unity, arguing that black rejection of McWhorter would result in a Democrat taking his place in the legislature. He emphasized that the black community had to stand together to resist Democratic designs. Returning to speak in December, Turner again pled for unity, and just before the election Colby and McWhorter publicly embraced, calling the election the "final struggle."[44]

The Saturday night before the election Abram Colby returned home from church, and as he approached his house the dogs in his yard began barking. His son opened the door, and a shot rang out. The bullet narrowly missed Colby and his son. Colby grabbed his gun and ran upstairs to return fire when a fusillade of bullets struck the house. Before Colby could respond the attackers slipped away. Shaken but uninjured, Colby voted in the election. Then his supporters convinced him to leave the county for his own safety. In the election black voters firmly supported the Republican party, and both McWhorter and Colby won by substantial margins.[45]

Outside Greene County, however, Republican political power began to collapse. Governor Bullock delayed the assembly of the new legislature as long as possible, then in October 1871 fled the state. In November a Democratically controlled legislature assembled in Atlanta bent upon "redeeming" the state. Over the next year the legislature considered hundreds of bills as the newly dominant Democratic legislators struggled to undo the effects of Reconstruction. Colby and several other black legislators were present, but unable to stem the rising tide.[46]

In 1871, because of continuing violence directed at his house, Abram Colby moved with his family to Atlanta. This finally gave the white conservatives a way to defeat Colby. Using the state law requiring local residency, Democrats were able to prevent Abram Colby from running for office again in Greene County. Unable to defeat Abram Colby at the polls, Democrats defeated him through the application of a minor law. In 1872 Jack Heard, a younger and less influential black leader, ran for the House seat in Colby's place.[47]

Meanwhile, Robert L. McWhorter repudiated the Republican party and Governor Bullock and refused to run again in 1872, so white Republican Greene Thompson was nominated to run with Jack Heard. Once again black voters dominated the election in Greene, and both men won, while in neighboring counties throughout eastern Georgia Republicans suffered disastrous defeats in 1872. Against great odds the freedpeople of Greene County had won another political victory. By this time, however, Abram Colby had realized that political victory and resistance to violence would not be enough if the legal system failed to give black people justice. He had resisted terrorism, but the violence continued. He had won political victory but found it hollow. Only the legal system offered hope for justice, and by 1872 Colby knew this hope was futile.[48]

In the fall of 1871 a joint congressional committee investigating political terrorism in the South had come to Atlanta. Abram Colby testified, along with dozens of other freedmen, about the situation in Georgia. When asked why he never went to court about the Klan attack, Colby explained that he knew of no judge or court that would punish his attackers, that even the federal grand jury called in Atlanta to investigate the violence had Klan sympathizers on it, including James R. Sanders, a leader of the Ku Klux Klan in Greene County and Colby's opponent in the 1870 election. When asked if there were any judges he trusted, Colby tried to explain that the problem was larger than the men involved, the problem was the legal system itself. The entire legal system in Georgia, both state and federal, would never give black people justice. Only the resumption of military rule and the imposition of a new legal system, argued Colby, could give the freedpeople any hope for legal justice. The faith Abram Colby once had in the equity of the legal system, the hope that an attorney representing blacks might allow fair play, had been crushed.[49]

The legal system not only failed to protect blacks from violence, it also gave white landowners the means to regain a great deal of control over their agricultural laborers, control legitimated by the law's promise of equity. In 1870 only four freedmen owned land in Greene County, and in 1880 less than forty out of a black population of 11,974 owned land. Greene County's blacks owned so little property of any kind that in 1882, seventeen years after emancipation, the value of their total property in Greene averaged less than

$5 per person, while that of whites averaged more than $330 per person. Living in such poverty, Greene's freedpeople essentially possessed only their ability to labor. This did give them some power: most blacks worked less as freedpeople than they had as slaves and through sharecropping and tenancy arrangements maintained a measure of autonomy. White landowners, however, worried that they could no longer control their workers as completely as they had under slavery, so they continually sought ways to reduce the freedpeople's autonomy. As one planter put it, "There is a sufficient amount of labor . . . if it could be judiciously controlled." Ultimately, the law proved the most effective means of control.[50]

Georgia had a well-established system of tenancy before the Civil War, and between 15 and 20 percent of Greene's farm operators in 1860 were tenants. The tenancy system, however, operated peripherally to the plantation system of agriculture, providing some white farmers with little more than a living. The laws of tenancy were of little concern to large plantation owners. Emancipation changed this dramatically, and during the 1870s tenancy and sharecropping became the dominant system of labor in Greene County. By 1880 approximately 70 percent of all farm operators in Greene County were tenants, and more than two thirds of the tenants were sharecroppers, almost all of whom were black.[51]

Although the law already gave landlords great advantages in their relationship with tenants, in the decade following emancipation, both Georgia's judiciary and legislature acted to increase that advantage. In 1866 the first postwar Georgia legislature passed a law giving landlords a furnishing lien on tenants' crops. Suddenly, landlords obtained an automatic property interest in crops that had before belonged completely to the tenant, giving landlords the legal right to exercise some control over the disposition of those crops.[52]

The Georgia Supreme Court also acted to increase the power of landlords after the Civil War. First, in a series of cases in 1870 and 1871, the court ruled that the state homestead exemption did not apply to a tenant's crops. Unlike other property, held the court, tenants' crops could not be protected from debts owed the landlord. Then, in 1872, the Georgia Supreme Court handed down its most powerful ruling in favor of landlords. In *Appling* v. *Odom*, the court held that sharecroppers were not tenants but merely wage laborers. Thus, the landlord owned *all* of a sharecropper's crop and only had to pay him, as wages, what was left after deducting all debts from the cropper's share. Thus, sharecroppers had no possessory rights in the land they tilled, their jobs could be terminated at will, and they owned none of the crop they raised until they received a part as wages.[53]

Tenants and sharecroppers were thus reduced to almost complete dependency upon their landlords. In Greene County, virtually all black farmers were landless and had little or no property to use as collateral for credit, so they had to enter the crop lien system that forced them into servility. This process took time, but ultimately it began to tell. Through the late 1860s and well into the 1870s the *Greenesboro Herald* carried many complaints about the problem of labor control, but by 1881 announced "we understand the schedule has changed in this county. The farmers had to hunt up the negroes to labor for them, now it is the negroes that are hunting up the farmers for homes next year." White elites controlled the legal system, and through it, far more effectively than through terrorism or politics, they regained control over their black laborers.[54]

The last struggle for Greene County's black voters came in the fall of 1874. Political terrorism played little part in the election that year; instead, manipulation of the legal system crushed the freedmen's political hopes. In the October state election former Freedmen's Bureau agent John Sullivan and black Republican Jack Heard lost to planter Democrats L. B. Willis and L. D. Carlton. Of more than twenty-five hundred men registered, less than sixteen hundred cast votes, two-thirds of them for Democrats. The *Herald* attributed Democratic victory to white solidarity and to "black men with white hearts" who voted Democratic, but actually legal subterfuge made the victory possible. In two of the county's six precincts there were no Republican votes, and in a third precinct only one Republican vote. Local election managers simply allowed whites to vote early, telling black voters to wait their turn. Then, under Georgia's election laws that allowed local managers to set the hours for voting, they closed the polls. Frustrated black voters looked to Jack Heard for leadership, but he declined to lead any protest. Heard believed the cause was lost, so turned his energies to making peace with white leaders and promoting black emigration to the West.[55]

On the morning of November 3, more than three hundred black voters awaited the opening of the poll at Union Point determined to defeat whites' strategy of the month before by voting as soon as the poll opened. Local election managers conferred, then simply refused to open the poll, again an arguably legal act under the state election law. Outraged black voters called a protest meeting the following Saturday night, and there turned to a middle-aged artisan named Montgomery Shepherd for leadership. Shepherd spoke to the crowd, then led them in a midnight protest demonstration through the streets of Union Point. Some of the crowd, armed with pistols and clubs, marched into the white residential section and threatened the homes of several local leaders. About three o'clock Sunday morning the last of the protesters went home.[56]

Later that day Montgomery Shepherd and several other freedmen were arrested and locked in the local jail. In response to rumors of an attempt to free the prisoners, a posse of twenty-five white men rode up from Greenesboro, and Governor James Smith put five hundred militiamen on alert in Augusta. There was some violence; unknown persons fired on election manager William Reynolds from ambush, and an incendiary set fire to L. D. Carlton's barn, but no rescue effort developed. The prisoners all received stiff sentences for riot from the county court. Montgomery Shepherd received the maximum sentence possible, five hundred dollars in fines and twelve months on the chain gang. Less than a month later a small item in the *Herald* reported "convict killed." Montgomery Shepherd, while working with the chain gang, was killed trying to escape. "All right, set 'em up again," commented James B. Park, the *Herald*'s editor.[57]

Although Greene County blacks voted in large numbers until the passage of a new voter registration law for Greene County in 1885, they never again acted with the unity of purpose they had during the decade following emancipation. Robert L. McWhorter managed to find "redemption," joined the Democratic party in the late 1870s, and won election as a state senator from Greene's district. He died in 1908, "a distinguished and beloved citizen." Jack Heard served in the House until 1874, and no African American has since represented Greene on the state level. Heard ultimately reached accommodation with Greene County's white elite and became their anointed leader of the black community. Tom Catching remained loyal to the Republican party, and in 1872 local Klansmen drove him from the county, bankrupt and destitute.[58]

After leaving the legislature in 1872, Abram Colby disappeared. His son William, however, apparently continued to live in Atlanta and took part in politics, as had his father. In 1894, William Colby attended the Georgia Peoples' party convention in Atlanta as a delegate from Fulton County. During this convention, the Populists made great show of including blacks in their party, even appointing a black man to their executive committee. William Colby decided, however, that this was all a sham. The final straw came when a Populist leader ordered Colby to the back of the hall "with the other nigger delegates." Colby left the convention and told the *Atlanta Journal* that he completely rejected the Populist party. Then, in an ironic twist of fate, William Colby swore to use all of his influence for the Democratic party, the same party that had tried to destroy his father. The *Journal*'s only comment was, "Colby is said to be a very influential politician among his race."[59]

Notes

1. U.S. Congress, *Joint Select Committee on the Condition of Affairs in the Late Insurrectionary States, Georgia* (Washington, D.C., 1872), 1113, 1114, 697 (hereafter cited as *KKK Testimony*); D. A. Newsom to Rufus Bullock, September 13, 1869, D. A. Newsom and W. H. McWhorter to Rufus Bullock, September 22, 1869, Governors' Incoming Correspondence, Georgia Department of Archives and History, Atlanta (hereafter cited as GDAH).

Greene's seat has had three spellings over the past two centuries. Originally "Greenesborough," about 1850 this changed to "Greenesboro," which prevailed until about 1900 when the U.S. Postal Service changed the spelling to "Greensboro." Throughout this essay the spelling "Greenesboro" will be used.

2. *KKK Testimony*, 696–99.

3. Ibid., 1113.

4. Ibid., 697, 1113.

5. Ibid., 697, 698; *Daily New Era* (Atlanta), December 30, 1870.

6. Russell Duncan, *Freedom's Shore: Tunis Campbell and the Georgia Freedmen* (Athens: University of Georgia Press, 1986); Edmund L. Drago, *Black Politicians and Reconstruction in Georgia: A Splendid Failure* (Baton Rouge: Louisiana State University Press, 1982); Eric Foner, *Reconstruction: America's Unfinished Revolution, 1863–1877* (New York: Harper and Row, 1988); Ruth Currie-McDaniel, *Carpetbagger of Conscience: A Biography of John Emory Bryant* (Athens: University of Georgia Press, 1987); Thomas Holt, *Black over White: Negro Political Leadership in South Carolina during Reconstruction* (Urbana: University of Illinois Press, 1977); Peter Kolchin, *First Freedom: The Response of Alabama's Blacks to Emancipation and Reconstruction* (Westport, Conn.: Greenwood Press, 1972). All the above take black political activity seriously, but at best consider law as another instrument used by white leaders to bludgeon recalcitrant freedpeople. Eric Foner's superb *Nothing But Freedom: Emancipation and its Legacy* (Baton Rouge: Louisiana State University Press, 1983) takes a more perceptive view of the role of law in black political movements. E. P. Thompson's *Whigs and Hunters: The Origin of the Black Act* (New York: Pantheon Books, 1975) provides a fine model for understanding the interplay of law and political consciousness in western society.

7. Abigail Colby headstone, Greenesboro City Graveyard, Greenesboro, Georgia; John Colby's Will, Will Book G, Greene County, Georgia, 94–95; *KKK Testimony*, 696.

8. John Colby's Will, 95; "Population" and "Slave Schedule," in "Returns of the United States Census, Greene County, Georgia," Seventh Census, 1850; "Agriculture," in "Returns of the United States Census, Greene County, Georgia," Seventh Census, 1850; *KKK Testimony*, 696.

9. *KKK Testimony*, 696, 702, 706.

10. "Population," "Agriculture," and "Social Statistics," in "Returns of the United

States Census, Greene County, Georgia," Eighth Census, 1860. Per capita wealth for all inhabitants was more than $700, while if only whites are considered, per capita wealth was about $2,200.

11. *The War of the Rebellion: Official Records*, series 1, vol. 44 (Washington, 1893), 270–71; Dr. Thaddeus Brockett Rice and Carolyn White Williams, *History of Greene County* (Macon, Ga.: J. W. Burke Co., 1961), 414; Arthur F. Raper, *Tenants of the Almighty* (New York: Macmillan, 1943), 70–72.

12. Orville Vernon Burton, "The Rise and Fall of Afro-American Town Life: Town and Country in Reconstruction Edgefield, South Carolina," in Orville Vernon Burton and Robert C. McMath, Jr., eds., *Toward a New South: Studies in Post-Civil War Southern Communities* (Westport, Conn.: Greenwood Press, 1982), convincingly explains why freedpeople were drawn to the towns. Canaan, "a land flowing with milk and honey," reflects the religious content of the freedpeople's concept of liberty. Whites, however, tended to use the term derisively. See Exodus 3:8.

13. Sidney Andrews, *The South Since the War* (Boston: Ticknor and Fields, 1866), 352–53.

14. *Colored American* (Augusta, Ga.), December 30, 1865, January 6, 1866.

15. *Proceedings of the Freedmen's Convention of Georgia Assembled at Augusta, January 10, 1866* (Augusta, Ga., 1866), 4 (hereafter cited as *Proceedings, January 1866*). The Georgia Equal Rights Association apparently had no official ties to the National Equal Rights Association of Frederick Douglass, Elizabeth Cady Stanton and others, but the similarity in name suggests a knowledge of the organization among the freedpeople and a desire to emulate the Equal Rights Association's goals.

16. *Proceedings, January 1866*, 18–20.

17. *Georgia Code, 1867*, 14–15, 331–35.

18. Superior Court Proceedings, Greene County, Georgia, March Term, 1866.

19. *Proceedings, January 1866*, 17; *KKK Testimony*, 701; William S. McFeely, *Yankee Stepfather: General O. O. Howard and the Freedmen* (New York: W. W. Norton and Co., 1968), 149–65.

20. County Court Proceedings, Greene County, Georgia, June Term through December Term 1866. The county court held a term every month beginning in June 1866.

21. County Court Proceedings, Greene County, Georgia, June Term through December Term, 1866; Richard Quinney, "The Ideology of Law: Notes for a Radical Alternative to Legal Oppression," in Charles E. Reasons and Robert M. Rich, eds., *The Sociology of Law: A Conflict Perspective* (Toronto: Butterworths, 1978), 39–71; Abram Colby to Mr. G. L. Eberhart, March 1, 1866, Greensboro Georgia Letters, Records of the Bureau of Refugees, Freedmen, and Abandoned Lands, Record Group 105, National Archives, Washington, D.C.

22. Abram Colby *et al.* to Davis Tillson, August 3, 1866, U.S. Department of War, Bureau of Refugees, Freedmen, and Abandoned Lands, Records of the Assistant Commissioner for the State of Georgia, Unregistered Letters Received 1866, Record Group 105, National Archives.

23. R. H. Gladding to Rufus Bullock, November 29, 1869, Georgia Governors' Papers, GDAH; Drago, *Black Politicians*, 26.

24. *Proceedings of the Convention of Georgia Equal Rights and Educational Association*, Macon, Ga., October 30, 1866 (Augusta, 1866); Kenneth Coleman, ed., *A History of Georgia* (Athens: University of Georgia Press, 1977), 210–11.

25. Thomas R. R. Cobb, *On Slavery* (1859); Barbara J. Fields, "Ideology and Race in American History," in J. Morgan Kousser and James M. McPherson, eds., *Region, Race, and Reconstruction: Essays in Honor of C. Vann Woodward* (New York: Oxford University Press, 1982), 142–60; *Herald* (Greenesboro, Ga.), July 6, August 10, 1867.

26. *Herald*, August 24, September 7, 1867.

27. *Herald*, July 20, October 12, November 2, 1867. Because of the size and power of the Equal Rights Association in Greene County, the Union League never really developed as an independent force in the community.

28. *Herald*, November 9, 16, December 14, 1867; 1860 manuscript census, Greene County, "Population"; Issac A. Hall to Prov. Governor Ruger, June 3, 1868, Governor's Incoming Correspondence, GDAH.

29. *Herald*, December 14, 1867.

30. *Herald*, February 27, 1868; Stanley K. Deaton, "Violent Redemption: The Democratic Party and the Ku Klux Klan in Georgia, 1868–1871" (M.A. thesis, University of Georgia, 1988), 10–12, 26.

31. *Herald*, March 28, 1868; *KKK Testimony*, 696–97.

32. "Population" and "Slave Schedules," in "Returns of the United States Census, Greene County, Georgia," Eighth Census, 1860; St. Clair Abrams, *Manual and Biographic Register of the State of Georgia, 1871–72* (Atlanta, 1872), 22–23; *Georgia's General Assembly of 1880–81* (Atlanta, 1882), 77–80; *Herald*, March 26, 1868.

33. *Herald*, April 2, 23, 30, May 14, 1868; Deaton, "Violent Redemption," 33.

34. *Journal of the House of the State of Georgia, 1868* (Atlanta, 1868), 7–13, 49–52, 93, 201, 218.

35. *Herald*, August 27, 1868; Drago, *Black Politicians*, 49; *Journal of the House of the State of Georgia, 1868* (Atlanta, 1868), 224.

36. Edwin S. Redkey, *Respect Black: The Writings and Speeches of Henry McNeal Turner* (New York: Arno Press, 1971), 15, 27; Currie-McDaniel, *Carpetbagger of Conscience*, 95.

37. *Herald*, Sept. 17, 1868; Drago, *Black Politicians*, 53.

38. Numan V. Bartley, *The Creation of Modern Georgia* (Athens: University of Georgia Press, 1983), 62; *The Condition of Affairs in Georgia: Statement of Hon. Nelson Tift to the Reconstruction Committee of the House of Representatives, Washington, February 18, 1869* (Freeport, N.Y.: Books for Libraries Press, 1869, reprint 1971), 138; Joe McWhorter to John J. Knox, November 1, 1868, John H. Sullivan to J. H. Cathey, October 29, 1868, Governor's Incoming Correspondence, GDAH; *Herald*, September 17, October 22, 29, 1868.

39. Deaton, "Violent Redemption," 38–40; *Herald*, November 5, 1868.

40. *Herald*, December 3, 1868; D. A. Newsom to R. B. Bullock, July 24, 1869,

Abram Colby to Governor, August 23, 1869, R. H. Gladding to R. B. Bullock, September 22, 1869, Governor's Incoming Correspondence, GDAH.

41. *KKK Testimony*, 1111–19; *Herald*, September 16, 1869; Affidavit of Jordan Williams, August 25, 1869, Governor's Incoming Correspondence, GDAH.

42. *KKK Testimony*, 697–704.

43. Georgia Executive Records, Proclamation of November 29, 1869, GDAH; Coleman, ed., *A History of Georgia*, 214; *KKK Testimony*, 700.

44. *KKK Testimony*, 703–6; *Herald*, August 31, November 17, December 8, 15, 1870; W. A. Pledger to Hon. A. Pratt, November 18, 1875, John Emory Bryant Papers, Special Collections, Duke University Libraries, Durham, N.C.

45. *KKK Testimony*, 697–99; *Daily New Era* (Atlanta), December 30, 1870.

46. Atlanta *Constitution*, January 13, 1872; Coleman, ed., *A History of Georgia*, 215–16; Savannah *Morning News*, August 28, 1872.

47. *KKK Testimony*, 699–700; Atlanta *Constitution*, November 7, 1872.

48. *KKK Testimony*, 699–700; Atlanta *Constitution*, November 7, 1872.

49. *KKK Testimony*, 697, 700, 701.

50. Raper, *Tenants of the Almighty*, 365, 372; *Herald*, August 10, 1882; *Southern Cultivator*, 30, no. 5 (May 1872). For excellent accounts of the struggle to control black labor, see Charles L. Flynn, Jr., *White Land, Black Labor: Caste and Class in Late Nineteenth-Century Georgia* (Baton Rouge: Louisiana State University Press, 1983), and Roger L. Ransom and Richard Sutch, *One Kind of Freedom: The Economic Consequences of Emancipation* (New York: Cambridge University Press, 1977).

51. Frederick A. Bode and Donald E. Ginter, *Farm Tenancy and the Census in Antebellum Georgia* (Athens: University of Georgia Press, 1986), 151.

52. *Georgia Laws, 1866*, 141. For an account of the further development of these laws see Jonathan M. Bryant, "A Dangerous Venture: Three Legal Changes in Post-bellum Georgia" (M.A. thesis, University of Georgia, 1987), 26–41; and Jonathan M. Bryant, "'A County Where Plenty Should Abound': Race, Law, and Markets in Greene County, Georgia, 1850–1885" (Ph.D. diss., University of Georgia, 1992), 133–236.

53. *Davis* v. *Terry*, 41 Ga. 95 (1870); *Taliaferro* v. *Fry*, 41 Ga. 622 (1871); *Appling* v. *Odom*, 46 Ga. 583 (1872).

54. *Herald*, December 22, 1881.

55. *Herald*, October 8, 15, 1874; *Daily Chronicle and Sentinel* (Augusta, Ga.), December 3, 1874.

56. *Herald*, November 12, 1874; *Daily Chronicle and Sentinel*, November 10, 1874.

57. *Herald*, November 12, 19, 26, December 3, 1874; *Daily Chronicle and Sentinel*, November 10, 13, 18, 1874; Atlanta *Constitution*, Nov. 10, 1874.

58. *Georgia Laws, 1884–1885*, 615–17; Raper, *Tenants of the Almighty*, 127–29; *Herald-Journal* (Greenesboro, Ga.), May 29, 1908; John W. T. Catching to Gov. James M. Smith, June 3, 1872, Governor's Incoming Correspondence, GDAH.

59. *Atlanta Journal*, May 17, 1894. Abram Colby does not appear in the Soundex Index to the 1880 census for Georgia. Possibly he moved to another state, died, or

was killed, but I can find no evidence of his fate. During the summer of 1990 I spent several weeks researching in Greene County and interviewed many older residents, both white and black. The black community remembered nothing of Abram Colby. His story was so thoroughly unknown that at one point I returned to my car and pulled out xeroxes of old documents to reassure myself that Colby had indeed existed. Only one white man, Carey Williams, Jr., the ninety-year-old former editor of the *Herald-Journal*, recalled any of Colby's story. "That nigger congressman?" he said. "They killed him." Whatever Abram Colby's fate, perhaps most shocking of all is the destruction of his memory among the black citizens of Greene County.

A Georgia Governor
Battles Racism

Rufus Bullock and the
Fight for Black Legislators

Russell Duncan

Sitting onstage just behind the speaker, the distinguished master of cere-
monies, Rufus Brown Bullock, listened to Booker T. Washington give the
speech of his life. The audience applauded enthusiastically the black man's
words that his race was an economic ally, not the enemy, of southern white
society. "In all things that are purely social, we can be as separate as the fin-
gers, yet one as the hand in all things essential to mutual progress. There is
no defence or security for any of us, except in the highest intelligence and
development of all."[1]

Washington may have accommodated too much in this chance to speak
for black people to a nationwide audience, and he told white people only
what they wanted to hear. But Bullock must have been thrilled to watch a
former slave give the keynote address opening the 1895 Atlanta Cotton States
and International Exposition. Like Washington, Bullock had come to advocate equal if separate coexistence for blacks and whites in the South. Like
Washington, Bullock was a principled but practical man.

A quarter of a century earlier Bullock, Georgia's only Republican governor ever, had joined black leaders Henry McNeal Turner, James M. Simms,
and Tunis G. Campbell to promote full equality and equal citizenship for
all Americans. Eventually, he came to realize that most white Georgians—
indeed most white Americans—were incapable of living out their expressed

creed that "all men are created equal." So Bullock made the best of the times. He found it expedient to save black lives and help black people advance at the most deliberate speed. He came to this accommodation as a result of a long career in the business world, where the marketplace promoted compromise, and after sixty-one years of reconciling what ought to be with what was possible.

Bullock was not a native Georgian, but he had lived in Augusta since 1859, when he moved south to expand the freight business of the Adams Express Company. During Reconstruction, his enemies were never sure of how to condemn him and alternately referred to him as "carpetbagger" and "scalawag." In later years, Margaret Mitchell knew that simply to describe him as "Republican" was epithet enough to link him with "Carpetbaggers, Yankees, and negroes." [2]

Born in 1834 and raised in Albion, New York, a town on the Erie Canal, Bullock learned about abolition, business, and free labor ideology from his parents, peers, and teachers. He knew soon-to-be industrialist George Pullman. He conversed with visitors who departed canal boats, and he heard stories about manifest destiny, moral uplift, and free soil. Albion was part of the "burned-over district"—so named because of the intense heat of evangelism that swept the area during the Second Great Awakening. Also, Albion lay just west of Rochester, a center of abolitionist activity and pivot point for Frederick Douglass's efforts. Bullock received a practical education in equality by attending an integrated academy whose teachers hid fugitive slaves in their schoolhouse until they could "be put upon the night train for . . . liberty." [3]

Bullock found employment with a local telegraph company just seven years after Samuel Morse invented the device. Bullock's successes led to new opportunities, first as manager of the American Telegraph Company's Philadelphia office and later with the Adams Express Company, which hired him and sent him to Augusta to expand lines and business in a new market. When the Civil War erupted, Bullock continued his business operations, then under the aegis of the Southern Express Company. After 1865, Bullock saw the chance both to reshape Georgia in the North's free labor mode and to make money. He became a city councilman, served as president of a bank, ran a manufacturing company, and headed a railroad construction project. After Congress took charge of Reconstruction in 1867, friends urged him to run for governor. He reluctantly agreed. [4]

Elected governor in April 1868 by newly enfranchised black voters, upcountry whites, and a handful of white Radicals, Bullock came under attack from Democratic counterstrikes to remove Republicans from the Georgia

Rufus Brown Bullock.
Photographic files, Hargrett Rare Book and
Manuscript Library, University of Georgia Libraries.

government. But before they removed him, Democrats focused upon the two black senators and twenty-nine black representatives—the first black men to be elected to state offices ever, but, and more importantly, men who were put into office by the ballots of former slaves. Bullock and his enemies realized that the early fight over black rights and power in Georgia centered on whether or not these black Republicans could keep their legislative seats.

Democrats abhorred the presence of blacks in the statehouse and had been ready to expel them since the opening session in May 1868. The political rewards of doing so were considerable, for it would raise the stock of Democrats among white Georgians and undermine the "equality" of the hated Thirteenth and Fourteenth Amendments; and, in accordance with Georgia law, it would replace the expelled members with men who had received the second-highest number of votes in the election—all Democrats—and thereby reinstall the old conservative leadership in power. Then, no matter what the governor attempted, they could override him.

As early as July 8, the fourth day of the session, Democrats asserted that blacks were ineligible under the state constitution. Less than three weeks later, on July 26, the Senate tabled a resolution by Milton Chandler of Washington that sought to remove black senators from their seats. On September 3, members of the Georgia House voted to expel all twenty-nine black legislators as ineligible for office on condition of race under the state constitution and Georgia law. When Speaker of the House Richard McWhorter, a moderate Republican, ruled that the black legislators could not vote on their own eligibility, he ensured expulsion. Many Republicans then failed to vote on the question at all; some were resigned to the reality that their votes could not prevent the inevitable, while others feared being branded "nigger lover" or being murdered by the Klan—as Republican senatorial candidate George W. Ashburn had been in Columbus on March 31. Bullock later testified before the Joint Committee on Reconstruction that many Republicans failed to cast ballots after receiving "letters advising them to prepare to meet their Maker, &c., if they dared to vote to keep negroes in their seats." The final vote to expel in the House was eighty-three to twenty-three. The Senate followed suit and on September 12, by a vote of twenty-one to eleven, expelled its two black senators, Tunis Campbell and George Wallace. The votes clearly show that on the question of racial equality, only thirty-four white Republicans were committed to the Radical program. The moderates agreed with the Democrats that freedom was enough; to make former slaves their political equals simply went too far.[5]

Blacks did not acquiesce quietly in their expulsion. Senator Campbell loudly protested the action as "illegal, unconstitutional, unjust and oppressive." The most prominent black leader in the House, Henry McNeal Turner, spoke of the paradox in the expulsion by noting that while many legislators have been removed for committing crimes, "it has remained for the State of Georgia . . . to call a man before the bar, and there charge him with an act for which he is no more responsible than for the head which he carries upon his shoulders. . . . It is very strange, if a white man can occupy on this floor *a seat created by colored votes, and a black man cannot do it.*"[6]

In an effort to regain their seats, the expelled legislators sent Campbell and his son, a member of the House, to Washington, D.C., to lobby for congressional interference into Georgia affairs. For five weeks the Campbells pleaded with senators Charles Sumner, E. D. Morgan, and others for some protection in their rights as citizens, as did James Simms, Henry Turner, and other black Georgians. It would be over a year before Congress returned them to their seats.[7]

Bullock reluctantly did his duty and submitted the names of the Democrats who had finished second in the late election to take the seats of the expelled Republicans. The House was then overwhelmingly aligned against any Republican program, and political animus further intensified with Bullock's outspoken objections to the General Assembly's action. He reminded the legislators of his "solemn oath" to uphold the constitution and his intention to do so. He declared that he would not be "a silent spectator" to their prejudiced actions in excluding "electors who are not of Anglo-Saxon blood from the right of representing the voters by whom they were legally and constitutionally elected." Bullock tried to disarm the ridiculous assertion that a constitution had to specifically grant rights to citizens under a "specific enactment." He proposed that "it might with more propriety be argued that a Constitution framed by delegates who were voted for by 85,000 black men and 25,000 white men and ratified by the votes of 70,000 black men and 25,000 white men, did not carry with it that privilege to the white elector because it was not affirmatively stated."[8]

Bullock reminded the legislators that during the 1868 constitutional convention Democratic delegate James Waddell's motion that "white men only shall be eligible to office . . . in this State" was defeated overwhelmingly, 113 to 19. Bullock said that "the framers of the Constitution made no distinction between electors, or citizens, on account of race or color, and neither can you without violating it." He chided them for their failure to live up to republican ideals. Bullock cited sections of the Georgia law, Irwin's Code, which granted to all citizens the right to hold office "unless specifically prohibited by law." He concluded by pleading with them "to pause in the suicidal course upon which you have entered."[9]

His words fell upon unsympathetic, but not deaf, ears. There were signs that Bullock might even be impeached if he pursued his denunciation of the legislature. Indeed, as early as August 24, Savannah Republican Charles H. Hopkins told him of the impending expulsion of black legislators and warned: "You will be impeached, . . . your enemies have all their plans well laid to destroy you." Democratic Senate leader Milton Candler rebuked the governor for his "interference" in legislative matters and told him to mind his own business. The Democratic press inflamed whites by calling Bullock "a sincere and consistent advocate of negro supremacy in the South. He hates the white people . . . so intensely that he would prefer to see all the offices in the State filled by the most ignorant and corrupt of the black race."[10]

Labeling the expulsion "the great wrong," Bullock reached a crisis that became a turning point in his political and personal life. A close friend remembered that Bullock "had to decide a vital question. He had to either go back entirely on the men who had elected him or he had to take sides with the negroes in their contest with the white people. . . . He was bound to do the latter, and after that decision it was a bitter and deadly fight. There was no compromise possible. It was war."[11]

Bullock realized that to control Georgia's economic development he must maintain political power. He had been a reluctant politician, but once in office he threw himself into his job and took charge of the state's reconstruction. And yet, his defense of black rights was deeper than just an attempt to remain in power. Forced to examine his fundamental beliefs, Bullock realized, perhaps for the first time, that justice required equal rights for all men. He believed in the Union, in the Constitution, and in obedience to law. He believed in progress and the advancement of the nation under its original revolutionary creed. He came to see the injustice of racial arrogance. In a time and a place where everything was increasingly defined in terms of black or white, Bullock went against the current to support the freedpeople and the Constitution and he remained steadfast even though admitting, "Earnest appeals were made to me by frightened and discouraged Republicans to acquiesce in this outrage." With his sense of propriety bruised but his insistence on doing what was right unshaken, he could not retreat to a philosophy of "whatever is good for business and damn the rest."[12]

Bullock was able to see a broader duty beyond the narrow interests of self, business, or party. From this point, where he supported the rights of black men to hold office in Georgia—where he supported the principles for which Republicans stood—Bullock set a course he would have to defend the rest of his life. Once he concluded that blacks should have an equal chance in American life, he became outspoken for equal treatment in regard to race. He became the black man's friend and devoted his time as governor to achieving as much as possible for blacks and for business. But his path was hazardous.[13]

Just one week after the Georgia Senate completed the removal of blacks from the General Assembly, a number of white men in the south Georgia town of Camilla killed or wounded nearly forty Republicans. Known thereafter as the "Camilla Massacre" or the "Camilla Riot," according to one's perspective, the violence of September 19, 1868, awakened northern consciousness while simultaneously warning all Georgians that participation in Republican politics imperiled life and property.[14]

The Ku Klux Klan under Grand Dragon John B. Gordon perpetrated innumerable outrages on Republicans in Georgia as Bullock stood helpless to stop the intimidations. The occupation army under the command of George Meade in Atlanta was reluctant to intervene, would not respond to Bullock's incessant requests for help, and stood by as Democrats and their terrorist wing intimidated, beat, and murdered with impunity. In 1871, Henry Turner estimated that fifteen hundred to sixteen hundred Georgia blacks had been killed by the Klan. Bullock's secretary of state, David G. Cotting, informed the governor that "no human being will ever know the number of murders committed in Georgia. . . . The murderers and buzzards only can give a guess."[15]

Bullock's first hundred days as governor would have destroyed a lesser man. He had little support from the legislature, the military, or Congress. He had been unsuccessful on the eligibility question, on the expulsion of black legislators, and in his efforts to stem Klan violence.

Bullock realized that the state still might be saved if he could keep its affairs before the northern public. Democrats accused him of manufacturing outrages, but with Klan violence rising, there was little need for anything but the truth. The expulsion, violence, and fraud that gave Georgia to Democrat Horatio Seymour instead of Republican Ulysses S. Grant in the 1868 presidential election helped Bullock convince Congress that Georgia needed further reconstruction. During the next sixteen months Bullock occupied himself with efforts to restore the expelled legislators to their rightful seats and remove those white Democrats who were ineligible. Under the test oath provisions of the July 2, 1862 statute, as incorporated into the March 23, 1867 Reconstruction Act and the Fourteenth Amendment, no person who had once sworn to uphold the Constitution but then had supported the South by arms or aid could be elected to public office without having the disability removed by two-thirds vote of Congress. Bullock sought congressional interference to uphold the so-called "test oath" whereby members had to swear that they were eligible under the law. In this effort he was not alone.[16]

Soon after their expulsion, black legislators met in convention in Macon, where Henry M. Turner urged them to be alert for Republican "vipers" who voted alongside Democrats. Many of the black leaders spent much of the next year in Washington imploring Congress to support Bullock, whom they trusted more than any other white man in the state. Their faith in him was well placed. This issue of black officeholding distinguished him from the majority of white Republicans and explains why black Georgians continued to believe in Bullock after they lost faith in other white party leaders. Committed to a true reconstruction, the governor sought to reinstate blacks even if it meant alienating white members of his party.[17]

And that was what it meant. Many white Republicans feared that further congressional interference in Georgia affairs, even if necessary to protect freedmen's rights and Republican lives, would be a major political blunder. Joseph E. Brown, the ever-resilient Democratic war governor turned Republican Chief Justice of Georgia's highest court, understood the economic and personal intimidation that Democrats could impose upon freedmen. He wrote Bullock that the success of the Republican party no longer depended solely on the black vote but also upon a divided white vote. He observed that planters "will always control tenants and laborers" and concluded that Congress should "act cautiously" to "take no step backward" to "undo what has been done." Brown explained that peace and the future of the party was at stake. Congressional interference, he predicted, "would raise such a storm and so embitter the feelings of our people" that the Republican party would be cast out at the next election.[18]

Bullock thanked Brown for his views but proceeded with his course. Had he followed Brown's advice and courted white Georgians at the expense of the freedmen, perhaps the state's Republican party might have remained viable in the post-Reconstruction years. But that would mean abandoning equality, something Bullock had determined to defend. Thirty years later, an admirer recalled Bullock's course of action: "Undaunted by obloquy and although deserted by some of his best friends, Governor Bullock stood out conscientiously and manfully for the rights of the negro representatives in the legislature." [19]

While some Republicans compromised to retain power, Bullock stuck to his beliefs. Historian Michael Perman, using the terminology of political scientists, has written that after 1868 the Republican party moved from being an "expressive" party to become a "competitive" party. An expressive party, he explains, maintains its consistency and ideological principle above all other issues, including broadening its membership and winning elections. Conversely, a competitive party constantly adjusts its stance and principles to win elections. Clearly, the national Republican party increasingly became dominated by non-Radicals, headed by Ulysses S. Grant, and thus made the transition from expressive to competitive.[20]

In Georgia, Joseph Brown led the competitive wing, those willing to compromise equality in order to remain in power. He wrote President Grant about the Radicals' failure to compromise and shared his fears with Massachusetts senator Henry Wilson: "I respectfully say that a few extreme men, mostly, popularly called carpetbaggers are not the best judges of what will promote our interests or the interest of the government." Brown hoped that most Georgians eventually would settle to the center—or Centrist position—equidistant from the extremes of Klan violence and Radical egalitarianism.[21]

It was Brown's wing who joined Democrats to put competitivists (Centrists) in the U.S. Senate and expel the black legislators. Increasingly, as Bullock insisted that Georgians follow the Reconstruction Acts, borderline Radicals drifted to the center or became Democrats. Bullock understood the consequences and recalled that his action in defending the political rights of blacks "was intensely unpopular at the time, and . . . large numbers of white men who had accepted the reconstruction policy, condemned my course in behalf of the colored men and withdrew from the party." Some who were not rewarded with patronage positions left Bullock. Others feared that congressional interference would precipitate open rebellion within the state. As more Republicans moved to the center, they split the party and ensured Democratic victories.[22]

Bullock did not join the defection to the Centrists but retained his expressive views. Because he stuck to principles, many of his friends and fellow Republicans accused him of destroying the party in Georgia, and many historians have, too. But Bullock understood the essence of the American creed. Radical U.S. Senator Samuel C. Pomeroy of Kansas agreed with Bullock that if the party abandoned its principles, "the party itself would not be worth preserving. The strength of the Republican party consists in its adherence to principle, and to that embodiment of its principles, equality of rights among men." [23]

Less than a week after Brown counseled him not to seek congressional intervention, Bullock went to Washington. There he reminded the legislators that under a section of the 1867 Reconstruction Acts, Georgia was to remain in provisional status until Congress tendered seats to her representatives. Although the House had admitted the representatives from Georgia, the Senate had not yet seated its elected senators, Joshua Hill and H. V. M. Miller; thus, Georgia remained in limbo. Bullock told Congress that Georgia's legislature had not been "organized in accordance with the Reconstruction acts," because the test oath had been ignored. He asserted that the legislature had compounded this iniquity by expelling its black members. Bullock asked Congress to assert its authority over Georgia by reseating the rightful members and requiring all legislators to take the test oath.[24]

Leading the opposition to Bullock's plan, Joe Brown stated his case in a letter to Senator Joshua Hill. While conceding that some of Georgia's state legislators sat illegally, Brown believed that the governor's "proposition to declare all that has been done in Georgia illegal and remand the state back under military government" was unwise. Brown feared that "our people will lose all patience and become desperate under the belief that we are never to have stability." He told Hill that, in his opinion, "the reconstruction acts no where require us to give the negroes the right to hold office." Brown gave Hill permission to use the letter as he saw fit to prevent Congress from acquiescing to Bullock's requests. Other Georgia Republicans of the Centrist stripe joined Democratic letter writers to oppose the Radical plan. With such conflicting counsel, members of Congress had a difficult time deciding what to do.[25]

Bullock remained in Washington and joined eight other Georgia Republicans who testified on conditions in Georgia before the Joint Committee on Reconstruction. On December 19, Bullock repeated his criticism of Meade's failure to require legislators to take a valid test oath and charged that there were "not less than 40 in the House and 15 or 18 in the senate" who were unable to take the oath. Responding to a question from committee chair George Boutwell, who asked for suggestions as to what should be done, Bullock answered only that the nation "carry out the laws literally, and to admit to the legislature only those who could take the oath required by law. By these means the colored members who were expelled will be reinstated."[26]

Bullock wanted Congress to execute the law by having the military commander reassemble the original 1868 legislature and then investigate each member's right to be seated. He trusted in the efficacy of the oath as the vehicle to effect a true reconstruction and opposed "any new legislation to bring about results which would have been accomplished by the legislation already had." Democrats had proven beyond a doubt that they intended to use all methods available—intimidation, obloquy, election fraud, perjury, judicial corruption, lawless sheriffs, assault, murder, and collusion of all sorts—to hold on to the old ways. Bullock understood their resistance to change, but the Civil War mandated change; progress would not come unless Radical Republicans sat in the state legislature. Clearly, Bullock's insistence on the oath was a partisan measure that would result in more "loyal Union men" gaining office. But they had rightful claims to those offices. By supporting the oath, Bullock acknowledged the primacy of law.[27]

Eight other Georgians answered questions before the Joint Committee. James Simms of Savannah, an expelled member of the legislature, spoke about the intimidation and violence toward black voters and the fact that powerful Democrats condoned such action, if only by their silence. In obvious reference to the Camilla massacre, Henry McNeal Turner told of freedmen's political meetings, which were enthusiastic yet controlled: "At no meeting did the colored people ever inaugurate strife or collision with the whites." Amos Akerman amplified Simms's analysis, saying, "there are two and only two very disturbing elements in our southern society": Democratic politicians and sons of wealthy men who saw their "easy lives" threatened by the results of the war. John E. Bryant, a failed officeholder who increasingly disagreed with Bullock over the direction of the Republican party, disagreed with Simms and Akerman and testified that he felt that the leading Democrats did not control their constituents and could not prevent violence in the state. While arguing that Georgia's constitution surely gave blacks the right to hold office, Bryant contended that more congressional interference would "stir up the people." The other four Georgians focused their remarks on the violence and fraud that attended the 1868 presidential election. The Joint Committee accepted into evidence documents, memorials, petitions, and letters, some assembled by the Georgia Republican party, from other Georgians, military officers, and Freedmen's Bureau agents. The testimony and documents present a sordid portrait of a recalcitrant Georgia where Republican lives and votes had little value.[28]

Georgia congressman Nelson Tift of Albany presented the most effective argument for the Democrats and Centrists, and undoubtedly his efforts confused the issue and created further congressional indecision. Tift, a lifelong Democrat, represented Georgia's Second Congressional District; he probably was one of those fraudulently elected since even though his twenty-two-county district had a black majority of over eighty-one hundred votes, he "won" the election by twenty-five hundred votes. He labeled Bullock a "traitor" who used "false pretexts and false testimony" to persuade Congress. Democratic newspapers followed Tift's lead and filled their columns with fustian innuendo about a "slander mill" originated and operated by the governor. The *Augusta Chronicle* fumed: "Outrages of the most horrible description, and murders [of] the most cold-blooded [kind] were manufactured in Atlanta . . . and sent Northward . . . for Congressional consumption."[29]

To counter Republican testimony and documentation, Tift distributed a questionnaire among "the best citizens of the state" asking whether all citizens, black and white, Republican and Democrat, had equal protection and security in Georgia. Tift's letter held up the specter of "the dictatorship of a provisional governor, with the army and navy of the United States to enforce his edicts." Predictably, respondents answered almost uniformly that no violence or even discrimination existed in Georgia; indeed, Georgians did not resist the laws of Congress and had good government under the existing legislature. Joseph E. Brown, however, dissented.[30]

Brown wrote that in the last election "a great deal of lawlessness and crime . . . has gone unpunished." Brown blamed the situation on election excitement, "bitter and vindictive" leaders, and local law officers who "yielded to the strength of the current, and neglected to discharge their duties with firmness and strict impartiality." Brown forthrightly stated that, in his opinion, "the whole mass of the people are controlled by passion or prejudice . . . beyond the corrective power of congressional legislation or military dictatorship." While he argued against a re-Reconstruction, Brown believed that Congress had the power to reseat the black legislators and expel illegal members in the Georgia legislature. Anything further would give Democrats a "cause" and hurt Republican chances to split them. While Brown's response acknowledged the turbulence in Georgia, Tift used it to bolster his case that Congress should recognize Reconstruction as complete and enact no further legislation.[31]

In a long letter to the Reconstruction committee, Bullock refuted Tift's representations and denied that he wanted a resumption of military rule. Bullock challenged Tift's argument that Georgia had complied with every particular of the Reconstruction Acts: "If this statement can be true, it must be admitted that the laws of Congress, instead of accomplishing reconstruction, have effectively secured the destruction of the hopes, expectations, and prayers of the loyal men, who have suffered ostracism, outrage, and, in many instances, death."[32]

Bullock emphasized that blacks were citizens who had been denied their rights to hold office. He denounced the questionnaires as invalid and said that of those judges, mayors, ordinaries, and others who answered, only six were Republicans. Some respondents wrote entirely against Tift and some were misrepresented. Bullock cited the "evidence" of ordinary Lewis Jackson of McIntosh County, a freedman, who supposedly agreed with Tift, who "denies, on oath, ever having made any reply whatever to the interrogations of Mr. Tift . . . and pronounces . . . [his questionnaire] a forgery."[33]

After listening to the arguments, two of the nation's most powerful and consistent Radicals, Senator Charles Sumner and Representative Benjamin Butler, presented bills in the Senate and the House supporting Bullock's request for another Reconstruction in Georgia. But a full year would pass before Congress would reach that conclusion.[34]

On January 13, 1869, Bullock presented his first annual message to the General Assembly. He began by reading the letter he wrote to Congress asking for a literal interpretation of the Reconstruction Acts. Then he scolded the legislators for the expulsion of black members and called for them to "take the initiative" and reseat their black counterparts. Referring to the murders of freedmen in Camilla and to the recent New Orleans race riot, Bullock demanded that the government tighten officeholding and voting requirements for former Confederates: "With me, no more amnesty or removal of disabilities till the life of the humblest individual who walks on God's foot-stool, be he black or white, is as sacred in Camilla, Georgia, or in New Orleans, Louisiana, as it is in . . . Amesburg in Massachusetts." Bullock promised the lawmakers that if they would recognize their ex-slaves as equal citizens of Georgia he would support removal of all political disabilities. He warned them that if the state refused to act, the national government would intervene.[35]

Despite this forceful plea, the General Assembly failed to act and Congress

dallied. Perhaps a part of the latter's inertia lay in the fact that Andrew Johnson was a lame duck president and Republicans preferred to wait for Grant to
take office in March. During this period of obstinate inaction, state Republicans wrote many letters supporting the Sumner and Butler bills and pleading
for action. One blamed Meade: "The curse of present troubles grew out of
shirking a plain duty by neglecting to apply the 14th Article or Amendment
when the Legislature was first organized." Bullock told Benjamin Butler that
many feared Grant might refuse to support intervention and hoped that Congress would take the chance that Johnson might sign the bill. The governor
suggested disfranchising "all the rebs who still persist in their opposition to
Congress" and pointed out that enfranchising them had only led to violent
opposition to Reconstruction. He felt confident that "prompt action will save
many lives & make a loyal state." Clearly, he had given up hope that Georgia
Democrats would do justice.[36]

Savannah Republican Charles H. Hopkins wrote Butler in support of Bullock, praising him as "the champion of the weak and oppressed in this State."
Hopkins predicted, "Should your bill fail in Congress their [the black legislators'] last hope will have expired." Expelled representative Henry Turner told
Butler of his impatience with a turtle-like Congress: "If it is a fact that the
party for whom we have sacrificed every thing is going to desert us . . . then it
is high time we knew it." Then in a flurry that must have bruised Butler's ego
and moved him to greater action, Turner ended his letter: "Thousands have
already declared that the Republican party have led us into the wilderness
and deserted. And the democrats are daily taunting us with it, by saying, *Now
where is your damned Radical party. Why don't Beast Butler, and old Sumner come
to your aid etc.*"[37]

While Congress deliberated, the Georgia House and Senate supported a
resolution that a test case be tried before the Georgia Supreme Court to decide if black men were eligible to hold office. The legislators believed that this
would show good faith and keep the federal government deadlocked. Legislators also hoped that Chief Justice Joseph Brown would sway the court in
their favor and declare blacks ineligible. After all, only one year before, he
had told north Georgia whites that the black man was ineligible for office.
Democrats must have delighted to see him squirm.[38]

Bullock believed that Democrats had adopted the resolution for a trial case
"without any intention on their part to abide by such decision." He vetoed
the resolution and returned it with the explanation that the original organization of the legislature without application of the test oath was the main
issue. Thus, he continued, "evil results" have followed. Bullock then went
into a long and tightly reasoned argument to show why the legislature was

unlawfully constituted. Since the Georgia House had maintained in July that "all persons now in their seats are eligible," Bullock argued that the subsequent decision to remove blacks was obviously based on racism. As proof of black eligibility, he cited the Fourteenth Amendment, the test oath, and the Georgia Constitution, as well as the fundamental principle that individuals in a democracy can elect whomever they wanted to represent them. He conceded that in due judicial time a case now pending in Savannah would reach Georgia's highest court and the legal opinion of the state would decide the eligibility question. But until then, he asked them to proceed quickly to do what was right.[39]

With the governor and the legislature at an impasse and before the Savannah case reached Georgia's high court, Congress sent the Fifteenth Amendment to the states for ratification. That amendment specifically granted the right to vote regardless of "race, color, or previous condition of servitude." Surely, with the fight raging over black rights, Democrats in both houses of the Georgia legislature would refuse to support the amendment. But when Georgia voted not to ratify, it was Bullock, not the Democrats, who defeated the amendment. Bullock knew that Democrats would support ratification, for to oppose it would risk further intervention by a Congress that seemed willing to acquiesce in the seizure of the Georgia legislature.

On March 10, Bullock transmitted the amendment to the General Assembly but warned them that ratification without reorganization and reseating could not be taken seriously. He argued that for democracy to work, blacks must participate in the government and hold seats, so "that their voices may be heard in your halls and their votes recorded on public measures." He emphasized, "This Amendment is specifically designed to secure political privileges to the colored man." Bullock told them he cherished this amendment because it embodied the spirit of the American creed that "all men are created equal" as "the very foundation of Republican Government." He reminded the lawmakers that "the colored race is free" and that this amendment would complete their transition from slavery.[40]

Bullock's message to the Georgia legislators followed the Republican convention held in Atlanta on March 5, where 238 delegates from 104 counties drafted and sent a resolution to Congress claiming that the loyal men of Georgia had been denied representation by the usurping legislature. The delegates cited their fears of terrorism and murder but declared themselves "totally opposed to the remanding of our State to military government and only ask such interference . . . as may be necessary to a thorough and Moral execution of that portion of the Reconstruction acts which should control the organization of the General Assembly." They praised the Fifteenth Amendment as "a measure of right and justice and [we] shall recommend its adoption when we have a legislature that will, in good faith, provide for its enforcement." Bullock held the upper hand. For if the General Assembly did not reorganize itself, Radicals in the Georgia Senate could defeat the Fifteenth Amendment. Because northern Republicans viewed the amendment as a way to consolidate party strength in the North, they would surely intervene in Georgia affairs if the amendment were defeated.[41]

The General Assembly refused to reorganize itself, apply the test oath, or reseat its black members as Bullock requested. It probably would have defeated the Fifteenth Amendment had not the threat of a return to military rule been eminent. So Democrats decided to support the amendment, reasoning that they could always disregard it as they were ignoring the Fourteenth. On March 11 the Democrat-controlled Georgia House voted sixty-seven to fifty-nine in support of the amendment, and sent it to the senate where it failed by thirteen to sixteen votes with fifteen abstentions. Seven senate Radicals voted to defeat the amendment, and nine more failed to vote on the question. Bullock explained by letter to Congress why "ardent Republicans and hearty friends" of the amendment refused to vote or voted against ratification: the Georgia legislature was an illegally constituted body of men who evaded the law and true Republicans could not now support the amendment while these villains are "cooly trampling" on the Fourteenth Amendment, "*which they had only a few months before made a pretense to ratifying.*"[42]

On April 9, 1869, the fourth anniversary of the surrender at Appomattox, Indiana senator Oliver P. Morton introduced a bill requiring Virginia, Mississippi, Texas, and Georgia to ratify the Fifteenth Amendment as a precondition to reentering the Union. Bullock returned to Washington to lobby for the bill and was so active that the *New York World* even credited him with authorship. The Senate passed the bill 40 to 9. In the House, Butler presented a similar bill, which passed 121 to 51. One newspaperman commented that "Governor Bullock seemed, in fact, to be managing the bill in the house. He was on the floor all day, and was consulted by Butler at every stage. His presence was . . . the boldest piece of lobbying ever witnessed in Congress." The reporter misstated the situation; Bullock's presence or absence made no difference. The overwhelming vote for the bill indicated that Butler had little need of Bullock's help to secure passage. Nevertheless, the governor's efforts indicate the degree of his commitment to true reconstruction in Georgia.[43]

While Congress debated freedmen's rights under law, Democratic violence and murders continued in Georgia and were undoubtedly encouraged by congressional inaction. Daily, Bullock received letters begging for assis-

tance and repeatedly asking, as did black minister Adam Palmer of Waynes-
boro, "Is there no help for us[?] Must we thus endure and see our people
murdered and slain and sacrifice our own lives and all we have to the malice
and hatred of lawless and unGodly men or else become exiles in our own
country[?] Is there no power to give us protection?"[44]

Two Georgia state legislators and Radical Republicans, Benjamin Ayer
and Joseph Adkins, were killed en route home from Washington, D.C., where
they had supported Bullock's lobby. Commenting on the murders, the *New
York Times* matter-of-factly stated that "Republicans who desire legal reconstruction in Georgia are rapidly 'perishing by the wayside.'" Augusta Republican A. L. "Fatty" Harris expressed his frustration to fellow Radical
Benjamin Conley: "Do you not think Congress will see the *necessity* of doing
something now? . . . Four years of bloody war to prove *wrong* was *right*, and
still they are trying to do the same thing by assassination. How long must
such things be? . . . We expect Gov. B's return tomorrow if he is not killed on
the way."[45]

Meanwhile, the test case challenging the right of blacks to hold office
reached the Georgia Supreme Court. After freedman Richard W. White of
Savannah had been elected clerk of the superior court of Chatham County,
William J. Clements, a white who had finished second in the voting, filed
suit questioning White's eligibility. The case came to trial in Savannah on
March 4. Amos T. Akerman, whom Grant would appoint attorney general in
1870, argued White's case before the court.[46]

Akerman referred to the vote in the constitutional convention on the clause
that would have specifically granted black officeholding. He insisted that the
delegates had refused to include a specific statement in the constitution because it would be "superfluous" and certainly "negroes would be eligible to
office even though that section were stricken out." Akerman failed to influence the jury, who decided that White, who had seven-eighths white ancestry,
was "a person of color" and thereby ineligible for office. After Judge William
Schley named Clements the rightful winner, White appealed the case to the
Georgia Supreme Court.[47]

In June, Georgia Supreme Court justices Joseph Brown, Henry McCay,
and Hiram Warner heard the case; undoubtedly, they had already come to
individual conclusions. In the gubernatorial race of 1868 and in his letter
to Joshua Hill, Chief Justice Brown had denied that blacks had the right to
hold office. If he maintained that position, White would lose. But Brown's
January letter to Nelson Tift, which had been introduced into evidence before the Joint Committee on Reconstruction, argued for reseating the black

legislators and asked for no new reconstruction policy. Brown had to decide in White's favor, because to do otherwise might spur Congress to intrude further in Georgia affairs.

Hiram Warner, a Democrat, rigidly opposed black officeholding. Warner had been demoted from his position as chief justice when Bullock named Brown to that position.[48]

The third justice, Henry Kent McCay, had been a delegate to the constitutional convention of 1867–68 and therefore knew intimately the intentions of the convention on the question of black officeholding. He had supported Bullock for governor and agreed with Congressional Reconstruction. In writing the principal opinion for *White v. Clements*, McCay agreed that although the 1868 constitution had not specifically granted the right to hold office to blacks, it did not need to. McCay ridiculed the racist assumption that whites got their rights from God, but blacks had to be granted rights by the state. He wrote that blacks "form a portion of the body politic" and thereby have the right to hold office. He stated that blacks contributed at least three-fourths of the vote that ratified the constitution and thereby had "made" the constitution. It was ludicrous to think that they would vote for a basic law which denied their right to representation by a man of their choosing. Brown concurred with McCay; Warner dissented. Thus by a vote of two to one, the high court decided that White and, by implication, all blacks could hold office in Georgia. With this decision the action of the legislature in expelling its black members appeared in an even harsher light.[49]

After the decision, Bullock refused to call a special session of the Georgia legislature. As the *Augusta Chronicle* reported, he was compelled to wait: "The expelled negroes are not now members, and any call which he could lawfully make would apply to those who were *actual* members at the time of the last adjournment. To call that body together as it was constituted, would expose Bullock to almost certain hazard of *impeachment*." For months, Democrats had been proposing just that. Bullock read the papers, understood the Democratic temper, and realized that men who killed and intimidated might well impeach an unpopular governor. So Bullock preferred to wait for Congress to act and refused to convene the hostile legislature.[50]

A month earlier, after hearing of the Adkins and Ayer murders, Massachusetts senator Henry Wilson wrote to Grant about the continuing Georgia bloodbath: "Can nothing be done to stop these outrages in Georgia? These political murders should cease. . . . Martial law is this day needed in that, the worst of all the States." Grant forwarded the letter to William T. Sherman, who, in turn, sent it to the army commander in the South, General Alfred H. Terry. By early July, Terry had investigated the condition of affairs in Georgia and informed Bullock that it would be "fruitless" to prosecute anyone who has previously committed outrages upon Republicans because the local machinery of sheriffs, marshalls, and community leaders were Democratic. Bullock wrote Ben Butler that Terry had decided to recommend return of military rule for Georgia. He hoped Grant would send in the army so that blacks would gain their constitutional rights, Republicans would be protected, and Georgia would be saved "from the political control of the Rebel Democracy."[51]

By mid-August, Terry completed his investigation and filed his report. He described Georgia as a lawless region where killings were "frequent" and where local magistrates and government leaders failed to carry out their responsibilities under the laws. Those civil officers who were not participating members or spiritual allies of the Ku Klux Klan were so intimidated by robed night riders as to be ineffective. Terry described Bullock as a governor who would "gladly interpose" to protect all citizens, but "he has power neither to act directly in bringing offenders to justice nor to compel subordinate officers to do their duty." Terry supported a reorganization of the Georgia legislature as Bullock suggested.[52]

Bullock anxiously awaited the next session of Congress. In late November he wrote Georgia representative Wesley Shropshire, "I profoundly hope and trust that there may be backbone and nerve enough in the National Legislature, to give our Georgia rebels back seats."[53]

Clearly, Bullock wanted a military overseer for Georgia; but that is not to say that he wanted military government. He realized that Terry's opinion might convince Congress to act, and so he supported it. In December 1869, Bullock explained to the *New York Times* that "the time has come when Congress must go backward or forward." He emphasized that he neither wanted harsh terms "nor do we desire military government. . . . All we ask or desire is that congress shall provide for the enforcement of its laws." Others asked for stronger action. In a letter to Butler, Republican party chairman Foster Blodgett displayed a reluctant acquiescence to a military government "until the lawless and rebellious spirit . . . shall be eradicated." Obviously, after a year of waiting, Bullock and Blodgett would accept anything as an improvement over the status quo.[54]

On December 6, 1869, President Grant made his only real contribution to Congressional Reconstruction. Undoubtedly, he came to this decision reluctantly and after weighing a great deal of conflicting information as to the true situation in Georgia. In fact, one letter from elected, but as yet unseated, Senator Joshua Hill described violence in his state as "occasional" and insisted that "men are taking the advice of Webster to his farmer John

Taylor [to] talk of oxen and horses and deep plowing instead of politics."
Eventually Grant came to believe the opposite and in a message to Congress
recommended, "It would be wise to pass a law without delay for the Georgia Governor to convene the original members of the legislature and require
each to take the oath prescribed in the reconstruction acts"—exactly what
Bullock had asked Meade to do in 1868.[55]

Grant's decision supporting the return of Georgia to military supervision
also secured the deciding vote necessary to ratify the Fifteenth Amendment.
Bullock and Blodgett's plan to have the Radicals defeat the amendment nine
months earlier had succeeded. For had those Radicals voted for an amendment which they really wanted, Grant and other Centrists would not have
needed one more state to ratify. Because they needed the vote of Georgia
to secure the Fifteenth Amendment and to consolidate their position in the
North, national Republican Centrists joined Radicals in remanding Georgia
to military rule. For their part, Radicals were most interested in protecting
southern blacks.[56]

Three days before Christmas 1869, Congress acted upon Grant's suggestions and required Georgia to reconvene the original 1868 legislature,
reorganize under the test oath, and ratify the Fifteenth Amendment. Many
Georgians, black and white, played key roles in that decision, but none
more so than Governor Bullock. Following heated debates over states' versus national rights, the Senate voted 45 to 9 and the House concurred 121
to 51 to reimpose military rule. Georgia Radicals hailed the governor for his
tireless efforts. Congressman Charles H. Prince of Augusta, a Republican
who served in the 1868 constitutional convention, wrote to Benjamin Conley
to glorify Bullock as "deserving of great praise from our party in Ga. on account of his untiring energy. . . . The more I see of him the more I am led to
admire him." [57]

Democrats went into a rage. Newspapers throughout Georgia howled
against Bullock as being the architect of this further Reconstruction. Klansman editor Isaac W. Avery of the *Atlanta Constitution* lamented, "To-day is
seen the sad, piteous, shameful spectacle of her Executive conspiring with
her enemies for the overthrow of her liberties. Plotting, scheming, bribing,
truckling, maligning, toiling for her injury and abasement, . . . the government of a million virtuous people is demolished by the act, and anarchy and
the rule of ignorance substituted thereof. . . . Her rulers are against her, not
for her; they are seeking personal aggrandizement, not the public weal." [58]

Avery and other white supremists never understood Bullock's belief that
the Civil War had mandated a free labor system where men of all races should
be treated fairly. Avery's "public weal" did not include the rights of half the

state's population, those who were now free of slavery's bonds. Bullock did indeed take a partisan stand in favor of Radical Reconstruction; his enemies gave him little option. In fact, collusive Democratic polemicists wounded Bullock's sense of honor and fair play and so drove him ever closer to men who seemed to agree with him. Thus Bullock clung to others who were being abused, tended to disregard all criticism of them as fabrication, and had a difficult time distinguishing honest from dishonest motives where these friends were concerned. A few of the men who gained Bullock's trust did not deserve it, but Avery overstated when he charged that all Radicals sought self-aggrandizement.

The same day that President Grant signed "An Act to Promote the Reconstruction of Georgia," Bullock issued a call for those legislators elected in June 1868 to convene in Atlanta on January 10, 1870. Bullock also urged Grant and Sherman, as General of the Army, to appoint General Terry as the on-site commander to oversee the reconstruction of Georgia. On Christmas Eve, Grant formally put Terry in charge of ensuring the state's compliance with the law.[59]

On January 10, the members of Georgia's original 1868 legislature met in Atlanta. Clerks called the name of each elected member to come forward and take the test oath. This procedure depended upon the honesty of the oath takers; it soon became clear that that was not enough. Democrats who were not eligible simply took the oath as if they were. Senator Campbell stood and protested the seating of seven senators and later asked Bullock and Terry to purge the unqualified.[60]

More decisive than Meade had been in 1868, Terry intended to make Georgians comply with the law. On January 13, he appointed a three-man board of military officers, Maj. Gen. Thomas H. Ruger, Brig. Gen. T. J. Haines, and Maj. Henry Goodfellow, to investigate the eligibility of the legislators. Bullock actively pursued the expulsion of those ineligible by sending Terry a list of sixteen house members who had sworn to uphold the Constitution and then participated in the rebellion. Following Georgia precedence and instead of calling for new elections, Bullock advocated replacing legislators found ineligible with those who finished second in the April 1868 election. Unsure of what to do, Terry wrote Sherman for advice and then accepted Bullock's plan—a decision with important ramifications in the future. Bullock wrote Ohio congressman William Lawrence that Democrats had perjured themselves, evidently believing that no one had the authority to expel them. Clearly no Georgia jury would convict them. Bullock supported Terry's board with the understatement, "The situation here is critical." Democratic newspapers resounded with accusations against Terry and

Bullock. The *Augusta Chronicle* screamed about "plunder," called Bullock a "consumate ass, robber and villain," and referred to Georgia Radicals as a "gang of crawling scum." In the end, Terry's board found nineteen house members and five senators unable honestly to take the oath.[61]

Terry purged the twenty-four Democrats and replaced them with the Republican runners-up from the 1868 election. That, in addition to the reseating of thirty-one black legislators, gave Bullock a working majority in both houses of the General Assembly. On February 1, 1870, nineteen months after Bullock's original protests that some legislators sat illegally, and seventeen months after the expulsion of the black legislators, Georgia had a General Assembly organized in accordance with the 1867 Reconstruction Acts. Bullock could be proud of his efforts on behalf of equality and justice for black Georgians, and yet his determined stance in their favor rent the Republican party in favor of the Centrists. In Congress, many protested Terry's actions, denied that the Act of December 22 gave any authority for a purge, and questioned the seating of election runners-up instead of requiring new elections. When the Senate Judiciary Committee began to investigate, Bullock defended Terry's reorganization and, revealing his own polarized political view, asserted that no one disapproved except "the rebel democracy and four recreant republicans whom they have purchased."[62]

The day following the reorganization, February 2, Bullock addressed the legislature. He described the long struggle as a battle between those who supported Reconstruction and those who opposed it. He said his party was the "party of peace" and would accept everyone who supported "equal rights and republican liberty." Bullock sounded the theme of free labor, stressed the importance of the working man, supported free public education for all, and insisted that "a citizen's worth, shall be determined by his own efforts and his own character, neither advanced nor retarded by his birth."[63]

The legislature quickly ratified the Fifteenth Amendment and, to show that the ratification of the Fourteenth Amendment had been effected by an illegal legislature, re-ratified it. Military supervision was withdrawn, and Georgia once again became an equal state in the Union in July 1870. By the 1870 legislative elections, resurgent Democrats with the help of their militant wing, the Ku Klux Klan, stole the vote and called for the governor's head. Bullock held out until October 31, 1871, when, with impeachment certain and imprisonment possible, he resigned and fled north. By November 1, Georgia Redeemers celebrated with one Atlanta editor that the Radicals "are gone—gone so far into the past that fame, with the trumpet of a thousand Gabriels, will never be able to resurrect them, and again set them up as Mentors to frame laws to govern the people of this State."[64]

In 1895, when Booker T. Washington finished his ten-minute address, Bullock rushed forward to congratulate him. They stood together hand in hand for a moment not speaking. Both understood that while wanting equality for blacks, Washington spoke the reality of turn-of-the-century America. The promise and ideals of Reconstruction seemed far away. An acknowledgement of gradualism replaced demands for immediate equality.[65]

Bullock, of course, had returned to Georgia, had stood trial and been acquitted, and had taken a prominent role in building Atlanta's business interests. He continued to support black advancement. Bullock fought discrimination in public accommodations, was a lifelong supporter of Atlanta University, and helped convince Booker T. Washington to come to Atlanta in 1895.[66]

Blacks remained in the Georgia legislature until 1907—the year Bullock died—when state law again disfranchised black voters. It is sadly coincidental that blacks gained the right to vote and hold office in the year of Bullock's ascendancy to the governor's chair and lost those rights the year he died. It was a full one hundred years between Bullock's term and that of another Georgia liberal, James Earl Carter, before any Georgia governor would stand up outspokenly for the constitutional guarantees of one man, one vote.

Notes

1. Booker T. Washington, *Up From Slavery: An Autobiography* (New York: Doubleday, 1901; reprint, New York: Bantam Books, 1967), 156.

2. Margaret Mitchell, *Gone With the Wind* (New York: Macmillan, 1936), 842.

3. Russell Duncan, *Entrepreneur for Equality: Governor Rufus Bullock, Commerce, and Race in Post–Civil War Georgia* (Athens: University of Georgia Press, 1994), 2–8, quote from p. 6.

4. Ibid., chapters 1 and 2.

5. *Journal of the House of the State of Georgia, 1868* (Atlanta: Public Printer, 1868), 121–30, 138, 222, 229, 242–44, 272–73, 277–80. Strangely not using the "rule" that one drop of black blood makes a person black, the House allowed four mulattoes to keep their seats; Testimony of Governor Bullock, "Condition of Affairs in Georgia," 40th Cong., 3rd Sess., House Miscellaneous Document no. 52, part 2, 6.

6. *Journal of the Senate of the State of Georgia, 1868* (Atlanta: J. W. Burke, 1868), 277–81; Turner quoted in W. E. B. Du Bois, *Black Reconstruction in America: An Essay toward a History of the Part Which Black Folk Played in the Attempt to Reconstruct Democracy in America, 1860–1880* (New York: Russell and Co., 1935), 501–2.

7. Russell Duncan, *Freedom's Shore: Tunis Campbell and the Georgia Freedmen* (Athens: University of Georgia Press, 1986), 53–55; Benjamin Conley et al., to the Congress of the United States, September 18, 1868, "Condition of Affairs in Georgia," 86–87.

8. *New York Times,* September 14, 1868; *Georgia Senate Journal, 1868,* 324–27;

Bullock to Georgia House of Representatives, September 9, 1868, Georgia Executive Department, Minutes, 1866–1870, microfilm, 179–83, Georgia Department of Archives and History, Atlanta (GDAH).

9. Ibid.; Volney Spalding to William E. Chandler, September 1, 1868, and John H. Caldwell to William Claflin, September 1, 1868, William E. Chandler Papers, Library of Congress (LC).

10. C. H. Hopkins to Bullock, August 24, 1868, Ga. Exec. Dept., Incoming Correspondence, Bullock, 1868–1871, GDAH; *Augusta Chronicle*, September 11, 1868.

11. Rufus Brown Bullock, "Letter from Rufus B. Bullock, of Georgia, to the Republican Senators and Representatives in Congress Who Sustain the Reconstruction Acts. Dated Willard's Hotel, May 21, 1870" (Washington, D.C.: Chronicle Print, 1870), 4; Newspaper clipping, January 2, 1878, in Henry W. Grady Papers, Emory University, Atlanta.

12. Ibid.; Richard L. Zuber, "The Role of Rufus Brown Bullock in Georgia Politics" (M.A. thesis, Emory University, 1957), 109–10; Clark Howell, *History of Georgia* (Chicago: S. J. Clarke, 1926), 600.

13. Numan V. Bartley, *The Creation of Modern Georgia* (Athens: University of Georgia Press, 1983), 65–66; *Contemporary American Biography* (New York: Atlantic Publishing Co., 1895), 68–69.

14. Duncan, *Entrepreneur for Equality*, 114–17; Lee W. Formwalt, "The Camilla Massacre of 1868: Racial Violence as Political Propaganda," *Georgia Historical Quarterly* 71 (Fall 1987): 66–71.

15. Duncan, *Entrepreneur for Equality*, 70–75; Cotting quote from p. 75. For the best study of the Klan in Georgia, see Stanley K. Deaton, "Violent Redemption: The Democratic Party and the Ku Klux Klan in Georgia, 1868–1871," (M.A. thesis, University of Georgia, 1988).

16. Reconstruction Act of March 23, 1867, "Iron Clad" Test Oath, and Fourteenth Amendment, in Walter L. Fleming, ed., *Documentary History of Reconstruction: Political, Military, Social, Religious, Educational and Industrial, 1865–1906* (1907; reprint, New York: McGraw-Hill, 1966), 1:191–92, 407–11, 479.

17. Edmund L. Drago, *Black Politicians and Reconstruction in Georgia: A Splendid Failure* (Baton Rouge: Louisiana State University Press, 1982), 53–56. Of Georgia's black leaders, only A. A. Bradley of Savannah broke openly with Bullock. Their feud reached back to the 1868 constitutional convention when Bullock led the move to expel Bradley for insulting other convention members. See Drago, *Black Politicians*, 62–63; Eric Foner, *Reconstruction: America's Unfinished Revolution, 1863–1877* (N.Y.: Harper and Row, 1988), 342.

18. Joseph E. Brown to Bullock, December 3, 1868, Joseph E. Brown Papers, Atlanta Historical Society.

19. *Contemporary American Biography*, 69.

20. Michael Perman, *The Road to Redemption: Southern Politics, 1869–1879* (Chapel Hill: University of North Carolina Press, 1984), 5–30, 42–50.

21. Joseph E. Brown to Ulysses S. Grant, May 10, 1869, Brown Family Papers,

University of Georgia, Athens; Joseph E. Brown to Henry Wilson, December 19, 1868, Rufus Brown Bullock Papers, Henry E. Huntington Library, San Marino, Calif.

22. Bullock to the Editor, *Atlanta Constitution*, May 4, 1896; Volney Spalding to W. E. Chandler, August 14, 1868, William E. Chandler Papers, LC; John H. Caldwell, *Reminiscences of the Reconstruction of Church and State in Georgia* (Wilmington, Del.: J. Miller Thomas, 1895), 14.

23. Olive Hall Shadgett, *The Republican Party in Georgia: From Reconstruction through 1900* (Athens: University of Georgia Press, 1964), 49–51; Elizabeth S. Nathans, *Losing the Peace: Georgia Republicans and Reconstruction* (Baton Rouge: Louisiana State University Press, 1968), vii, 147; Ruth Currie-McDaniel, *Carpetbagger of Conscience: A Biography of John Emory Bryant* (Athens: University of Georgia Press), 89–91; Pomeroy quoted in Michael Les Benedict, *A Compromise of Principle: Congressional Republicans and Reconstruction, 1865–1869* (New York: W. W. Norton, 1974), 326.

24. *New York Times*, December 8, 1868; *Congressional Globe*, December 7, 1868, 1–5, 43, 568; December 10, 1868, 43; *Journal of the Senate of the United States*, 40th Cong., 3rd Sess., 5–6, 18, 141–42; William A. Russ, Jr., "Radical Disfranchisement in Georgia, 1867–71," *Georgia Historical Quarterly* 19 (September, 1935): 196–98.

25. Joseph E. Brown to Joshua Hill, December 7, 1868, Brown Family Papers, University of Georgia.

26. Testimony of Governor Bullock, "Condition of Affairs in Georgia," 1–6, quotes from pp. 2, 3; *Congressional Globe*, December 7, 1868, 10.

27. Ibid.

28. Testimony of James M. Simms, Henry M. Turner, Amos T. Akerman, V. A. Gaskill, John E. Bryant, James A. Madden, S. P. Powell, and A. W. Stone, "Condition of Affairs in Georgia," 6–48, documentary evidence, 48–139; *Congressional Globe*, 40th Cong., 3rd Sess., Pt. 1, 3–4; *Journal of the Senate of the United States*, 40th Cong., 3rd Sess., 192, 334.

29. Alexander Stephens to James Brooks, July 24, 1868, Felix Hargrett Collection, University of Georgia; *Report of Madison Bell, Comptroller General of the State of Georgia. From August 11, 1868, to January 1, 1869* (Atlanta: Samuel Bard, 1869), table A; "Condition of Affairs in Georgia," 140–237; *Augusta Chronicle*, September 9, 1869.

30. Zuber, "Role of Rufus Brown Bullock," 49–52; Nelson Tift to Mother, April 24, 1869, Nelson Tift Letter, University of Georgia. Early "Lost Cause" historians of Georgia helped perpetuate the myth of a "slander mill"; see Howell, *History of Georgia*, 601–2.

31. Joseph E. Brown to Nelson Tift, January 2, 1868 [1869], "Condition of Affairs in Georgia," 141–46.

32. "Letter from Governor Bullock, of Georgia, in Reply to the Statement of Hon. Nelson Tift to the Reconstruction Committee of Congress," February 26, 1869, "Condition of Affairs in Georgia," 1–4.

33. Ibid.

34. *Congressional Globe*, 1869, 27, 38, 74, 171, 1506; "A Bill to Enable the People of Georgia to Form a State Government Republican in Form," January 5, 1869, Butler Papers, LC.

35. Bullock Annual Message, January 13, 1869, Ga. Exec. Dept., Minutes, 1866–1874, GDAH; John Hope Franklin, *Reconstruction: After the Civil War* (Chicago: University of Chicago Press, 1961), 63–64.

36. Bullock to Benjamin F. Butler, February 7, 1869, J. L. Dunning to Benjamin F. Butler, February 3, 1869, Butler Papers, LC.

37. C. H. Hopkins to Benjamin F. Butler, February 14, 1869, Henry M. Turner to Benjamin F. Butler, February 19, 1869, Butler Papers, LC.

38. Bullock to General Assembly and Senate, February 15, 1869, Ga. Exec. Dept., Minutes, 1866–1874, GDAH.

39. "Letter from Governor Bullock, of Georgia, in Reply to the Statement of Hon. Nelson Tift," 3, Ga. Exec. Dept., Minutes, 1866–1874, GDAH; *New York Times*, February 15 and 16, 1869.

40. Nathans, *Losing the Peace*, 154; Bullock to General Assembly, March 10, 1869, Ga. Exec. Dept., Exec. Sec. Letterbooks, GDAH; *New York Times*, March 11 and 20, 1869.

41. *New York Times*, March 10, 1869. For a lucid explanation of Congressional support of the Fifteenth Amendment as a way to consolidate Republican party power in the North, see William Gillette, *The Right to Vote: Politics and the Passage of the Fifteenth Amendment* (Baltimore: Johns Hopkins University Press, 1969).

42. Eugene Davis to Edward McPherson, July 26, 1869, Ga. Exec. Dept., Exec. Sec. Letterbooks, GDAH; *Journal of the House of the State of Georgia, 1869* (Atlanta: Public Printer, 1869), 575–80; *Journal of the Senate of the State of Georgia, 1869* (Atlanta: Public Printer, 1869), 652–58. In the House vote, three members voted to ratify but stipulated that they interpreted the proposed amendment as not granting office-holding rights to blacks.

43. Gillette, *Right to Vote*, 98–101; Howell, *History of Georgia*, 611–12.

44. Adam Palmer to Bullock, August 24, 1869, Ga. Exec. Dept., Incoming Corr., Bullock, 1868–1871, GDAH.

45. John W. Oneil et al., to Senate and House of Representatives, January 1, 1869, and Bullock to General Commanding, undated (2 letters, in September 22 and November 20, 1869 folders), Ga. Exec. Dept., Incoming Corr., Bullock, 1868–1871, GDAH; Joshua Hill to President Grant, May 24, 1869, Joshua Hill Letter, University of Georgia; Allen W. Trelease, *White Terror: The Ku Klux Klan Conspiracy and Southern Reconstruction* (N.Y.: Harper & Row, 1971), 232–34. For the Adkins's assassination see Ku-Klux Report, *Report of the Joint Select Committee to Inquire into the Condition of Affairs in the Late Insurrectionary States.* 42d Cong., 2d Sess., No. 22. 13 vols. (Washington, D.C.: U.S. Government Printing Office, 1872), 7: 1023–26; *New York Times*, May 17, 1869; A. L. Harris to Benjamin Conley, May 11, 1869, Benjamin Conley letters, Atlanta Historical Society.

46. William S. McFeely, "Amos T. Akerman: The Lawyer and Racial Justice,"

in J. Morgan Kousser and James M. McPherson, eds., *Region, Race, and Reconstruction: Essays in Honor of C. Vann Woodward* (New York: Oxford University Press, 1982), 395–415.

47. *Can a Negro Hold Office in Georgia? Decided in the Supreme Court of Georgia, June Term, 1869* (Atlanta: Daily Intelligencer, 1869), 18–19, 65–79; Henry R. Goetchius, "Litigation in Georgia during the Reconstruction Period, 1865–1872," *Report of the Georgia Bar Association* (N.p., 1897), 34–35. For a full description of proceedings of the case see *White v. Clements,* Georgia Supreme Court, *Reports of Cases in Law and Equity Decided Before the Supreme Court of Georgia . . . 1869* (Macon, Ga.: Burke, 1870), 232–85.

48. Appointment of Hiram Warner, August 14, 1868, Ga. Exec. Dept., Minutes, 1866–1874, GDAH, 164.

49. Appointment of H. K. McCay, August 14, 1868, Ga. Exec. Dept., Minutes, 1866–1874, GDAH, 164; Alexander A. Lawrence, "Henry Kent McCay: Forgotten Jurist," *Georgia Bar Journal,* undated, 6–10, in "Henry K. McCay," file 2, Names, GDAH; *White v. Clements* in *Reports of Cases in Law and Equity . . . 1869,* 232–85.

50. Zuber, "Role of Rufus Brown Bullock", 58; Eugene Davis to J. M. Bishop, July 9, 1869, Ga. Exec. Dept., Exec. Sec. Letterbooks, GDAH, 286; *Augusta Daily Chronicle,* June 30, 1869; W. Calvin Smith, "The Reconstruction 'Triumph' of Rufus B. Bullock," *Georgia Historical Quarterly* 52 (December, 1968): 416.

51. Henry Wilson to U. S. Grant, May 14, 1869, *Report of the Secretary of War,* vol. 1, 89, 41st Cong., House of Representatives, Executive Document, 1869–1870; Bullock to Benjamin F. Butler, July 8 and August 2, 1869, Butler Papers, LC.

52. A. H. Terry to William T. Sherman, August 14, 1869, *Report of the Secretary of War,* vol. 2, 89–95.

53. Bullock to Wesley Shropshire, November 24, 1869, Ga. Exec. Dept., Exec. Sec. Letterbooks, GDAH, 367.

54. Foster Blodgett to Benjamin F. Butler, November 6, 1869, Butler Papers, LC; Bullock to the Editor, *New York Times,* December 4, 1869.

55. *Congressional Globe,* 41st Cong., 2nd Sess., 4; William Gillette, *Retreat From Reconstruction, 1869–1879* (Baton Rouge: Louisiana State University Press, 1979), 86–89.

56. Gillette, *Right to Vote,* 48–50; Smith, "Reconstruction 'Triumph,'" 414–23.

57. Tunis G. Campbell, *Sufferings of the Rev. T. G. Campbell and His Family in Georgia* (Washington, D.C.: Enterprise Publishing Co., 1877), 10; *Congressional Globe,* December 16, 17, 20, 21, and 22, 1869, 165–66, 201–6, 209–18, 222, 224–25, 232, 246–47, 275–93, 325; C. H. Prince to Benjamin Conley, December 18, 1869, Conley letters, Atlanta Historical Society.

58. Isaac W. Avery, *The History of the State of Georgia from 1850 to 1881* (New York: Brown and Derby, 1881), 421.

59. Bullock Proclamation of December 22, 1869, Ga. Exec. Dept., Minutes, 1866–1874, GDAH, 448; James E. Sefton, *The United States Army and Reconstruction, 1865–1877* (Baton Rouge: Louisiana State University Press, 1967), 201–2; William T.

Sherman to General A. H. Terry, December 24, 1869, *Records of the Adjutant General's Office, 1780s–1917*, Record Group 94, microcopy 565, roll 38, National Archives.

60. Appointment of J. G. W. Mills and A. L. Harris, January 8, 1870, Ga. Exec. Dept., Minutes, 1866–1874, microfilm, GDAH, 455; General A. H. Terry to Bullock, January 8, 1870, Ga. Exec. Dept., Bullock, Incoming Corr., GDAH; *Atlanta Daily New Era,* January 11, 1870; Campbell, *Sufferings,* 10–12; Zuber, "Role of Rufus Brown Bullock," 65–69.

61. Military District of Georgia, General Order no. 3, January 13, 1870, in N. L. Angier, *The Georgia Legislature, Legally Organized in 1868* (Washington, D.C.: Gibson Brothers, 1870), 13; Bullock to General Terry, January 15, 1870 (2 letters) and January 19, 1870, Rufus Brown Bullock, File II, Names, GDAH; Bullock to William Lawrence, January 20, 1870, Hamilton Fish Collection, LC; W. C. Morrill to Simon Cameron, January 15, 1870, Simon Cameron Papers, microfilm, LC; *Augusta Chronicle,* January 14, 15, and 19, 1870; Avery, *History of Georgia,* 430–32.

62. Military District of Georgia, General Orders nos. 9, 10, 11, and 13, January 25, 28, and 31, 1870, in Angier, *The Georgia Legislature,* 15–16; *Georgia House Journal, 1870,* 3–72; Bullock to Senators Trumbull, Stewart, Edmonds, Conkling, Carpenter, and Rice, January 28, 1870, and Bullock to J. M. Thayer, January 28, 1870, Ga. Exec. Dept., Exec. Sec. Letterbooks, GDAH, 101–3, 105–7; Bullock to General Terry, February 1, 1870, Rufus Bullock, File II, Names, GDAH; *Congressional Globe,* 41st Cong., 2nd Sess., 576, 1029, 1128; Wallace C. Smith, "Rufus Brown Bullock and the Third Reconstruction of Georgia, 1867–1871" (M.A. thesis, University of North Carolina, 1964), 100–101; Russ, "Radical Disfranchisement," 201–3.

63. *New York Times,* February 17, 1870; Bullock to General Assembly, February 2, 1870, and Amendment Ratification, February 2, 1870, Ga. Exec. Dept., Minutes, 1866–1874, GDAH, 488, 490–98; Russ, "Radical Disfranchisement," 202–4.

64. *Georgia House Journal, 1870,* 72–78, 81; *Atlanta Daily Sun,* November 2, 3, and 5, 1871. For a recent treatment of the Democratic campaign against Bullock, see William Harris Bragg, "The Junius of Georgia Redemption: Thomas M. Norwood and the 'Nemesis' Letters," *Georgia Historical Quarterly* 77 (Spring 1993): 86–122.

65. Louis R. Harlan, John W. Blassingame, et al., eds., *The Booker T. Washington Papers* (Urbana: University of Illinois Press, 1976), 1:79 and 4:54; Washington, *Up From Slavery,* 86, 153–67, 225.

66. Duncan, *Entrepreneur for Equality,* chapters 7 and 8.

"The Negroes Cannot Navigate Alone"

Religious Scalawags and the Biracial Methodist Episcopal Church in Georgia, 1866–1876

Daniel W. Stowell

In 1866, amid the destruction and despair of Confederate defeat, a handful of southern Methodist ministers and laymen began an attempt to reestablish the Methodist Episcopal Church in Georgia on a biracial basis. In a period of upheaval and uncertainty in race relations, these "religious scalawags" hoped to alleviate the hostility between whites and the newly freed black population in the South, while evangelizing and educating the freedmen.[1] They also sought to become peacemakers between the northern Methodist Episcopal Church and the Methodist Episcopal Church, South, with the hope of effecting a reunion of the two largest branches of American Methodism.

The religious scalawags conceived of religious reconstruction as a broad revitalization of southern society, rather than as a policy of concentrating solely on the freedmen. Their idealistic vision enjoyed several years of success. Within two years, the denomination had over one hundred traveling and local preachers and over ten thousand members in the state. Blacks and whites belonged to the same Georgia Conference, though rarely to the same congregations. However, they could not overcome centuries of southern racial prejudice in a decade. Sectional animosity continued virtually unabated. The Georgia Conference continued to grow through the end of the decade, but the movement began to wane in the 1870s. From a high point of over 21,000 members in 1869, the denomination in Georgia shrank to under 16,000 in 1875 and in that year also voted to request division along geographical/racial lines. By the autumn of 1876, the experiment was over; racial segregation had won in the Methodist Episcopal Church in Georgia.

The experience of the Methodist Episcopal Church in Georgia prompts a reconsideration of the conventional portrait of black and white religious life during this period, when freedmen segregated themselves into racially separate denominations. Members of both races joined together to build a denominational structure in Georgia. Southern white ministers, not northern missionaries, joined with black ministers to organize and maintain the denomination in the decade following the Civil War. They established the Methodist Episcopal Church in Georgia on a biracial basis with a majority of its membership consisting of freedmen.[2]

Although the 1876 division of the denomination marked the defeat of this experiment, in January 1866 the prospects for racial harmony in a unified southern Methodism were far from bleak. Seven ministers of the Methodist Episcopal Church, South met Bishop Davis W. Clark and the Reverend James F. Chalfant of the Methodist Episcopal Church in Atlanta to organize the Western Georgia and Alabama Mission District. Chalfant was pastor of one of the largest and most prominent Methodist churches in Cincinnati.[3] Bishop Clark informed the men that Chalfant, the superintendent of the new mission district, would hold a quarterly meeting and allow them to join the Methodist Episcopal Church. All of the men did, expressing the belief that "the promotion of Christ's kingdom . . . may be done more efficiently by establishing missions & endeavoring to spread the Gospel under the auspices of the M.E. Church than they are affecting in the relation they formerly sustained." Several thought they might establish congregations among both blacks and whites in many areas, obtain a few church buildings, and do "a vast amount of good" even where they could not procure church buildings immediately.[4]

In this first meeting the new representatives of the Methodist Episcopal Church in Georgia drafted a "Report on the State of the Work and Demand for Laborers." The lengthy document offered a statement of purpose for the religious scalawags in Georgia. Rather than try to overthrow the southern church, they hoped they could aid in effecting a speedy reunion of the two Methodisms. They lauded southern Methodism's antebellum efforts among the slaves and viewed their new mission as a continuation of these missionary labors: "We as Southern ministers have been in this work. . . . We have stood by the dying slave as he lay in his hut upon his pallet of straw and endeavored to soften the closing hours of his long night of toil with the hopes of a better life." Now, "rejuvenated by the Providential openings before us, reconsecrated, and, as we trust, rebaptized with the Holy Ghost," they were "ready again to engage in this holy work under new and more hopeful auspices." The efforts of missionaries to slaves had never been a popular task, yet "somehow their ministry could only be fulfilled in preaching to the Negroes." These missionaries had always been careful to avoid any criticism of the institution of slavery, for such sentiments would surely have killed the movement. However, the field was more promising in 1866 than it had been before the war because many closed plantations were now open to "a missionary of the Cross."[5]

The report also issued a call for teachers of freedmen. The blacks "must be a power in society either for good or evil." If they could be "elevated, enlightened and civilized, they will become a power for good." If not, they would be a power for evil in southern society, "indulging their characteristic vices—licentiousness, falsehood, and theft." Teachers could become a three-fold blessing, according to the report, because they would "conserve the best interests of the South, promote the true welfare of the blacks and advance the Kingdom of Christ." This early pronouncement reflected a strong and continuing concern among the religious scalawags for the education of the freedmen, in addition to their evangelization. It was also thoroughly imbued with the paternalism that eventually undermined and divided the biracial church in Georgia.[6]

Armed with this statement of purpose and committed to planting churches among both white and black Georgians, the religious scalawags sought to reestablish the Methodist Episcopal Church in the state. One of the most energetic of their number was John H. Caldwell. While organizing a large congregation of blacks in La Grange, he also helped to establish black churches in several surrounding counties, gave advice to freedmen and fellow ministers, and served as an important link with both the Freedmen's Bureau and the northern Methodist press.[7]

Like his fellow religious scalawags, Caldwell staunchly believed they were working toward the greater good of their native South and looked expectantly to the day when their fellow southerners would agree. "God is with us, I know of a truth," he wrote. "The South is yet enslaved by her old ideas. The truth alone can make her free. . . . I love her—she is my native land—and while my people all denounce me as a traitor to her, I feel I am one of her best friends, because I am laboring incessantly for her true emancipation."

John H. Caldwell.
Andrew College, Cuthbert, Georgia.

His brother Charles M. Caldwell confidently looked "for a better day when the blind prejudices of the people will give way and reason take the place of passion, and Christians unite for the prosperity of Zion."[8]

John W. Yarbrough, a veteran southern Methodist minister in Oxford, Georgia, also desired a reunion between the northern and southern churches, but his black congregation did not want to wait. Yarbrough had overseen "colored" congregations before the Civil War and had also served as a presiding elder for several years. His appointments for 1866 from the southern church were the Covington and Oxford colored charges, but the freedmen therein wished to transfer to the Methodist Episcopal Church immediately. Yarbrough had served them "very faithfully and acceptably" and was "willing to join that Church and serve them as their pastor."[9]

Yarbrough wrote to Chalfant explaining his reasons for seeking a position in the Methodist Episcopal Church. He had always regretted the division of the church in 1844 and sought to return to the church from which he had been separated. Though he would be "cut off" from many friends and relatives, "I want to do something for the poor colored people and the Church South has not the ability to help us if they had the will. My charge will follow me." Yarbrough was certain of his position among the blacks: "I know more of the colored people than any one that you could send unless he be taken from among them and I have a stronger hold upon them than anyone I know."[10] A sense of duty to evangelize the freedmen, coupled with the Church, South's inability and indifference, compelled John Yarbrough to leave that church and join the Methodist Episcopal Church. He understood the hostility he would face from his southern brethren; a fellow minister of the Church, South, not knowing he was planning to join the Methodist Episcopal Church, wrote him: "These northern missionaries are instigated of the devil and are in league with hell."[11]

In the spring of 1866, Yarbrough wrote his son George and son-in-law Atticus Haygood, both rising young ministers in the southern church, to explain that he had become "a *convert* to that old doctrine of Methodism, indeed I never believed *unwaveringly* in slavery. When I have seen negroes on the block, and in the market I have doubted." He also sent a farewell letter to his fellow ministers through the columns of the *Southern Christian Advocate,* offering an explanation for returning to "the old church in which I was converted and ordained." He had "never ceased to regret" the 1844 division of the Methodist Church and believed that the churches must reunite "or both branches must suffer." In conclusion, Yarbrough insisted that he could "labor more successfully with the colored people by going back," as they preferred the "old Church" to the Church, South.[12]

While John Caldwell and John Yarbrough were both men of substantial talent and stature within the southern church, the majority of religious scalawags were average traveling preachers, local preachers, or perhaps even laymen who saw a providential opportunity in the entrance of the Methodist Episcopal Church into the southern field. However, they were quickly frustrated in their attempts to reach southern whites. The southern religious press portrayed them as "aggressors" and "marauders," bent on destroying the southern church and overthrowing southern social customs. They did seek to educate the freedmen and often favored black suffrage, but in the early stages they took a moderate stand in regard to the southern church and the social order. Neither did the northern religious press represent their views; it was too uncharitable in its treatment of the southern people. The religious scalawags were southerners, and as such they did not seek to alienate their fellows by harsh rhetoric. Rather, they hoped to free white southerners from their hatred of northerners and their prejudices toward blacks, attitudes that hindered their spiritual growth.

Although opposed by many whites, the Methodist Episcopal Church did attract other Georgians, both white and black. The religious scalawags proceeded with the work of gathering and ministering to these scattered and persecuted flocks. Yet these men also had a larger intent in their work: the religious reconstruction of the southern states. This process involved much more than bringing together and preaching to a few white Methodists and a few hundred freedmen. It required a moderation in the prejudice and sectionalism of southerners to enable them to grow in spiritual matters and become an effective part of the nation once again. The reconstruction would culminate in a reunification of the sections "in spirit" as they were being unified politically.

A sizable number of white Methodists in northern Georgia favored the Methodist Episcopal Church, but those in central and southern Georgia were indifferent or even hostile to the northern church. Ministers of the Methodist Episcopal Church to the south and east of Atlanta worked almost exclusively among the black population. The mood of much of Georgia was demonstrated by the hostility which Fosh Burrow, a black preacher in the Methodist Episcopal Church, encountered on his trip to Columbus, Georgia. He had great difficulty finding a place to stay the night and saw few prospects for the church in that city. He also learned that "all the country below Columbus is very much opposed to our Church."[13]

Several influences hindered whites from joining the Methodist Episcopal Church. John Caldwell noted in April 1866 that some who were "with us in heart" sought a good opportunity to join, others waited for the excitement of the times to die down, while many still awaited a reunion of the two branches of Episcopal Methodism. Some Georgians simply felt that the Methodist Episcopal Church was making a temporary foray into the state and that the effort would soon dissolve, an opinion that the leaders of the Church, South encouraged in their congregations. Other preachers wrote of more serious impediments to effective recruitment. Samuel D. Brown in Polk County found "the common people anxious to be members of our church but they dread the abuse & that is all that keeps them back." Richard H. Waters in Jonesboro sought to attract those who wavered by starting a school for poor white children: "I know that a thing of that sort will do as much or more to get hold of the people here than anything we could do. They look on with jealousy at the instruction of the negro" when their own children go uneducated.[14]

Concern for reaching the poor class of whites appears in the letters of several of the religious scalawags. Cornelius W. Parker in Griffin voiced serious reservations about southern society: "The white people who sympathize with us can't express themselves for fear of suffering hunger, as they would be dropped. Those who join us suffer in patronage. Poor people are not free."[15] Those who affiliated with a northern religious body faced the same ostracism and persecution as did southerners who joined the Republican party. John Caldwell also noted the class distinctions in the appeal of the Methodist Episcopal Church: "Except in the portions of the South [mountains] and among the class [poor] designated, our Church has but a faint prospect of success with the native white population."[16]

Prospects among the freedmen were much more encouraging for the religious scalawags. Few black Methodists wanted to remain connected with the church of their masters. During the Reconstruction period, four separate Methodist churches sought these black prospects: the Methodist Episcopal (ME) Church, the African Methodist Episcopal (AME) Church, the African Methodist Episcopal Zion (AMEZ) Church, all northern organizations; and the Colored Methodist Episcopal (CME) Church, sponsored by the Methodist Episcopal Church, South for its former black members. The latter church was unacceptable to many freedmen because of its ties to the Church, South.[17]

In Georgia the primary rivalry arose between the ME Church and the AME Church. Beginning on the field earlier with more men and money, the ME Church often "won" local contests for black Methodist congregations. In early 1866 northern Georgia was virtually unpenetrated by any outside Methodist missionaries. The indigenous religious scalawags of the Methodist Episcopal Church alone provided an alternative for black Methodists to the Methodist Episcopal Church, South. The freedmen responded enthusiastically. Even before the organizational meeting of the mission district in January 1866, several black ministers came to John Caldwell seeking to unite with the ME Church. The freedmen in Polk County continually petitioned S. D. Brown to come to "this, that, or the other place" to preach to them, until he complained, "I scarcely have time to read my Bible." John Yarbrough agreed to go with his black congregation when they joined the ME Church. In writing to the superintendent, he recalled that Georgia law prescribed a $500 fine and imprisonment for teaching a black to read and asked, "Do you wonder at their going to the M.E.C.?"[18]

In northern and central Georgia the religious scalawags received entire black Methodist congregations into the Methodist Episcopal Church. In Rome Andrew W. Caldwell, a brother of Charles and John Caldwell, attempted to receive a society of black Methodists. A large autonomous black congregation had existed there before the war, presided over by a preacher supplied by the Georgia Conference of the Church, South. The African Methodist Episcopal Church also wanted to add this group of blacks to its fold in the South. Many of the leaders at first favored joining the African church. Caldwell, however, told them of the ME Church and its "kind offers to them." Some had never heard of the denomination, while others had been advised that it was "a political and dangerous concern." Caldwell's discussion convinced most of the leaders. Demonstrating his paternalistic attitudes, Caldwell wrote that the freedmen were "a fold without a shepherd, drifting they know not whither, and I find they have scarce enough to know they cannot manage for themselves. . . . They seem to be anxious for me to take charge of them and this I will do God permitting me to the best of my ability." [19]

In nearby Cartersville, he had to face the combined opposition of the AME Church and the Methodist Episcopal Church, South. An African Methodist missionary, supported by a southern Methodist preacher, claimed for his church a structure built by the freedmen and prevented Caldwell from using it. The AME missionary informed him that he could organize Sabbath schools, but these must remain under the control of the AME Church. Refusing such an arrangement, Caldwell began meetings in the open air. [20] Caldwell felt the only hope for the Methodist Episcopal Church in Cartersville lay in building a house and opening a school "free for all." The Freedmen's Bureau, however, was reluctant to aid him until a teacher had been engaged; "If the Bureau could understand the true state of things, and could see the influence Southern rebel Methodists are exerting through the agency of the Africans, I believe it would aid us in our efforts to pour peace and comfort into the hearts of the people," he complained to Chalfant. He wrote to the State Superintendent of Education for the Freedmen's Bureau, G. L. Eberhart, informing him of the situation in Cartersville and seeking assistance to build a schoolhouse for "*all* freedmen without *distinction* as to *sect.*" Caldwell also wrote to Chalfant seeking funds because it would be "best for our Church, and Freedmen's Aid Society to establish their schools with the Church," and afterward apply to the Freedmen's Bureau for support, thereby retaining ultimate control of the school in Methodist hands. [21]

While Andrew Caldwell sought to receive entire congregations of black Methodists in Rome and Cartersville, his brothers farther south began with only a handful of black members and built upon this small base. Charles Caldwell had been a local preacher in the Methodist Episcopal Church, South when he followed his brother John into the Methodist Episcopal Church. Superintendent Chalfant assigned him to Newnan, and he began work in February 1866. He traveled through Fayette, Meriwether, and Coweta counties, finding much opposition from the whites, but "the colored people are all anxious for me to serve them and receive them into the M.E. Church." An exception to the hostility of the whites came from Mr. Park Arnold, who had owned over three hundred slaves. He invited Caldwell to preach to the blacks on his plantation because "he wishes them to have religious instruction." Arnold's attitude was rare, however, as many planters "put a prohibition upon the colored people leaving the plantations either at night or on Sabbath to hear the missionary."[22]

Another method by which the religious scalawags tried to accomplish the work of religious reconstruction was the camp meeting. The practice of meeting for several consecutive days had been utilized by the Methodists since 1800 to "keep alive the emotional intensity and sense of power" of the great revivals.[23] While the camp meeting was not an uncommon Methodist activity, the one organized by John Caldwell and his brother Charles in the summer of 1866 was quite unique. Plans for the rally in August began months before in the mind of John Caldwell. He invited prominent political leaders and asked Benjamin H. Hill to address the freedmen on their "legal rights, duties, & obligations." By inviting these men, Caldwell tried to soothe white fears about the aims of the movement, but in doing so he also displayed an interest in political matters that later proved so destructive to the Methodist Episcopal Church in Georgia.[24]

The camp meeting, held within the city limits of La Grange, began on the second Thursday of August and ran until the following Sunday. On Thursday and Friday attendance ranged from seven to eight hundred blacks. On Saturday, however, blacks from "all the adjoining counties and Alabama" poured into La Grange, coming from as far away as Atlanta, Montgomery, and even Selma, until over three thousand had gathered for the meeting. They joined a procession of Sunday school scholars led by Mrs. Caldwell to hear an address. As John Caldwell later wrote, "Such a spectacle had never been witnessed in 'Dixie' in the days of slavery." Although the political leaders Caldwell invited did not attend, several sent supportive letters which were read to the crowd. John Caldwell then delivered an address to the freedmen on "their civil relations, duties, and responsibilities." White representatives from La Grange came to hear the speech and were surprised not to hear "a political harangue" as they had expected. When these representatives reported to other whites in La Grange, Caldwell wrote, "prejudice at once began to give way."[25]

By Sunday morning the assembly had swelled to between five and six thousand. At eleven o'clock Charles Caldwell delivered a stirring sermon: "He held five thousand people entranced, chained, as it were, to their seats for more than an hour." In the afternoon the brothers Caldwell administered the Lord's Supper and baptized many of the freedmen. Since "the Baptists were all out," six thousand blacks and one thousand whites attended to "witness the spectacle." One hundred seventeen people joined the church, while hundreds more mourned or "groaned out unutterable prayers for mercy." On

Sunday night John Caldwell gave an account of the "Old Methodist Church," arguing that "the old Church, our Mother, had come to reclaim her Southern domain, wrenched unjustly from her grasp by an arrogant and cruel slave power." Caldwell also explained "her plans and purposes in coming to the South—namely, to elevate, educate and Christianize these poor blacks whom the slave power would never suffer to be educated at all." [26]

The importance of the revival lay in the opportunity it offered southern ministers in the ME Church to demonstrate their intentions. They contended that such an immense gathering of freedmen without incident was a testimony to their peaceful and conservative intentions. Not only did such an assembly provide unparalleled opportunities for evangelization by drawing blacks from miles around, it also provided a forum for the religious scalawags to express their objectives to both blacks and whites. Thus, the camp meeting allowed the religious scalawags to overcome in some areas the lack of a public outlet normally provided by a religious newspaper. The La Grange camp meeting from the beginning was a "hazardous experiment," but the results were impressive in its effect on the entire area: "As an experiment the meeting was more than a success, it was a triumphant vindication of our cause." Some freedmen who had joined the AME Church "have discovered their mistake, and are sending me messages to come and organize them." Further, according to the Caldwells, the gathering seemingly reduced the prejudices of some white southerners: "Many who opposed us bitterly now say that I am doing a noble work for the negroes of the country." [27]

The La Grange meeting in 1866 was so successful that large camp meetings were held in several towns in the late summer of 1867, the largest in September in Newnan, under the direction of Charles Caldwell. In preparation, Caldwell was instrumental in the passage of the following resolution by the freedmen in Newnan at a quarterly conference meeting:

> [W]e as a colored people will at all times and under all circumstances so demean ourselves towards the white people of this country as to give no just cause for oppression, And that we will at all times treat the white people with that courtesy and respect which is due them as our Superiors in Intelligence, Wealth & Education. And we do hereby pledge ourselves to discountenance any colored man or woman and to withdraw from the Society of the same who shall hereafter act in any way unbecoming towards the white people of this community.[28]

This resolution represents the lengths to which the religious scalawags and perhaps their black congregations were willing to go to mollify southern whites. That the religious scalawags would accept and encourage its passage demonstrates that they held to a firmly paternalistic vision of their role in revitalizing southern society.

At the camp meeting in September, nine white preachers and twenty black preachers and exhorters addressed a crowd of four to six thousand people, and almost two hundred people joined the church. When John Caldwell returned to La Grange after the meeting, two of the cars in the train were filled with freedmen from Grantville, Hogansville, and La Grange, who sang at each stop as white passengers mocked, cursed, or sat speechless "with moistened eyes." This "portable camp meeting," as one observer labeled it, continued until the train arrived in La Grange.[29]

The most successful method for Methodist expansion in Georgia was the organization of schools to educate blacks in a religious atmosphere. In a letter to Bishop Edmund S. Janes in late 1865, Caldwell stressed the importance of schools to the progress of the church: "To begin right here in Georgia, let us begin with education." The establishment of schools became a major concern of all the religious scalawags as they perceived the importance of education to the freedmen's future. Andrew Caldwell noted that in Rome all the freedmen "unite in one thing, and that is a great desire to have their children educated." When Methodist missionaries provided schools and teachers for the freedmen, they quickly acquired a congregation within the community.[30]

The Freedmen's Bureau, established in 1865, played an important if uneasy role in successful Methodist efforts to furnish education to the freedmen. The arrangements for a school and church for freedmen in Grantville and Whitesville were typical of the process. John Caldwell collected $300 from the freedmen in Grantville and $400 from those in Whitesville. His Superintendent, James F. Chalfant, persuaded the Missionary Society of the Methodist Episcopal Church to provide $350 for the former and $300 for the latter place. After these funds had been pledged, Caldwell wrote to the Freedmen's Bureau Superintendent of Education asking that the Bureau match these contributions for the two communities. The Bureau granted the money with the provision that the lot be deeded to black trustees. A pattern emerged in which the freedmen collected what they could for schools, after which the Methodist Missionary Society and the Freedmen's Bureau would appropriate equal sums to complete the project.[31] These two agencies, along with the Freedmen's Aid and Church Extension Societies of the ME Church, were vital sources of support for the fledgling efforts in a hostile environment and provided links to governmental and northern philanthropic funds that were essential to the maintenance of the Methodist Episcopal Church in Georgia in the first two years after the war.

Several of the preachers proposed to start day schools for white children to ease tensions between the races. Cornelius Parker began efforts in Griffin: "I am teaching a free (missionary) school for the poor whites & I believe it will do good. I can hear it spoken of favorably all around. It softens prejudice." Five months later he still sought support for a white school to lessen hostility: "The people accuse us of partiality to the colored & say we do not care what becomes of the poor white children." Richard Waters agreed that poor whites "look on with jealousy at the instruction of the negro," and he asked for help in starting a school for white children in Jonesboro. John Caldwell had more grandiose plans for white education when he proposed that the Methodist Episcopal Church buy the La Grange Female College and establish an institution for white children.[32]

Despite these promising beginnings, the preachers of the ME Church faced a variety of obstacles which, between 1868 and 1875, combined to thwart their ministry in Georgia. The poverty of the people among whom they labored, the withdrawal of ecclesiastical and governmental support, and the hostility of white southerners exerted pressure on the movement from without. Within the group, paternalism and politics contributed to the failure of their vision of religious reconstruction by alienating the two groups to whom they tried to minister. By the mid-1870s the position of the Methodist Episcopal Church in Georgia clearly revealed the failure of the religious scalawags to achieve their goals of Methodist fraternity and widespread black evangelization.

The people among whom the ministers of the Mission District labored, both black and white, were extremely poor. John Yarbrough in a letter to Superintendent Chalfant, rejected Chalfant's idea that the freedmen could contribute something substantial to the support of the work there with a resounding, "I tell you they *cannot!*" Samuel Brown emphasized that "dearth is spread over this country," yet "our people tell me that they intend to try to pay something for the support of the gospel by the close of the year." Later he wrote that he had to travel by foot but was "determined never to give up the fight whether my people can feed my horse or no."[33]

The organization of the Georgia Mission Conference in October 1867 delighted the religious scalawags, but this development also marked a turning point in the history of the Methodist Episcopal Church in Georgia. After the promotion of the work in Georgia to the status of a conference, aid from northern sources dwindled. Other external forces worked against the fledgling conference as the operations of the Freedmen's Bureau, a major ally, declined after 1867 and ceased altogether in 1870, and the support and protection afforded by the Republican state government vanished with Democratic redemption in 1871. The efforts at redemption from 1868 to 1871 marked increasing hostility against all things "northern," including the Methodist Episcopal Church.

The combination of the Freedmen's Bureau, military rule, and a Republican state government provided a measure of physical support and protection from 1866 to 1870. These forces allowed the religious scalawags some degree of safety in pursuing their efforts for reconciliation through evangelization and education. To insure his ability to labor in La Grange and surrounding areas, John Caldwell carried "a written order of military aid from Gen. Tillson through Mr. Eberhart at any moment I should call for it." Local whites undoubtedly resented these applications for military protection. Once the federal troops and Republican politicians were removed, they reasoned, these traitors to the South and southern Methodism would have little to protect them. By 1871 the religious scalawags were indeed "left to the mercy of the unreconstructed" as they had earlier feared.[34]

Southern whites used a variety of methods, from intimidation to violence, to destroy the work of the Methodist Episcopal Church and other northern churches and aid societies. The inability of religious scalawags to overcome this hostility disillusioned and embittered them, forcing them into a closer alliance with Radical Republicans. One of their opponents' most effective weapons was economic pressure. Charles Caldwell wrote to Superintendent Chalfant that the people in Newnan threatened to discharge any of their black employees "if they do not quit my church and quit going to my meetings." In their dependence upon white employers, black laborers had little recourse when whites applied such pressure. This tactic also proved useful in attacking the religious scalawags themselves. Andrew Caldwell lamented that to support the work of the Methodist Episcopal Church "is almost the same as to rush upon starvation at once." He presented the case of an exhorter in his area who had lost his job and had been refused employment by others because "he is in union with us, and in sympathy with the government."[35]

No less serious than economic intimidation was the burning of churches and schools. The Ku Klux Klan or other secret groups in Georgia burned several buildings used by the Methodist Episcopal Church. On July 2, 1866, Richard Waters wrote to the superintendent that the brush arbor where he had preached to the blacks had been burned down. On July 16 he bought a house for $320 to be used as a church. At midnight that same night it was burned down by unknown whites. Cornelius Parker in Griffin also reported that his schoolhouse/church was burned. In his letter to Chalfant, he enclosed an article from the local newspaper on the blaze, which stated that the cause of the fire was unknown but speculated that the "carelessness" of blacks living in the building probably caused it. As to rumors that white men set it on fire because it contained a black school, the paper scoffed, "We don't believe any such tale." The editor also believed that the "accident" would be reported as "evidence of the disposition on the part of the people to do injustice to the blacks. We know that no such feeling exists here."[36]

In addition to problems with the general white population, the religious scalawags in Georgia faced the more distressing opposition of other Christian churches, especially the Methodist Episcopal Church, South and the African Methodist Episcopal Church. The curious alliance between these two churches was designed to prevent the Methodist Episcopal Church from gaining large numbers of freedmen as members, a circumstance both churches wanted to avoid for different reasons. The Church, South feared the influence of the "radical" northern Methodists over the freedmen, while the AME Church realized that northern Methodists were attracting substantial numbers of its potential membership in the South. The southern Methodists directed many of their black members into the AME Church, fearing that if left alone, many of the freedmen might join the ME Church. The African Methodists exhibited due appreciation for this support, while also hoping to acquire the church buildings held in trusteeship for black congregations by the Church, South. The southern Methodists saw the alliance as a method of thwarting the activities of the Methodist Episcopal Church in the South. Although they claimed support for the AME Church, in the General Conference of 1866 the southern Methodists refused to turn over their black membership and property to the African Methodists; instead they chose to allow their black members to organize separate but affiliated conferences which became the Colored Methodist Episcopal Church at the General Conference of 1870. The religious scalawags believed that the southern people, both black and white, had to be rescued from those who would lead them.[37]

In the face of poor funding, threats, social ostracism, and fierce opposition from the Church, South and the AME Church, the religious scalawags continued their work of religious reconstruction in Georgia. They found adherents among the mountain whites and the large number of freedmen who sought new church relations. Through lectures, sermons, camp meetings, and schools, the Methodist Episcopal Church received individual converts and even entire congregations and attempted to overcome the bitter spirit of the white South toward northerners and southern freedmen. By October 1867 its ranks had grown to include thirty-seven traveling preachers (including nine black preachers), sixty-six local preachers, and over ten thousand members and probationers.[38]

To counter the economic and physical opposition of native whites, some of the religious scalawags turned to political action as a remedy for the abuses which they and the freedmen suffered. They believed that the civil and religious rights of the freedmen were intimately connected with the success of the Republican party in the state and the congressional plan of Reconstruction. Without their civil rights, these men reasoned, the freedmen would be unable to protect their religious freedoms. The missionary endeavors of the ministers of the ME Church gave them a ready political audience, as historian William Warren Sweet observed: "Nothing could have been better fitted for the organization of the Negro into groups for the purpose of their political control by white leaders than their organization into congregations under the guidance of the white missionary." [39]

Though the religious scalawags undoubtedly had a strong influence over their listeners, they considered themselves to be acting for the benefit of the freedmen in discussing political matters. John Caldwell wrote, "I felt it my duty to lecture the people on the present nature of affairs in the country, inform the people of their enfranchisement," and urge them to qualify themselves "for the right exercise of the most exalted prerogative of freedom." By late 1867, when the mission district became a mission conference, Caldwell was optimistic: "It is only a question of time for [southerners'] prejudices to be subdued and under the Civil Reconstruction process if it proves successful, there must and will be great and salutary changes." In the current political contests, he saw "the dying agonies of slavery and the rebellion. They will expire together the moment Congress accepts the new constitutions of reconstructed states." [40]

The ministers of the Methodist Episcopal Church in Georgia also participated in political activities through secret groups of Unionists and freedmen in the South known as Union or Loyal Leagues designed to support political reconstruction and counter the Ku Klux Klan. The activities of the Union League in Georgia inspired both fear and anger in native whites. Southerners viewed it as a troublesome organization designed to manipulate blacks. The religious scalawags' association with the Union League hindered their ability to minister to native whites. Nevertheless, several of the preachers participated in the organization of Loyal or Union Leagues in the spring of 1867. Cornelius Parker in Griffin wrote G. L. Eberhart of the Freedmen's Bureau that "we initiated 20 colored men into the Union League Saturday night. . . . They are pleased." The Union Leagues also drew in black support for the ME Church. Richard Waters in Jonesboro boasted, "We have the biggest Union League in the least time in this town perhaps you ever saw and yet they come by companies. Now with the right sort of management the whole Methodist fraternity is ours." John Murphy working in Fairburn rejoiced that "the Union League works admirable for our Church." In La Grange, where John Caldwell labored, "the Republican Party, through the League, became practically supreme."[41]

While the religious scalawags who participated in political activities felt their actions were justified in furthering the work of religious reconstruction, they failed to understand the effect their political involvement would have on the Methodist Episcopal Church in Georgia. To southerners, and especially to southern Methodists, the efforts of the ME Church in the South "smacked of carpet-bagging" and "the parallel between radical reconstruction and the reconstruction of the M. E. Church was obvious to all."[42] The connections of the northern church "with a political party and military might" which were established during the war, continued during the Reconstruction period and "constituted one of the principal grounds of the Southern church's objection to their presence in the South."[43] In Georgia the religious scalawags did little to alter these perceptions; instead, they increased the association in the minds of southerners between their church and radical politics. Such a position probably drew some blacks to their church, but it alienated more southern whites and undermined efforts at reconciliation with southern Methodists. Political differences reinforced and intensified existing difficulties between the two Methodisms in Georgia. According to John Caldwell, one prominent southern Methodist in Georgia told him that "if I had not attempted to complicate the Church relations with the political questions I would now have half the Georgia Conference with me. But who can believe this?"[44]

While alienating southern whites with their political activities, the religious scalawags also alienated southern blacks through their paternalism and refusal to allow blacks supervisory powers. In November 1866, Dr. Daniel Curry, the influential editor of the New York *Christian Advocate*, published an editorial that urged the formation of biracial conferences in the South and even the establishment of biracial congregations. The question should now be answered by the church "whether we are ready to grant true and real equality to colored members in our Churches." For Curry, the answer was emphatically yes. A few days later, Yarbrough wrote to Superintendent Chalfant: "Dr. Curry is out with an article in favor of conferences compounded of white and black. That suits me; the negroes cannot navigate alone." Yarbrough had translated Curry's egalitarian appeal into a mandate for paternalistic biracial conferences. Freedmen's Bureau Superintendent of Education G. L. Eberhart later wrote Chalfant that he understood Yarbrough to be "as much controlled by prejudice as those southerners who make no pretensions to friendship."[45] Yarbrough's past deeds had displayed his deep concern for the religious welfare of the freedmen, but his attitude was that of a father toward his children.

Yarbrough, however, was not alone in his paternalistic attitudes. Other religious scalawags questioned the fidelity of the freedmen to the ME Church. Andrew Caldwell in Rome requested money to buy a lot on which to build a church for the freedmen. The blacks of the area could afford to buy the lot also, but "I think it best all things considered for the Church to buy the lot, and let them build the house. . . . If they pay nothing for the ground they can never hereafter lay any claim to it." Cornelius Parker put it more bluntly: "I think that they will stick to us as long as they see any benefit coming & when they think they can stand alone away they'll go." [46] Holding these opinions of their black brethren, the religious scalawags failed to provide black preachers with paths for advancement, reinforced black dependence on white leaders, and encouraged the process of segregation within the Georgia Conference.

As early as 1869 the fledgling conference, like others in the South, was beginning to polarize along racial lines. The physical setting of the Georgia Annual Conference that year illustrated this growing trend toward disintegration. Originally scheduled for Lloyd Street Church in Atlanta, the conference was transformed into a camp meeting at Rataree's Grove, five miles from Atlanta. Two large brush arbors were built on the campgrounds about a quarter of a mile apart. "Two services per day were held in each so that the races worshipped simultaneously, but separate. Business sessions were attended by the two races jointly in a rude building mid-way between the two camps." At this conference, nine black preachers introduced a petition requesting that "districts be manned by colored ministers, and that as soon as may be proper in your judgment, we be organized into a separate conference." The conference gave some sanction to the plan by organizing one black district with Adam Palmer, a black preacher, as presiding elder. [47]

During the October 1871 Georgia Conference, John Yarbrough and Richard Waters introduced a resolution to instruct their delegates to the 1872 General Conference "to move that Body to authorize the setting off of a colored annual conference in Georgia" and that the preachers in Georgia discuss the issue among themselves and come to the next conference prepared to take action. After discussion the resolution was adopted by the conference. The 1872 General Conference, meeting in Brooklyn, New York, in May, authorized the racial division of the Missouri and St. Louis Conferences if the bishops felt "the interests of the work required it," but declined to separate other conferences. In doing so, the General Conference also issued the "magna charta" of black rights in the Methodist Episcopal Church. Blacks were entitled to ordination with white men in annual conferences, appointment as presiding elders, election to the General Conference, and eligibility to "the highest office in the Church."[48]

The subsequent October meeting of the Georgia Annual Conference and those in 1873 and 1874 again passed resolutions requesting a racial separation of the conference. The 1875 conference contemplated the racial segregation of the Georgia work, but some black members and northern preachers voted down a proposal by other blacks and white religious scalawags for a racial division of the conference. Blacks also tried to gain control of both seats in the lay delegation to the 1876 General Conference, further irritating the southern white preachers. The two sides compromised on asking for a geographical rather than a racial division. Opponents of segregation also passed a resolution disclaiming "any movement which looks to the separation of our work into a white and colored conference." The 1876 General Conference approved the separation of the southern conferences provided that the action was "requested by a majority of the white members, and also a majority of the colored members."[49]

The Georgia work of the Methodist Episcopal Church was immediately split into the Georgia Conference and the Savannah Conference, presumably along geographical lines.[50] In the midst of the fall meetings of these new conferences, however, a commission of ministers from both met in Augusta to adjust the boundaries of the two bodies. Citing the fact that "the conference lines are irregular and inconvenient, giving much needless travel to ministers in the work," and the desire of a number of black ministers and congregations in the Georgia Conference to transfer to the Savannah Conference, the commission voted to transfer the La Grange district from the Georgia to the Savannah Conference. It also declared that the Savannah Conference "shall have free access to all the people of color throughout the State of Georgia without regard to geographical lines," and that the Georgia Conference would have charge of all white Georgians. No person could be denied membership, however, on the basis of "race, color or previous condition." Presiding Bishop Levi Scott approved the action of the joint commission, and the racial division was completed.[51]

By 1884 twenty-five of the twenty-eight conferences in the former slave states contained only black or only white ministers and members. The effects of this segregation lingered for many years in the Methodist Episcopal Church, for "what was at first a brotherhood, knowing no race or color, gradually developed into a race problem within the Church." The religious scalawags, in trying to appeal to white southerners, shared responsibility for this problem because a majority of both black and white members had to favor the division of the Georgia Conference for it to be accomplished.[52]

By 1876 the groups that the religious scalawags hoped to reconcile were alienated from one another and from these peacemakers. The membership of the Methodist Episcopal Church had declined from a high point in 1869 of over 21,000 members and probationers to fewer than 16,000 in 1876. Most of the religious scalawags remained in a truncated, all-white Georgia Conference with fewer than 5,000 members. In the same period, the Church, South in Georgia gained over 34,000 white members, while it lost nearly 15,000 black members. As the membership of the Methodist Episcopal Church, South in Georgia grew dramatically, the conferences of the Methodist Episcopal Church could only try to retain their small membership and await the denominational reunion and racial understanding which their ministers had been unable to accomplish.[53]

While external forces did much to hamper their efforts, the religious scalawags themselves bear much of the responsibility for the failure of their vision of religious reconstruction. Believing that the best interests of their black members required their involvement in Republican politics, they actively supported political goals, thus alienating many white southerners who hated and feared military rule and congressional Republicans. Seeking to draw more white support, the religious scalawags later disavowed any political intentions and supported the complete segregation of the Methodist Episcopal Church in Georgia by the organization of a separate black conference. They failed to understand the destructive effect segregation would have on their goal of alleviating racial prejudices. Their sense of paternalistic responsibility also hindered their work among the freedmen.

The tragedy of the Reconstruction history of the Methodist Episcopal Church in Georgia lies in the inability of its ministers, both black and white, to reconcile the two goals of Methodist reunion and racial harmony. Decades later, when the two Methodisms moved toward reunion, the position of black members in the ME Church continued to cause consternation among southern white Methodists.[54] Perhaps the religious scalawags could have done no more than they accomplished. Yet they were motivated by a sincere desire for Methodist reunion and a genuine concern, albeit tainted with paternalism, for the welfare of the freedmen. That the attempt to promote sectional unity and racial harmony was made at all by a group of white Georgians in the 1860s and 1870s attests to the courage and convictions that these men held in the difficult years of Reconstruction.

Notes

1. The term "religious scalawag," applied to white southern ministers who joined northern denominations, is useful for two reasons. The mass of southern whites viewed these ministers in much the same way as they did southern whites who joined the Republican party—as traitors to their section and to the memory of the Confederacy. The term also easily differentiates between this group and northern ministers who came into the South after the war, an important distinction for the purposes of this essay.

2. The conventional portrait of black and white religious life in the South during Reconstruction posits a massive black exodus from the white denominations that by the early 1870s left virtually no black members in white denominations. The exact reasons for the black exodus are assigned alternately to the intense hostility of whites to any association with the freedmen and to the freedmen's desire for their own denominational organizations. Northern-born teachers and missionaries of both races came into the South preaching social equality and ministering almost exclusively to the freedmen. For elements of this view, see Hunter Dickinson Farish, *The Circuit Rider Dismounts: A Social History of Southern Methodism, 1865–1900* (Richmond: Dietz Press, 1938); Ralph E. Morrow, *Northern Methodism and Reconstruction* (East Lansing: Michigan State University Press, 1956); Rufus B. Spain, *At Ease in Zion: A Social History of Southern Baptists, 1865–1900* (Nashville: Vanderbilt University Press, 1961); Kenneth K. Bailey, "The Post–Civil War Racial Separations in Southern Protestantism: Another Look," *Church History* 46 (1977): 453–73; Joe M. Richardson, *Christian Reconstruction: The American Missionary Association and Southern Blacks, 1861–1890* (Athens: University of Georgia Press, 1986); Katharine L. Dvorak, "After Apocalypse, Moses," in John B. Boles, ed., *Masters and Slaves in the House of the Lord: Race and Religion in the American South, 1740–1870* (Lexington: University Press of Kentucky, 1988), 173–91; Katharine L. Dvorak, *An African-American Exodus: The Segregation of the Southern Churches* (Brooklyn: Carlson Publishing, 1991); and William E. Montgomery, *Under Their Own Vine and Fig Tree: The African-American Church in the South, 1865–1900* (Baton Rouge: Louisiana State University Press, 1993). This essay does not argue that the conventional portrait is entirely inaccurate. Rather, it adds another dimension to the turbulent religious history of the period and qualifies some of these scholars' broader generalizations.

3. The 1865 Minutes of the Cincinnati Annual Conference list James F. Chalfant as the Corresponding Secretary for the Church Extension Society and as pastor of Trinity Church, the third largest in membership of eleven churches in the Cincinnati area. The 1866 Minutes list him as the Superintendent of the Georgia and Alabama Mission District, Huntsville, Alabama. Methodist Episcopal Church, *Minutes of the Cincinnati Annual Conference*, 1865, 1866.

4. Minutes of Western Georgia and Alabama Mission District, January 24, 1866, organizational meeting, Methodist Episcopal Church, Records of the Tennessee Conference, The Georgia and Alabama Mission District, The Reverend James F. Chalfant, Superintendent, 1865–1867, Incoming Letters to the Rev. James F. Chalfant,

1865–1878, Atlanta University Center Woodruff Library, Archives Department, Atlanta, Georgia (hereafter referred to as Chalfant Correspondence).

5. "Report of the Committee on the State of the Work and the Demand for Laborers under the Auspices of the Methodist Episcopal Church," January 1866, Chalfant Correspondence. By 1844 the mission to the slaves was established throughout the South, with eighty missionaries ministering "to over 22,000 slave members and preaching to thousands more." Donald G. Mathews wrote that "no numbers of stars in a minister's 'crown' could make it very pleasant to risk health and life in miasmatic swamps for the honor of being called a 'nigger preacher.'" Yet men such as John H. Caldwell and John W. Yarbrough did engage in this perilous work. Caldwell later noted the difficulties of the situation: "The slightest imprudence, an inadvertent remark, a hint of anything wrong in the institution of slavery or the conduct of either master or overseer, would have been the spark to precipitate a fatal explosion." The purpose of this work, according to Mathews, was not "emancipation, but conversion, and pastoral care," thus helping the slaves "in the only way they knew how." The later work of Caldwell, Yarbrough, and others among the freedmen can be understood as a continuation of this commitment to "conversion and pastoral care." Donald G. Mathews, *Slavery and Methodism: A Chapter in American Morality, 1780–1845* (Princeton: Princeton University Press, 1965), 70, 75–76; John H. Caldwell, "Relations of the Colored People to the Methodist Episcopal Church, South," *Methodist Quarterly Review* (July 1866), 430. See also Donald G. Mathews, "The Methodist Mission to the Slaves, 1829–1844," *Journal of American History* 51 (March 1965): 615–31.

6. "Report of the Committee on the State of the Work and the Demand for Laborers," Chalfant Correspondence.

7. J. H. Caldwell to Bishop E. S. Janes, November 24, December 1, 1865, Chalfant Correspondence; J. H. Caldwell to G. L. Eberhart, January 18, 31, March 27, April 17, May 7, 1867, J. H. Caldwell to J. R. Lewis, August 5, October 5, 1867, United States Department of War, Bureau of Refugees, Freedmen, and Abandoned Lands (BRFAL), Records of the Superintendent of Education for the State of Georgia, 1865–1870, Record Group 105, National Archives, available on microfilm (M-799). For an analysis of Caldwell's break with the southern church and the reaction to his decision, see Daniel W. Stowell, "'We Have Sinned, and God Has Smitten Us!': John H. Caldwell and the Religious Meaning of Confederate Defeat," *Georgia Historical Quarterly* 78 (Spring 1994): 1–32.

8. J. H. Caldwell to J. F. Chalfant, July 3, 1866; C. M. Caldwell to J. F. Chalfant, March 19, 1866, Chalfant Correspondence.

9. J. Knowles to J. F. Chalfant, January 3, 1866, Chalfant Correspondence.

10. J. W. Yarbrough to J. F. Chalfant, January 27, 1866, Chalfant Correspondence.

11. Quoted in J. W. Yarbrough to J. F. Chalfant, February 26, 1866, Chalfant Correspondence.

12. J. W. Yarbrough to J. F. Chalfant, May 24, 1866, Chalfant Correspondence; J. W. Yarbrough, "A Farewell Letter," *Southern Christian Advocate*, March 9, 1866.

13. F. Burrow to J. F. Chalfant, July 16, 1867, Chalfant Correspondence.

14. J. H. Caldwell to J. F. Chalfant, April 2, 1866; R. H. Waters to J. F. Chalfant,

August 7, 1866; S. D. Brown to J. F. Chalfant, August 28, 1866; R. H. Waters to J. F. Chalfant, June 11, 1866, Chalfant Correspondence. Waters wrote in August that the mission district needed to hold an annual conference to convince Bishop Pierce of the Church, South and others that "we are making tracks never to go back."

15. C. W. Parker to J. F. Chalfant, November 30, 1866, Chalfant Correspondence.

16. J. H. Caldwell, letter, *Christian Advocate* (New York), December 6, 1866. The Methodist Episcopal Church in Georgia purposely refused to give a racial breakdown of its membership statistics. However, there is no indication that local congregations were biracial and the areas of white and black membership were somewhat geographically distinct. After 1876 white churches remained in the Georgia Conference while black churches formed the Savannah Conference. By tracing congregations backward from this racial division, it is possible to estimate the racial composition of the Georgia Annual Conference between 1867 and 1876. For most of the period white members comprised from 14 to 20 percent of the membership of the conference. During this decade the white membership never numbered more than 3,800, and when the conference divided in 1876, only 2,761 whites remained in the Georgia Conference. At the same time, the all-black Savannah Conference had 12,881 members.

17. For examinations of these denominations' efforts among southern blacks after the Civil War, see Morrow, *Northern Methodism and Reconstruction*, 125–80; Clarence Walker, *A Rock in a Weary Land: The African Methodist Episcopal Church during the Civil War and Reconstruction* (Baton Rouge: Louisiana State University Press, 1982); David M. Bradley, *A History of the A.M.E. Zion Church*, 2 vols. (Nashville: Parthenon Press, 1956–1970); Othal Hawthorne Lakey, *The History of the CME Church* (Memphis: CME Publishing House, 1985), 23–46, 131–278; and Harry V. Richardson, *Dark Salvation: The Story of Methodism as It Developed among Blacks in America* (Garden City, N.J.: Doubleday Anchor, 1976), 191–250.

18. J. H. Caldwell to J. F. Chalfant, January 8, 1866; S. D. Brown to J. F. Chalfant, August 28, 1866; J. W. Yarbrough to J. F. Chalfant, February 26, 1866, Chalfant Correspondence.

19. A. W. Caldwell to J. F. Chalfant, December 26, 1866, Chalfant Correspondence.

20. A. W. Caldwell to J. F. Chalfant, April 19, 1867, Chalfant Correspondence.

21. Ibid.; A. W. Caldwell to G. L. Eberhart, April 16, 1867, BRFAL, Records of Supt. of Ed. for Georgia; A. W. Caldwell to J. F. Chalfant, undated letter after April 1, 1867, Chalfant Correspondence. Funds were obtained from the Freedmen's Bureau on the promise from officials of the Methodist Episcopal Church that the church building would also be used for a regular day school.

22. Minutes of Western Georgia and Alabama Mission District, January 24, 1866 organizational meeting; C. M. Caldwell to J. F. Chalfant, March 19, July 2, 1866, Chalfant Correspondence.

23. Donald G. Mathews, *Religion in the Old South* (Chicago: University of Chicago Press, 1977), 52. For an examination of antebellum camp meetings, see Charles A.

Johnson, *The Frontier Camp Meeting: Religion's Harvest Time* (Dallas: Southern Methodist University Press, 1955), and Dickson D. Bruce, Jr., *And They All Sang Hallelujah: Plain-Folk Camp-Meeting Religion, 1800–1845* (Knoxville: University of Tennessee Press, 1974).

24. J. H. Caldwell to J. F. Chalfant, June 26, 1866, Chalfant Correspondence.

25. J. H. Caldwell to J. F. Chalfant, undated letter (written in mid-August 1866), Chalfant Correspondence.

26. Ibid.

27. Ibid.; J. H. Caldwell to J. F. Chalfant, August 20, 1866, Chalfant Correspondence.

28. C. M. Caldwell to J. F. Chalfant, August 31, 1866, Chalfant Correspondence.

29. J. H. Caldwell to J. F. Chalfant, September 17, 1867, Chalfant Correspondence. J. H. Caldwell's summary of eight camp meetings held in western Georgia in 1867 estimated the combined attendance of the meetings at over fifteen thousand. *American Union* (Griffin, Ga.), October 11, 1867. Charles M. Caldwell expected disturbances by whites at the meeting and wrote Col. Caleb C. Sibley, the assistant commissioner of the Freedmen's Bureau for Georgia, requesting "a few men . . . in order to prevent an anticipated row, at the coming camp-meeting." C. M. Caldwell to C. C. Sibley, September 11, 1867, BRFAL, Records of the Assistant Commissioner for the State of Georgia, 1865–1870, Record Group 105, National Archives, available on microfilm (M-798).

30. J. H. Caldwell to Bishop E. S. Janes, December 1, 1865, Chalfant Correspondence; A. W. Caldwell to G. L. Eberhart, April 9, 1867, BRFAL, Records of the Supt. of Ed. for Georgia. For studies of northern educational efforts among the freedmen, see especially Jacqueline Jones, *Soldiers of Light and Love: Northern Teachers and Georgia Blacks, 1865–1873* (Chapel Hill: University of North Carolina Press, 1980); Robert C. Morris, *Reading, 'Riting, and Reconstruction: The Education of Freedmen in the South, 1861–1870* (Chicago: University of Chicago Press, 1981); and Richardson, *Christian Reconstruction.*

31. J. H. Caldwell to Maj. J. R. Lewis, August 5, 1867; J. R. Lewis to J. H. Caldwell, August 7, 1867, BRFAL, Records of the Supt. of Ed. for Georgia. See also A. W. Caldwell to J. R. Lewis, August 28, 1867, BRFAL, Records of the Asst. Comm. for Georgia. A. W. Caldwell wrote that a lot had been secured for $100 and deeded to black trustees. The Missionary Society of the Methodist Episcopal Church pledged $500; if the Bureau would match this amount, Caldwell would build a house "which can answer the double purpose of Church and school-house."

32. C. W. Parker to J. F. Chalfant, June 16, 1866, November 14, 1866; R. H. Waters to J. F. Chalfant, June 11, 1866; J. H. Caldwell to J. F. Chalfant, May 30, 1867, Chalfant Correspondence. Georgia Conference minutes for 1867 indicated "some schools among the poor whites have been established, but the provision for their support is inadequate." Methodist Episcopal Church, *Minutes of the Georgia Annual Conference,* 1867, 14.

33. J. W. Yarbrough to J. F. Chalfant, November 4, 1866; S. D. Brown to J. F.

Chalfant, August 28, 1866, May 4, 1867, Chalfant Correspondence. James M. Hall, working in northern Georgia, received support from his congregations in a combination of cash and produce. At Tunnel Hill, the people gave him eight dollars and two pounds of wool; at Red Clay, one dollar, one-half bushel of dried apples, one bushel of Irish potatoes, and one pound of wool. J. M. Hall to J. F. Chalfant, December 31, 1866, Chalfant Correspondence.

34. J. H. Caldwell to J. F. Chalfant, July 3, 1866, Chalfant Correspondence. John H. Caldwell's support in 1866 was from the Freedmen's Bureau, as Brig. Gen. Davis Tillson served as Assistant Commissioner for Georgia from September 1865 through January 1867 and G. L. Eberhart was Bureau Superintendent of Education for Georgia from October 1865 through August 1867. Elizabeth S. Nathans, *Losing the Peace: Georgia Republicans and Reconstruction, 1865–1871* (Baton Rouge: Louisiana State University Press, 1968), 32–33.

35. C. M. Caldwell to J. F. Chalfant, July 31, 1866; A. W. Caldwell to J. F. Chalfant, August 30, 1867, Chalfant Correspondence.

36. R. H. Waters to J. F. Chalfant, July 2, 16, 17, 1866; C. W. Parker to J. F. Chalfant, May 23, 1866, clipping from *Tri-Weekly Star* (Griffin, Ga.), Chalfant Correspondence. White southerners used violence against freedmen, scalawags (religious and political), and northerners to accomplish a variety of political, economic, and social goals. See Allen W. Trelease, *White Terror: The Ku Klux Klan Conspiracy and Southern Reconstruction* (New York: Harper and Row, 1971).

37. Morrow, *Northern Methodism and Reconstruction*, 137–38; Walker, *A Rock in a Weary Land*, 93–99. The American Missionary Association, representing Congregationalists and Presbyterians, also engaged in this rivalry for black members. See Jones, *Soldiers of Light and Love*, 153–58.

38. Methodist Episcopal Church, *Minutes of the Georgia Annual Conference*, 1867, 18.

39. William Warren Sweet, "Methodist Church Influence in Southern Politics," *Mississippi Valley Historical Review* 1 (March 1915): 554–55; The religious scalawags also depended on the Freedmen's Bureau, backed by congressional Republicans, for continued support in building new schoolhouses and churches. Donald G. Jones, *The Sectional Crisis and Northern Methodism: A Study in Piety, Political Ethics and Civil Religion* (Metuchen, N.J.: The Scarecrow Press, 1979), 30; Henry M. Johnson, "The Methodist Episcopal Church and the Education of Southern Negroes, 1862–1900" (Ph.D. diss., Yale University, 1939), 184.

40. J. H. Caldwell to J. F. Chalfant, March 4, 1867; J. H. Caldwell to W. Prettyman, October 2, 1867, Chalfant Correspondence. Caldwell also wrote, "I sincerely hope that [the freedmen] may show in the great experiment about to be made at the ballot box, that they are worthy to be trusted with the free man's most sacred prerogative—the right of franchise." J. H. Caldwell to J. R. Lewis, October 5, 1867, BRFAL, Records of the Supt. of Ed. for Georgia.

41. C. W. Parker to G. L. Eberhart, April 8, 1867, BRFAL, Records of Supt. of Ed. for Georgia; R. H. Waters to J. F. Chalfant, March 20, 1867; John Murphy

to J. F. Chalfant, April 16, 1867, Chalfant Correspondence; Michael W. Fitzgerald, *The Union League Movement in the Deep South: Politics and Agricultural Change during Reconstruction* (Baton Rouge: Louisiana State University Press, 1989), 31, 58–59; Roberta F. Cason, "The Loyal League in Georgia," *Georgia Historical Quarterly* 20 (June 1936): 125–53. Cason does not specifically name J. H. Caldwell as a leader of the Union League in La Grange, but given his involvement in political issues from mid-1867, he was a likely supporter, if not leader, of the Union League.

42. William A. Russ, Jr., "The Failure to Reunite Methodism after the Civil War," *Susquehanna University Studies* 1, no. 1 (1936): 15–16.

43. Richard M. Cameron, *Methodism and Society in Historical Perspective* (Nashville: Abingdon Press, 1961), 198. Victor Howard examines the role of radical members of northern denominations on the course of political reconstruction in *Religion and the Radical Republican Movement* (Lexington: University Press of Kentucky, 1990). Howard's "radical Christians" had gained control within the Methodist Episcopal Church by the end of the Civil War and strongly supported the religious scalawags in their efforts in the South.

44. J. H. Caldwell to J. F. Chalfant, April 22, 1867, Chalfant Correspondence. The man to whom Caldwell referred was Rev. John M. Bonnell, the president of Wesleyan Female College in Macon. Some of Caldwell's Republican political activities can be traced in Nathans, *Losing the Peace*, and Ruth Currie-McDaniel, *Carpetbagger of Conscience: A Biography of John Emory Bryant* (Athens: University of Georgia Press, 1987).

45. Daniel Curry, "The Church and the Freedmen," *Christian Advocate* (New York), November 8, 1866; J. W. Yarbrough to J. F. Chalfant, November 19, 1866, Chalfant Correspondence; G. L. Eberhart to J. F. Chalfant, April 17, 1867, BRFAL, Records of the Supt. of Ed. for Georgia.

46. A. W. Caldwell to J. F. Chalfant, August 10, 1867; C. W. Parker to J. F. Chalfant, June 23 (1866?), Chalfant Correspondence.

47. Edmund J. Hammond, *Methodist Episcopal Church in Georgia* (n.p., 1935), 124–26; Methodist Episcopal Church, *Minutes of the Georgia Annual Conference*, 1871, 13; *Methodist Advocate* (Atlanta), September 15, 1869.

48. Methodist Episcopal Church, *Minutes of the Georgia Annual Conference*, 1871, 13; "magna charta" of black rights quoted in Oliver S. Heckman, "Northern Church Penetration of the South, 1860–1880" (Ph.D. diss., Duke University, 1939), 195. Erasmus Q. Fuller, the editor of the Methodist Episcopal Church's *Methodist Advocate* in Georgia, complained that the General Conference "practically took no action upon the question of the colored conferences." Many conferences which had requested division had few white members and were practically black conferences, he argued, and "they have never felt many of the embarrassments found in some localities," like the Georgia Conference. *Methodist Advocate*, June 26, 1872.

49. *Methodist Advocate*, November 6, 1872, November 12, 1873, October 27, 1875; Hammond, *Methodist Episcopal Church in Georgia*, 139; Frank K. Pool, "The Southern Negro in the Methodist Episcopal Church" (Ph.D. diss., Duke University, 1939),

214–33; William Gravely, *Gilbert Haven, Methodist Abolitionist: A Study in Race, Religion, and Reform, 1850–1880* (Nashville: Abingdon Press, 1973), 231; Morrow, *Northern Methodism and Reconstruction*, 196; Methodist Episcopal Church, *Journal of the General Conference*, 1876, 331.

50. Methodist Episcopal Church, *Journal of the General Conference*, 1876, 372, 377. The Georgia Conference initially consisted of the Atlanta, Dalton, and Ogeechee districts; while the Savannah Conference embraced the Rome, Macon, Augusta, and Savannah districts.

51. "Division of Georgia Conference," *Methodist Advocate*, November 8, 1876; Hammond, *Methodist Episcopal Church in Georgia*, 139.

52. Dwight W. Culver, *Negro Segregation in the Methodist Church* (New Haven: Yale University Press, 1953), 59; John H. Reed, *Racial Adjustments in the Methodist Episcopal Church* (New York: Neale Publishing Co., 1914), 58. Reed's volume gives insight into the position of blacks within the Methodist Episcopal Church from a prominent black minister's view. Reed attributes the fact that the Methodist Episcopal Church still had no black bishops in 1914 to a trend toward reunion with the Methodist Episcopal Church, South, an organization that would disapprove of such a development. The Methodist Episcopal Church did elect two black bishops, Matthew W. Clair, Sr., and Robert E. Jones, in 1920. Richardson, *Dark Salvation*, 271–72.

53. Methodist Episcopal Church, *Minutes of the Annual Conferences*, 1865–1875; Methodist Episcopal Church, South, *Minutes of the Annual Conferences*, 1865–1875.

By 1876 several of the original religious scalawags had left their positions. Charles M. Caldwell returned to secular employment to support his family. John H. Caldwell entered politics in 1868 and transferred to a conference in Delaware in 1872. John W. Yarbrough returned to the Church, South in 1872, perhaps because he saw little hope for the reunion which he had so desired. In a September 1872 letter to the *Methodist Advocate*, he announced that he was returning to the southern church "for reasons sufficient to my own mind." He had strong family ties with the Church, South as three sons and two sons-in-law were southern Methodist ministers. Several others who remained in the Georgia Conference of the Methodist Episcopal Church soon entered semiretired, or supernumerary, positions. The 1871 Georgia Conference *Minutes* listed William Brewer, A. W. Caldwell, and C. W. Parker as either superannuated (worn-out) or supernumerary (semiretired). J. W. Yarbrough, letter, *Methodist Advocate*, September 25, 1872; Methodist Episcopal Church, *Minutes of the Georgia Conference*, 1871, 16.

54. The Methodist Episcopal Church and the Methodist Episcopal Church, South did reunite in 1939, after years of negotiation. Culver, *Negro Segregation in the Methodist Church*, 60–78.

The Ties That Bind

Educated African-American Women in Post-Emancipation Atlanta

Jennifer Lund Smith

In 1894, Mattie F. Childs, an Atlanta University student, addressed the crowd gathered for Emancipation Day exercises taking place at the school with a speech entitled, "The Progress of the Colored Woman Since 1863." No doubt she drew applause from the women in the crowd with the words, "Suddenly snatched from the cursed bondage of slavery, placed in the blessed light of freedom, with God as helper, we have patiently and arduously toiled upward, and tonight we can look in the face of any man and boldly say: 'We are rising'. . . . *Slowly*, but *surely* it is dawning upon the 'lords of creation' that Almighty God in his infinite wisdom did not make one sex inferior to another but made all men equal."[1] Though she lost some of her momentum proclaiming the equality of all *men*, Childs's speech clearly reflected a growing self-consciousness among educated African-American women. As the century drew to a close, the female graduates of Atlanta University in the audience were fully cognizant of the distance they had traveled together and the strength they had exhibited, and they took pride in their success.

The women who graduated from Atlanta University during its first fifteen years of existence were not even a generation removed from slavery. They came to the school a disparate group of individuals with varied backgrounds. The collective intellectual and ideological lessons they learned at Atlanta University fused them into a community of women aspiring to common goals. This essay is based on the experiences of twenty-five young women who attended Atlanta University during its early years and who then made the city their home. An examination of this select group of educated Atlantans, who would have considered themselves members of what W. E. B. Du Bois termed the "talented tenth," sheds light on the transforming effects of higher education on these women, on the forces that drew and held them together, and the impact of their experiences, individually and collectively, on their rapidly changing community.

When the American Missionary Association (AMA) founded Atlanta University in 1869, the city was in the midst of redefining itself. In the wake of the Civil War, Atlanta faced a new set of circumstances that provided its inhabitants, black and white, with propitious opportunities. The city rebounded from the war with remarkable growth. The boom in construction and the ever-increasing influx of new residents created a business environment particularly conducive to budding entrepreneurs. Freed people found Atlanta particularly welcoming; the absence of an antebellum black elite enabled successful new businessmen to rise rapidly to leadership status within the city's African-American community.[2]

Among the benefits Atlanta offered were numerous schools for African-American children. Ex-slaves recognized that education meant empowerment, and they made it one of their foremost priorities. Not only did they need to understand the labor contracts they signed each year, but many also hoped to assimilate into white society by proving their intellectual capabilities.

AMA missionaries began arriving in Atlanta in late 1865 to establish an educational system upon the foundation of those schools already organized by the freedpeople themselves. During the summer of 1865, Grandsion Daniels and his partner, James Tate, who would become an active political figure in the African-American community, established the city's first school for black children. The two men turned the school over to the AMA shortly after its first representatives arrived. Under the guidance of Frederick Ayer, a missionary who had gained his field experience working with Native Americans in Minnesota, the AMA brought organization, professionally trained teachers, and funding to educate the freedpeople in Atlanta. It also brought the free labor ideology northerners hoped to instill in recently emancipated southern African Americans.[3]

Under the auspices of the AMA, education in Atlanta flourished. Six months after the war's end, Frederick Ayer and his assistants taught reading, spelling, writing, arithmetic, geography, and occasionally some singing to an eager group which gathered in the local African Church. In 1869, the AMA opened Atlanta University with the aid of the Congregational Church on a sizable tract of land recently purchased for that purpose on the city's southwestern side. The first year eighty-nine students enrolled for classes; twenty-seven of them were women.[4]

Many of the parents of the young women who attended Atlanta University migrated to the city after the war to take advantage of the opportunities it offered. Men, women, and children who had been slaves only a few short years earlier poured into the revitalized metropolis from locations as near as the countryside of neighboring counties and as far as Virginia.

Along with ministers and those who had secured an education, a number of the freedmen who achieved financial success fairly quickly created an economic and social elite that tended to act as the voice of the African-American community. Within that community, many female graduates of Atlanta University, on the basis of their education more than their family's financial background, entered those select ranks as educators and civic leaders.[5]

The Escridge family's story is typical of the upward mobility possible in postbellum Atlanta. Soon after the war, Peter Escridge acknowledged his freedom by leaving rural Gwinnett County just north of Atlanta and moving to the city with his family, which included two young daughters. He used his accumulated savings as a blacksmith to purchase, with a partner, a modest amount of land in 1867. Over the next decade he amassed larger tracts of land and opened a grocery. Escridge achieved a level of financial success that he never could have realized in Gwinnett County, and he was able to send his daughters Effie and Emma to Atlanta University, where they graduated in 1878 and 1880, respectively. When he died in 1909, Escridge left $7,500 worth of property to be divided among his heirs.[6]

Peter Upshaw achieved a more modest level of success. He moved his family to Atlanta from Cassville, Georgia, just after the war and worked as a carpenter while his wife, Lila, stayed at home with their children: Martha (Mattie), Sarah, Arthur, and Thomas. Upshaw saved enough money to buy property on Vine Street and nearly doubled his financial worth from $400 to $730 during the 1870s. Themselves illiterate, Peter and Lila saw that their children received an education. By 1870 all four of their offspring, ranging in age from nine to fourteen, were attending school, with Mattie already enrolled at Atlanta University. She eventually taught in various schools in the city and became an indefatigable organizer in several women's clubs and reform societies.[7]

Not all parents of Atlanta University students prospered. Life in Atlanta proved more peripatetic and less lucrative for Isaiah Thomas. By 1870, Thomas, his wife, and their two young daughters had moved to Atlanta from Greensboro, Georgia. Thomas worked as a laborer moving from job to job, earning a living as a porter, an employee at a grocery, and later as a driver for a hardware company. By 1879 his effects totaled only twenty-five dollars. Yet his daughter Ella was able to attend Atlanta University, and she later taught in the city schools.[8]

The experiences of Atlanta's postwar migrants varied greatly, as the levels of income and education attained by the parents of Atlanta University students attested. While some found ways to purchase their own land, the majority did not. Yet these parents did share a universal concern to educate their children and a hope that this education would provide their offspring with opportunities that slavery had denied them.

University officials recruited their first students from the various AMA schools in Georgia. Most of the men and women who entered Atlanta University in 1869 were Atlantans, but the institution drew scholars from Savannah, Augusta, Macon, and Athens as well. The first year all eighty-nine students worked together in the Preparatory Department. Enrollment had doubled by the second year, thus necessitating divisions in the levels of study so that students tested for placement in a senior, middle, or junior class.[9]

Atlanta University expanded rapidly. In 1872, the university opened a Normal Department designed specifically to train teachers. Because northern missionaries could not possibly meet the educational demands of Georgia's black populace, Atlanta University graduates offered a valuable means of filling that vital need, and in doing so they could further disseminate the values the northern missionaries espoused. From its inception, the Normal Department was dominated by female students who underwent a rigorous review of the "common branches" with a "reference to teaching them." The students studied algebra, geometry, natural science, drawing, English literature, elements of Latin, the theory and practice of teaching, and mental and moral philosophy.[10]

The women who attended Atlanta University were expected to subscribe to the moral codes established by their northern missionary teachers. Heirs to the methods and beliefs of the reform movements of the early nineteenth century, northern instructors who ventured south sought to instill in their students values that they presumed would produce responsible members of society: thrift, temperance, cleanliness, and free labor ideology. University officials took care to enroll only men and women they deemed possessed of "good moral character," and in an effort to ensure that their students upheld the school's high standards of morality, officials required every pupil to "sign a pledge to abstain from the use of all intoxicating drink and tobacco in every form while a member of the school." [11]

The moral conduct required by the teachers at the school became more than a set of rules superimposed on the students; most internalized these values and came to expect from one another full adherance to the school's code of behavior. The case of Ann Brown illustrates this peer pressure. Despite her intellectual ability, Brown did not exhibit the scholarly zeal or, more significantly, the demeanor expected of an Atlanta University student. She was one of the few students who belonged to the Congregational church, but in 1871 the church declared that Brown had "associated herself with persons of bad reputation [and] had often attended public dancing parties and other places of bad repute." Not only that, she professed "no sorrow" and made "no promise of amendment." The church excommunicated her, and—no doubt as a result—she did not return to school nor did she ever become a member of the Atlanta University "community." As a woman who did not subscribe to the values of the rising black elite, Brown would have been an obstacle to their foremost goal: proving they were the intellectual and moral equals of their white counterparts.[12]

Despite Atlanta University's close affiliation with the Congregational church, the school enjoyed only modest success in converting its students to Congregationalism. Most preferred to attend the newly independent African-American churches that appeared following emancipation. The students did absorb their mentors' evangelical approach to social reform, however. The majority of women who graduated from Atlanta University became teachers and, bound together professionally and socially, they also worked through reform groups for the betterment of African Americans in Atlanta.

In 1873, Atlanta University graduated its first class of students. Full of knowledge and idealism, these men and women left the school eager to teach. Their presence in the city provided Atlanta with a unique advantage. Although the capital was more receptive to white northern educators than were many smaller towns and rural areas, freedpeople generally preferred to study with black teachers when given the option. They sensed both the racial and regional condescension of northern whites, and they were not always comfortable with the values promoted by northern missionaries. Most Georgia communities did not have enough African-American teachers with the skills to provide a thorough education. But because of the presence of Atlanta University, the city possessed an abundance of qualified teachers, and the black community pushed hard to see them appointed to positions in the black public schools.[13]

By the time Atlanta University held its first graduation ceremony, the city's African American leaders were already pressuring the Atlanta Board of Education to establish a public high school for black students. In 1874 they added the employment of black teachers to their list of goals. From its origin in

1869, the all-white board of education in Atlanta had exhibited a reluctance to educate the freedpeople at all, and it adamantly preferred white, southern teachers, regardless of the racial makeup of their pupils.

Pressure to provide funding for the education of African-American children arose from the black community's own middle class. Its leaders challenged the board's disingenuous assertion that the Freedmen's Bureau's endeavors to educate black children had proven so successful that the needs of the city's white children seemed "more immediate and pressing." After two years of resistance, the board began to make arrangements to assume responsibility for a few of the African-American schools in the city. Its first step consisted of asking the trustees of existing missionary schools to allow the Board of Education to use their buildings free of rent in exchange for providing administration. That proposal met with a mixed reaction. The Methodist trustees readily agreed and relinquished control of Summer Hill School. The AMA, however, resisted and only after a lengthy and bitter power struggle did they finally transfer control of their schools to the Board of Education.[14]

The freedpeople themselves continued to pressure the city with demands of their own. On September 17, 1872, a group of twenty-five black citizens, led by Rev. Frank Quarles of the Friendship Baptist Church, convened to discuss the need for a public high school. A week later they petitioned the Board of Education, asking that they either supply a high school for qualified African-American students or defray the expenses of their enrollment in Atlanta University's preparatory department. The board denied their request.[15]

The black community was more successful in their attempts to see African Americans employed in the public schools, but only after a long and arduous battle. In 1874, Reverend Quarles once again corresponded with the Board of Education, this time requesting that it hire black teachers for the Haynes Street School, which had recently opened for African-American children. The board reacted by postponing a discussion of the issue to an indefinite date that never arrived. The community persisted, however. A year and a half later, the Board of Education received a petition from Atlanta University graduates determined to teach in the public schools. Four male graduates, on behalf of themselves and nine unidentified others, notified the board of their qualifications and their desire to teach. Three months later a group of black ministers followed this request with another petition urging "that colored teachers be employed in all the colored schools under the charge of the Board."[16]

The board took no action until a year later when it announced its decision to consider hiring African-American teachers. Board members cited numerous reasons for its eventual decision to appoint black instructors. They acknowledged the community's desire for African-American teachers and noted the success of similar programs in Savannah and Macon. Perhaps more compelling was their suggestion to hire black teachers "on the grounds of economy." The public schools were experiencing severe financial stress, and the board planned to pay African Americans approximately one-third of what they paid white teachers. The decision was also a thinly disguised ploy to decrease the number of positions open to northern white teachers associated with the AMA.[17]

Although black women remained noticeably absent in this battle with the board, the fight ultimately resulted in their employment. The African-American community realized that obvious involvement on the part of women in the political negotiations with the board would appear "unladylike." Yet many of the petitioners for the employment of African-American teachers were the fathers of women who would later fill those positions. This suggests that prospective female teachers, using the voices of their fathers, worked actively behind the scenes toward their own employment.

It was not until the fall of 1878, five years after the first Atlanta University graduates were available as teachers, that the city's board of education actually hired two of them. During the summer of that year the board had administered exams for fourteen African-American applicants, nine of whom were graduates of Atlanta University's Normal Department. Atlantan Oswell A. Coombs received the highest score, but the board did not offer him a job, most likely in order to save money by hiring females. The two applicants selected as new teachers from this pool were the two highest scoring female Atlantans. Thus Indiana Clark and Ella Townsley, both Atlanta University graduates, became the first black women hired to teach in the Atlanta public school system. By the end of the summer, the board consented to employ three more Atlanta University alumnae, Julia Turner, Mattie Upshaw, and Elizabeth Easley.[18]

Two years after this breakthrough, the Board of Education conceded to demands from local black leaders and erected a new school building on the corner of Houston and Butler streets. In so doing, it took two more significant steps: the first construction of a school building specifically for African Americans, and the hiring of an entirely black staff. The board did stipulate, however, that two older schools for black children would employ white faculty only. The new two-story structure on Houston Street held eight classrooms and accommodated 450 pupils. The principal, R. H. Carter, was an Atlanta University graduate, as were at least five of the teachers hired that year.[19]

Most of Atlanta University's female graduates who went on to teach in the public school system left their jobs once they married. This pattern was typical among many, though certainly not all, women, white and black, whose husbands' economic status afforded them the opportunity to surrender their teaching positions. In 1882, the first year of its existence, the Mitchell Street school lost twelve of its twenty-four female teachers when they "crossed the river of matrimony to live in comfortable homes of their own." [20]

Not all women, however, gave up their teaching positions once they became wives. Despite marrying twice, Indiana Clark taught continuously in the Atlanta public school system for forty-one years and became one of the first black female principals in the public schools.[21] Upon her graduation in 1874, Mattie Upshaw took a teaching position at a private school on Loyd Street, and in 1878 she became one of the five other Atlanta University alumnae appointed as the first African Americans to teach in the public schools. In July 1881 she left teaching to marry Pierce Ford, a carpenter.[22]

After giving birth to four children, Ford resumed her career in 1892, temporarily filling the position of assistant principal in the public school system at Summer Hill School—after the board had issued a special dispensation for her employment as a married woman. In the fall, she transferred to Mitchell Street School where she taught first grade. At some point during the 1890s, Pierce Ford died, and by 1900 Mattie and her family were living with her father. In that year, she left the public schools to accept a teaching post at Morris Brown College, a private institution established in 1885.[23]

Attending Atlanta University became a tradition in the Upshaw and Ford families. Mattie's brother earned his degree in 1878 and became a clergyman. Her younger sister Sarah took classes in the Normal Department, and while she did not complete her degree, she became a teacher. Later, all three of Mattie's daughters graduated from the Normal Department and became teachers.[24]

Teaching offered both rewarding and frustrating challenges to the graduates of Atlanta University. In the public schools they taught a curriculum which included reading, grammar, arithmetic, American history, and geography. Those who taught the advanced levels also taught algebra and geometry, and Latin and Greek. They sought to reach the minds of young students who often found distractions in an environment not always conducive to learning. Despite the addition of a new school for black children located on Gray Street in 1890, African-American students suffered from chronic overcrowding in their classrooms. The board supported eleven schools for white children in the city, but only four schools for African-American pupils. The Houston Street School lacked "water closets," a deficiency that led to sanitation problems. Only the Gray Street School, the newest, could claim "the latest educational aids in the way of maps, globes, numeral frames, and charts," along with a heating system and new desks.[25]

For their work, African-American teachers earned a relatively small salary. The Board of Education paid them $300 per year, $200 less than white teachers received in identical positions. In the winter of 1878, the board found itself short of funds and requested that all its teachers continue working for the month of December at half their salary until additional money could be solicited from the city government. The teachers had little choice but to agree to a cut in their already modest incomes. Despite pressure from the black community in the form of an 1881 petition to increase the salaries of black teachers, the board refused to close the gap between the salaries of its white and black educators.[26]

Alternative nonpublic teaching positions did exist for Atlanta University graduates, and it was common for female graduates to shift between public and private schools. Some women operated their own schools. Mary Pope McCree, a member of the graduating class of 1880, ran a private school at Big Bethel AME Church until Rev. Wesley J. Gaines recruited her to serve as the first principal at Morris Brown College. In that capacity McCree filled its classrooms with her former students. Yet private schools lacked the funds to provide current books and teaching aids, and salaries remained meager.[27]

Whether employed by private or by public schools, the young women from Atlanta University battled discouraging odds in their mission to educate children of their own race. They persevered, however, and achieved results by forging a tight, supportive community. Ultimately, these women, even those who had resigned their jobs upon marrying, reached beyond the classroom and took their teaching skills into the surrounding neighborhoods by means of reform groups and women's organizations.

At the end of the nineteenth century, the consequences of urbanization gained national attention. Reform groups, dominated by women, proliferated in attempts both to instill prescribed moral values in the lower classes and to alleviate their suffering. Black Atlantans participated in urban reform and, in so doing, drew from a long tradition of African-American benevolent organizations and mutual aid societies.[28]

By their very existence, African-American associations had always been forced to address prejudice, but ironically, the Progressive Era, with its emphasis on providing aid to lower-class Americans, ushered in a new surge of overt displays of virulent racism. During the last decade of the nineteenth century, southern states disfranchised blacks and formalized Jim Crow laws to enforce segregation. The increasing estrangement of black and white Atlantans caused African Americans to turn to each other and prompted the elite to create reform societies to reach those whom white organizations overlooked.[29]

Many Atlanta University alumnae entered reform movements through their churches. One nondenominational organization that attended to indigent blacks in Atlanta was the Independent Order of Good Samaritans and Daughters of Samaria. The organization, comprised of both men and women, bought property and used it to care for the poor and sick in the city.[30]

Although benevolent societies comprised of both males and females existed, women took the initiative to organize reform groups of their own. One of the most emotionally charged issues of the day was temperance. While temperance was a popular concern of all women, the Women's Christian Temperance Union (WCTU) relegated the African-American chapters to a separate department. In March 1887 black women in Atlanta gathered at Friendship Baptist Church to organize the West Atlanta chapter of the WCTU, electing several Atlanta University graduates to leadership positions.[31]

The West Atlanta WCTU got off to a slow start, but when Mattie Upshaw Ford assumed the presidency, she put the Union to work. Between their frequent meetings, they taught the gospel of temperance and morality to such diverse groups as convicts on chain gangs and students at Atlanta University. In 1890 alone this ambitious group gave twenty-three talks on purity to the young women at the University. Lecture titles reflected the values to which they subscribed: "Engagements, What They Are"; "Engagements, What They Should Be"; "Care of Body" and "Baths"; "Mother's Influence" and "Motherhood"; "Unfermented Wine"; and "Character Building."[32]

In 1896 Atlanta University hosted the first annual Conference for the Study of Negro Problems. Female graduates of the university took an active role in collecting data and presenting papers on topics such as infant mortality and "Co-operation of Parents and Teachers." In 1899 Mattie Upshaw Ford sat on a panel in a session titled, "What Shall Our Children Do For a Living?" The participation of many female graduates of Atlanta University in these conferences reflects the intensity of commitment and responsibility to the community assumed by these women.[33]

In 1908, following the violent and destructive race riot that occurred in Atlanta in 1906, black women armed with ideas and enthusiasm generated at the Atlanta conferences undertook a massive effort aimed at social change in the city's African-American neighborhoods. Under the leadership of Mrs. Lugenia Burns Hope, wife of Atlanta University's president, they organized the Neighborhood Union. Appalled at the unsanitary conditions and the lack of entertainment for children, they established clubs to teach boys and girls practical skills and opened a health clinic.[34] Mattie Upshaw Ford was among the women who put her energies to work for the Neighborhood Union. She engaged in fund-raising efforts at Big Bethel Church and headed up the committee to tackle Atlanta's Fourth Ward, the area of the city the Neighborhood Union found most odious for its "dens of vice" and the "several inadequate, dilapidated, excuses for public schools for Negroes." In 1919, when the Union divided the city into zones to serve it more effectively, Ford chaired a zone, taking charge of investigating the living conditions of 1,185 Atlantans.[35]

Recognizing that they could gain strength in large numbers, women's organizations began joining together to form an association of women's clubs. In 1896 Mattie Ford represented Georgia as a delegate to the National Association of Colored Women (NACW). The larger goal of the NACW was to attain "full acceptance . . . into the American mainstream." The expansive network they created enabled communication among African-American women throughout the country. They provided one another with support and a sense of belonging that they did not find in white society.[36]

The women who graduated from Atlanta University during its first fifteen years subscribed to the belief that the advancement of African-American people depended on their ability to assimilate into white society and prove their equality. As teachers, they hoped to convey to their students the skills to rise above racial stereotypes and to inspire them to challenge white society's assumptions of their intellectual and social inferiority.

While enacting social reforms, Atlanta graduates worked within the confines of nineteenth-century expectations of female behavior. Attending to their husbands and families, they continued to work in the community through church organizations and as members of reform groups. Serving the needs of less fortunate black Atlantans offered this group of intelligent and educated women a chance to exercise their talents and share their concerns, as well as contribute to the African-American community.

Notes

1. Mattie F. Childs, "The Progress of the Colored Woman since 1863," *Bulletin of Atlanta University* 49 (January 1894): 5; Martha (Mattie) Freeman Childs, an Alabama native, apparently graduated from Atlanta University's College Department in 1895 and found employment teaching at Tuskegee the next year. *Catalogue of Atlanta University,* 1892–93, 1896.

2. Eric Foner, *Reconstruction: America's Unfinished Revolution, 1863–1877* (New York: Harper and Row, 1988), 397. On a later generation of the city's black elite, see August Meier and David L. Lewis, "History of the Negro Upper Class in Atlanta, Georgia, 1890–1958," a 1959 essay reprinted in Meier, *A White Scholar and the Black Community, 1945–1965* (Amherst: University of Massachusetts Press, 1992), 103–16.

3. Charles A. Bacote, *The Story of Atlanta University: A Century of Service, 1865–1965* (Atlanta: Atlanta University Press, 1969), 1–14; Myron Adams, *A History of Atlanta University* (Atlanta: Atlanta University Press, 1930), 2; Joe M. Richardson, *Christian Reconstruction: The American Missionary Association and Southern Blacks, 1861–1890* (Athens: University of Georgia Press, 1986), 164, 169. Adams hints that Tate and Daniels relinquished their school to the AMA because they recognized their limitations as teachers. A letter from one of the AMA missionaries suggests that it may instead have been the AMA that perceived them to be incompetent. A month after arriving in Atlanta, Rose Kinney told an AMA secretary: "We have had the assistance of two col[ored] men, but they are not as efficient as our teachers ought to be." It is quite possible these two men were Tate and Daniels (Rose Kinney to Mr. S. Hunt, Atlanta. American Missionary Association Archives, Amistad Research Center, New Orleans, La.; cited hereafter as AMA Archives). Tate may not have fit the AMA standards of an efficient teacher, but he did become a successful business-man in Atlanta who devoted himself to the cause of educating freedpeople in Georgia. He entered politics as a delegate to the Freedmen's Convention of Georgia in 1866, and later, in 1870, he campaigned for a seat in the state legislature. While his race was unsuccessful, he remained involved in politics throughout the 1880s. *Proceedings of the Freedmen's Convention of Georgia Assembled at Augusta, January 10th, 1866. Containing the Speeches of Gen'l Tillson, Capt. J. E. Bryant, and Others.* (Augusta, 1866), 4 (hereafter cited as *Proceedings of the Freedmen's Convention*); James M. Russell and Jerry Thornberry, "William Finch of Atlanta: The Black Politician as Civic Leader" in Howard N. Rabinowitz, ed., *Southern Black Leaders of the Reconstruction Era* (Urbana: University of Illinois Press, 1982), 323.

4. Report of Frederick Ayer, December 1865; Report of Rose Kinney, December 1865; Report of Jennie E. Barnum, 1865; AMA Archives; Bacote, *Story of Atlanta University*, 1–14; *Catalogue of Atlanta University*, 1868–1870.

5. Willard B. Gatewood attests to the importance of education in upward social mobility for those not born affluent in *Aristocrats of Color: The Black Elite, 1880–1920* (Bloomington: Indiana University Press, 1990), 247–48.

6. Fulton County Deed Book, J, 218; *Atlanta City Directory*, 1875–1889; Twelfth Census of the United States, Population Schedules, 1900: Georgia (hereafter cited as Twelfth Census); Fulton County Tax Digest, 1909; *Catalogue of Atlanta University*, 1875–1886.

7. Myron W. Adams, *General Catalogue of Atlanta University* (Atlanta: Atlanta University Press, 1929), 145; Fulton County Tax Digests, 1873–1877; Fulton County Deed Book, F-3, 333; *Catalogue of Atlanta University*, 1869–1874; Atlanta City Direc-

tory, 1889; Tenth Census of the United States, Population Schedules, 1870: Georgia (hereafter cited as Tenth Census).

8. Fulton County Tax Digest, 1879; *Atlanta City Directory*, 1867–1889; Tenth Census; Adams, *General Catalogue*, 140.

9. Adams, *History of Atlanta University*, 16–17; Bacote, *Story of Atlanta University*, 25, 28–29; *Catalogue of Atlanta University*, 1869–1873.

10. *Catalogue of Atlanta University*, 1869–1870, 10–11.

11. Ibid., 10–11. For a discussion of the goals of northern missionary teachers see Jacqueline Jones, *Soldiers of Light and Love: Northern Teachers and Georgia Blacks, 1865–1873* (Chapel Hill: University of North Carolina Press, 1980), especially chap. 7. Ralph E. Luker highlights the conservative methods of the AMA and other "social gospelers" in their aspirations to realize the more radical vision of elevating the status of freed people in *The Social Gospel in Black and White: American Racial Reform, 1885–1912* (Chapel Hill: University of North Carolina Press, 1991), chap. 2. For a description of more debilitating effects of the AMA's attempts to influence "almost every aspect of the freedmen's lives," see Richardson, *Christian Reconstruction*, 240–45.

12. Minutes of the First Congregational Church, Atlanta, 1869–1871, Georgia Department of Archives and History, Atlanta (GDAH).

13. Jones, *Soldiers of Light and Love*, 66, 111; Robert C. Morris, *Reading, 'Riting, and Reconstruction: The Education of Freedmen in the South, 1861–1870* (Chicago: University of Chicago Press, 1981), 90.

14. Pamphlet issued by the Atlanta Board of Education, GDAH (hereafter cited as Board of Education); Arthur Reed Taylor, "From the Ashes: Atlanta during Reconstruction, 1865–1876" (Ph.D. diss., Emory University, 1970), 243; Board of Education, September 26, 1872, April 29, 1880.

15. Quarles incorporated political activity into his duties as minister of the Friendship Baptist Church. Along with James Tate, he served as a Fulton County delegate to the Freedmen's Convention of Georgia in 1866. During the course of the meeting he was elected as one of the Association's vice-presidents. Quarles continued to head committees concerned with the conditions of education for African Americans and to present petitions to the Atlanta Board of Education on behalf of African Americans in the city during the 1870s. Taylor, "From the Ashes," 248; Board of Education, September 26, 1872, August 22, 1874, June 13, 1878; *Proceedings of the Freedmen's Convention*, 4, 21.

16. Board of Education, August 22, 1874, April 27, July 10, 1876.

17. Ibid., June 27, July 26, 1877.

18. Ibid., July 2, September 2, 26, 1878.

19. Ibid., June 30, July 30, 1881; Rev. E. B. Carter, *The Black Side* (Atlanta, 1894; reprint, Freeport, N.Y.: Viking Press, 1965), 232, 236.

20. In 1883 the Atlanta Board of Education voted to prohibit the hiring of any married female teachers. The ruling did exempt those who were already employed in the public schools, however. Five years later, in 1888, it amended its decision and

allowed the employment of individual married women contingent upon a special vote. Board of Education, August 24, October 26, 1882, January 1, 1883, February 23, 1888; Carter, *The Black Side*, 226, 240.

21. Board of Education, July 3, 1878, June 6, 1896; Adams, *General Catalogue of Atlanta University*, 56, 70, 142, 145; *Catalogue of Atlanta University*, 1867–1929. Indiana Clark married Richard J. Henry on July 24, 1895. Five years after his death in 1902, she married Howard Pitts. Both her husbands were widowers who had previously been married to Atlanta University graduates. Fulton County Marriage Book E, 418.

22. Fulton County Marriage Book B, 290; *Catalogue of Atlanta University*, 1867–1929; Twelfth Census; Adams, *General Catalogue*, 70, 145.

23. Board of Education, January 28, June 3, 1892; Twelfth Census; *Catalogue of Atlanta University*, 1899–1900; Annie B. Thomas, *Morris Brown College: From Its Beginning in 1885 to Time of Removal, 1932* (Atlanta: Morris Brown College, 1923), 29.

24. Adams, *General Catalogue*, 70, 145.

25. Board of Education, March 25, 1886, June 29, 1889, July 29, 1880; Carter, *The Black Side*, 224–26.

26. Board of Education, June 2, 1893, June 20, 1881, June 29, 1891.

27. Thomas, *Morris Brown College*, 19, 29, 51–52.

28. A growing literature on black women and turn-of-the-century reform efforts includes Kathleen C. Berkeley, " 'Colored Ladies Also Contributed': Black Women's Activities from Benevolence to Social Welfare, 1866–1896," in Walter J. Fraser, Jr., R. Frank Saunders, Jr., and Jon L. Wakelyn, eds., *The Web of Southern Social Relations: Women, Family, and Education* (Athens: University of Georgia Press, 1985), 181–203; Dorothy C. Salem, "To Better Our World: Black Women in Organized Reform, 1890–1920" (Ph.D. diss., Kent State University, 1986); Jean E. Friedman, *The Enclosed Garden: Women and Community in the Evangelical South, 1830–1900* (Chapel Hill: University of North Carolina Press, 1985), chap. 6; Cynthia Neverdon-Morton, *Afro-American Women of the South and the Advancement of the Race, 1895–1920* (Knoxville: University of Tennessee Press, 1989); Anne Firor Scott, "Most Invisible of All: Black Women's Voluntary Associations," *Journal of Southern History* 61 (February 1990): 1–22; Scott, *Natural Allies: Women's Associations in American History* (Urbana: University of Illinois Press, 1991); and several essays in Nancy A. Hewitt and Suzanne Lebsock, eds., *Visible Women: New Essays on American Activism* (Urbana: University of Illinois Press, 1993). On earlier African-American reform activity see Frederick Cooper, "Elevating the Race: The Social Thought of Black Leaders, 1827–1850," *American Quarterly* 24 (December 1972): 605–25.

29. On the relationship between Jim Crow and Progressivism, see Jack Temple Kirby, *Darkness at the Dawning: Race and Reform in the Progressive South* (Philadelphia: J. B. Lippincott Company, 1972); Dewey Grantham, *Southern Progressivism: The Reconciliation between Progress and Tradition* (Knoxville: University of Tennessee Press, 1983); and John Dittmer, *Black Georgians in the Progressive Era, 1900–1920* (Urbana: University of Illinois Press, 1977). On the long-term legacy of black reform efforts in

Atlanta during the Progressive era, see Ronald H. Bayor, "The Civil Rights Movement as Urban Reform: Atlanta's Black Neighborhoods and a New 'Progressivism,'" *Georgia Historical Quarterly* 77 (Summer 1993): 286–309.

30. Carter, *The Black Side*, 25–27.

31. Ibid., 43–45.

32. Ibid.; Eva Doris Adams, "Negro Social Life as Reflected by the Lives of the Students of Atlanta University, 1870–1900," (M.A. thesis, Atlanta University, 1968), 13.

33. *Atlanta Constitution* February 11, 1889, C-1; *Bulletin of Atlanta University*, 1897, 1899, 1900.

34. Louie Delphia Davis Shivery, "The History of Organized Social Work among Atlanta Negroes, 1890–1935" (M.A. thesis, Atlanta University, 1936), 40, 44. See also Jacqueline Anne Rouse, *Lugenia Burns Hope: Black Southern Reformer* (Athens: University of Georgia Press, 1989).

35. Shivery, "History of Organized Social Work," 64, 77, 95–98, 475, 484, 494.

36. Charles Harris Wesley, *The History of the National Association of Colored Women's Clubs: A Legacy of Service* (Washington, D.C.: National Association of Colored Women's Clubs, Inc., 1984), 51, 295, 297; Tulia Kay Brown Hamilton, "The National Association of Colored Women, 1896–1920" (Ph.D. diss., Emory University, 1978), 121.

Black Elitism and the Failure of Paternalism in Postbellum Georgia

The Case of Bishop Lucius Henry Holsey

Glenn T. Eskew

During the spring of 1858 the Methodist church in Athens, Georgia, sponsored a week-long revival exclusively for the slave and free black population
of the city. The warm May nights fostered the religious fervor of the crowd
gathered in the church to hear the two circuit riders who had been sent to
Athens by the plantation missions board of the southern Methodist church.
A young free black minister who would later have his own illustrious and
controversial career, the Reverend Henry McNeal Turner, preached to the
congregation. His powerful voice struck the innermost souls of many wor-
shippers, and by the end of the week nearly one hundred people had been
converted to Christ and had joined the Methodist church.

On the last day of the revival a white evangelist, the Reverend W. A. Parks,
delivered the Sunday sermon. At the end of the service, after most of the
congregation had departed, a sixteen-year-old slave tarried near the altar,
struggling "in an agony too great to describe." Noticing that the young man
had remained behind, Parks announced to those leaving, "Brethren, I believe God will convert this boy right now. Let us gather around him and pray
for him!" As the crowd surrounded the young mulatto slave, the minister
intoned to God to save his soul. The object of this attention later recalled,

in the traditional language of religious autobiography, that the "Lord rolled the burden of sin from my heart and heaven's light came shining in. O what a happy boy I was!" Tears coursed down the cheeks of the convert as he looked into the face of the evangelist, pointed his forefinger upwards, and said, "Brother, when you get to heaven, and the blessed Lord places a crown on your head, I will be one star in that crown." [1]

The young mulatto slave, Lucius Henry Holsey, later became a bishop in the Colored Methodist Episcopal (CME) Church in America and from this lofty position articulated a plantation mission ideology of paternalism as the best method for improving the situation of his fellow black southerners. He believed that by being "Christianized" and "civilized" blacks would be assimilated with whites. As long as whites treated him with a degree of respect, Holsey accepted the hegemony of planters; but in the late 1890s, when they adopted a new racial code that treated him like common black folk, he abandoned his hopes for assimilation and advocated black nationalism. Holsey's transformation suggests how one member of the aristocracy of color responded to what Rayford W. Logan called the "nadir" of black America. As Jim Crow eroded the paternalism that supported a three-tiered system of race relations, members of the mulatto elite apparently withdrew into their own closed communities, migrated north, or passed for white. Those who remained openly in the South cast their lot with African Americans. By 1920, when Holsey died, a rigid black-white line divided the nation as never before. [2]

Born near Columbus, Georgia, in 1842, Holsey was the son of his white master, James Holsey. He remembered his "aristocratic" father as a "gentleman of classical education, dignified in appearance and manner of life," who could neither black his own boots nor saddle his own horse. With muted contempt, Holsey added that his father "never married, but mingled, to some extent, with those females of the African race that were his slaves—his personal property." These included his mother, Louisa, a beautiful woman of "pure African descent." She was an "intensely religious woman, a most exemplary Christian" who belonged to the Methodist church. [3] In 1848 Holsey's father died, and Holsey became the property of his white cousin, T. L. Wynn, who lived in Sparta, in Hancock County, Georgia. Holsey's white ancestors had lived in Hancock County, and thus the slave grew up among relatives. Holsey served Wynn as a body servant until 1857 when his dying twenty-six-year-old master asked Holsey to choose his next owner from between two of Wynn's intimate friends. Holsey selected Richard Malcolm Johnston, a planter and teacher in Hancock County who had just accepted a professorship at Franklin College in Athens. [4]

Describing himself as the "property" of Johnston, Holsey recalled the move to Athens: "As an important part of his effects, I was carried along with him and his family as carriage driver, house servant, and gardener." His reference to being a "part of his effects" and Johnston's "property" demonstrates an awareness of the dehumanizing aspects of slavery, yet he recognized his favored status as a house slave by referring to his own importance. Three-fourths of the slaves in the South worked in the fields, and of the remaining one-fourth, only a few achieved the status of body servant or carriage driver. While mulatto slaves were not invariably house servants, those who were blood relatives of their owners often were.[5]

Holsey, whose red hair and blue-gray eyes identified him as a product of miscegenation, later wrote an essay on the topic in which he denounced the "shameful practice" because of its illegality. Obviously referring to his father, he described the "craving, heaving and impulsive passion of men, [which] goads them on to blacklisted indulgences that even racial prejudices, many of which are stronger than death, cannot restrain." After condemning miscegenation, Holsey then dismissed the concept of racial inferiority. While acknowledging racial differences, he identified them as "conditional and circumstantial rather than constitutional." Holsey argued that "no man is born higher, purer, and better than another, so far as his real nature and the faculties of his humanity are concerned. One man may be superior to another but this is in degree and not in kinds."[6] Throughout his life, Holsey struggled to correct this inequality, especially focusing on the promise of education. Yet as a fifteen-year-old slave, Holsey was illiterate.

After arriving in Athens, Holsey developed an "insatiable craving for some knowledge of books." Despite laws against slaves learning to read and write, Holsey determined to "take whatever risks" were necessary to achieve his goal. He purchased two Webster blue-back spellers, a copy of *Paradise Lost*, the Bible, and a dictionary. He enlisted the assistance of an old black man and several white children to teach him the alphabet and then taught himself how to read.[7]

Holsey's purchase of the Bible and *Paradise Lost* suggests that he learned to read following his conversion. In an effort to Christianize the slaves, the southern Methodist church had initiated plantation missions such as the one that sponsored the revival where Holsey was converted. Under the direction of Bishop William Capers, southern Methodists promoted a plantation mission ideology of paternalism with its mutual obligations and reciprocal duties that reinforced black subservience. By Christianizing and civilizing their slaves, southerners attempted to pacify the growing northern abolitionist movement while stabilizing their work force. The Methodist Episcopal Church, South (MEC,S), which was formed as a result of an 1844 schism in the national denomination over the issue of slavery, supported plantation missions. Between 1829 and 1864 the southern Methodist church spent $1.8 million on the effort and claimed, by the outbreak of the Civil War, 207,766 black members, of which 66,559 belonged specifically to the plantation missions. However practical Christianizing the slaves might have been, it is more likely that the black and white evangelists acted out of genuine missionary zeal.[8] Holsey praised "these men of God in [the] ante-bellum decades" as the "most apostolic since the days of Pentecost."[9] Holsey himself had experienced a "change of heart" after hearing the charismatic Turner.[10] Following his conversion, Holsey felt called "to preach the gospel" but saw "no opening for such a thing in the days of slavery." Yet a persistent hope remained that he would one day have an "opportunity to proclaim God's truth."[11]

With the outbreak of the Civil War, Johnston left Athens and took his family and slaves back to Hancock County. There Holsey met Harriett A. Turner (no relation to H. M. Turner), a young house slave formerly owned by Bishop George Foster Pierce of the MEC,S, who had given the young woman to his daughter as a wedding present. In 1862 Holsey married the fifteen-year-old Harriett, and a wedding ceremony was held for the two favored slaves in the "spacious hall of the Bishop's residence," Sunshine. Pierce personally conducted the service. Holsey recalled, "The Bishop's wife and daughters had provided for the occasion a splendid repast of good things to eat. The table, richly spread, with turkey, ham, cake, and many other things, extended nearly the whole length of the spacious dining hall. 'The house girls' and 'the house boys' and the most prominent persons of color were invited to the wedding of the colored 'swells.' The ladies composing the Bishop's family, dressed my bride in the gayest and most artistic style, with red flowers and scarlet sashes predominating in the brilliant trail."[12]

A strong friendship developed between Holsey and Pierce, who recognized the slave's hunger for knowledge, his strong Christian faith, and his evident leadership potential. The son of the Reverend Dr. Lovick Pierce, a leader of southern Methodism, George F. Pierce was born in Greene County, Georgia. Ordained a bishop in the MEC,S in 1854, Pierce had previously served as president of both Wesleyan College and Emory College. During the early postwar years, he took Holsey under his tutelage and trained him in theology. For the rest of his life, Pierce referred to Holsey as his pupil. The relationship between Holsey and Pierce reflected the interracial cooperation expressed through religion. By working together as evangelists, blacks and whites in biracial churches came closer to racial equality than in any other area of southern society.[13]

A deep faith sustained Holsey, and he experienced an almost "mystical" relationship with God. Holsey once recalled feeling "out of the body and in another sphere where God and angels stood nearer to men." These strong religious beliefs enabled Holsey to predict that assimilation would occur through Christianity: "Shem, Ham, and Japheth are all nearly in the same house and eating at the same table, saying the same prayers, singing the same songs, and worshipping the same God. . . . In the onward trend and rounding out of this great civilization, white and black, red and swarthy, with all the seven colors of the rainbow, shall be ground to dust and calcined by the stately tramp of a golden civilization, culminating in the external fixedness of the golden standard and crowned with the age of diamonds." [14]

Following emancipation, southern Methodist freedmen could leave the discriminatory MEC,S and join one of the black independents—the African Methodist Episcopal (AME) Church or the African Methodist Episcopal Zion (AMEZ) Church—or the northern Methodist Episcopal Church. Most left. By 1866, only 78,742 of the 207,766 black members of the MEC,S in 1860 remained in the church. That number dropped to 19,686 by 1869. In evaluating the inability of the plantation mission ideology to continue inculcating values of black subservience and white paternalism in the postbellum era, the bishops of the MEC,S feared that the African-American independents and northern branches of Methodism would radicalize the freedmen. Thus the leaders of the MEC,S decided to ordain black preachers and to organize a black branch of southern Methodism that would exist under the direct influence and indirect control of the southern white church. [15]

In 1868 Pierce conducted a review board of Methodists that examined Holsey and granted his ministerial license. Appointed to the Hancock County circuit, the young preacher led the newly organized Ebenezer Methodist Church made up of black former members of the white Sparta Methodist Church. Pierce gave land to the new black church that was led by his pupil, and a year later he administered deacon's orders to Holsey and other black ministers in the Georgia Colored Conference of the MEC,S. Appointed pastor of the black Andrew Chapel in Savannah, Holsey found when he arrived in the port city that the congregation was under the influence of the AME Church. Holsey struggled to sway the black communicants back to the MEC,S. In 1869 Pierce ordained Holsey as an elder, and at that time Holsey was elected delegate to the Organizing General Conference of the Colored Methodist Episcopal (CME) Church scheduled to convene the following December in Jackson, Tennessee. At the conference white leaders of the MEC,S ordained two black bishops, and the CME Church officially came under the direct control of African Americans. The black delegates to the conference determined not to use their churches for political purposes and in return received church property from the MEC,S. Three years later, in March 1873, the CME General Conference met in Holsey's parish, Trinity CME Church in Augusta, where Pierce assisted CME Bishop William Henry Miles in ordaining Holsey and two others as bishops in the CME Church.[16]

Critics of the CME Church claimed that the MEC,S had "set up" the separate church in order to "set off" its remaining black members. As Holsey explained in 1897: "I understand that we were 'set-up' and not 'set-off.' In no sense does this 'setting up' business destroy, neither was it intended to destroy the religious inter-racial relations that had obtained in days of old." As Holsey makes clear, the MEC,S could not have set off the CME Church because of the plantation mission ideology of paternalism. Atticus Greene Haygood, later a bishop of the MEC,S, explained that the CME needed the "help of its mother" and that if anyone thought that setting them up equated to setting them off in order to get "rid of a burden," then "let them repent of this evil thought."[17]

Many black communicants supported and others acquiesced in the MEC,S plan to set up the CME Church; but not all black members wanted to leave the MEC,S. Towards the end of his life, Holsey angrily recalled, "So far, therefore, as the Negro was concerned, many were pushed out of the Methodist Episcopal Church, South, against their will, and had to set up organizations of their own, duplicating the mother church as far as possible in all things that seemed legitimate and necessary for its development and its perpetuity." Apparently, some of the African Americans who joined the CME Church did so only because they could no longer stay in the MEC,S. They were not given this option.[18]

Although separated from the Methodist Episcopal Church, South, the Colored Methodist Episcopal Church retained strong ties to its white parent. CME Bishop Othal Hawthorne Lakey in his *History of the CME Church* noted that a "close affinity" between black and white Methodists had developed during slavery and that despite the social and political changes brought on by emancipation, "the personal relationships and the rapport that had been established during slavery for the most part continued." Lakey concluded that "many of the leaders of the M.E. Church, South, had brought them [African Americans] the Gospel, and had served them as pastors, presiding elders, and bishops. Hence, the ties between the former slaves and the Southern Methodists were religious as well as personal." Certainly Pierce had been Holsey's teacher, mentor, and friend.[19]

During the turmoil of the postwar years and Reconstruction, when many blacks struggled for independence from whites through active involvement in politics, an apolitical Holsey remained loyal "to those who appeared to be my enslavers and oppressors." He described the reaction of other African Americans to his loyalty to whites when he recalled in 1919 that "in the seventies and eighties I was very much slandered, persecuted, and rejected by my own race and people."[20] Holsey's favorable references to slavery seem puzzling. In one essay he wrote, "However unrighteous or repugnant to a Christian civilization the institution seems to have been, and whatever changes have come over the public mind since its abolition, one thing is clear, and that is, the Negro race has lost nothing by it, but has gained a thousand pounds sterling where it has lost a penny."[21] A second passage on slavery written by Holsey is of a more personal nature: "The training that I received in the narrow house of slavery has been a minister of correction and mercy to me in all these years of struggle, trial, labor and anxiety. I have no complaint against American slavery. It was a blessing in disguise to me and to many. It has made the negro race what it could not have been in its native land. Slavery was but a circumstance or a link in the transitions of humanity, and must have its greatest bearing upon the future."[22]

Both references to slavery reveal important elements of Holsey's personal philosophy. First, Holsey believed that, as a result of slavery, the black man was Christianized and thus saved from damnation, hence gaining a "thousand pounds sterling." Second, as a result of slavery, the black man was exposed to the "superior" white civilization. Holsey dismissed the concept of racial inferiority, but he believed that blacks could learn from the "superior training, [and] higher culture" of whites.[23]

From a black perspective, Holsey espoused what John David Smith has described as the postbellum "new proslavery argument." The case of Holsey suggests that some black people viewed slavery as a civilizing and Christianizing influence and thus not as unmitigated evil. Holsey's position as a highly respected bishop of the CME Church grew out of the acceptance by his black constituency of his views on slavery and race relations. CME members could have joined more activist sects but chose to remain in the smallest of the African-American Methodist denominations, the "old Slavery Church." Other bishops of the CME Church also expressed beliefs in keeping with those of Holsey and of the church's laity. Furthermore, Bishop Henry M. Turner of the AME Church accepted the slavery-as-school metaphor, as did the editor of the Indianapolis *Freeman*, George L. Knox, who had been a slave. Even Booker T. Washington, as Smith notes, thought of slavery as a "divine plan for black progress."[24] Thus Holsey was not alone in his attitudes.

Although it did not alter his belief in paternalism, a revealing incident occurred in 1875 when Bishop Holsey spent some time with northern Methodists at a camp meeting in Round Lake, New York. Holsey preached before

Bishop Lucius Henry Holsey. From the
Autobiography of Bishop Isaac Lane (Nashville, Tenn.:
Publishing House of the ME Church, South, 1916).

the thousands of mostly white people gathered at the resort. Later he reported, "The impression had been made on my mind that these Northern
white brethren would scorn us and would not receive us into their houses,
and accordingly I expected to meet with such treatment; but far from it. We
were kindly, cordially, and warmly received and entertained during the meeting. We were not treated as an inferior race of beings, neither were we known
by the color of the skin or the peculiarities of the hair, but as brethren in
the Lord. These good brethren did everything to make us happy." His surprise suggests the damn Yankee was not nearly the devil he had been led to
believe.[25]

When the CME Church was invited to participate in the first Ecumenical
Methodist Conference in London, England, Bishop Holsey traveled there
in September 1881 to represent his church. Delegates from nearly thirty
branches of Methodism worldwide attended the twelve-day meeting. Holsey
addressed the conference and then toured Europe, including Paris, where
one of his daughters studied piano. The next year, Holsey's nineteen-year-
old daughter, Louisa M. Holsey, a student at Atlanta University, died at home
in Augusta.[26] Holsey left the fifth General Conference of the CME Church

then meeting in Washington, D.C., to conduct the funeral. In his absence, the CME Church elected Holsey "fraternal delegate" to the MEC,S General Conference concurrently held in Nashville, Tennessee, and instructed him to appeal to the MEC,S for educational assistance. After returning to Washington and receiving these instructions, Holsey left for Nashville.[27]

Holsey had long been an advocate for educating his fellow freedmen, and he brought that concern to the 1882 MEC,S General Conference. As early as 1869 he had championed a school for black ministers and teachers to continue the evangelistic work of the plantation missions. Speaking before the assembled white clergy, Holsey explained the role of African Americans as threefold: "servants," "citizens," and "Church-children." He elaborated: "With this three-fold cable we are strongly bound together and united in a manner that cannot be analyzed or fully understood by a stranger. . . . It seems natural that we should follow you, and make ourselves a duplicate of you as far as we are able. We have looked, and still look, to you for guidance an [sic] counsel. We ask your sympathy, aid, and cooperation in redeeming your friends and former slaves from the long night of darkness and degradation. Who will come to the rescue? Who will hear the cries of the children of Ham?"[28] After thirteen years, the MEC,S had at last heard the cries of the CME Church and endorsed Holsey's concept of education. The General Conference collected $251 for CME educational purposes, but did little else for black schools.

The ground for this limited success had been prepared by Haygood who, in *Our Brother in Black*, first published in 1881, had called on the white mother church "to establish a great 'training-school' for this colored daughter." During the summer of 1882 Haygood assisted his mentor Pierce and others on the MEC,S educational commission, which chartered Paine Institute in Augusta. Pierce was the senior bishop in the MEC,S and chaired the meeting that established the school and appointed Holsey to the board of trustees. Yet Pierce did not see education as leading to assimilation. Haygood later accused Pierce of throwing "cold water on the negro education business" and thus failing to support Paine Institute. Pierce viewed blacks as inferior and their efforts to achieve equality as committing "violence (contrary to) the ordination of nature."[29] Whether Holsey recognized this characteristic of his friend remains uncertain.

Holsey, in line with the guiding principles of Paine Institute, proposed that southern white teachers be employed to train the black students. Many African Americans ridiculed the concept as an extension of the "Southern sentiment" expressed during slavery. Some black people referred to Holsey and the black supporters of what was called the Paine Idea as " 'Democrats,' 'bootlicks,' and 'white folks' niggers,' whose only aim was ultimately to remand the freedman back to abject bondage." Holsey responded to his critics in a statement that reflected his personal views of Reconstruction: "It ought to be said, however, that after emancipation the Negroes held themselves aloof from the Southern people to such extent that no proposition made by the latter could reach the former. Consequently, the margin for evangelistic labors among Negroes by Southern white people was narrow." In other words, the struggle for black independence from whites during Reconstruction hindered the Christianization of freedmen. Holsey's defense of the Paine Idea exhibits his trust in white men: "From the time of the emancipation of the slaves by the fortunes of war, I have not seen any reason why the Southern people should not be the real and true friends of the Negro race. The very religion that they taught, and practiced, and preached to the Negroes, directed them to be the friends of the ex-slaves. Consequently, I can see no reasons why they should not teach Negroes in the school room."[30]

The Paine Idea demonstrated an unusual feature that set Paine Institute apart from the other institutions founded for black education during the period. In essence an extension of the plantation mission ideology of paternalism, the school represented a biracial attempt by indigenous white southerners to educate the black man. Holsey advocated white assistance, and he sought a mutual relationship between southern black and white people working together to improve the situation of African Americans and by extension of the South. The *Augusta Chronicle* welcomed the school, noting that "it will be greatly to the negro's advantage that those who best know him and his wants should teach him; and it is much better for the white people that the negro should find his teacher in the superior race in whose midst he lives."[31]

Not everyone shared Holsey's vision. Many of the white elite in Augusta opposed the education of African Americans, and black people disliked the Paine Idea so much that in order to get students Holsey had to pay them to attend class. Nevertheless, the bishop persisted. He sent his own children to school there, and his daughter, Katie M. Holsey, graduated in the first class in 1886. Ultimately he placed the institution on firmer financial footing with the help of patrons and a successful fund-raising campaign. The school was renamed Paine College in 1903, and the MEC,S continued to support it financially. Until 1971 the president was always a white southern Methodist.[32]

From the beginning Paine Institute offered a classical curriculum in keeping with Holsey's original concept of a liberal arts college that crowned an education system of elementary, secondary, and industrial schools—a concept similar to Thomas Jefferson's model for the University of Virginia. Like W. E. B. Du Bois, Holsey did not disparage industrial education, but, unlike Booker T. Washington, Holsey rejected exclusive reliance upon manual training. By the end of his life Holsey had established several industrial schools across Georgia, in particular in 1892 the Holsey Normal and Industrial Academy at Cordele and the Helena B. Cobb School at Barnesville; yet the Paine Idea remained focused on the training of black ministers and teachers by southern whites.[33]

As corresponding secretary, Holsey wielded extensive power in the CME Church, yet infighting among its members suggested his weakened control over the denomination. At the General Conference of 1894, Holsey's candidate to succeed Bishop William Henry Miles was selected in a heated contest. Despite Holsey's opposition a resolution to create a "Committee on the State of the Country" passed by a slim margin. These spirited political debates contradicted the CME's "disposition to separate herself from every question that was political in tendency." Suffering from tuberculosis, Holsey asked the conference for a break from his episcopal duties so that he could recuperate in New Mexico—a trip he was financially unable to take. His health had declined throughout the 1880s; an earlier request for a respite had been denied in 1890 by the College of Bishops, but it had reduced his workload. During his convalescence, Holsey focused on writing. He returned to his episcopal burden in the fall of 1896, about the time he launched a new church newspaper, the *Gospel Trumpet*, to counter Charles Henry Phillips's editorials in the *Colored Methodist Episcopal Christian Index*. A future bishop in the CME Church, Phillips used his position as editor to campaign for higher office, consequently placing himself at odds with Holsey.[34]

Soliciting funds for the construction of a major building on the Paine campus to be named after the late Bishop Haygood, Holsey addressed the MEC,S General Conference of 1898. He envisioned that Paine would prepare black missionaries to go to Africa and redeem the "fatherland"; but he dismissed the idea of emigration to Africa, which had been proposed by Bishop H. M. Turner of the AME Church as a solution to the failure of Reconstruction. Holsey acknowledged that "the Negro is here and *en masse* he is here to stay. He is an important part of the body politic. . . . As such he is a factor in the growth and development of this great civilization." During his speech, Holsey summarized his philosophy and subsequent teachings: "The Negro did not march out of slavery empty-handed, but . . . came out with deep touches of your Christianity and flashes of your civilization, and received an upward propulsion that he could not have obtained in his native land." Referring to master-slave reciprocity, Holsey argued that "emancipation did not abrogate moral obligation." Despite the changed relations between the races, southern whites were obligated to assist African Americans in the "dawn"

of their "Christian civilization." Reemphasizing the goal of racial cooperation with the ultimate hope of assimilation, Holsey concluded: "You need
our brawn and muscle; we need your brain and culture. You need our sinews
of brass and bones of iron. We need your steady hand to prosecute the noble
ends of life, and the triumphs of a Christian civilization. You have the mental
force, we have the physical power, and I come to plead for a combination
of both." [35] Although appealing to white ministers and laymen to contribute
to the construction of Haygood Memorial Hall, Holsey's articulation of the
plantation mission ideology of paternalism stemmed from his own personal
belief rather than from a cynical desire to raise monies.

Holsey's *Autobiography, Sermons, Addresses, and Essays*—first published in
1898, reprinted in 1899, and used as a text for MEC,S seminary students—
advocated Christianizing and civilizing African Americans. Written during
the 1880s and 1890s, the essays reflect what Dr. George Williams Walker,
the white president of Paine Institute, called a "faithful product of the missionary zeal of this church [MEC,S] that was awakened by Bishop Capers in
founding the missions to the slaves." From the beginning, Holsey adhered to
the paternalistic ethos that pervaded the doctrine and practice of the CME
Church. That ethos lay behind his support of the Paine Idea in education. As
secretary of the College of Bishops for forty years, Holsey controlled church
policy. He selected MEC,S literature, doctrine, and even ministers as teachers in the CME Church. In 1894 he published *A Manual of the Discipline of
the Colored Methodist Episcopal Church in America*, which was a revision of the
1874 MEC,S *Manual of Discipline*, and several hymnals including the popular
Songs of Love and Mercy. As Lakey noted, Holsey gave the CME Church "its
definition and provided the rationale for its being." [36]

Holsey's leadership in the church made him a prominent member of
the mulatto elite in Augusta, a thriving black community. Spared by Gen.
William T. Sherman's March to the Sea during the Civil War, postbellum
Augusta quickly returned to business and experienced financial success that
was shared by some blacks in the city—especially the few free persons of
color who had owned property before the war. These light-skinned, upper-
class Negroes were the pillars of black society in Augusta, and they controlled
the few influential African-American institutions in the city, such as Trinity
CME Church, Paine Institute, and Ware High School.[37] Race relations in
Augusta—for the time and place—were considered mutually satisfactory for
black and white people. The black principal of Ware, H. L. Walker, noted
in 1894 that "in Augusta you will find two races of people living together
in such accord and sympathy as are nowhere else to be found in all this
Southland." Indeed, many African Americans found Augusta "the garden

spot of the country" in regard to race relations. Despite separate schools and hotels, public transportation remained unsegregated. A few blacks owned businesses that catered to an integrated clientele. Several black newspapers were published in the city, and the Republican party continued to operate until displaced by the People's party.[38]

African Americans exercised a decisive balance of political power in Richmond County and even supported a reform element in the Democratic party opposed to the corruption of the ruling Bourbon Democrats. But both reform and regular Democrats opposed Thomas E. ("Tom") Watson and the Populist movement. With heavy-handed corruption the Democrats crushed the Populists in 1896. The Democratic "reform element" then sought to maintain "honest, local reform government" by disfranchising the black and poor white Populists.[39] Black political allegiances shifted in the 1890s as the race politics of the Democrats turned harsher.

In the Tenth Congressional District, the Republican party had supported Watson in the elections of 1892 and 1894. Many ministers endorsed the People's party in 1896 because its platform opposed convict lease and advocated temperance. As economic conditions worsened during the decade, black workers lost ground to new white wage earners. Some Negro monopolies failed as competition with white tradesmen and a decline in white customers undermined black artisans. Hard pressed, the mulatto elite in Augusta condemned the corruption of the Democratic party and urged African Americans to support the Populists.[40]

It appears that in 1896 Holsey abandoned his apolitical stance: he endorsed the People's party because he was disenchanted with Bourbon Democracy, opposed to convict lease, and in favor of prohibition. The actions of Augusta's aristocracy of color, which joined the revolt against the Democratic party, influenced Holsey as well. For whatever reasons, this atypical Populist became directly involved in politics. In 1896 his new publication, the *Gospel Trumpet*, began to express—however inconsistently—disenchantment with planter hegemony.

The People's party, Holsey wrote, "allows free speech to the black man as well as to the white man." It was the "political emancipator from the bondage of slavery and ostracism of the Negro vote and all other votes in the state of Georgia." On racial exploitation, Holsey explained that the black man's "wages, when he has any, are so low, and the discrimination against him is so great, universal and unyielding, that often he is baffled, confused, and dispirited. There is but little to encourage and inspire him as a man and a citizen in this land of oppression and where he is made the dumping ground for every moral evil, and the scavenger for the rot and virus of society." Out of desperation, some black people turned to crime, but unlike white men who "steal fifty and a hundred thousand dollars, and are hardly ever hurt by it" because of a legal system that protects them, the "poor Negro, half starved, half naked, and half paid for his labor, steals a hog, a cow, or a sheep, or perhaps, a few melons or a handful of fruit, goes to the 'gang' or the penitentiary for months and years." [41]

Condemning the Bourbon Democrats for the "shameful, degrading, and disgusting" convict lease system that allowed "plutocrats, nabobs, millionaires, and gold magnates" to exploit a disproportionate number of black convicts for "blood money," Holsey acknowledged the Populist party as "anxious to correct the evil, and remove the shame and disgrace from the great state of Georgia." Holsey accused the Bourbon Democrats of making a mockery of the "awful splendors of statesmanship" previously exhibited by the "angelic Stephens, the archangel Ben Hill, and the mighty Cobbs, whose undimmed radiance in the galaxy of shining stars is always brilliant." [42] Referring to former Confederate vice president Alexander Hamilton Stephens, former Confederate senator Benjamin Harvey Hill, former Confederate generals Howell Cobb and Thomas R. R. Cobb, Holsey defended the Old South's planter aristocracy and thus revealed the long-term effects of paternalism while expressing his growing disaffection with the ruling Bourbon Democrats. He approved of the election of Republican William McKinley in 1896 because he supported the gold standard and disliked the Democrats' sectional politics. Holsey's shifting political opinion reflected the unraveling of his worldview. The political turmoil created by the Populist movement, and the concomitant change in race relations, apparently encouraged him to question his basic assumptions.

Discrimination, segregation, and ostracism increased in the late 1890s as white "reformers" implemented a new racial code. In 1897 the Richmond County school board voted to close the all-black Ware High School. The closing of this symbol of interracial cooperation shocked African Americans in Augusta, whose leaders filed a lawsuit to secure implementation of "separate but equal" treatment under the law as pertaining to education. Holsey's old friends among the black elite—Joseph W. Cumming, James S. Harper, and John C. Ladeveze—financed the legal challenge, which reached the U.S. Supreme Court in 1899. In *Cumming v. Richmond County Board of Education* the Court ruled that the closure of Ware High School did not constitute state-supported racial discrimination in education; nevertheless the decision ushered in an age of unequal funding. After 1897 a new era in race relations began in Augusta. While a boycott by black people prevented the segregation of streetcars in 1898, the city enforced separate seating following a murder, a lynching, and a riot in 1900. The year before, the creation of an all-white Democratic primary effectively removed African Americans from local politics. By the turn of the century, there was a new racial code that viewed the black community as monolithic, and class differences among blacks were no longer recognized by whites. Holsey, who by virtue of his elite status and paternalistic relationship with whites had been spared some of the indignities suffered by average African Americans, was suddenly placed on an equal footing with common black folk, and his new status proved quite unsettling. Two of the three light-skinned friends of Holsey's who had fought and lost the *Cumming* case left Augusta and passed for white. Unable, and perhaps unwilling, to deny his race, Holsey recanted his earlier belief in assimilation. From his new home on Auburn Avenue in Atlanta, where he had moved in 1896, Holsey struggled with the so-called race problem.[43]

The change in the racial attitudes of the white South forced the mulatto Holsey to identify with full-blooded African Americans. Denouncing what he recognized as a "vast legalized scheme throughout the South to set the iron heel more permanently and desperately upon the head of the black man as a race, and as individual characters," Holsey confessed that "there would be hope to the rejected and aspiring Afro-American if good character and becoming behavior would or could count for anything in the civic arena. But we are now confronted by conditions where merit in the black man does not weigh one iota in human rights, and very little in human life, if that life and character is under a black or brown skin."[44] Drawing on personal experience, Holsey lamented, "Learning, personal accomplishments, the achievement of wealth, the reign of morality, and skilled handicraft amount to nothing whatever in the black man. Merit and fitness for citizenship and advanced qualifications for the high and holy functions of civil life cannot win for him the rights and safety that is the natural and God-given inheritance of all. Nowhere in the South is the black man as safe in his person and property as is the white man." Holsey continued, "Black men and black women, though cultured and refined, are treated as serfs and subjected to every imaginable insult and degradation that can be invented or discovered by an ill-plighted and perverse ingenuity."[45]

Revealing his earlier belief that through the plantation mission ideology black people would achieve assimilation, Holsey admitted that he had supposed that "whenever the negro is prepared for the duties and responsibilities of citizenship, by culture, wealth and moral standing, and that whenever he becomes a skilled artisan and scientific farmer, then as a race the white people of the South will bestow upon him equal political privileges with themselves." As race relations achieved a new low by the turn of the century,

Holsey realized the sham of his convictions. "How, then," he demanded, "can the Afro-American rise to the dignity of good citizenship and aspire to its possibilities, when political rights, privileges and agencies are taken from him?"[46]

Finding little solace in the paternalistic relations he had long maintained with whites, Holsey despaired, "No man of color, no matter how cultured and worthy, or however accomplished, refined and fitted, has ever been allowed to occupy the same civic plane with the white man of the South for a single hour." Where once he had advocated assimilation, now Holsey saw racial prejudice as making it "impossible for the two separate and distinct races to live together in the same territory in harmonious relations, each demanding equal political rights and equal citizenship." Holsey dismissed his favored status as a mulatto, which had reinforced his faith in paternalism, instead claiming that "the ruling race" rejected mixed bloods "to the same extent as the typical negro." With a finality that belies his earlier belief in assimilation, Holsey resolved, "The white people of the South have not been willing in the past; they are less willing now, and reason and experience teaches us that they will not be willing at any time in the endless future for the race of black men to become their political equals, or occupy the same plane of freedom and citizenship, with themselves, no matter how well qualified they may be for it." Holsey concluded that there would never be peace between the races in the United States until "black Ham and white Japheth dwell together in separate tents."[47]

The grisly lynching of Sam Hose on Sunday, April 23, 1899, in Newnan, Georgia, typified the decade's dehumanization of African Americans and demonstrated the barbarity that many white southerners accepted. One account of the atrocity reported that some "2,000 people surrounded the small sapling to which he [Hose] was fastened and watched the flames eat away his flesh, saw his body mutilated by knives and witnessed the contortions of his body in his extreme agony."[48] A week later in the *Atlanta Constitution,* columnist John Temple Graves called for the separation of the races: "These two opposite and inherently antagonistic races cannot grow up side by side on equal terms of law and possession in the same territory."[49] Through a letter to the editor of the *Constitution,* published August 30, 1899, Holsey publicly responded to Graves and the lynching of Hose with his call for a separate black state within the United States.[50]

In a speech of August 18, 1899, Holsey announced his support for "separation and segregation" of the races with the goal of establishing a black state where, as "governor, legislator and judge," the African American "could be a man among men." Holsey justified his demand by explaining that "each year the racial differences are rendering it more and more impossible for the whites and the blacks to occupy the same territory, and there is nothing for the black man to do but to move or remain here as an oppressed and degraded race." For Holsey, "segregation" meant the separation of the races, which would end the perceived Negro "menace" to white civilization while preventing the "complete serfdom" of the African American. Holsey identified the Oklahoma and New Mexico territories as possible locations for the proposed black state. He believed that only the United States had the authority to solve the "race problem" and that blacks "should remain in their own country." According to his plan, the federal government would establish the segregated territory and protect the blacks from whites, who were to be denied citizenship unless married to African Americans. The separate black state would then function like other states in the Union.[51] Retaining his elitist perspective, Holsey desired that the voluntary citizenry meet certain requirements, such as having "a reputable character, some degree of education, and perhaps a competency for one year's support."[52]

The likelihood of Holsey's plan ever being implemented was remote. Some twenty years earlier, Atticus Haygood had dismissed such an idea from a racist perspective that captured the white sentiment of the time: "The preposterous scheme of colonizing the whole six millions of our negro fellow-citizens in some part of the United States, as Arizona, for example, has been mentioned a few times. Such a scheme could never originate in the serious thinking of any representative Southern man. For the Southern people, with all that has been said and thought about them, know the negro too thoroughly and love him too well to wish him such a fate. What utter nonsense! what inhuman folly! A negro State! A little Africa in America!" Newspaper editor George L. Knox presented one black view when he described Moses Madden's 1920 plan to create a black state near the Rio Grande as "an unmistakable attempt at Jim Crowing our people." Yet for Holsey such segregation of the qualified, educated, and financially secure—the Negro upper class—would allow at least some African Americans to experience first-class citizenship.[53]

Holsey's dramatic response to the nadir of race relations was no more drastic than the actions taken by other members of the mulatto elite during this twilight of the aristocracy of color. The antebellum three-tiered system persisted in the postbellum period. Despite political cooperation during Reconstruction, the mulatto elite had distanced itself socially from the black masses in part because of the continuity of paternalism, which reinforced segregation within the black community. As Willard B. Gatewood has demonstrated, the aristocracy of color had self-consciously created a complex class structure that was almost impenetrable from below. Jim Crow removed this third class. By redefining southerners as either black or white, segregation destroyed the paternalism that had allowed upper-class blacks to maintain a separate world sanctioned by whites. After the turn of the century, class divisions survived in the black community, but the aristocracy of color passed away.[54]

Gatewood notes that the mulatto elite responded in several different ways to the nadir, and it appears that the degree to which whites "capitulated to racism" influenced the reactions of the black aristocrats. In border state cities such as Louisville and Baltimore a milder form of segregation developed. In both, streetcars remained integrated and black men voted, thanks in part to the efforts of the mulatto elite who organized protests against Jim Crow. In New Orleans and Charleston, where the three-tiered system had flourished, the mulattoes' response to segregation was more severe. New Orleans Creoles at first fought discriminatory laws, taking the case of Homer A. Plessy to the U.S. Supreme Court; but following the Court's "separate but equal" ruling, they withdrew into their private world and refused to associate with the larger African-American community. The non-Creole black Pinckney Benton Stewart Pinchback, a former governor of Louisiana, sold his elegant mansion on Bienville Street near the New Orleans Customhouse and abandoned the South for the relative security of Washington, D.C. Like others of the mulatto elite, he escaped through migration. Nevertheless, despite the openness of the U.S. capital during Reconstruction, the atmosphere there chilled as the century ended. In Charleston, the drawing of the color line forced many elite light-skinned African Americans to move north and pass for white. Whole families escaped this way, but those who chose to remain espoused collective activism. Black sociologist Horace Mann Bond concluded that between 1880 and 1925 those mulattoes who wanted to and could passed for white and those who remained in the black community organized for "racial survival."[55]

Booker T. Washington advocated the easiest, and probably safest, way to survive—accommodation. Some of the aristocracy of color, especially in the Deep South, chose this route and became Bookerites. They merged with a rising black middle class represented by the National Negro Business League. Yet others found Washington's compromise on equality intolerable, and when the Niagara Movement evolved into the National Association for the Advancement of Colored People in 1909, the black elite had an alternative to Washington's accommodationist Tuskegee Idea. Indeed, a list of early members who formed local NAACP chapters reads like a Who's Who of aristocrats of color. With the death of Washington in 1915, the NAACP moved quickly to become the dominant civil rights organization in the South. By the 1920s, the old mulatto elite had either faded into a larger white world or been forced into a union with the black masses. The remnants of the aristocracy of color made common cause with the new black bourgeoisie to lead the twentieth-century fight for assimilation.[56]

Holsey had rejected assimilation, yet his demand for a separate black state was not as unusual as it may seem. While his plan differed from Turner's call for an African emigration movement, the two had similarities. Both Holsey and Turner sought to escape from an oppressive white society into a black world where African Americans could exert their rights as citizens. Both believed that God had used slavery to Christianize and civilize African Americans but that white America had failed to give black people the opportunity to exercise self-government and control. Both accepted white assistance in black efforts at separatism, both rejected assimilation, and both admitted that their programs would meet opposition from the Negro elite.[57] Yet Turner had formulated his separatist ideas more than twenty-five years before Holsey reluctantly converted to black nationalism.

August Meier has suggested that racial separatism such as Holsey proposed was an extreme variant of the ideas of racial solidarity, self-help, and group economy that many blacks in the 1890s adopted as a defense against worsening race relations. While a gradualist on matters of race, Holsey, like others of the mulatto elite, until the mid 1890s held assimilation as an uncompromisable goal and thus looked somewhat askance on Booker T. Washington's accomodation. Only when Holsey's dream appeared too elusive in the face of stark white racism did he turn to separatism. Holsey fits the description of nineteenth-century black nationalists presented by Sterling Stuckey in *The Ideological Origins of Black Nationalism*. According to Stuckey, the components of a black nationalist ideology included "a consciousness of a shared experience of oppression at the hands of white people, an awareness and approval of the persistence of group traits and preferences in spite of a violently anti-African larger society, a recognition of bonds and obligations between Africans everywhere, [and] an irreducible conviction that Africans in America must take responsibility for liberating themselves." As Edwin S. Redkey notes in *Black Exodus*, whether practical or not, the importance behind the Back-to-Africa movement and other efforts at black nationalism lies in their reflection of a "widespread dream of economic and political power, of independence and manhood."[58] Through the creation of a separate black state, Holsey sought these rights.

In 1903 Holsey and Turner contributed to a symposium on "The Possibilities of the Negro" organized to show the African American as " 'not a beast,' but a man." Holsey eloquently stated his program for a separate black state, and Turner did likewise for emigration to Africa.[59] According to biographer John Brother Cade, after 1903 Holsey made "no other serious attempt . . . to advance the 'segregation' theory as the best method of settling the Negro problem in America." Following the Atlanta race riot of September 1906, which occurred on Decatur Street a few blocks from Holsey's house and in which some thirty-five black people were killed by white mobs, Holsey joined a group of leading black and white citizens at a mass meeting where they urged their fellow Atlantans to obey the law. Frustrated with his failed efforts at black nationalism, Holsey grew increasingly pessimistic. Personal problems, ranging from his declining health to his weakened control of the CME Church, contributed to his bitterness. After he advocated separation, Holsey began to distance himself from Paine College, becoming hostile toward the institution by 1910.[60]

In 1919 and 1920, Holsey rewrote his autobiography, but the revised version was never published and now appears to have been lost. Having gained access to the unpublished manuscript from Holsey's daughter, Katie Holsey Dickson, Cade cited several long excerpts from it in his biography of Holsey.[61] The selections reveal a man attempting to rationalize his life.

Thinking back in 1919, Holsey explained that the CME Church needed the sanction of the planter class, so he designed it "to be so organized, constructed, and directed that it would be means of propaganda to make and maintain, as far as possible, the reign of peace and harmony." Whether or not Holsey intended to admit that he had assisted white southerners in using the CME Church to control part of the black community is open to debate. The CME Church certainly functioned in that capacity by defending planter hegemony. With an uncharacteristic cynicism, Holsey reflected on his past actions: "I have always been impressed and so understood from boyhood, that no matter what might take place in the rise or fall of American civilization; and no matter what social or political changes or upheavals might appear, the white man of the South would be on the top. I think I had a prophetic vision and rather an unclouded view of those things to come that would affect the religious and political condition of the people of color, and it was folly, if not madness, to ignore and set at nought such a conclusion."[62] Thus he explained his support for interracial cooperation that buttressed the plantation mission ideology of paternalism.

Here is the remarkable story of a self-educated slave, Lucius Henry Holsey, who became bishop of a church and founded several schools. Yet today he seems unattractive for his opposition to Reconstruction and his defense of planter hegemony. The Methodist plantation mission to the slaves could not have produced a more perfect product than Holsey. His personal relationships with elite whites shaped his self-perception and epitomized the debilitating effects of paternalism. Although he never experienced equality with whites, he remained loyal to a concept of mutual obligations that elevated himself and other aristocrats of color while relegating common blacks to a subservient position—loyal, that is, until the late 1890s when white society adopted a new racial code that dumped him into a monolithic black mass. Forced to rethink his perception of race, Holsey in 1899 advocated a separate black state as the solution to the race problem. When the private privilege of the mulatto elite no longer existed, Holsey advocated removal from the South rather than acceptance of second-class citizenship. The dramatic shift in Holsey's philosophy from assimilation to separation underscores the crisis faced by the aristocracy of color as the final vestiges of the antebellum three-tiered system of race relations disappeared. Despite the rationalizations of a dying Holsey in 1919, his fundamental belief in the equality of the races never wavered; only his view on how to achieve equal rights changed.

While Holsey's plan for an African-American state expressed a desire for black nationalism, it demonstrated that Holsey still believed in the be-nevolence of the United States government. Despite his condemnation of Bourbon Democracy, he never quite brought himself to repudiate planter hegemony or paternalism. Holsey seemed to characterize the white elite as the African American's best friend. Yet the actions of those very whites dem-onstrated the failure of postbellum paternalism. While some members of the planter class such as Pierce, Haygood, and other MEC,S bishops attempted, through the founding of the CME Church and other proposals, to recreate the master-slave relationship of reciprocal duties that had existed before the Civil War, the effort received little support. No longer was religion perceived as the proper method of social control. Instead, the white community used violence instituted through the state with its penal system and through the vigilance committee with its lynch law. In large measure for the white South, the religious imperative behind the mutual obligations of the plantation mis-sion ideology of paternalism ended with emancipation.[63]

To his five-year-old granddaughter, Kate Dickson McCoy-Lee, the gray-ing bishop appeared the sun-baked color of an Egyptian. From his "won-derful garden" on Auburn Avenue (the current site of the sarcophagus of the Reverend Dr. Martin Luther King, Jr.) she remembers eating "beautiful strawberries." Since childhood Holsey had worked outdoors as a cure for his tuberculosis, which was aggravated by his earlier, difficult years as a circuit rider. Hemorrhages left him helpless, and as he grew older, the hemorrhages increased. By his death at age seventy-eight on August 3, 1920, other African

Americans had taken over the debate on the race problem. Holsey's obituaries remembered his church work and not his call for a separate black state.[64] Perhaps the disparity between his early and late teachings prevented a full assessment of his contributions. Holsey's hopes for assimilation achieved through Christianity and education foundered on the reality of white racism in the late nineteenth century. Although he lived until 1920, Holsey's earlier dream remained shattered. Nearly forty years passed before another preacher from Georgia articulated the struggle that others had continued to wage and brought the dream closer to reality.

Notes

1. Michael L. Thurmond's chapter "Lucius Henry Holsey: The Slave Who Founded A College," in Thurmond, *A Story Untold: Black Men and Women in Athens History* (Athens, Ga.: Clark County School District, 1978), originally suggested the subject of this essay. The sources on Holsey are scarce. Many original manuscripts were destroyed in August 1968 in a fire that razed Haygood Memorial Hall on the Paine College campus in Augusta, Georgia. Much of the material used by John Brother Cade in his sympathetic account of Holsey's life, *Holsey—The Incomparable* (New York: Pageant Press, Inc., 1964), was destroyed at that time. Lucius Henry Holsey, *Autobiography, Sermons, Addresses and Essays*, 2d ed. (Atlanta: The Franklin Printing and Publishing Co., 1899), includes sermons and essays collected from among his works and apparently written between 1873 and 1898, although they are all undated. Several of the essays were written as speeches made before the general conferences of the Methodist Episcopal Church, South. A limited edition of Holsey's brief autobiographical sketch and a new introduction by Paine College professor George E. Clary, Jr., recently appeared as L. H. Holsey, *The Autobiography of Bishop L. H. Holsey* (Keysville, Ga.: Brier Creek Press, 1988). The account of Holsey's conversion is taken from Holsey, *Autobiography*, 18; quotations are from Alfred Mann Pierce, *A History of Methodism in Georgia* (Atlanta: North Georgia Conference Historical Society, 1956), 132–33; and originally appeared in William Pope Harrison, ed., *The Gospel Among the Slaves* (Nashville, Tenn., 1893; reprint, New York: AMS Press, Inc., 1973), 350–53, see also 384–88 in chap. 18, "Testimony of Prominent Freedmen"; Mungo Melanchthron Ponton, *Life and Times of Henry M. Turner* (Atlanta, 1917; reprint.) New York: Negro University Press, 1970), 155–58; and for a discussion of the revival and Turner's impression of Athens, see Stephen Ward Angell, *Bishop Henry McNeal Turner and African-American Religion in the South* (Knoxville: University of Tennessee Press, 1992), 27–30. The author thanks Numan V. Bartley, John B. Boles, W. Fitzhugh Brundage, Jonathan Bryant, Sheree H. Dendy, Eugene D. Genovese, William F. Holmes, John C. Inscoe, Virginia Kent Anderson Leslie, William S. McFeely, August Meier, and Bennett H. Wall for their helpful comments.

2. Historians tend to agree with C. Vann Woodward's analysis of a "capitulation to racism" as argued in his seminal work, *The Strange Career of Jim Crow* (New York: Oxford University Press, 1955), but the black elite's response to the "nadir" remains an open question. In his book *The Negro in American Life and Thought: The Nadir, 1877–1901* (New York: Van Nostrand Reinhold 1954), 79–96, Rayford W. Logan describes "The Nadir Under McKinley." For a discussion of postbellum paternalism see George M. Fredrickson, *The Black Image in the White Mind: The Debate on Afro-American Character and Destiny, 1817–1914* (New York: Harper and Row, 1971), especially chap. 7, "The New South and the New Paternalism, 1877–1890," 198–227. In *The Crucible of Race: Black-White Relations in the American South since Emancipation* (New York: Oxford University Press, 1984), Joel Williamson characterizes three strains of white thought on race—conservative, liberal, and radical—that vied for dominance in the South during this period. Between 1897 and 1907 the radicals held sway over the region, instigating lynchings and other forms of violent racial oppression. In his *New People: Miscegenation and Mulattoes in the United States* (New York: Free Press, 1980), Williamson analyzes the antebellum three–tiered system of race relations that created a separate sphere for free blacks—often mulattoes—between the larger slave and white worlds. He describes the disintegration of mulatto society and the emergence of rigid segregation at the turn of the century. In the classic *Negro Thought in America, 1880–1915: Racial Ideologies in the Age of Booker T. Washington* (Ann Arbor: University of Michigan Press, 1963), 161–255, August Meier suggests that the black mind itself divided over the issue between the conservative ideas of Booker T. Washington and the radical challenge of W. E. B. Du Bois. John Dittmer, *Black Georgia in the Progressive Era, 1900–1920* (Urbana: University of Illinois Press, 1977), suggests that the black nationalism of Holsey and Turner offered a third solution in addition to those presented by Washington and Du Bois, especially for the black "poor and uneducated, who had little concern for philosophies of accommodation or protest" (p. 177); and Willard B. Gatewood notes in *Aristocrats of Color: The Black Elite, 1880–1920* (Bloomington: Indiana University Press, 1990), chap. 11, that the black elite's response to Jim Crow varied.

   3. Holsey, *Autobiography*, 9.

   4. Charles Henry Phillips, *The History of the Colored Methodist Episcopal Church in America* . . . (Jackson, Tenn., 1898; reprint, New York: Arno Press, 1972), 213; Elizabeth Wiley Smith, *The History of Hancock County, Georgia* (Washington, Ga.: Wilkes Publishing Co., 1974), 2:90, 97; Buster W. Wright, *Burials and Deaths Reported in the Columbus (Georgia) Enquirer, 1832–1872* ([Columbus, Ga.]: Wright Printers, 1984), 221; and Rhea Cumming Otto, *1850 Census of Georgia: Hancock County* (Savannah, Ga.: Mrs. Walker W. Otto, 1980), 18, 41. For a description of Hancock County, see James C. Bonner's essay, "Profile of a Late Antebellum Community," in Elinor Miller and Eugene D. Genovese, eds., *Plantation, Town, and County: Essays on the Local History of American Slave Society* (Urbana: University of Illinois Press, 1974): 29–49; John William Gibson and William Henry Crogman, *Progress of a Race, or the Remarkable Advancement of the American Negro* . . . (Atlanta, 1902; reprint, Miami, Fla.: Mnemosyne

Publishing Inc., 1969), 532–34, mentions Wynn's owning Holsey's mother. For information on the white and mulatto branches of the Wynn family and on the aristocrats of color in Hancock County, see Adele Logan Alexander, *Ambiguous Lives: Free Women of Color in Rural Georgia, 1789–1879* (Fayetteville: University of Arkansas Press, 1991); Holsey, *Autobiography*, 10, 16; and Mark Schultz's essay in this volume. After the Civil War, Johnston became a famous local colorist whose writings included *Dukesborough Tales*, published under the pseudonym Philemon Perch (Baltimore: Turnbull Brothers, 1871); and *Old Times in Middle Georgia* (New York and London, 1897). See also the *Autobiography of Col. Richard Malcolm Johnston* (Washington, D.C.: The Neale Co., 1900); and Edwin Anderson Alderman and Joel Chandler Harris, eds., *Library of Southern Literature*, 13 vols. (Atlanta: Martin & Hoyt Co., 1907), 6:2781–85.

5. Holsey, *Autobiography*, 16; and Eugene D. Genovese, *Roll, Jordan, Roll: The World the Slaves Made* (New York: Pantheon, 1974), 328–30. Although little is known of Holsey's father, the information on Wynn and Johnston suggests that they were indulgent masters. See Genovese's discussion of paternalism, *Roll, Jordan, Roll*, 3–7. Over one-third (39 percent) of all mulattoes in the United States lived in the Deep South, and most were slaves. See Williamson, *New People*, 24–26.

6. The essay, "Amalgamation or Miscegenation" appeared in Holsey, *Autobiography*, 233–38 (first quotation, 238; second, 233; third and fourth, 234). For a physical description of Holsey by his granddaughter, Kate Dickson McCoy-Lee, see Virginia Kent Anderson Leslie, "Woman of Color, Daughter of Privilege: Amanda America Dickson, 1849–1893" (Ph.D. diss., Emory University, 1990), appendix II–1, 139–43.

7. Holsey, *Autobiography*, 16–18 (quotation, 16); and William A. Hotchkiss, *A Codification of the Statute Law of Georgia* . . . (New York: John F. Trow & Co., 1845), 772. For a discussion of slaves' self-education, see Janet Duitsman Cornelius, *When I Can Read My Title Clear: Literacy, Slavery, and Religion in the Antebellum South* (Columbia: University of South Carolina Press, 1991).

8. In his "Testimony" included in Harrison, ed., *Gospel Among the Slaves*, 384–86, Holsey explained that he learned to read in order to read the Bible. Having financed missionaries to the Native Americans since 1819 (Bishop Capers originally served as a missionary to the Indians beginning in 1821), the Methodist church expanded its activity to include Africa in 1832 and China in 1848 as well as the plantation South. After its formation in 1844 the MEC,S continued financing foreign missions although not at the same level as the plantation missions. See James Cannon III, *History of Southern Methodist Missions* (Nashville, Tenn.: Cokesbury Press, 1926); and William May Wightman, *Life of William Capers* (Nashville, Tenn.: Publishing House of the M.E. Church, South, 1902), 291–96. Wightman was ordained a bishop in the MEC,S in 1866 and knew Capers personally. Caper's catechism for slaves reinforced the servile status of blacks. See William Capers, *Catechism for the Use of the Methodist Missions* . . . (Nashville, Tenn., 1861), 13. For a discussion of the catechism, see Othal Hawthorne Lakey, *The Rise of "Colored Methodism": A Study of the Background and the Beginnings of the Christian Methodist Episcopal Church* (Dallas, Tx.: Crescendo Book Publications, 1972); for an account of the schism, see Donald G. Mathews, *Slavery and Methodism:*

A Chapter in American Morality, 1780–1845 (Princeton, N.J.: Princeton University Press, 1965). Mathews argued that the southern Methodists established the plantation missions as an answer to the growing antislavery movement; see also James P. Brawley, *Two Centuries of Methodist Concern: Bondage, Freedom, and Education of Black People* (New York: Vantage Press, 1974). Several scholars have developed the argument that planters used Christianity as a means of social and labor control. See Genovese, *Roll, Jordan, Roll*, 183–93, on Methodism, 233–35, on slave resistance, 658–59; see also E. P. Thompson, *The Making of the English Working Class* (New York: Pantheon Books, 1964), 34–42. Like Capers, the Reverend Charles Colcock Jones, a Presbyterian from Georgia, argued in his treatise, *The Religious Instruction of the Negroes in the United States* (Savannah, Ga., 1842; reprint, New York: Negro University Press, 1969), 104–5, 156–71, 206–11, that through Christianization slaves would have a "better understanding of the relation of master and servant: and of their reciprocal duties" (206), and that the "pecuniary interests of masters" would be "advanced as a necessary consequence" (208) while contributing "to safety" (210). An excellent study of Jone's paternalism is Erskine Clarke, *Wrestlin' Jacob: A Portrait of Religion in the Old South* (Atlanta: John Knox Press, 1979). Clarke recognized the irony involved in the plantation missions in that whites were concerned with the salvation of their slaves and not just the desire to make them obedient and dependent servants. See also Blake Touchstone, "Planters and Slave Religion in the Deep South," in John B. Boles, ed., *Masters and Slaves in the House of the Lord: Race and Religion in the American South, 1740–1870* (Lexington: University Press of Kentucky, 1988): 99–126.

9. Holsey, *Autobiography*, 255.

10. Ibid., 18; Ponton, *Life and Times of Turner*, 156.

11. Holsey, *Autobiography*, 11; Hotchkiss, *Codification of the Statute Law*, 840–41.

12. Holsey, *Autobiography*, 11–12 (quotation), 18. R. M. Johnston gave another account of the wedding. Johnston's property adjoined Pierce's plantation, and, as a result, "there were several intermarriages between his Negroes and mine. I once attended one between one of mine, Lucius (now one of your colored bishops) and Harriet, a fine woman belonging then to the Bishop. He performed the ceremony in his mansion, after which the bridal party with Negro[es] and the whites spent the evening together until a late hour. He seemed to have partaken of some of the joyousness of our humble dependents." Johnston described Pierce as a kind master who preached paternalism. Johnston added that if someone mistreated a slave, knowledge of the transgression would get around and that the offender, "stepping into the Methodist church at Sparta might hear words from Pierce on the treatment of slaves, that would make him feel like hastening to undo or repair any wrong he may have done." See R. M. Johnston to A. G. Haygood, February 12, 1885, folder 1, box 1, Atticus Greene Haygood Papers, Special Collections Department, Robert W. Woodruff Library, Emory University, Atlanta. For information on the life of Harriet Turner Holsey, see Sara Jane McAfee, *History of the Woman's Missionary Society in the Colored Methodist Episcopal Church*, rev. ed. (Phenix City, Ala.: Phenix City Herald, 1945, c1934).

13. Following emancipation, Holsey remained with his former master, R. M. Johnston, renting land as a tenant farmer until 1868. His wife did the laundry of students taught by Johnston at his school, Rockby. George Gilman Smith, *The Life and Times of George Foster Pierce* . . . (Sparta, Ga.: Hancock Publishing Co., 1888); Othal Hawthorne Lakey, *The History of the CME Church* (Memphis, Tenn.: CME Publishing House, 1985), 127, 246–47 (Lakey is a bishop in the CME Church); Smith, *History of Hancock County*, 2:123–24; Phillips, *History of CME Church*, 213; Isaac Lane, *Autobiography of Bishop Isaac Lane* . . . (Nashville, Tenn.: Publishing House of the M.E. Church, South, 1916), 152. In his *Autobiography* (11), Holsey described Pierce as a "wonderful preacher, with wide influence, and august presence. Everybody loved, respected, and some almost adored him"; see also 10, 15, 20. For a discussion of antebellum biracial religion, see John B. Boles's "Introduction," and Randy J. Sparks, "Religion in Amite County, Mississippi, 1800–1861," in Boles, ed., *Masters and Slaves*, 1–18, 58–80; and Katharine L. Dvorak, *An African-American Exodus: The Segregation of the Southern Churches* (Brooklyn, N.Y.: Carlson Publishing, Inc., 1991), 59–60, 156.

14. Lakey, *History of the CME Church*, 396 (first two quotations); Holsey, *Autobiography*, 278 (third quotation). See the essay, "The Trend of Civilization," *ibid.*, 273–78, in which Holsey predicted a new civilization where "racial prejudice must fall and bow to the better and higher interests of man" (277).

15. Statistics from Dvorak, *An African-American Exodus*, 121. Dvorak argues that the CME Church was organized after a failed attempt by black members within the MEC,S to achieve ecclesiastical equality; William B. Gravely, "The Social, Political and Religious Significance of the Formation of the Colored Methodist Episcopal Church (1870)," *Methodist History* 18 (October 1979): 3–25, especially 15–16. Gravely asserts that the property question led to the formation of the separate black church; Holland N. McTyeire, *A History of Methodism* . . . (Nashville, Tenn.: Southern Methodist Publishing House, 1884), 666–71 (McTyeire was ordained a bishop in the MEC,S in 1866); Brawley, *Two Centuries of Methodist Concern*, 411–13; Katharine L. Dvorak, "After Apocalypse, Moses," in Boles, ed., *Masters and Slaves*, 186; C. Eric Lincoln and Lawrence H. Mamiya, *The Black Church in the African American Experience* (Durham, N.C.: Duke University Press, 1990), 60–61.

16. Holsey, *Autobiography*, 11–20; Forrest Shivers, *The Land Between: A History of Hancock County, Georgia, to 1940* (Spartanburg, S.C.: Reprint Company, 1990), 216–17. In *Ambiguous Lives*, Adele Logan Alexander notes that members of the CME chose their denominational name because they "considered themselves 'colored' rather than 'African'" (p. 159) Alexander also recounts an anecdote that characterizes the elitist nature of Ebenezer, also called Holsey Memorial Church:

"A heavyset, dark-skinned woman wearing a bandanna around her head, an apron, and generally shabby clothing supposedly rushed into the service at the Ebenezer church and positioned herself in a front-row pew, interrupting Bishop Holsey's sermon. Her color, her unpolished manner, and her dress immediately told the more affluent and lighter-skinned parishioners, decked out in their finest attire, that she was neither a member nor an invited guest. The woman fanned herself, gasped for breath, and tried to recover from her exertions while the minister and church members stared in stunned silence following her unexpected intrusion. Then, slowly, a solemn hymn reportedly swelled around the visitor as the congregation began to sing: 'None but the yellow, None but the yellow, None but the yellow . . . shall see God' " (162). Holsey worked under the auspices of the MEC,S in Savannah, and the church ultimately regained control of Andrew Chapel, which it gave to the CME Church. See Haygood S. Bowden, *History of Savannah Methodism from John Wesley to Silas Johnson* (Macon, Ga.: J. W. Burke Company, 1929), 139, 141. The renegade congregation then formed St. Phillip's AME Church. Whereas the AME Church actively supported the Republican party during Reconstruction, the CME Church maintained an apolitical policy reflecting the conservative nature of its members, many of whom had ties to the white elite. Consequently, the MEC,S gave its former plantation mission properties to the CME Church. See Angell, *Bishop Henry McNeal Turner*, 104–5; Clarence E. Walker, *A Rock in a Weary Land: The African Methodist Episcopal Church During the Civil War and Reconstruction* (Baton Rouge: Louisiana State University Press, 1982); Phillips, *History of CME Church*, 26, 57–60; and Lakey, *History of the CME Church*, 36, 126, 159–61, 220; on paternalism and the formation of the CME Church see Lakey, *Rise of "Colored Methodism"*; and Eula Wallace Harris and Maxie Harris Craig, *Christian Methodist Episcopal Church: Through the Years*, rev. ed. (Jackson, Tenn.: CME Publishing House, 1965), 54–55.

17. Holsey, *Autobiography*, 247; Atticus G. Haygood, *Our Brother in Black: His Freedom and His Future* (Nashville, Tenn., 1881; reprint, Nashville: Southern Methodist Publishing House, 1887), 236–37. Haygood wrote: "The 'Colored Methodist Episcopal Church in America' that was 'set up'—I hope not 'set off'—needs the help of its mother."

18. Quotation from Cade, *Holsey—The Incomparable*, 71. By 1892 only 357 black communicants remained in the MEC,S. Dvorak, *African-American Exodus*, 168.

19. Lakey, *History of the CME Church*, 127.

20. Holsey, *Autobiography*, 10; the 1919 quote from Holsey is taken from a citation of his unpublished revised autobiography in Cade, *Holsey—The Incomparable*, 53. Apparently an exception to the rule, Holsey's apolitical views during Reconstruction differed greatly from those of other black preachers. Edmund L. Drago, *Black Politicians and Reconstruction in Georgia: A Splendid Failure* (Baton Rouge: Louisiana State University Press, 1982), especially 24–25, 33–34, 46–47.

21. Holsey, *Autobiography*, 253.

22. Ibid., 10.

23. Ibid., 235. See Holsey "Amalgamation or Miscegenation" for his rejection of racial inferiority (233–38). However, Holsey described African Americans as a "semi-civilized people" (22).

24. John David Smith, *An Old Creed for the New South: Proslavery Ideology and Historiography, 1865–1918* (Westport, Conn.: Greenwood Press, 1985), especially 197–

238. Smith paraphrases Washington on 206. Smith emphasizes blacks who rejected the revised "old creed" especially the slavery-as-school analogy, and deemphasizes those who accepted it. In his more recent work, Smith addresses the acceptance of the proslavery creed by the mulatto conservative William Hannibal Thomas. John David Smith, "'How I Became a Doubting Thomas'—Methodological Problems with Local Black History Research" (unpublished paper). For studies of the "old creed" see William Sumner Jenkins, *Pro-Slavery Thought in the Old South* (Chapel Hill: University of North Carolina Press, 1935); and Larry E. Tise, *Proslavery: A History of the Defense of Slavery in America, 1701–1840* (Athens: University of Georgia Press, 1987). For the other bishops' views on slavery, see Charles Henry Phillips, *From the Farm to the Bishopric: An Autobiography* (Nashville, Tenn.: Parthenon Press, 1932), 7–8; and Harrison, ed., *Gospel Among the Slaves*, 380–82; for a less favorable picture see Monroe Franklin Jamison, *Autobiography and Work of Bishop M. F. Jamison . . .* (Nashville, Tenn.: Publishing House of the M.E. Church, South, 1912), 32; for "old Slavery Church" see Phillips, *History of Colored Methodist Episcopal Church*, 72. In 1884, the CME Church claimed some 155,000 laymembers, as opposed to 391,044 for the AME and 300,000 for the AMEZ churches. McTyeire, *History of Methodism*, appendix A. On Turner, see Edwin S. Redkey, *Black Exodus: Black Nationalist and Back-to-Africa Movements, 1890–1910* (New Haven, Conn.: Yale University Press, 1969), 35–36; and Angell, *Bishop Henry McNeal Turner*, 263; Willard B. Gatewood, Jr., ed., *Slave and Freeman: The Autobiography of George L. Knox* (Lexington: University Press of Kentucky, 1979); and Knox's essay "The American Negro and His Possibilities," in D. W. Culp, ed., *Twentieth Century Negro Literature* (Atlanta: J. L. Nichols & Co., 1902), 454–63. Indeed, aristocrats of color perceived themselves as carrying white culture and civilization to the black world; see Gatewood, *Aristocrats of Color*, 27–29; and Williamson, *New People*, 130.

25. Phillips, *History of CME Church*, 100. Toward the end of the decade, Holsey wrote an article on Methodist theology, "Wesley and the Love Feast," which he intended to be his (and the CME Church's) contribution to the *Wesley Memorial Volume*, a collection of essays edited by the Rev. James Osgood Andrew Clark of the MEC,S to commemorate the building of the Wesley Memorial Church in Savannah, Georgia. Instead of including Holsey's theological paper in the collection of essays, Clark replaced it with another essay by Holsey, "Wesley and the Colored Race." The substitution of subject matter—a black man's statement on race relations rather than his ideas on religion—sadly demonstrates Holsey's role in the church while suggesting that he envisioned equal footing as a theologian. See J. O. A. Clark, *The Wesley Memorial Volume* (New York: Phillips & Hunt, 1880), 256–67; and L. H. Holsey to J. O. A. Clark, January 29, March 19, April 11, 1879, box 2, James Osgood Andrew Clark Papers, Special Collections Department, Robert W. Woodruff Library, Emory University.

26. Holsey, *Autobiography*, 28–30; and "World Methodist Conference" in Nolan B. Harmon, ed., *The Encyclopedia of World Methodism*, 2 vols. (Nashville, Tenn.: Abing-

don Press, 1944), 2:2600–2602. Apparently called "Ruth" by her family, Louisa "was becoming widely acclaimed as a talented musician." Of Lucius and Harriet Holsey's other children, James Henry graduated from Howard University and opened a dental practice first in Augusta, then in Atlanta; Katie M. married Charles Dickson, the grandson of white Hancock County planter David Dickson, but divorced him and afterward lived with her father; the Rev. C. Wesley served as the CME presiding elder of the Augusta District but failed in his attempt to be chosen bishop in 1922; and Ella B., Claud Lucius, and the painter and publisher Sumner L. moved to Boston, Massachusetts. Two other children died shortly after birth. Quotation from Cade, *Holsey—The Incomparable*, 148; *Atlanta Independent*, May 7, 1904; Leslie, "Woman of Color, Daughter of Privilege"; and Lakey, *History of the CME Church*, 392.

27. Phillips, *History of CME Church*, 124–27; George Esmond Clary, Jr., "The Founding of Paine College—A Unique Venture in Inter-Racial Cooperation in the New South (1882–1903)" (Ed.D. diss., University of Georgia, 1965), 39–40; see also William L. Graham, "Patterns of Intergroup Relations in the Cooperative Establishment, Control and Administration of Paine College (Georgia) by Southern Negro and White People: A Study of Intergroup Process" (Ph.D. diss., New York University, 1955).

28. Holsey, *Autobiography*, 23; Cade, *Holsey—The Incomparable*, 80–81; Phillips, *History of CME Church*, 84–85; "Bishop Holsey's Address" before the MEC,S General Conference of 1882, meeting in Nashville, is reprinted in full as appendix B in Lakey, *History of the CME Church*, 667–70 (quotation from 669–70); see also 442–49. Holsey used the racist rhetoric of the day by describing African Americans as the descendants of Ham. See Thornton Stringfellow, "The Bible Argument: Or Slavery in the Light of Divine Revelation" in E. N. Elliott, ed., *Cotton Is King, and Pro-slavery Arguments* . . . (Augusta, Ga.: Pritchard, Abbott, Loomis, 1860), 461–92.

29. C. T. Wright, "The Development of Education for Blacks in Georgia, 1865–1900" (Ph.D. diss., Boston University, 1977), 162–66; Clary, "The Founding of Paine College," 64–65; Haygood, *Our Brother in Black*, 236–37. Haygood, who was a paternalist, dedicated his life to improving the condition of southern blacks, and he was at times ostracized for his efforts, being called the "Nigger Bishop." In *Our Brother in Black*, Haygood stressed the need for racial toleration, acceptance of black land ownership, and support for African-American schools. A native of Georgia and president of Emory University, Haygood served as the first general agent of the John F. Slater Fund, which emphasized manual education for blacks. See John E. Fisher, *The John F. Slater Fund: A Nineteenth Century Affirmative Action for Negro Education* (Landham, Md.: University Press of America, Inc., 1986); Meier, *Negro Thought in America*, 90–99; quotations on Pierce cited in Harold W. Mann, *Atticus Greene Haygood: Methodist Bishop, Editor, and Educator* (Athens: University of Georgia Press, 1965), 190; Elam Franklin Dempsey, [ed.], *Atticus Greene Haygood* (Nashville, Tenn.: Parthenon Press, 1940), 182–97. In *Crucible of Race*, 88–93, Joel Williamson presents Haygood as the quintessential racially liberal clergyman who personified the continuity of paternalism. This view is evident in Haygood's January 17, 1888 letter to Rutherford B.

Hayes, then a board member of the Slater Fund: "Our people will come to *their* duty slowly—but the debate is over as to the general question." The MEC,S had decided to support black education, and Haygood, Pierce, Holsey, and others had requested $250,000 from the Slater Fund for Paine's initial endowment. Pierce and Haygood's protege, Bishop Warren A. Candler, did not support higher education for African Americans, and the school did not receive the grant from the Slater Fund. Haygood criticized Pierce in a letter to Hayes; see Louis D. Rubin, Jr., ed., *Teach the Freeman: The Correspondence of Rutherford B. Hayes and the Slater Fund for Negro Education, 1888–1893* (Baton Rouge: Louisiana State University Press, 1959), 6.

30. Holsey, *Autobiography*, 25 (first two quotations), 24 (third quotation), 23 (last quotation); in his *Autobiography*, 21, CME Bishop Lane described the African-American opposition to the denomination: "We were severely criticized and maligned because we did not rebel and secede. Other independent Negro Methodist Churches had rebelled and seceded, and because we chose to be regular and orderly we were charged with being sympathizers with slavery. In many places we were called Democrats and the like." Bishop W. H. Miles recalled an altercation with some black Methodists in East Texas: "One very old lady, bending over a long staff, said: 'My God, brethren; I am a radical all over! Go away from here, you conservatives!' " See *Colored Methodist Episcopal Christian Index*, June 12, 1873, quoted in Phillips, *History of Colored Methodist Episcopal Church*, 72–73.

31. Clary, "Founding of Paine College," 143–51; and *Augusta Chronicle*, March 6, 1883, p. 4; see also Paul R. Griffin, *Black Theology as the Foundation of Three Methodist Colleges: The Educational Views and Labors of Daniel Payne, Joseph Price and Isaac Lane* (Landham, Md.: University Press of America, Inc., 1984).

32. Holsey, *Autobiography*, 23–27; Cade, *Holsey—The Incomparable*, 78–102, 148; and Lakey, *History of the CME Church*, 442–49. In 1885 the MEC,S Rev. Moses U. Payne of Missouri donated $25,000 to the school, which was named after Bishop Robert Paine of the MEC,S, who had presided over the organization of the CME Church; see Clary, "Founding of Paine College," 7–12, 42, 69–74.

33. Curriculum of Paine College for 1887, outlined as appendix 6 in Clary, "Founding of Paine College," 161–62 and 107–10; Cade, *Holsey—The Incomparable*, 79–80; and Lakey, *History of the CME Church*, 394. Meier, *Negro Thought in America*, remains the seminal work on the conflicting ideologies of Washington and Du Bois.

34. Phillips, *The History of CME Church*, 164–71 (first two quotations are on 171), 176, 191; and Phillips, *From the Farm to the Bishopric*, 128–31. Phillips also supported self-segregation in response to white discrimination but opposed legal Jim Crow. See Meier, *Negro Thought in America*, 49, 56; Lakey, *History of the CME Church*, 317–36. A bimonthly that ran for six years, the *Gospel Trumpet* first published on September 2, 1896. Apparently there are no extant copies.

35. See "Speech Delivered Before Several Conferences of the M.E. Church, South," in Holsey, *Autobiography*, 239–48 ("fatherland" on 243, first quotation 242, second, third, fourth and fifth quotations 243, last quotation 246). Holsey raised about $8000 in support of the building; see Phillips, *History of CME Church*, 217.

36. Walker wrote the introduction to Holsey, *Autobiography*, 5–7 (quotation on 5), and he concluded that Holsey discerned in slavery a "providential blessing to both white and black—a harsh measure to bring the ignorant Negro in contact with the educated Caucasian" (p. 5); Cade claims that the MEC,S used Holsey's *Autobiography* as a seminary text; see *Holsey—The Incomparable*, 42; Lakey, *History of the CME Church*, 392 (second quotation), 116, 246–47; Lakey referred to Holsey as the "driving force of the CME Church" (ibid., 33); L. H. Holsey, *A Manual of the Discipline of the Colored Methodist Episcopal Church in America* (Jackson, Tenn.: Colored M.E. Church in America, 1894). Holsey added a preface and a revised ritual to the MEC,S hymnbook and published it as the CME *Hymn Book* in 1891. In collaboration with Fayette Montgomery Hamilton, Holsey wrote the hymn "O Rapturous Scenes," which is the unofficial anthem of the CME Church. See *The Hymnal of the CME Church* (Memphis, Tenn.: CME Publishing House, 1987); and F. M. Hamilton and L. H. Holsey, *Songs of Love and Mercy* (Memphis, Tenn.: CME Publishing House, 1968). Holsey also published a collection of inspirational poems and prose, *Little Gems* (Atlanta: Privately published, 1905).

37. On the mulatto elite in Augusta see Gatewood, *Aristocrats of Color*, 90–91, 158; Howard N. Rabinowitz, *Race Relations in the Urban South, 1865–1890* (Urbana: University of Illinois Press, 1980), 189, 248–49; Richard Henry Lee German, "The Queen City of the Savannah: Augusta, Georgia, During the Urban Progressive Era, 1890–1917" (Ph.D. diss., University of Florida, 1971), 37; Leslie, "Woman of Color, Daughter of Privilege," 245; and Horace Calvin Wingo, "Race Relations in Georgia, 1872–1908" (Ph.D. diss., University of Georgia, 1969). The noted educator John Hope grew up among Augusta's aristocracy of color; see Ridgely Torrence, *The Story of John Hope* (New York: Macmillan Company, 1948).

38. *Augusta Chronicle*, October 10, 1880, p. 7; J. Morgan Kousser, "Separate but *not* Equal: The Supreme Court's First Decision on Racial Discrimination in Schools," *Journal of Southern History* 46 (February 1980): 17–44; see also Kousser's unpublished California Institute of Technology Working Paper no. 204 (March 1978), 4–7, 15–19 (quotations on 15). (This paper is a similarly titled, unedited version of the *JSH* essay.) Torrence quotes Augusta native Dr. Channing Tobias as saying, "It was possible for a Negro in the Augusta of John Hope's boyhood to aspire to the heights and to receive encouragement from white people in so doing"; *The Story of John Hope*, 59. The leading black newspaper in Augusta, the Reverend William Jefferson White's *Georgia Baptist*, was published from 1881 to 1909.

39. German, "The Queen City of the Savannah," 45, 65–66, 130–36; C. Vann Woodward, *Tom Watson: Agrarian Rebel* (New York: Macmillan Company, 1938), 241–42, 265–69, 286–87; and Wingo, "Race Relations in Georgia," 85–93.

40. John Michael Matthews, "Studies in Race Relations in Georgia, 1890–1930" (Ph.D. diss., Duke University, 1970), 55–74. On blacks and prohibition see Dittmer, *Black Georgia in the Progressive Era*, 112–13; and Edward Aaron Gaston, "A History of the Negro Wage Earner in Georgia, 1890–1940" (Ph.D. diss., Emory University, 1957), 232–35, 278–88.

41. Two editorials by Holsey from the *Gospel Trumpet:* "The Negro and Democ-

racy in Georgia" and "The Convict Lease System," are excerpted by Cade in *Holsey—The Incomparable*, 126–37 (quotations are on 129, 136, and 137).

42. Ibid., 130–31; on the Bourbon Democrats, see Kenneth Coleman, ed., *A History of Georgia* (Athens: University of Georgia Press, 1977), 207–308.

43. Augusta was not alone in the dramatic transition in race relations. For a complex analysis of segregation that generally supports Woodward's thesis in *Strange Career of Jim Crow*, see John William Graves, "Jim Crow in Arkansas: A Reconsideration of Urban Race Relations in the Post-Reconstruction South," *Journal of Southern History* 55 (August 1989): 421–48, revised in *Town and Country: Race Relations in an Urban-Rural Context, Arkansas, 1865–1905* (Fayetteville: University of Arkansas Press, 1990); Kousser, "Separate but *not* Equal," 27–28, 42–44; Kousser, Working Paper No. 204, 13–15, 45–46. The black newspaper the *Georgia Baptist* reprinted an article concerning a murder and lynching that so outraged elements of the white community that a mob formed and attacked the editorial offices. Two days later the Augusta City Council segregated the streetcars. See *Augusta Chronicle*, June 3, p. 1, and June 5, 1900, pp. 3, 5; and August Meier and Elliott Rudwick, "The Boycott Movement Against Jim Crow Streetcars in the South, 1900–1906," *Journal of American History* 55 (March 1969): 756–75. See also *Cumming v. Richmond County Bd. of Educ.* 175 U.S. 528 (1899). The reasons for Holsey's move to Atlanta are unclear but could be church-related. According to *Howard's Directory of Augusta . . . 1892/3* (Augusta, Ga.: Chronicle Job Printing Co., 1892), 273, Holsey lived at 1633 15th St., which was near the campus at Paine Institute. The house, which later served as the parsonage for Williams Memorial CME Church, no longer stands. *Atlanta City Directory* (Atlanta: Franklin Printing and Publishing Co., 1899), 23:801, lists Holsey's Atlanta address as 335 Auburn Avenue. The Reverend Dr. Martin Luther King, Jr., Center for Nonviolent Social Change now occupies the site of Holsey's house. For information concerning the elite African-American community on Auburn Avenue, see August Meier and David Lewis, "History of the Negro Upper Class in Atlanta, Georgia, 1890–1958," *Journal of Negro Education* 28 (Spring 1959): 128–39.

44. L. H. Holsey, "Race Segregation," in *The Possibilities of the Negro in Symposium . . .* ([Atlanta]: Franklin Printing and Publishing Co., 1904), 99–119 (quotation on 102); see also Clarence A. Bacote, "Negro Proscriptions, Protests, and Proposed Solutions in Georgia, 1880–1908," *Journal of Southern History* 25 (November 1959): 471–98.

45. Holsey, "Race Segregation," in *Possibilities of the Negro*, 102–3.

46. Ibid., 105.

47. Ibid., 100, 106, 107, 110, 119.

48. *Atlanta Constitution*, April 24, 1899, p. 1; Hose was one of twenty-seven people lynched in Georgia in 1899. Coleman, ed., *History of Georgia*, 286.

49. *Atlanta Constitution*, April 30, 1899, p. 9.

50. Ibid., August 30, 1899; W. E. B. Du Bois responded similarly. See *Dusk of Dawn: An Essay toward an Autobiography of a Race Concept* (New York: Schocken Books, 1971).

51. "Bishop Holsey on the Race Problem" and "Bishop Holsey's Plan," both on

p. 4 of the *Atlanta Constitution*, August 30, 1899; and L. H. Holsey, *The Racial Problem* (Atlanta: S. L. Holsey, 1899). This pamphlet reprints Holsey's letters (August 30 and September 29, 1899) to the *Constitution*, that newspaper's editorial response, the opinion of the *Augusta Chronicle*, and the *Chicago Times-Herald* coverage of the August 18, 1899 speech—apparently the first public expression of his views on racial separation—that Holsey delivered before a meeting of the Afro-American Council. Quotations are from Holsey, *Racial Problem*, 14, 15, 16, 17.

52. Holsey, "Race Segregation," *Possibilities of the Negro*, 116.

53. Haygood, *Our Brother in Black*, 20; and Gatewood, ed., *Slave and Freeman*, 36.

54. Michael P. Johnson and James L. Roark, eds., *No Chariot Let Down: Charleston's Free People of Color on the Eve of the Civil War* (Chapel Hill: University of North Carolina Press, 1984); and Johnson and Roark, *Black Masters: A Free Family of Color in the Old South* (New York: W. W. Norton, 1984) describe the three-tiered system in South Carolina. While in *New People*, 3, 82, 108–9, Williamson argues that most mulattoes permanently merged with freedmen during Reconstruction, Thomas Holt convincingly demonstrates that class differences prevented racial bonding in *Black over White: Negro Political Leadership in South Carolina During Reconstruction* (Urbana: University of Illinois Press, 1977). Holsey fits Gatewood's analysis: "The rising tide of racism and the fading of hopes for an integrated society, as well as the decline in the economic base of the old upper class, eroded the prestige and influence of a group that had nurtured ties with whites and advocated assimilation into the larger society." Gatewood, *Aristocrats of Color,* 335; on class structure, see 23–29; on decline, see 332–40. For a contrary view on race and class, see Rabinowitz, *Race Relations in the Urban South*, 333–36, where he contends that whites failed to recognize black class differences.

55. George C. Wright, *Life Behind a Veil: Blacks in Louisville, Kentucky, 1865–1930* (Baton Rouge: Louisiana State University Press, 1985), chap. 2; William George Paul, "The Shadow of Equality: The Negro in Baltimore, 1864–1911" (Ph.D. diss., University of Wisconsin, 1972), 3–4, 287–92; Arthé Agnes Anthony, "The Negro Creole Community in New Orleans, 1880–1920: An Oral History" (Ph.D. diss., University of California, Irvine, 1978), 39–58; and James Haskins, *Pinckney Benton Stewart Pinchback* (New York: Macmillan Publishing Co., Inc., 1973), 249–58. Pinchback's friend, former Mississippi congressman John Roy Lynch, sold his plantations in Natchez, moved to Washington, and found refuge as paymaster in the United States Army. See John Hope Franklin, ed., *Reminiscences of an Active Life: The Autobiography of John Roy Lynch* (Chicago: University of Chicago Press, 1970), xxvi–xxix; Constance McLaughlin Green, *The Secret City: A History of Race Relations in the Nation's Capital* (Princeton, N.J.: Princeton University Press, 1967), 119–54; and Mary Church Terrell, *A Colored Woman in a White World* (reprint, New York: Arno Press, 1980/c1940). As Washington resident Mary Church Terrell learned, no matter how aristocratic they appeared, mulattoes could not escape proscriptions based on race, which supports Woodward's point that "Jim Crow laws applied to *all* Negroes." See Woodward, *Strange Career of Jim Crow*, 107; Gatewood, *Aristocrats of Color*, 301–2; and Edmund L. Drago, *Initia-*

tive, Paternalism, and Race Relations: Charleston's Avery Normal Institute (Athens: University of Georgia Press, 1990), 2–5, 81–82, 137–40. In an interesting twist Drago analyzes the "Yankee paternalism" of the American Missionary Association. Bond quoted in Williamson, *New People*, 103.

56. Meier, *Negro Thought in America*, 161–255; Gatewood, *Aristocrats of Color*, 311–21, 332–40.

57. On Turner see Angell, *Bishop Henry McNeal Turner*, 119–22, 134–38, 173–75, 262–65; Redkey, *Black Exodus*, 35–40, 99–107; Ponton, *Life and Times of Turner;* and E. Merton Coulter, "Henry M. Turner: Georgia Negro Preacher-Politician During the Reconstruction Era," *Georgia Historical Quarterly* 48 (December 1964), 371–410. On western settlement and the idea of a separate black state, see Nell Irvin Painter, *Exodusters: Black Migration to Kansas After Reconstruction* (Lawrence: University Press of Kansas, 1986). According to Sterling Stuckey, *The Ideological Origins of Black Nationalism* (Boston: Beacon Press, 1972), 11, receiving assistance from whites was one of the tenets of nineteenth-century black nationalism. Turner said that the black "so-called leading men worshipped white" (Redkey, *Black Exodus*, 39) and thus favored integration, and Holsey likewise identified the potential source of opposition to his plan:

"It will come from that class of Negroes who live in the cities and condensed centers of population where they have police protection, and are doing fairly well. They have but little cause for complaints. They care but little for the down trodden and debased millions of their race who are dying by peace meal [*sic*] in the rural districts where the great mass of the Negro race lives, or rather where they merely breathe in poverty and ignorence [*sic*], and die in despair, ignominy and shame. Strange to say some of these objectors are editors of papers, teachers, preachers, and political office holders. They do not go in the rural districts of the black belts, and are ignorant of the true state of affairs. They know nothing of the real condition of the oppressed and suffering millions of their race, and since they do not feel the sorrow, the unrest, nor see the distress, ignorance and squalidness of the millions, they object to every thing that may be proposed to settle the race problem." Holsey, *Racial Problem*, 17.

58. Meier, *Negro Thought in America*, 65–68, 146–49. Meier recognizes the subtle distinction between black paternalism advocating assimilation and Washington's accommodation (p. 234). No record of any correspondence between Holsey and Washington exists in Louis R. Harlan et al., eds., *The Booker T. Washington Papers*, 14 vols. (Urbana: University of Illinois Press, 1972–1989); nor did Holsey correspond with Du Bois, according to Herbert Aptheker, ed., *The Correspondence of W. E. B. Du Bois*, Vol. 1 (Amherst: University of Massachusetts Press, 1973). On territorial separation and a sense of black distinctiveness, see John H. Bracey, Jr., August Meier, and Elliott Rudwick, eds., *Black Nationalism in America* (Indianapolis, Ind.: The Bobbs-Merrill Company, Inc., 1970), especially 156–210; Stuckey, *Ideological Origins of Black Nationalism*, 1–2, 6 (first quotation); and Redkey, *Black Exodus*, x (second quotation), 288.

59. The proceedings and other papers were published in *The Possibilities of the Negro* (quotation, 1); Holsey's paper is "Race Segregation," 99–119; and Turner's is "Races Must Separate," 90–98.

60. Cade, *Holsey—The Incomparable*, 116; see also L. H. Holsey, "Will It Be Possible for the Negro to Attain in this Country unto the American Type of Civilization?" in Culp, ed., *Twentieth Century Negro Literature*, 46–48. In this essay, written in 1901, Holsey appears to pull back from his demand of separatism. *Atlanta Independent*, October 6, 1906, refers to a meeting at the Wheat Street Baptist Church, where "Bishop L. H. Holsey made some fitting remarks, which meant much to the interested audience." See also Ray Stannard Baker, *Following the Color Line: An Account of Negro Citizenship in the American Democracy* (New York, 1908; reprint, Williamstown, Mass.: Corner House Publishers, 1973), 3–25, especially 20; Charles Crowe, "Racial Violence and Social Reform—Origins of the Atlanta Riot of 1906," *Journal of Negro History* 53 (July 1968): 234–57; and Crowe, "Racial Massacre in Atlanta, September 22, 1906," ibid., 54 (April 1969), 150–73. For a hair-raising account of the Atlanta race riot, see Walter White, *A Man Called White: The Autobiography of Walter White* (New York: Viking Press, 1948); on Holsey's activities within the CME Church, see *Atlanta Independent*, November 18, 1905, April 28, 1906, November 22, 1913.

61. Cade, *Holsey—The Incomparable*. The quotations from the unpublished revised autobiography are identified as such by Cade in the text or in the footnotes. In the bibliography to "Founding of Paine College" Clary refers to the missing manuscript as being in the possession of Cade, who is now deceased. In his history, Lakey also quotes Cade's *Holsey—The Incomparable* for references to the manuscript. Apparently the unpublished revised autobiography no longer exists.

62. Cade, *Holsey—The Incomparable*, 60–61 (quoted from the unpublished revised autobiography).

63. Clary compares the MEC,S financial support of plantation missions with its postbellum financial support for black education, and his findings demonstrate the failure of paternalism:

Plantation Missions   1844–1864 $1,706,207.70
Paine and Lane Institutes   1882–1903 $ 160,000.00

Clary concludes that the MEC,S "had committed itself to support Negro education, and when every extenuating circumstance is taken into consideration, its support of this work was indeed 'painful and pitiful.'" Clary, "Founding of Paine College," 95–96.

64. Leslie, "Woman of Color, Daughter of Privilege," 139–43; Cade, *Holsey—The Incomparable*, 44; and *Atlanta Independent*, August 7, 1920, p. 1, editorial on p. 4. The *Atlanta Journal* obituary of August 4, 1920, is almost completely inaccurate. Holsey's funeral took place on August 6, 1920, in the West Mitchell Street CME Church, with burial in Atlanta.

Interracial Kinship Ties and the Emergence of a Rural Black Middle Class

Hancock County, Georgia, 1865–1920

Mark R. Schultz

In the summer of 1921, Jean Toomer came to Hancock County, Georgia, to serve as interim head of the Sparta Agricultural and Industrial Institute for Negroes. A northern "black" man of European, African, and Native American descent, Toomer was searching for the meaning of race—his personal meaning of race—in America. The year he spent in the plantation belt catalyzed his writing abilities and inspired *Cane*, a brilliant and innovative blend of fiction and folklore regarded as one of the first masterpieces of the Harlem Renaissance. One of *Cane*'s central themes addresses sexual relationships between rural black and white southerners and the ambiguous social position occupied by their light-skinned children. Like Toomer himself, his interracial characters were notably wealthier than the majority of black southerners. They owned grocery stores and wagon shops. They were educated, owned pianos, and displayed heavy, oak-framed portraits of their white ancestors on their mantelpieces. Also like Toomer, they sometimes had to endure crises of cultural and personal identity.[1]

The southern mulatto elite that Toomer represented in life and art has appeared often in literary works.[2] These fictional narratives are frequently laced with cryptic hints of antique kinship ties with planter aristocrats. Yet, while long taking for granted the existence of the mulatto elite, historians have only recently begun to explore its ties to the planters.[3] With a few exceptions, the mechanisms accounting for the economic success of the mulatto elite have been either obliquely insinuated or limited to the "exceptional" history of an individual, especially in the historiography of the postbellum period.[4]

The model of strict racial endogamy represents only the outlines of the actual "southern experience." Despite anti-miscegenation laws, interracial sexual contact—and sometimes monogamous relationships—continued to occur between rural white men and black women in the lower South after emancipation. Despite the economic, legal, and social gulf that separated black and white worlds, many rural southerners were aware of their biological kinship with individuals of a different race. Finally, despite the threat of social sanction, "white" biological fathers of "black" children in the nineteenth- and twentieth-century South sometimes accepted or constructed for themselves roles as social fathers. "Kinship," as these men constructed it, often led them to extend economic assistance to their "black" children. Interracial kinship also sometimes extended to recognized relationships between all the various components of extended families, including cousins. Although the children of an interracial couple were usually defined as "colored," they sometimes had resources, through their white kin, normally unavailable to African Americans.[5] By using oral histories of interracial families from rural Georgia I will argue that, taken together, these private, interpersonal acts of assistance made a considerable contribution toward the formation of the rural black middle class in the Deep South between 1865 and 1920.[6]

This essay is an exploratory study, with limited parameters. As used here, "interracial kinship ties" refers exclusively to biologically linked relationships between black and white southerners that were invested with meaning by the participants as some construction of "family." The individuals involved recognized one another—in some way "belonged" to one another—so as to make them in some way responsible for one another's welfare. "Kinship" has been historically constructed in many different ways. Because of limited evidence, I do not presume to define the internal worlds of meaning given to interracial kinship by those who recognized such ties. Also, due to the limits of my methodology, I am unable to address relationships between white women and black men. While Martha Hodes has indicated that these relationships existed in the antebellum period, I have been unable to locate concrete references to such couples in the family narratives of rural Georgians.[7]

In exploring the meanings given to interracial kinship, one must be careful not to conflate biological kinship with sociological kinship. Although a significant number of white fathers gave material assistance to their children by black women, it seems that most neither assisted nor recognized their children. Frederick Law Olmsted noted that the great majority of mulatto children born to Virginia slaveholders were neither emancipated nor given special consideration as slaves. His observations can be generalized. Many, perhaps most, mulatto children never even learned the identity of their fathers—including Frederick Douglass, born in 1818, and Booker T. Washington, born around 1856. Georgia sharecropper Ed Brown, born in 1908, remembered that his mother had once pointed out his white father during a trip to town. But Brown never learned more about his father, and the tall white man in a big Stetson hat and overalls "never owned up to [him] in no way."[8]

Very probably, most southerners, white and black, had unrecognized biological kin on both sides of the race line, which might range from children to unknown distant cousins. It is a truism that in small towns and rural areas everyone is related to everyone else. In the South, the unspoken (and false) conceptual limitation on this maxim has been the division of "white" and "black" people into neatly separate "everyones." In actuality, the lines of kinship were spun out wildly in all directions, especially during the colonial period, until a great web of biological belonging tied nearly all southerners together. Usually the descendants of interracial unions became socially "black," although thousands of light-skinned individuals chose to become "white." Socially meaningful interracial kinship obviously made up only a few strands of this great web of belonging.

For the purpose of this study, interracial kinship will be considered to have been without social significance—even if recognized by a white father—if it did not lead to material assistance given by the father to the mother or children.[9] Katie Hunt, born in 1891 in middle Georgia, remembers the frequent visits her white grandfather John Henry Neal made to her family's home. Hunt's father, Burrell Neal, would see his father coming and abruptly leave the house. According to Hunt, "he just despised his father" because his mother "talked about how she was mistreated" by John Henry under slavery. The family received no assistance from him, perhaps because Burrell would not accept any. Although the kinship tie seemed to be recognized, the only material exchange seemed to have been the meals that Hunt and her mother shared with John Henry.[10]

The meaning of miscegenation in North America has changed with its historical context. While the bulk of interracial sexual encounters occurred in the seventeenth and eighteenth centuries in the Chesapeake region of Virginia and Maryland, they involved Europeans and Africans of similarly lowly estate. Accordingly, the mulatto children born in this period did not have influential contacts available to them through their kin. Their inter-racial parentage had no social significance.[11] By the late eighteenth and early nineteenth century, anti-miscegenation laws had come to curb the sexual behavior of the majority of Americans.[12]

Upper-class white male slaveowners of the lower South, however, began to develop a new pattern of interracial sexual activity with their female slaves. Most of the activity seems to have been promiscuous and random. These planters gave little evidence of having a sense of fatherly responsibility for their children in the slave quarters. However, a second distinct pattern emerged marked by long-term and sometimes monogamous relationships between upper-class white men and their mulatto domestic servants. This pattern seems to have been a widespread variation on the system of con-cubinage that elite slaveowners had developed earlier on Latin American and Caribbean estates as well as in French Louisiana.[13] These relationships often led to some construction of a socially significant "father" role by the white men involved in them, and sometimes to constructions of "interracial kinship" by their white relatives.[14]

With emancipation, the frequency of interracial sex declined sharply, as African Americans gained possession of their own bodies and the freedom to move. Still, antebellum kinship ties continued to be recognized by some families in the postbellum period—sometimes with implications for the ma-terial welfare of the black kin. Additionally, some white and black southerners continued to initiate new couplings and new interracial families well into the twentieth century.[15]

The historiography of the antebellum period has already described various ways by which masters who felt tied by kinship to one or more of their slaves could assist them. Joel Williamson, the leading historian of North American miscegenation, wrote that most slaves who were emancipated were mulattoes, usually the children of their owners. Some were given education or special training to allow them to earn money to purchase their own freedom. Others were emancipated outright, often through wills. Some emancipated children of slaveowners were given land on which to farm or were established in busi-ness in a city by their white kin. "Black" persons recognized as "family" by white persons were even named as chief beneficiaries in wills. Repeatedly, in certain circumstances, white men acted in accord with their personally con-structed identity as kin of black persons rather than their identity as whites with a material interest in slavery.[16]

The settlement of wills reveals a second generation of interracial family in direct contact with one another. Executors were often directed to free their half-brothers and sisters. While many such wills were no doubt broken, many others were carried out. In an 1856 will, after recently passed state laws made emancipation difficult, one planter in the South Carolina upcountry instructed his white son to treat his slave mistress and her children (the son's half-brothers and sisters) with indulgence and never to allow them to become "the Slaves of Strangers." Sometimes interracial kinship was recognized by men and women who in some way accepted identities as half-brothers and sisters, uncles, aunts, or cousins of individuals with a different racial status. According to Williamson, white men involved with only one black woman usually avowed their children either publicly or to a friend or relative. Sharing the same plot of soil, both black and white families were often made aware of each other, creating the possibility both of jealous conflict and of the construction of meaningful kinship ties generations after the deaths of the sexually involved individuals.[17]

During the antebellum period, many of the emancipated children of slave-owners moved to free states. Others concentrated in southern urban areas, notably Charleston and New Orleans. This mulatto elite developed exclusive business and social circles, provided excellent educations for their children, and maintained themselves in comfort, if not in wealth.[18] Only by hard work, cooperation with one another, and shrewd maneuvering were they able to withstand the assaults made on them by hostile whites. Yet, in spite of a racist environment, they expanded whatever material advantages they had received from their white kin and came to dominate the free African-American community. With the coming of Reconstruction, these mulatto communities provided much of the leadership of African Americans throughout the South.[19]

While many mulatto children of planters built business communities in urban centers, others followed the only other route to economic security—agriculture.[20] In rural plantation-belt communities, interracial kinship ties afforded meaningful assistance for upwardly mobile black southerners. Most southerners lived in such areas well into the twentieth century, and the majority of interracial contacts also occurred there.

Hancock County, Georgia is located in the middle of the plantation belt, fifty miles southeast of Atlanta, in some of the richest land in the state. Accordingly, it was one of the wealthiest counties in Georgia as long as the South's economy rested on the cotton industry. Although enclaves of white and, later, black yeoman farmers contended for space, large plantations dominated much of Hancock's land and population from the antebellum period until the 1940s and 1950s. The county held a clear black majority from the time of its settlement by Europeans and Africans. From 1830 to 1900, the percentage of black residents rose from 61 to 75 percent before declining slightly in the twentieth century. Due to the considerable wealth of its self-consciously paternalistic, politically Whiggish white minority and the poverty of its black majority, Hancock resembles the economic and demographic patterns of the Georgia and South Carolina lowcountry where interracial kinship ties have been most frequently described. Yet it also remained representative of any number of planter-dominated counties throughout the Deep South's plantation belt.[21]

As elsewhere, some of the most powerful white men of antebellum Hancock County entered into sexual unions with slave women. Some of these men assumed various social responsibilities as "father" to their children of color, which enhanced their children's material condition. While Glenn Eskew's essay in this volume describes the minimal advantages that Lucius Henry Holsey of Hancock County received from his planter father, James Holsey, other children of antebellum interracial unions received far greater consideration. Scholars have already provided richly documented accounts of several of the most prominent examples of Hancock's antebellum interracial kinship ties.

Adele Logan Alexander has detailed the interracial history of the Hunt family of Hancock County. Following seemingly casual sexual liaisons with two of his slave women in the 1820s, Judge Nathan Sayre established a life-long, seemingly monogamous relationship with Susan Hunt, a free woman of African and Cherokee descent. Instead of living in a rural area like all other interracial families examined in this study, Sayre, Hunt, and their three children lived in a mansion in Sparta, Hancock's county seat. He quietly provided for the education of his children and, at his death in 1853, saw that they received his estate through James Hunt, another white planter. Susan Hunt then moved to a house near James Hunt and his brother, Henry Hunt. Henry, a bachelor, carried on a long-term alliance with Susan's daughter Mariah from the early 1850s until his death in 1889. James, who was a childless widower, developed a relationship with Susan and at his death in 1879 bequeathed his estate, including about one thousand acres of farmland, to her and to their children. Building on the considerable foundations laid by interracial, kinship-based bequests, the black Hunts gained prominence as educational leaders in Georgia.[22]

Neither the Hunts' wealth nor that of any other Hancock County family could compare to the estate of the "prince of farmers," David Dickson. According to Virginia Kent Leslie, Dickson ruled over an antebellum plantation that included 250 slaves, and left a postbellum estate valued between half a million and one million dollars. In 1849, Dickson, still a bachelor at forty, took a thirteen-year-old African-and-Portuguese slave girl, Julia Lewis, as his mistress. Years later, he married a white woman, but she died soon after, leaving him no legal heirs. His only child, Amanda, was by Julia.[23]

Amanda America Dickson grew up in an isolated world of her father's creation. She was educated at a private school that Dickson built, dressed in the height of fashion by her own seamstress, and generally adopted the lifestyle of an aristocratic lady—within the vast boundaries of her father's estate. A marriage which David Dickson arranged for her with his white nephew, Charles Eubanks, deteriorated after a couple of years. When she returned home with her two children, Charles and Julian, David took them to New Orleans to be declared "white" and gave them his own name. Unimpressed, white Hancock residents continued to consider Dickson's family "colored." His grandsons later relocated, Charles to California and Julian to South Carolina. Apparently, they redefined themselves as "white." Amanda remained with her father until his death in 1885.

By that date, it had become quite difficult for white men in the South to bequeath their estates to their children of a different racial status. When Dickson's white relatives learned that he had willed nearly his entire fortune to his African-American daughter and grandsons, they attempted to break the will, and nearly succeeded, after appealing all the way to the Georgia Supreme Court. But, because they failed, David Dickson's stubborn construction of himself as the father and grandfather of black persons temporarily altered the class structure of the black community in Hancock. Amanda Dickson later moved from the rural estate to Augusta where she remained until her death, an enormously wealthy woman of color.[24]

Dickson's commitment to recognize and care for Amanda and his grandchildren well after the end of slavery suggests that some of the constructions of interracial kinship from the antebellum period were durable enough to survive in or adapt to the new context of freedom. While the frustrated white Dicksons did not honor David Dickson's construction of interracial family, other white men and women did recognize kinship relationships between themselves and their biological "black" extended family.

In Warren County, on the east border of Hancock, a white half-brother of a black man recognized his interracial kin through material assistance. In slavery, Matthew Hubert and his family had owned his half-brother Paul Hubert and his family. After freedom, Matthew urged his black relatives to remain on his land. When Paul's children insisted that their family relocate, Matthew negotiated with a planter three miles away to let the black Huberts rent some land. He also gave them cotton reportedly worth three hundred dollars, a tremendous gift in a wrecked economy. The family sold the cotton, bought seed, fertilizer, a plow, and a mule and began their drive to economic independence. They worked as a unit and saved money until Paul died, whereupon his sons moved west to rent land in Hancock.[25]

Zach Hubert, the first of Paul's sons to move, returned to the original plantation for technical farming advice from a white family member of his own generation, his cousin Henry Clay Hubert. He also used Henry as a contact to inquire into the possibility of buying farmland. Henry informed him that some men in Hancock were willing to sell land to freedmen. Zach visited Sparta, the county seat, and located Henry L. Burke, a white lawyer from Virginia who was speculating on uncleared land. In 1871, Zach and two of his brothers agreed to purchase 174 acres at the relatively high price of ten dollars an acre and on an unusually difficult three-year payment schedule. By working continuously to clear land, farm, and support themselves off the land, they managed to meet the deadline. Up to this juncture, their white kin had played an instrumental role in the upward mobility of the black Hubert family.[26]

However, when the lawyer refused to turn over the deed after Zach made the last payment on schedule in 1874, there is no evidence that the white Huberts intervened in any way on their relatives' behalf. The black Huberts had to make contacts of their own to locate another lawyer to defend their claim to the land. In 1876, after working as renters on land they had already purchased, they secured the legal services of Poulton Thomas of the nearby town of Crawfordville and threatened Burke into turning over the deed. When Zach and his brothers publicly fought a white man to secure title to their land, they had to do so without assistance from their white kin. Yet, without the aid they had received from their white relatives, they might never have been in a position to make such a claim in the first place.[27]

Over the ensuing decades, Zach and Camilla amassed an estate of over one thousand acres. All twelve of their children graduated from college. Several of them entered careers in higher education; some built farms on a scale similar to Zach's; one became director of the New York Urban League. At least two of Zach's brothers also became landowners and bequeathed the security of that status to their children.[28] Despite the white Hubert's apparent lack of involvement in the defining conflict of their lives, Zach and Henry regularly exchanged visits and farming advice. Furthermore, they publicly referred to each other as "cousin."[29] Caught between their shared identity as kin and their polarizing, politicized identity as "white" and "black," their relationship must have been fraught with tension and contradiction, as were the interracial kinship ties that other families inherited from slavery.

As the Huberts' narrative illustrates, black farmers' kinship ties to white planters did not guarantee them indpendence. They still had to fight the boll weevil, gain access to credit, and make their way through a racist society that threatened to undermine their position at every turn. Acts of assistance by their white kin leveled the playing field only to a degree. And ultimately, in each family's history, the most closely related interracial kin died off and the ties attenuated. Black families who gained independence through this avenue had to continually devise new strategies to adapt to a changing structure of opportunity. Additionally, it should not be assumed that interracial kinship played a significant economic role outside the plantation belt. Loren Schweninger has found that the overwhelming majority of black landowners arose in the upper South. There, where the economic system was less oppressive, black farmers seemingly found routes to independence within the system. In the Deep South, where black farmers were systematically impeded in their quest for land, interracial kinship played an important role in opening the first door. Yet, in a racist society, identification with such ties carried many emotional contradictions.[30]

Thomas Dickson of Hancock County, one of David Dickson's white relatives, gave his "black" son, Gordon Dickson, the use of a small plot of land, a house, and some seed money shortly after the Civil War. This small gift boosted Gordon over the quagmire of debt and tenantry from which most freedmen and their descendants never escaped in lifetimes of toil. Gordon married Julia Hillman, herself the daughter of a white planter and a free woman of African and Cherokee heritage. Beginning with a purchase of one hundred acres for 6,500 pounds of middling lint cotton in 1882, Gordon and Julia worked feverishly to build up an estate of at least eight hundred acres, and possibly as much as two thousand acres, by the early decades of the twentieth century. Eventually, they purchased Julia's father's house for their family of eighteen children. Although Gordon and Julia had been unable to secure educations for themselves, their children attended school, several of them received at least some college training, and one son became a medical doctor. Many of them worked for years with their father on shares until each of them inherited a plot of their own land when their parents died.[31] Their parents' hard work, building on a gift from their white grandfather, earned them as secure a position as African Americans were capable of attaining in a hostile environment.

Yet Gordon Dickson and his family chose to deemphasize the kinship tie that bound them to white ancestors and contemporaries. In the 1910s, one of his daughters attending Spelman College in Atlanta complained to a teacher that other students were teasing her because her name bound her suggestively to her white kin, especially to the renowned David Dickson. The teacher suggested that she change the spelling of her name to "Dixon" to camouflage the association. When she returned to Hancock, the rest of her family, including Gordon, emulated her example.[32] The recognized claim of interracial kinship, critical in establishing a secure first foothold for the Dixon family's upward climb, became a social liability once they had attained economic security. Still, the Dixon family history exemplifies the continuity of antebellum interracial kinship ties into the postbellum period.

Many African Americans, like Dixon, received only modest assistance from their white kin, compared with the large bequests given by Sayre, the Hunts, and David Dickson. Yet these acts were not insignificant. Often these small gifts provided a foothold of opportunity by which motivated individuals could begin to climb. Some black southerners believed that white planters simply did not cheat their black children as they did other tenants or renters. Others may have provided their children of color a degree of protection from hostile whites in making their own way in the world.[33] Compared with the majority of freedmen, who had nothing but their labor to assist them in overcoming absolute poverty, those with white parentage sometimes found that even a slight edge could make a great difference in a competitive capitalist economy.

Furthermore, the postbellum South did not operate as an unobstructed free market economy. First, business was enacted on a personal basis. For both black and white farmers within the lower South, relationships with individuals of wealth and authority often proved crucial to economic success. Credit was more often extended by private individuals than by banks. The interpretation of contracts and other powers of the courts, the granting of military deferments, and the upkeep of selected roads were all within the influence of the planters and their allies. Second, the planters were allowed great personal power over dependent laborers. The tenant system gave them opportunities to absorb their tenants' profits and thereby maintain them as cheap, reliable labor. A cycle of debt trapped most tenants. A gift of land, even a small one, or an opportunity to rent good land could mean the difference between a life of dependence and a chance at self-direction. Unlike tenants, landowners and renters could select which cash crops to plant. They could plant as much as they wished for home consumption. They could keep from being cheated by ginning their own cotton, marketing the crops themselves, shopping where they wanted, and keeping their own books. Furthermore, they controlled their children's educational opportunities and usually chose to send their children through grade school and sometimes high school and college. Dependent laborers such as sharecroppers and wage laborers normally could not control any of these areas of their lives.[34]

Roy Roberts, born into a black family in neighboring Warren County in 1915, remembered that his father told him that he was a cousin of the McGregors, a white family of wealthy planters on the Hancock County line. In recognition of that relationship, the McGregors allowed the Roberts family to supplement their thirty-acre farm by renting them as much land as they could work and allowing them to cut wood on their land without charge. Roberts's family gained control of their own lives by controlling their own land. "Most black people hired themselves out to whites," remembered Roberts. "If they said 'get up at six o'clock and go to work,' they had to get up. If they said 'fifty cents a day,' that's all they got. But we didn't have to get up for nobody, because we were home. We had our own land—our own everything—and it made a difference. It made a difference." [35]

Besides the general institutional challenge of tenancy, poor black farmers faced additional difficulties in gaining economic independence that white landless farmers did not have to overcome. A black man who had the price of a piece of property could not automatically purchase it, as sociologist Arthur Raper learned in the 1920s and 1930s while studying Greene County, which borders Hancock to the north. The prospective landowner had to be sponsored by a white man who would make arrangements for him and vouch for him as a "reliable," conservative man. Then he had to gain the acceptance of the white farmers whose land lay near the proposed plot. Finally, he usually paid more than market value for the property on an accelerated payment schedule. This difficult process was greatly facilitated if a black farmer had white kinship ties. Raper noted that five black families had told him that they had acquired their land directly from white relatives. [36]

The cotton culture presented a highly selective window of economic opportunity for black Georgians from the 1880s until the boll weevil arrived in the early 1920s. Afterward, the weevil, the decline of cotton prices, and the "long southern depression" began to close this window, and the implementation of the agribusiness-oriented programs of the New Deal clanged it shut. Still, a number of families climbed through while it remained open. A stable, landed black rural elite had formed by 1910, its fortune balanced upon cotton prices. For the generation entering adulthood after World War One the cities, not the farms, held the real opportunity and there, interracial kinship ties were of no consequence. Before the war, however, economic progress came in rural areas like Hancock County, often through traditional, familial means.

The rise of the wealthiest black families in late-nineteenth-century Hancock can be traced to assistance rendered by white kin who continued to recognize previously established kinship ties. The five black men owning the most assets in Hancock in 1910 were: Julian H. Dickson, with property valued at $17,000; Richard I. Johnson, $10,185; Gordon Dixon, $5,416; Sherman Ingram, $4,235; and Henry L. Wynn, $3,935.[37] Although Wynn had died by 1920, the other four men still stood on the topmost rung of the county's black economic ladder in that year, each with over $10,000 in taxable assets. As described above, Julian Dickson was launched into wealth as the beneficiary of his white grandfather's will, while Gordon Dixon laboriously built upon the small gift of his white father. According to oral sources, the other three men also received aid from white kin at the initial stage of their rise to wealth.[38]

Richard Johnson came to control much of the business sector in Sparta. Although he had appeared in the 1890 tax digest without any assets, by 1900 Johnson owned $800 worth of city property, over $700 in cash and $900 in merchandise.[39] According to Katie Hunt, who knew Johnson in the 1910s, he was generally reported to have had a white father who gave him economic assistance. Yet, even then, she did not know the identity of Johnson's father or the means by which he helped his son. She had heard that his wife, Claude Little, was the mulatto daughter of a Hancock judge who also may have assisted the Johnsons. James McMullen, a black county educator and businessman who lived across the street from Johnson, related that Johnson conducted his business through white employees. Ultimately, Johnson found it too difficult to hold white men responsible for his financial affairs. In the 1930s, he and his family moved first to Atlanta to redefine and reestablish themselves as white, and then, upon their "exposure" as "black," to California, where they remained. Although familiar with the business life of the county, McMullen knew few details of the way the interracial ties worked in behalf of the Johnson family, stating merely that such assistance was usually given quietly, through either outright gifts, direct loans, or influence in securing loans.[40]

The children and grandchildren of Sherman Ingram state that a wealthy white planter, Tom Ingram, loaned his mulatto son, Sherman, the funds he used to set up a sawmill in the northern part of Hancock.[41] Soon he bought a second mill and began to purchase large tracts of timberland. By 1920, he owned over 1,000 acres of land and was worth over $11,000.[42] Henry and Delia Wynn, like Julian Dickson and Richard Johnson, have no descendants remaining in Hancock. However, contemporaries report that they, too, were known to have had access to the resources of white kin. In the Wynn's case, it was Delia's white father who was reported to have extended aid to the Wynns. Her interracial kinship ties brought them the funding they needed to set up a mortuary.[43] Evidently, some white southerners assumed responsibility for the material welfare not only of their black sons, but of their black daughters as well.

Other black families that rose to economic independence in Hancock and surrounding counties during the same period also describe aid given at a critical point in their climb. Although such transactions served as powerful social forces and shaped the business dynamics of communities such as Sparta, it is virtually impossible to determine their relative frequency.[44] This is because they took place privately, even secretly, due to the public ideology which forbade (and denied the existence of) such ties. However, in describing interracial ties in the first part of the twentieth century, one retired black businessman stated that "most of the big men in the county had black women." Although connections between the white and black community were rarely displayed publicly, one could tell which black people had access to interracial kinship ties. "You could tell by the color of the children and you could tell by how well they'd get along."[45]

Most of the socially significant postbellum interracial relationships seem to have been constructed between wealthy planters living in rural areas and mulatto domestic servants. The relationship between a white planter and sawmill owner, Lynn Rives, and a light-skinned black woman, Della May Flagg, is representative. According to Flagg, born in 1902, she and Rives lived in adjacent houses on his remote plantation in the country. She cooked for Rives, a public bachelor, and generally acted as his domestic servant. In appearance, their relationship resembled that of any number of southerners and conformed to the Georgia statute outlawing mixed-race marriages or sexual relationships. In actuality, their monogamous union began in the early 1920s, produced two daughters, and lasted for nearly forty years. In the late 1950s, Rives, then in his seventies, married a white woman. The creation of this legal union meant that neither Flagg nor their children and grandchildren were in line to inherit Rives's estate. Yet, he had already found small ways to assist them financially. Rives bought clothes, shoes, and school supplies for their two daughters and later for their grandchildren. He rented land to his daughters' families and purchased land to resell to each of them when they sought to become landowners. In the words of Rives's black grandson, Obilee Rhodes, Jr., "he was the banker for us. He would finance for us."

Lynn Rives's brother also had a long-term relationship with a black woman, and he also took responsibility for their children.[46] Some white families developed patterns in which more than one male acknowledged interracial paternity and carried out responsibilities as sociological fathers. Besides the Rives brothers, the Hunts and Dicksons also fit this pattern in which brothers maintained interracial families.

The postbellum families described in this essay are not examples of "concubinage." In concubinage, a man simultaneously maintained two families, a legal family and an "outside" family. While Rives married late in life, most of the white men and black women described in this essay are listed in the census manuscript as "single" throughout their lives. Moreover, according to family and community oral traditions, in most cases both partners maintained monogamous commitments to each other until death. Such fidelity may have emerged after emancipation sharply restricted white men's control over the sexuality of a number of women. These relationships may have become widespread in certain areas. A white woman from the Yazoo–Mississippi Delta wrote a letter to a newspaper in 1907, complaining that miscegenation was "common" in her community. She stated: "If a man isolates himself from feminine society, the first and only conclusion reached is, 'He has a woman of his own' in saddle of duskier shade."[47]

Lynn Rives slighted his children in his will, but other white men carried out conventional familial obligations for their interracial families upon their deaths. William Maxey, born in 1805 in Greene County, was such a man. His family moved two counties to the west to Jasper County in 1812, and it was there that he rose in the world as a prosperous merchant, with real estate valued at $10,000 and personal property at $27,764 in 1860. The Civil War reversed his fortunes and by the time he died in 1873, he owned only a 750-acre plantation, valued at around $4,000. Officially, he left no descendants, having never married. Yet, his will directed that his plantation go to a three-year-old black boy named William Henry Jordan. Maxey also appointed a guardian, Albert J. Talmadge, to ensure that he received an education. The boy's mother, Antoinette Jordan, who lived next door to Maxey, was given Maxey's house, lot, and furnishings in trust. Upon her death, they were to pass to William Henry or to any of her other five children, should he die without heirs.[48]

Sam Durham, who lived near the small town of Maxeys in Oglethorpe County, also ensured that his full estate passed to his children of color. Besides carrying on a long and famous family tradition as a medical doctor, Durham was also a dairy owner, planter, and partner in a bank. Next to his house he built a house for Sarah B. Mason, a woman of Spanish and African heritage who acted as his housekeeper. Together, they had eight children, the first born in 1886. Durham sent his oldest daughter to college in Atlanta and trained her to be a midwife and his medical assistant. His two daughters, Bridie Jackson and Queene Mason, remained with him after his sons moved away and Sarah Mason died. Perhaps for this reason, they were the only beneficiaries of his will. In it, he did not name them as daughters, but rather directed that his entire estate be split between them "for faithful services during my last long and protracted illness." In 1925, two years before he died, Durham sold his three plantations to two of his friends, one of whom he named executor of the will. Immediately after Durham's death, his daughters bought back the property. Perhaps Durham used trusted third parties to camouflage the illegal transfer of wealth to his two "black" daughters.[49]

In at least one case, the economic benefits of interracial kinship ties devolved to the children and grandchildren of an interracial couple only after the first generation had been economically exploited by the white grandfather. Clifford Smith, a Hancock man of distant African heritage, stated that his white grandfather, David Dickson, a poor coattail relative of his rich namesake, had a lifelong relationship with Julia Lockland, a poor black woman. Dickson had been born in 1856, just four houses away and five years before Lockland. Once Dickson told Smith that he had never been with a woman other than Lockland. At the least, the census manuscripts list him as a bachelor throughout his life. Smith's mother, the couple's first child, was born in 1879. Dickson lived near but not with Lockland and their ten children, and visited only at night. Yet he directed their labor until they earned enough money to buy 600 acres in 1899. Essentially, the Locklands were free labor to Dickson. Smith describes the conditions on the farm as "slavery." David's brother, Greene Dickson, lived nearby and had a similar arrangement with another black woman, Sarah Brinkley. The two Dickson brothers would be in the field themselves before light, but by nine in the morning each day, Smith remembered, they would be back on their front porch. "Chewin' tobacco was his biggest trade," recalled Smith, "that and talking."[50]

When Julia Lockland died in 1899 at the age of forty, the Lockland children, who were never allowed much time for school, continued to work the farm, bringing the profits and a share of the garden crops to their father. "His children worked for and bought his land for him," Smith stated. Dickson, as a white man, could purchase property with relative ease. "He bought it with talk, but they did the work." When Dickson deeded the land to his children near the end of his life, Smith remembers his mother saying, "We worked enough to pay for the land twelve times over." Undoubtedly they did. However, in the end, they did obtain the title. Most black farmers without white contacts, even an exploitive, distant father, were never allowed a chance to gain title to the land they worked.[51]

The experience of another interracial family, the Guills, was far different. Frank Guill, the son of a hard-drinking ex-Union soldier and a wealthy Hancock heiress, and Pearl Gordon, a beautiful mulatto woman, began their family in 1905 with the birth of the first of their eight children. They worked

part of their 176-acre farm themselves and contracted with four or five tenant families on the remainder. According to one of his sons, Frank may also
have spent some time as overseer of the county chain gang.[52]

Perhaps because of Frank's wealthy family, perhaps because of his threatening occupation, the Guill family seemed to have enjoyed a distinctively
public but unmolested experience. They shared a house. Pearl took Frank's
name, as did their children; the eldest son was named Frank Guill, Jr.; the
eldest daughter, Nancy, after her paternal grandmother. The intersection of
race and kinship in the extended family created an intricate tangle of lives.
While their parents never worshipped together, the children alternately attended a white Baptist church with their father and a black Baptist church
with their mother. Although formal visits were infrequent between the various Guill and Gordon families, the multihued extended family gathered to
celebrate Frank's birthday annually with a picnic and baseball game. Frank
and Pearl's children described frequent informal visits and lifelong friendships among themselves and their kin on every side. While definitions of race
never ceased to be a factor in their relationships, definitions of kinship also
decisively structured their interaction.[53]

Most of their children got only high-school training; however, Frank and
Pearl sent their youngest daughter to New York to attend college. When their
parents died in the mid-1930s, the children inherited the family farm as a
collective trust. The sons found skilled positions, as soldiers, welders, chefs,
and a building contractor. The oldest daughter became a nurse; the others,
homemakers. They could move back and forth freely between different racial
identities. They were "black" in the public world of Hancock, usually "black"
but sometimes "white" outside the county, and they had an irreducibly complex racial identity within the extended family. When the second eldest, Leo,
joined the army during World War I, his recruiter quite reasonably refused to
believe that he was "black" and enlisted him as "white." After his honorable
discharge papers were sent to the courthouse in Hancock County, the clerk,
in indignant red ink, scratched out his "X" in the "white" box and marked
the "black" box. Still, Leo received his pension at a higher rate of pay. Sometimes, when it was useful to do so, they became "white"; otherwise, as Frank
and Pearl's grandson Benjamin Alexander Glascoe relates, "they socialized
themselves as black" and "made a conscious choice to remain in the black
community."[54]

Some prominent white men had sufficient economic, political, and social
power to protect their relationships with black women from interference.
Many of the wealthiest planters controlled credit for all families in a community, white and black. In describing why the fairly open interracial re-

lationship between his maternal grandparents went undisturbed, Laramon Durham said, "The white community was working for them, and those who were not wished to hell they were."[55] As Katie Hunt explained the public relationship between Frank and Pearl Guill, "If anyone had money, they'd do what they wanted."[56]

David B. Hill also had money. In the 1880s and 1890s, he owned three thousand acres in the southernmost part of Baldwin County, which borders Hancock to the west. Hill, easily the largest landowner in his district, also owned a mill, a cotton gin, and a drug store in Milledgeville, the county seat. But instead of living in town, he lived in rural seclusion with a light-skinned African-American woman, Elvira Hill, and their seven children. The oldest, Stephen Hill, was born in 1860, when his mother was twenty-two and his father, thirty years old. Unlike most interracial children, the Hills did not attend a black school. Instead, David built a private school and hired a private teacher for them. Upon his death in 1901, David left his children a remarkable will. While most white men left their estates to their children in oblique ways, David's will not only openly identified his familial relationships with his children and their mother, but it named three of his children, Madison, Stephen, and Nora Hill, as his executors. He passed his plantations directly to his six surviving children in equally divided plots. Elvira was to have received a share as well, but she died the year before David. Their children all remained on the land, the sons farming in their own right, the daughters renting their land to other farmers.[57]

Elsewhere in Baldwin County, Joshua Ellis established himself in farming after serving in the Confederate Army.[58] While not as wealthy as Hill, he became one of the richest men in his district, accumulating 407 acres, a mill, and a store by 1890. Shortly after the war, he also began to raise a family of seven children with Charity Ingram, a mulatto woman who was born in 1844, one year after Joshua. The 1900 census manuscript describes them as sharing a house, with Charity listed as Joshua's servant and their children as boarders.[59]

When Joshua Ellis died in 1916, he bequeathed his estate directly to his children under the cover of a legal fiction. His will cited Charity Ingram and each of their children by name, but did not give any indication of consanguinal kinship, although it named his two youngest sons, Thomas and Julius Ingram, as executors. Ellis explained that the will was "an expression of my gratitude to [Charity Ingram] for long years of service to me and work in my interests." Except for outstanding debts and five dollars that were directed to Ellis's brother, his family received his entire estate. The children, some of whom took their mother's name, some their father's, and some the hyphenated "Ellis-Ingram," all succeeded as prosperous farmers, educators, or skilled tradesmen, and became community leaders in Baldwin County. Their children, in turn, received college educations and most of them left the area to join the urban middle class in the North and the South.[60]

With one antebellum exception, all interracial families whose residential arrangements could be discovered for this essay were isolated in rural areas. Few of the families located in the census manuscript had white neighbors. Most were surrounded instead by the houses of black tenants, cotton, corn, and cane fields, and woodland. Perhaps if such relationships remained discreet, local whites who may have disapproved chose instead to exercise "selective inattention."[61] At any rate, the interracial families of planters, even if generally known within a community, were seemingly allowed to remain a locally contained "open secret." Segregation, after all, was an urban, Progressive, middle-class reform measure. Observance of anti-miscegenation laws, or at least the avoidance of interracial kinship ties, may have been more characteristic of the towns than the countryside. The human geography of the rural plantation belt featured white aristocratic planters surrounded by African-American farmers, interacting in ways that were partly traditional, partly modernizing. When white planters began to alter these demographic conditions by increasingly moving to the towns as absentee landlords after 1900, these relationships became less common. Eight of the ten postbellum mixed relationships described in this essay were initiated between 1860 and 1900. Only two of the unions described here existed after 1921.

In rural communities, segregation was not the primary vehicle enforcing the inferior status of African Americans. Instead, personal, face-to-face rituals of violence and paternalism upheld white supremacy. In the experience of many rural southerners, interracial social contact continued to be regular and intimate. By stating that rural southerners participated in a highly personal interracial community, one is by no means implying that these communities were egalitarian or that they were experienced by African Americans as benign. Indeed, in most traditional societies, community is hierarchical.[62]

In the rural South, with wide spaces, diffuse population, few phones, and no paved roads, racial mores seem to have been enforced by white residents locally rather than by a systematic, centralized regional authority. William McFeely has observed that slavery was "often homemade, rather than cut from a standard pattern," and in many respects, so were the racial codes of the postbellum rural South."[63] Considerable variation in standards occurred from locale to locale. In many isolated rural areas, certain white men were allowed space in which to maintain long-term relationships with black women and sometimes to act as sociological fathers to their children of color. In other areas, they were attacked by white vigilantes.[64]

Some who did experience aggression from segments of the white community had resources with which to defend themselves. Francis Julian (Jules) Skrine of Hancock County was the son of John D. and Betsy Skrine, substantial Hancock farmers of 200 acres in 1874. Jules had a black half-brother named Quamley Skrine, so it may not have been a great surprise to his parents when, sometime in the 1880s, he moved into a house with Louisiana Taylor, a woman of Native American and African descent who was working as a day laborer on his father's farm.[65] As Jules and Louisiana's family grew to include thirteen children, their assets also grew. Between 1891 and 1900, they acquired 200 acres valued at nearly $1,000; by 1910, they owned 250 acres and other property valued at a total of nearly $2,000. Louisiana died that year at the age of forty-five and Jules began to drink the family property away. According to Lucius Skrine, their grandson, "When she died, he died. He just lost control." By the time he died, the land was eaten away by debts and there was little to bequeath to their children.[66]

While Jules did not leave an inheritance of land directly to his children, he left them his name and provided for them during his life. He discouraged education for his oldest children, pushing them into the field or kitchen, but some of the younger ones were more fully schooled.[67] However, as each of his children married and moved out, Jules built them a house on the family property and offered to work with them on a rent or share basis. At least two of his sons, Thomas and Pelham, bought farms from their father. All of the children became homeowners.[68]

Although in later years they lived in adjacent houses, early in Jules and Louisiana's apparently monogamous relationship they had openly shared a house with their children. According to family oral traditions, the family faced challenges to its integrity from white interlopers. Shortly after they had begun their relationship, a group of "paddyrollers" visited their home and threatened bodily harm if they continued to live together openly. Jules reportedly replied that Louisiana was his wife and that they would live together as long as they cared to. He then spun the threat around and warned the men not to return on pain of buckshot. The family was not threatened by violence again. His grandchildren remember him as a hard-living, barroom-brawling, hardscrabble hell-raiser of a man. Gaston Skrine, born in 1910, recalled that his grandfather would take his sons "to town to drink and fight with the white boys on Saturday nights." Evidently, his threats were credible.[69]

Some other interracial families cultivated a reputation as "too dangerous to control." Gaston Skrine remembered two extended interracial Hancock families that went generally unmolested. The Boyer and Harper families each had branches that specialized in moonshine. "If you bothered one Boyer," Skrine recalled, "you done bothered all the Boyers. They'd stick together, white and black." Like the Boyers, the Harpers were known to spill blood if anyone interfered with them. County law enforcement officials were too frightened of these backwoods families to attempt to curtail their public moonshine operation, much less their connubial arrangements.[70]

When southern white men resorted to violence to defend the integrity of their interracial families from attack by other white men, they also challenged the assumptions of determinism held by modern historians. When southern white men took measures that ensured that their children of color would inherit family estates or benefit in other ways from their father's economic status, they not only circumvented state laws but also eluded capture by our current interpretive mechanisms. Their perceived personal identities of race, class, and gender no doubt brought them into tension with their sense of kinship. Yet the way they untangled these identities and resolved those tensions can be inferred from the stories of their lives. While subjectively experienced human identities are composed of inextricably intertwined strands of various social identities, ultimately the concrete nature of choice and action demand that individuals choose to ally themselves with concrete, socially defined groups. Although individuals' personal motivations may confound all attempts at dissection, actions produce observable results in the material world.

Some construction of interracial kinship is the simplest way to explain the actions of Jules Skrine, Frank Guill, and the other white planters who quietly (and somewhat conventionally) extended economic resources to their biological children of color. Far more than acknowledged by contemporaries or recognized by historians since, a significant number of black southerners received critical material assistance that allowed them to attain economic independence based on their kinship ties to white southerners. Of course, many—perhaps most—who were theoretically eligible to receive assistance from their white kin did not. Yet for those who did, the social category of kinship was, within a specific historical context, as important an experienced social reality as were the categories of race, class, and gender.[71]

If constructions of interracial kinship were important forces in shaping the experience of many postbellum rural southerners, it is worth asking why so little is currently known about them. During the 1920s, 1930s, and 1940s, many social scientists addressed miscegenation in the South. Too many squandered their energy in the trackless wastes of physical anthropology. Others, both sociologists and anthropologists, made frequent citations of sexual relationships between white men and black women. However, due to the dominance of structural theory during the first half of the twentieth century, social scientists argued that white southerners' interest in the (racially approximated) southern class system demanded that they maintain an unwavering defense of racial endogamy. In turn, racial endogamy and the concept of the "Solid South" provided the uncompromisable basis on which social scientists built explanations of southern race relations. Structuralist theories dovetailed neatly with the vast and very real resistance that many white southerners raised to miscegenation. Confronted by the enormous public evidence of violent atrocities and by equally violent political speeches in defense of endogamy, they shared our current reasonable assumption that socially significant interracial kinship could not have existed in such a rabidly racist climate. Through their peculiar lens, scholars were forced to consign manifestations of socially recognized interracial kinship (which many of them discovered) to the scrap heap of meaningless exceptionalism. Ironically, few could resist mentioning these stories, though few seemed to have noted the pattern drawn by their string of exceptions. Their assumptions precluded avenues of research that would examine the social roots of the mulatto elite. In order to maintain a useful general theory of southern social relations, one origin of the black middle class has been allowed to remain obscured by mystery.[72]

Also, historically, there has been a tendency to over-exceptionalize the African-American experience. While certainly African Americans have encountered a distinctively severe and persistent exploitation, their story has sometimes been fictionalized into opposing narratives of victimization and resistance. Within this harsh dichotomy, the multifaceted experience of human life is lost. African Americans have been rendered as "essentially," ahistorically "other." Important aspects of the African-American experience can be explored only by suspending the reflexive assumption of overwhelming "otherness."[73]

Much remains to be discovered concerning the demographic, social, and cultural context that gave rise to socially significant interracial kinship ties. More local case studies are needed to map the private patterns of race relations in the rural South. Too often the meaning of race and race relations in the postbellum South has been constructed from afar, built upon general theories of exploitation and supported by illustrations from publicly announced ideology. While southern anti-miscegenation ideologies reliably express the programs of various social reformers in various periods, they less reliably reflect the experience of other southerners during these periods.

Anti-miscegenation laws are no more proof of endogamy than temperance laws are evidence of teetotalism. The story must be built from the ground of concrete human experience up, not from the sky of normative edicts down.

Notes

1. Jean Toomer, *Cane*, with an introduction by Darwin T. Turner (New York: Liveright, 1975). See especially "Becky," "Esther," "Blood-Burning Moon," and "Kabnis." On Toomer's own Georgia ancestry, see Kent Anderson Leslie and Willard B. Gatewood, Jr., " 'This Father of Mine . . . a Sort of Mystery': Jean Toomer's Georgia Heritage," *Georgia Historical Quarterly* 77 (Winter 1993): 826–41. I wish to thank Kathleen Conzen, Jacqueline Dowd Hall, Thomas Holt, Kent Leslie, Cathy McDonnell, William McFeely, James Roark, Frank Summers, and Joel Williamson for reading various drafts of this essay and making substantial contributions to whatever is good in the finished product. I, of course, am solely responsible for whatever is not.

2. Charles Waddell Chesnutt, *The Wife of His Youth and Other Stories of the Color Line* (Boston: Houghton Mifflin, 1899); William Faulkner, *Absalom, Absalom!* (1936; reprint, New York: Modern Library, 1951); *Go Down Moses* (New York: Random House, 1942); *Intruder in the Dust* (New York: Random House, 1948); Lyle Saxon, *Children of Strangers* (Boston: Houghton Mifflin, 1937); Robert Penn Warren, *Band of Angels* (New York: Random House, 1955); Raymond Andrews, *Rosiebelle Lee Wildcat Tennessee* (1980; reprint, Athens: University of Georgia Press, 1988).

3. Other explanations for the rise of the mulatto elite do exist. It has been suggested that "white" people, in some "natural" way, find darker-colored people psychologically disturbing, and therefore lighter-complexioned African Americans encountered less racial hostility and so fared relatively well economically. However, the prevalence of miscegenation in colonial America and the common nineteenth- and early-twentieth-century attacks on mulattoes as a weak, "mongrel race" suggest that this argument amounts to theoretical mysticism. Furthermore, it is not clear why an encounter with a social inferior who more closely resembled oneself should evoke a sense of comfort rather than one of unease. Even if European Americans, and even some African Americans, have at times seemed to give preferential treatment to mulattoes, this phenomenon can be explained materially. Ultimately, it is much easier to ascribe any preferential bias in favor of light-complexioned African Americans to a recognition of their generally privileged economic status than to reverse the causal connection. As Thomas Holt wrote, "Color was merely an indicator of a whole complex of interrelated variables of class and acculturation" (*Black Over White: Negro Political Leadership in South Carolina during Reconstruction* [Urbana: University of Illinois Press, 1977], 61). In the larger society, mulattoes may have been socially preferred because they were economically advantaged, not economically advantaged because they were socially preferred.

The second alternative to material assistance from white kin argues that mulatto people, because they were often given favored status as slaves, learned to master cultural skills that made them more familiar and hence more acceptable to European Americans. But why were light-skinned individuals disproportionately presented with an opportunity to absorb a cultural style that would purportedly benefit them in dealing with European Americans? The simplest explanation is that they were chosen because they were kin.

4. Joel Williamson, *New People: Miscegenation and Mulattoes in the United States* (New York: New York University Press, 1980), provides the essential starting point for studies of miscegenation and the economic rise of the mulatto elite. He establishes the existence of an antebellum pattern of material assistance given by white planters to their children of color. Other important works in the antebellum period are Eugene Genovese, *Roll, Jordan, Roll: The World the Slaves Made* (New York: Random House, 1974), 413–31; Ira Berlin, *Slaves without Masters: The Free Negro in the Antebellum South* (New York: Pantheon Books, 1975); Gary B. Mills, "Miscegenation and the Free Negro in Antebellum "Anglo" Alabama: A Reexamination of Southern Race Relations," *Journal of American History* 68 (June 1981): 16–34; Suzanne Lebsock, *The Free Women of Petersburg: Status and Culture in a Southern Town, 1784–1860* (New York: W. W. Norton, 1984); Michael P. Johnson and James L. Roark, *Black Masters: A Free Family of Color in the Old South* (New York: W. W. Norton, 1984); Michael P. Johnson and James L. Roark, *No Chariot Let Down: Charleston's Free People of Color on the Eve of the Civil War* (Chapel Hill: University of North Carolina Press, 1984); and Lois Virginia Meacham Gould, "In Full Enjoyment of Their Liberty: The Free Women of Color of the Gulf Ports of New Orleans, Mobile, and Pensacola, 1769–1860" (Ph.D. diss., Emory University, 1991). Studies that cover the postbellum period include Willard B. Gatewood, *Aristocrats of Color: The Black Elite, 1880–1920* (Bloomington: Indiana University Press, 1990), especially 15–22; Virginia Kent Anderson Leslie, "Woman of Color, Daughter of Privilege: Amanda America Dickson, 1849–1893" (Ph.D. diss., Emory University, 1990); Adele Logan Alexander, *Ambiguous Lives: Free Women of Color in Rural Georgia, 1789–1879* (Fayetteville: University of Arkansas Press, 1991); Martha Hodes, "Sex across the Color Line: White Women and Black Men in the Nineteenth-Century American South" (Ph.D. diss., Princeton University, 1991).

5. In every way that is historically significant, I understand racial categories to be the results of social construction and not of biological production. It is meaningless to refer to the "black" children of a "white" father in any biological sense. When I use racially descriptive terms, I refer to a socially designated racial status, not to a biological identity. Similarly, when I write "miscegenation," I refer to mating across socially and not biologically defined boundaries. Among the families in this study, the meaning of race is especially problematic. Many of the black women involved in these relationships were themselves of interracial parentage. Their children were often light enough to become socially white if they moved and chose to "pass." Some did, either for life or for a train ride, making race not only meaningless for them in the biologi-

cal sense but also highly problematic in the social sense. I refer to them as "black" rather than "white" because the larger society into which they were born considered them "colored." I rarely refer to them as "mulatto" because the great majority became "voluntary negroes," and ultimately joined their persons and their wealth with the larger "black" community. The most influential discussion of contemporary theories of race is Barbara J. Fields, "Ideology and Race in American History," in J. Morgan Kousser and James M. McPherson, eds., *Region, Race and Reconstruction: Essays in Honor of C. Vann Woodward* (New York: Oxford University Press, 1982), 143–78.

6. By "black middle class," I refer to the social grouping identified by the southern sociologists of the 1920s, 1930s, and 1940s. This study is based on the tape-recorded oral testimony of men and women from Hancock County and surrounding counties who claim interracial ancestry. They identified their families as benefiting materially from interracial kinship ties, sometimes involving themselves directly, more often their parents or grandparents. While oral history is perhaps the only way to approach this area of research in this historical context, reliance on this methodology raises questions about the meaning of oral traditions. It is possible that the content of words such as "father" could change, especially considering the context of the paternalistic ethos of slavery.

Yet there are reasons to take their testimony at face value. The informants come from a culture with high genealogical awareness. Parts of their testimony were general knowledge within the local communities in which they lived. Furthermore, their narratives of interracial kinship were often corroborated by photographs of white and black ancestors and usually by their own obviously interracial physical appearance. Finally, details of stories were repeatedly confirmed in the tax digests, census manuscripts, deed records, and registers of wills. In the absence of any evidence to the contrary, I interpret all references to kinship in the conventional sense.

7. Such relationships did occur but would have been more socially vulnerable and less likely to act as a conduit of assistance between white and black family. Hodes, "Sex across the Color Line"; John Dollard, *Caste and Class in a Southern Town* (New Haven: Yale University Press, 1937), 167–68; Allison Davis, Burleigh B. Gardner, and Mary R. Gardner, *Deep South: A Social Anthropological Study of Caste and Class* (Chicago: University of Chicago Press, 1941), 27–31, 47. Toomer, *Cane*, "Becky." I heard two references to black male, white female couples in my interviews, but was unable to elicit any detail whatsoever.

8. Frederick Law Olmsted, *A Journey in the Seaboard Slave States* (New York: Dix and Edwards, 1856), 127, 601–2; William S. McFeely, *Frederick Douglass* (New York: W. W. Norton, 1991), 8, 13; Louis Harlan, *Booker T. Washington: The Making of a Black Leader, 1856–1901* (New York: Oxford University Press, 1972), 3; Jane Maguire, *On Shares: Ed Brown's Story* (New York: W. W. Norton, 1975), 12.

9. I realize that by using the generational transfer of material wealth as a lens through which to examine interracial kinship ties, I am choosing not to explore many important and interesting aspects of these ties. I recognize that this lens magnifies my view of the role of the white father and sharply limits that of the black mother in these

families. Furthermore, I recognize that the role of fatherhood involves more than the generational transfer of material wealth. It seems logical, however, to initiate a study of postbellum interracial kinship with an examination of such transfers. These stories persist in family oral traditions, often after many other details have been forgotten, and they provide a consistent thread by which to connect the experience of almost all of the long-term interracial families that I found. Furthermore, oral narratives of material transfers can often be verified through county records. Other aspects of sociological parenthood are more difficult to document. Finally, my argument for the importance of these transfers as a meaningful explanation of the rise of the mulatto elite in the lower South justifies the study in its own right.

10. John Henry Neal was a brother-in-law of William Northen, who was elected governor of Georgia in 1890 and 1892. Interviews with Katie Hunt, Washington, D.C., June 14, 1990 and September 12, 1992. Although born in 1891, Mrs. Hunt was still fully alive in 1993.

11. Williamson, *New People*, 33–42; Allan Kulikoff, *Tobacco and Slaves: The Development of Southern Cultures in the Chesapeake, 1690–1800* (Chapel Hill: University of North Carolina Press, 1986), 386–87, 395–96. The colonial creation of a large mulatto population is historically significant only in demonstrating that Europeans and Africans in North America encountered no "natural" barrier to sexual intimacy before the raising of social taboos against miscegenation. As Marvin Harris argues, "In general, when human beings have the power, the opportunity and the need, they will mate with members of the opposite sex regardless of color or the identity of grandfather" (*Patterns of Race in the Americas* [New York: Walker Press, 1964], 68–69).

12. Beginning in Virginia in 1662, the colonial assemblies initiated a series of laws which made miscegenation increasingly difficult. By 1725, all the colonies had enacted laws prohibiting marriage between "white" and "black" persons, although the legal status of "mulattoes" remained a semantic tangle. The acts are generally interpreted as an attempt by the landed elites to socially isolate the African-American slaves as their primary labor supply. Williamson, *New People*, 7–13; Edmund S. Morgan, *American Slavery, American Freedom: The Ordeal of Colonial Virginia* (New York: W. W. Norton, 1975), 327–36.

13. Carl N. Degler, *Neither White nor Black: Slavery and Race Relations in Brazil and the United States* (New York: Macmillan, 1971); Verena Martinez-Alier, *Marriage, Class and Colour in Nineteenth-Century Cuba: A Study of Racial Attitudes and Sexual Values in a Slave Society* (London: Oxford University Press, 1974); Gary B. Mills, *The Forgotten People: Cane River's Creoles of Color* (Baton Rouge: Louisiana State University Press, 1977); John Blassingame, *Black New Orleans, 1860–1880* (Chicago: University of Chicago Press, 1973), 17–21.

14. Williamson, *New People*, 14–56; Genovese, *Roll, Jordan, Roll*, 413–31; Berlin, *Slaves without Masters*, 151–167; James Hugo Johnson, *Race Relations in Virginia and Miscegenation in the South, 1776–1860* (Amherst: University of Massachusetts Press, 1970); Mills, "Miscegenation and the Free Negro."

15. The sharp postbellum decline in the incidence of miscegenation is paralleled

by an even sharper decline in the already slender historiographical literature exploring interracial kinship ties. Autobiographies of African-American southerners provide the only postbellum studies currently available. Examples of postbellum interracial kinship ties are found in Anne Moody, *Coming of Age in Mississippi* (New York: Dial Press, 1968); Theodore Rosengarten, *All God's Dangers: The Life of Nate Shaw* (New York: Knopf Press, 1974); Susan Tucker, *Telling Memories among Southern Women: Domestic Workers and Their Employers in the Segregated South* (New York: Schocken Books, 1988); Raymond Andrews, *The Last Radio Baby* (Atlanta, Ga.: Peachtree Publishers, 1990); and Sarah and A. Elizabeth Delaney, *Having Our Say: The Delaney Sisters' First Hundred Years* (New York: Kodansha America, 1993).

16. Williamson, *New People*, 14–15, 23, 43, 56; Berlin, *Slaves without Masters*, 151–52; Johnson and Roark, *Black Masters*, 6, 11, 15; Alexander, *Ambiguous Lives*.

17. Quote from Orville Vernon Burton, *In My Father's House Are Many Mansions: Family and Community in Edgefield, South Carolina* (Chapel Hill: University of North Carolina Press, 1985), 186–89; Williamson, *New People*, 43; Genovese, *Roll, Jordan, Roll*, 415, 419.

18. Johnson and Roark, *Black Masters*, passim.

19. Williamson, *New People*, 14, 56. For a nuanced history of the role of the mulatto elite in Reconstruction politics, see Holt, *Black Over White*.

20. By 1910, 426,449 black Southern farmers—nearly a quarter of all black agricultural workers—owned their own land; Loren Schweninger, *Black Property Owners in the South, 1790–1915* (Urbana: University of Illinois Press, 1990), 183–84; Robert Tracy McKenzie, "Freedmen and the Soil in the Upper South: The Reorganization of Tennessee Agriculture, 1865–1880," *Journal of Southern History* 59 (February 1993): 63–84. Schweninger and McKenzie explicitly argue that the freedmen gained a meaningful foothold on the soil. McKenzie furthermore describes the ways in which freedmen in Tennessee used the small acreages they purchased to maintain a significant degree of independence from external control.

21. Forrest Shivers, *The Land Between: A History of Hancock County, Georgia to 1940* (Spartanburg, S.C.: The Reprint Co., 1990). Hancock County holds a reputation among surrounding counties for having an unusually strong tradition of recognized interracial kinship. However, I believe that Hancock's experience of recognized interracial kinship is representative of much of the plantation belt. In my four years of conducting extensive oral interviews in Hancock, I have encountered evidence of similar kinship ties in five of the seven counties bordering on Hancock. For this essay, I tracked down a few of these interracial families to confirm that Hancock County is typical of the surrounding area. Hancock's reputation probably stems from the local fame of the will by which the region's richest planter, David Dickson, bequeathed his vast fortune to his "black" family. Dickson's celebrity, and the breathtaking completeness of his gift, turned a somewhat acceptable, quietly private exchange into an "embarrassing" public affair. On the public stage, a "kinship" issue was reconstructed as a "race" issue.

22. Alexander, *Ambiguous Lives*, passim.

23. Leslie, "Woman of Color, Daughter of Privilege"; interviews with Hancock

natives Frank Guill, Jr., Sparta, November, 1988; John Gaissert, Sparta, November, 1988; Clifford Smith and Eva Smith, rural Hancock, September 11, 1992.

24. Jonathan M. Bryant, "Race, Class and Law in Bourbon Georgia: The Case of David Dickson's Will," *Georgia Historical Quarterly* 71 (Summer 1987): 226–42. Amanda Dickson's husband, Nathan Toomer, was the father of Jean Toomer. Jean's mother, Nina Pinchback Toomer, was Nathan's second wife, who he married less than a year after Amanda's death in 1893. Leslie and Gatewood, " 'This Father of Mine . . . a Sort of Mystery,'" 826, 831–33.

25. Lester F. Russell, *Profile of a Black Heritage* (Franklin Square, N.Y.: Graphicopy, 1977), 16–33. Russell wrote the family history, based primarily on interviews with family members. See also Mark R. Schultz, "A More Satisfying Life on the Farm: Benjamin F. Hubert and the Log Cabin Community" (M.A. thesis, University of Georgia, 1989).

26. Russell, *Profile*, 37–49.

27. Ibid., 49–53; Deed Record U, 413–14, Sparta Court House, Hancock County.

28. Russell, *Profile*, passim; Hancock County Tax Digests, 1874–1960, Georgia Department of Archives and History, Atlanta; interviews with grandsons of Zach and Camilla Hubert: Willis Hubert, Springfield, Ga. (in Hancock), February, 1989; Wilson Hubert, Savannah, Ga., February, 1989.

29. Russell, *Profile*, 40, 60.

30. Schweninger, *Black Property Owners*.

31. The Dixon family history was written by a daughter of Gordon and Betsy Dixon, Mary J. Dixon Williams, *A Profile of the Dixon Family* (Smithtown, N.Y.: Exposition Press, 1980); "The Dixon Family Portrait (A Chapter)," brief family history written by family members for a family reunion, Springfield, August, 1992; Deed Record, Sparta Court House; Hancock County Tax Digest, 1874–1960; interviews with grandchildren of Gordon and Betsy Dixon: Samuel Williams, Springfield, many interviews, 1988–1992; Thomas Dixon, Springfield, August, 1992; Elizabeth Dixon Walker, Springfield, August, 1992.

32. Interview with Samuel Williams, Springfield, Ga., March 1989. While almost all my contacts for this study seemed willing to openly discuss their interracial heritage, a few requested anonymity. Many grandchildren and great-grandchildren of mixed couples indicated that some of the children of these couples had been noncommunicative about the details of their parents' relationship. When asked to interpret this silence, my contacts offered two different theories. First, it was regularly noted that in the rural South from 1890 to 1940, adults generally did not openly discuss certain personal issues in the presence of children. While most southern families had highly developed storytelling traditions involving events from the family history, certain areas—economic matters, or personal relations such as intrafamily conflict, conjugal relationships, and sexuality—were taboo subjects for children. When adults were talking "personal business," children often had to leave the room. From other interviews I have done, this observation seems to be generalizable throughout the area and not limited to interracial families.

Second, some informants speculated that their parents or grandparents were em-

barrassed by their interracial status because of the possibility that others might associate them with the "socially illegitimate" interracial children of white fathers who
did not claim their children.

The central thesis of Williamson's *New People* offers a third interpretation. Toward
the end of the nineteenth century, the self-conscious attempt by mulattoes to carve
a distinct intermediate racial status in America failed. Jim Crow legislation and "one
drop" definitions of race converged to redefine light-skinned African Americans as
simply "black." Gradually, mulatto people came to embrace an Afrocentric identity
for themselves. In the context of the changing meaning of African-American identity,
individuals whose immediate family tree included a European-American male might
have felt uncomfortable.

33. Davis, Gardner, and Gardner, *Deep South,* 38–39.

34. For a description of the challenges faced by the majority of freedmen in their
quest for land, see Gerald David Jaynes, *Branches without Roots: Genesis of the Black
Working Class in the American South, 1862–1882* (New York: Oxford University Press,
1986), and Roger L. Ransom and Richard Sutch, *One Kind of Freedom: The Economic
Consequences of Emancipation* (New York: Cambridge University Press, 1977). These
perceptions are also based on extensive interviews with black and white retired Hancock farmers of all types of land tenure, and on interviews with David Dyer, white
supervisor of agricultural extension in Hancock during the 1940s and 1950s, and with
Samuel Williams, colored agricultural extension agent during the same period.

35. Interview, Roy Roberts, Thomson, Ga., August 31, 1992.

36. Arthur Raper, *Preface to Peasantry: A Tale of Two Black Belt Counties* (Chapel
Hill: University of North Carolina Press, 1936), 121–24. See also Hortense Powder-
maker, *After Freedom: A Cultural Study in the Deep South* (1939; reprint, New York:
Atheneum, 1968), 96–97.

37. Hancock County Tax Digest, 1910. According to Schweninger, 1910 marked
the apogee of black landholding in America. At least one of these men, Julian Dickson,
and perhaps all, held property outside of Hancock.

38. Hancock County Tax Digest, 1920. Zach Hubert, described earlier, was the
ninth wealthiest black person in the county in 1920, with $6,310 in assets.

39. Hancock County Tax Digests, 1890, 1900. Johnson appeared in the 1890 digest
only for payment of the poll tax.

40. Interviews, Katie Hunt, Washington, D.C., August 1, 1992; James McMullen,
Sparta, September 11, 1992.

41. Interviews, Katie Hunt, Washington, D.C., August 1, 1992; Samuel Williams,
Springfield, August 1, 1992; Albert Ingram, rural Hancock, September 15, 1992;
Mariah Castleberry, Sherman Ingram's daughter, Springfield, September 15, 1992;
Arment Chatman, Sherman Ingram's granddaughter, Sparta, September 18, 1989.

42. Hancock County Tax Digest, 1900, 1910, 1920.

43. Interview, Katie Hunt, Washington, D.C., August 1, 1992.

44. Jonathan Bryant has discovered that many of the first wave of freedmen who
gained title to land in Greene County stayed near the planters who had been their

masters and with whom they generally shared last names. See Bryant, "'A County Where Plenty Should Abound': Race, Law, and Markets in Greene County, Georgia, 1850–1885" (Ph.D. diss., University of Georgia, 1993), chapter 6. This may indicate interracial kinship ties as well as paternalism. Further, when I have informally spoken with black and white natives of various rural communities in the Deep South about this study, they have frequently cited additional examples of socially recognized interracial kinship ties with which they were personally acquainted.

45. Interview, Hancock, identity withheld by request. Often known only to the parties involved, interracial kinship ties are difficult to reconstruct. While oral history often provides the only lens through which to view these interracial acts of assistance, the time is rapidly passing in which it can be used. Even now the roots of the Deep South's rural black middle class lie in the shadowy field between memory and forgetting.

46. Interviews, Della May Flagg, rural Hancock County, September 1, 1992; Obilee Rhodes, Jr., August 31, 1992.

47. Letter published in the New Orleans *Times-Democrat*, June 21, 1907, reprinted in Ray Stannard Baker, *Following the Color Line: American Negro Citizenship in the Progressive Era* (New York: Doubleday, Page, 1908), 166.

48. Edith Maxey Clarke, *The Maxeys of Virginia: A Genealogical History of the Descendants of Edward and Suzannah Maxey* (Baltimore: Gateway Press, 1980), 796–98; Jasper County Wills, Book 14, 273–74; Jasper County Census Manuscript, 1870. My thanks to Kathleen Conzen for informing me of Maxey.

49. Durham was born in 1862, Mason in 1864. Interviews with Laramon Durham, grandson of Sam Durham and Sarah Mason, Winterville, Ga., March 11, 1993 and March 16, 1993; Durham had spent several years living with his aunt, Queene Mason, next door to his grandfather; Charles H. Calhoun, Sr., "Dr. Lindsey Durham: A Brief Biography" and "The Durham Doctors: Biographical Sketches," 1965, privately published manuscript in possession of the author; will of Sam Durham, Oglethorpe County Record of Wills, 1-G, 14–15 and Oglethorpe County Deed Record, WW, 575–76, and SS, 92, Oglethorpe County Courthouse, Lexington, Ga.; Oglethorpe County Tax Digest, 1920 and 1930, Georgia Department of Archives and History. My thanks to Jonathan Bryant for suggesting that I talk to Mr. Durham.

Due to Georgia state law, children of unmarried couples were unable to inherit property from their fathers. Additionally, the state forbade interracial marriages. As a result, white fathers of "black" children usually had to find ways to circumvent the law in order to transfer property to their children. *The Code of the State of Georgia*, 4th ed. (Atlanta: Jas. P. Harrison, 1882), 393, 418.

50. Sarah Brinkley was born in 1866, eight years after Greene Dickson. Sarah's mother, Malisee B. Brinkley, worked as the live-in cook for widower James Dickson and his five children, including David and Greene. Sarah therefore grew up in the same house as the Dicksons. Interviews, Clifford Smith, rural Hancock, December 1988 and August 10, 1992; Eva Smith, granddaughter of Greene Dickson, rural Hancock, August 10, 1992; Hancock County Census Manuscript, 1880, 1900.

51. By describing the mechanisms by which land passed from "white" men to their "black" children, I am by no means celebrating the relationships linking the Dickson men with their women and children. For the purpose of this essay, the only relevant question is whether or not kinship-based relationships to the Dickson men economically benefited some of their descendants. They did.

52. Frank Guill was born in 1875, Pearl Gordon in 1885. Interviews, Nancy Alma Jackson, oldest child of Frank and Pearl Guill, Sparta, August 28, 1992, and Frank Guill, Jr., rural Hancock, November 1988; Hancock County Tax Digest, 1874, 1878, 1891, 1900, 1910, 1920, 1930.

53. Interviews, Frank Guill, Jr., rural Hancock, November, 1988; Nancy Alma Jackson, Sparta, August 28, 1992; Edgar Guill, rural Hancock, August 27, 1992.

54. Soldiers Discharge Record 2, Hancock County Courthouse, Sparta; Interview, Benjamin Alexander Glascoe, grandson of Frank and Pearl Guill, rural Hancock, August 28, 1992.

55. Interview with Laramon Durham, grandson of Sam Durham and Sarah B. Mason, Winterville, Ga., March 16, 1993.

56. Interview, Katie Hunt, Washington, D.C., September 12, 1992.

57. Interview with Grover Hill, grandson of David and Elvira Hill, rural Baldwin County, January 7, 1993; Baldwin County Tax Digest, 1880–1900; Baldwin County Census Manuscript, 1900; Will of David B. Hill and Petition to have title executed, Superior Court, Baldwin County, Milledgeville, Ga.

58. Ellis served as a private in the Fifty-seventh Regiment of the Georgia Volunteer Infantry of the Army of Tennessee from May 10, 1862, until his capture on May 16, 1863; Lillian Henderson, ed., *Roster of the Confederate Soldiers of Georgia, 1861–1865*, vol. 5 (Hapeville, Ga.: Longino and Porter, 1960), 997.

59. Interviews with Otilia Edwards, family historian and great-granddaughter of Joshua Ellis and Charity Ingram, and with Richard Edwards, great-great-grandson of Ellis and Ingram, rural Baldwin County, January 21, 1993; Baldwin County Tax Digest, 1880–1900; Baldwin County Census Manuscript, 1900.

60. Will of Joshua Ellis and Petition to have title executed, Superior Court, Baldwin County, Milledgeville. Interviews, Otilia Edwards and Richard Edwards.

61. Blassingame, *Black New Orleans*, 209.

62. While no complete study of the dynamics of segregation as experienced in rural areas is available, the growing number of autobiographies of rural Southerners relate many incidents that highlight the ambiguous tension between regional racial ideology and local practice. See for example Rosengarten, *All God's Dangers;* Maguire, *On Shares;* Louise Westling, ed., *He Included Me: The Autobiography of Sarah Rice* (Athens: University of Georgia Press, 1989); Andrews, *Last Radio Baby.* See also Jacqueline Jones, "Encounters, Likely and Unlikely, between Black and Poor White Women in the Rural South, 1865–1940," *Georgia Historical Quarterly* 76 (Summer, 1992): 333–53; and the chapter entitled "Black and White, Distance and Propinquity," in Jack Temple Kirby, *Rural Worlds Lost: The American South, 1920–1960* (Baton Rouge: Louisiana State University Press, 1987).

The historiography of segregation indicates that the peculiar racial separation of public spaces was a phenomenon that expanded over space and time, as C. Vann Woodward first argued in *The Strange Career of Jim Crow* (New York: Oxford University Press, 1955). It began in the urban North (Leon Litwack, *North of Slavery: The Negro in the Free States, 1790–1860* [Chicago: University of Chicago Press, 1961]); proceeded to the urban South (Howard Rabinowitz, *Race Relations in the Urban South* [New York: Oxford University Press, 1978]); and moved into southern towns (John Cell, *The Highest Stage of White Supremacy: The Origins of Segregation in South Africa and the American South* [New York: Cambridge University Press, 1982]) and to a lesser degree into rural areas.

63. McFeely, *Frederick Douglass*, 5.

64. Localism rising from rural isolation is one of the central themes of William A. Link, *The Paradox of Southern Progressivism, 1880–1930* (Chapel Hill: University of North Carolina Press, 1992.) The history of interracial kinship ties also might be reconciled with the vast historiography describing violent white southern resistance to miscegenation through the use of Joel Williamson's theories of multiple white southern racial agendas or by David Potter's concept of southern "personalism." Williamson, *Crucible of Race: Black/White Relations in the American South Since Emancipation* (New York: Oxford University Press, 1984); David Potter, *The South and the Sectional Conflict* (Baton Rouge: Louisiana State University Press, 1968), 17–19. Note especially how personalism is used in Johnson and Roark, *No Chariot Let Down*, 10–15.

65. Jules was born in 1853, Louisiana in 1862. Their first child, Maud, was born in 1879.

66. *Tax Digest*, 1874, 1900, 1910; "The Skrine Roots," brief family history written by family members for a reunion, August 12, 1978; interviews, Lillie Parrish, West Palm Beach, Fla., September 10, 1992; Lucius Skrine, Springfield, Ga., August 29, 1992. All interviewees from the Skrine family are grandchildren of Jules and Louisiana.

67. Interview, Nina Ruth Howard, New York, September 9, 1992.

68. Interviews, Lucius Skrine, Springfield, Ga., August 29, 1992; Willie B. Skrine, Siloam, Ga., September 11, 1992; Gaston Skrine, Washington, D.C., September 11, 1992.

69. First quote, Willie B. Skrine, Siloam, Ga., September 1, 1992; second quote, Gaston Skrine, Washington, D.C., September 11, 1992; "The Skrine Roots."

70. Interview, Gaston Skrine, Washington, D.C., September 11, 1992.

71. Interracial kinship ties cannot be explained through the category of gender as merely a manifestation of interracial patriarchy. The "black" daughters of white men seemed to benefit materially from their interracial kinship ties. David Dickson, for example, bequeathed the majority of his estate to his daughter, Amanda America Dickson, and not to his two grandsons, although they were adults at the time. Similarly, the Hill and Ellis estates were divided among all the children, regardless of gender. The Durham estate was pointedly split between two daughters, leaving the sons completely out.

72. Baker, *Following the Color Line*, 164–66; Dollard, *Caste and Class*, 61–63, 134–72; Powdermaker, *After Freedom*, 96–97; Davis, Gardner, and Gardner, *Deep South*, 24–48, 244–48, 297–98, 406–8; Maurice R. Stein, *The Eclipse of Community: An Interpretation of American Studies* (Princeton: Princeton University Press, 1972).

73. In many different historical contexts, individuals have secured assistance in pursuing upward mobility for themselves or their children by developing kinship ties with an individual of higher socioeconomic status. This pattern has generally held throughout the Americas and Europe (as well as in Islamic cultures worldwide). Like many other people, African Americans have sometimes been the beneficiaries of upward-reaching interracial kinship ties. Sometimes, just as unremarkably, they have extended assistance through kinship ties to members of less advantaged groups. Near the turn of the twentieth century, W. E. B. Du Bois in Philadelphia and Ray Stannard Baker in Boston discovered that the vast majority of interracial marriages occurred between European-American immigrant women and more economically secure native African-American men. W. E. B. Du Bois, *The Philadelphia Negro: A Social Study* (Philadelphia: University of Pennsylvania, 1899), 361–66; Baker, *Following the Color Line*, 172.

"Some Women Have Never Been Reconstructed"

Mildred Lewis Rutherford,
Lucy M. Stanton, and the Racial Politics
of White Southern Womanhood,
1900–1930

Grace Elizabeth Hale

In the late nineteenth and early twentieth centuries, the American South experienced a profound identity crisis. Through economic exploitation and violent oppression, southern whites attempted to crush black southerners' explorations of the meaning of freedom. Yet deciding what type of society would be needed to maintain white supremacy did not settle the broader question that haunted white southerners: what, after defeat, occupation, and economic integration, would be the meaning of southern power in the future? As southerners struggled to articulate a present by arguing about their region's past, determining the meaning of race came to shape their visions of the future. In the first three decades of the twentieth century, two southern white women living in Athens, Georgia attempted to come to terms with these years of deep cultural confusion. Their vastly different representations of self and region reveal some of the complex connections between race and gender in the New South. Mildred L. Rutherford's speeches, pamphlets, and books and Lucy M. Stanton's paintings demonstrate the contradictory results of attempts to redraw the lines of gender difference in a region obsessed with race.

On the night of November 14, 1912, an expectant crowd packed the ballroom of the New Willard Hotel in Washington, D.C. A large woman, her grey hair piled high, her long skirt reminiscent of the style popular a century before, rose from her table and climbed the speaker's platform. The chattering laughter of renewed friendships stopped, and the women focused their attention on the featured speaker. Mildred Lewis Rutherford was not nervous. She had addressed many groups before in her various activities in her hometown of Athens, Georgia—the Ladies Memorial Association, women's groups at the First Baptist Church, the Daughters of the American Revolution, and the local and state divisions of the United Daughters of the Confederacy (UDC)—and had faced large crowds as vice-president of the national YMCA and a member of the National Board of Health two years earlier. Rutherford wore fresh flowers for inspiration, as always; their presence on her lapel seemed to strengthen her voice.[1]

Yet this night marked a turning point for the sixty-one year old "Miss Millie," as she was known to her friends, because she would speak here for the first time as historian general of the UDC, a group she would lead as historian general and then honorary president until her death in 1928. Resplendent in the costume of the Old South, she argued in a speech entitled "The South in the Building of the Nation" against the transformation of her region into anything "new": "There is no new South. The South of today is the South of yesterday remade to fit the new order of things. And the men of today and the women of today are readjusting themselves to the old South remade."[2] For Rutherford, the "new order of things" meant white southerners would simply rebuild what they had lost. War and Reconstruction had shattered an ordered way of life in which she had found security as a child, and like many southerners she believed what had changed was the meaning of race. The Confederate soldier, she said, "was compelled to establish the supremacy of the white man in the South." Since he was defeated, she implied, the men and women of "the old South remade" must take up the cause. For Rutherford, the breakdown of the South's racial order was the cause of postwar problems, and southern women had a vital role to play in restoring their homeland's past glory. In Rutherford's representations of self and region, the "Old South" was more than the southern past: it was her template for the southern future. Already a teacher, author, historian, and activist, as an "exponent of southern culture" Miss Millie had found her stage.[3]

That same fall another southern white woman seemed much less sure

Mildred Lewis Rutherford in lecture costume.
From *Four Addresses by Miss Mildred Lewis Rutherford
of Athens, Georgia* (Birmingham, Ala.: Mildred Rutherford
Historical Circle, 1916).

about both the place of white women in southern society and the meaning of the "New South." At the age of thirty-seven, Lucy M. Stanton did not wear a costume or address a large crowd. Her platform instead was the small wooden building, set far back on a wooded lot on Cobb Street in Athens, that served as both her painting studio and her home. Having just finished a cup of Souchong tea and a chat about suffrage with a young woman who had come to sit for her portrait, Stanton hurried to complete her uncommissioned work by the last sunlight streaming through her large north window. Her dress was more practical than stylish, more loose-fitting than flattering. Warmed by the heat of her primitive fireplace, her brown hair pulled back and her blue eyes sparkling, Stanton bent over her workboard in intense concentration. She wanted to finish the portrait of a local African-American man before dark.[4]

Her native region, she had written in her diary two years earlier, was the inspiration for her art: "The desire to interpret in paint and color the traditions of the South have, in some cases, overbalanced the obstacles . . . the universal is more easily seen through the deeply rooted local. . . . The South is virgin soil as far as interpretation in terms of paint is concerned. The things have never been painted before, never been seen before."[5] As with Rutherford, race was central to Stanton's conceptions of regional and personal identity. The South that "had never been seen before" was most often for Stanton the African-American community: "Here we have the life of this people, the bare dramatic facts of which have never been painted."[6] For Stanton, who grew to adulthood during the social and cultural confusion of the late nineteenth century, however, the southern future seemed unclear. While Rutherford attempted to impose on the present the order she found in the past through a rhetoric of white supremacy, Stanton revealed a much more confused sense of the past and present in her images. Through her paintings and her work as a suffragist, peace activist, and teacher, she tried to construct a decidedly different "New South," an alternative to the "old South remade" promoted by women like Rutherford. While for "Miss Millie" southern culture provided a stage and the southern "lady" a voice, for Lucy Stanton the South was a living canvas that her role as an elite white woman did not always prepare her to paint. Her paintings of African Americans and southern white women represented her response, a creative southern woman's ongoing attempt to find meaning in the chaos.[7]

Although they lived much of their lives in the same small college town in northeast Georgia, Mildred L. Rutherford and Lucy M. Stanton were different in many ways. Not quite ten years old when the Civil War began, Rutherford belonged to an older generation of white women than Stanton, who was born in 1875, ten years after the war had ended. "Miss Millie" also represented a different elite. In the late nineteenth and early twentieth centuries, elite status in the South existed in what might be described as a "doubled" class system. Antebellum elites often retained their power socially and culturally, even when the economic and political power that undergirded their position had given way. A new system of class relations, however, developed in the cities, often existing alongside or merging with older hierarchies. In Georgia, whose capital, Atlanta, was the self-pronounced center of the "New South," the existence of a "doubled" elite was especially pronounced.[8]

Rutherford's family had held a prominent position in the antebellum elite —her maternal uncles were the prominent slaveholders and Confederate leaders Thomas R. R. Cobb and Howell Cobb—and so her class position was based in the southern past, her security the result of family history as much as current financial standing. Unlike Rutherford, however, Stanton grew up in Atlanta and moved to Athens later, as a young woman. Her parents were members of the new southern urban elite that arose as cities like Atlanta became railroad centers in the flow of southern raw materials northward and northern manufactured goods southward. This new urban elite was highly unstable, struggling amid the financial shocks and political upheavals of the 1890s to consolidate its power. When her father suffered a financial and emotional collapse in 1895, Stanton's fragile place within the southern elite vanished. Only twenty years old, she did retain one important aspect of that elite status, however: her education.[9]

Despite their status as members of different generations and elites, Rutherford and Stanton received very similar educations in how to be southern "ladies." Indeed, the new urban elite may have hoped to acquire the status of the old elite by mimicking the gender conventions that had been such a vital component of antebellum southern culture. Both women learned how to be the "queen of the home," a "submissive," "innocent," "self-denying" being who needed men's protection yet nevertheless held responsibility for the difficult tasks of managing the household and bringing up the children. Education reinforced an image of white women as strong and capable, yet subservient to their men, an image rooted also in southern religion and kinship.[10] Interestingly, both Rutherford's and Stanton's families organized schools for women, and thus in their families kinship and education were literally intertwined. Both women attended and later taught at these female academies. "Miss Millie," in fact, spent most of her life at the Lucy Cobb Institute in Athens, serving as principal, president, and director. Stanton attended the Southern Baptist College for Women in Atlanta, founded by her father, and later served briefly as assistant art director after her stepmother's family assumed control of the school.[11]

Both the Lucy Cobb Institute and the Southern Baptist College were founded on the assumption that "the female mind is susceptible of the highest state of cultivation."[12] Yet while the pursuit of knowledge was certainly important, these academies celebrated their graduates for their social graces, not scholarly excellence. The "lady" was to be educated to help her husband, and the letter that prompted the founding of Lucy Cobb stated this purpose clearly: "we . . . contend that the more learned and better informed, the more capable and better fitted will they be for fitting their allotted stations in society. What man would object that his helpmate should be able to appreciate and understand—aye; even be able to assist him, if need be, in his various duties?"[13] These educators of southern white women, and by implication many parents, saw the ability to "turn labor into money" as a last resort in times of hardship and not as an additional, even desired skill for white women. Education and the attainment of skills became more important as the realities of poverty and the death of a generation of elite white men left many elite women "without anyone to depend on."[14] Yet self-support was not supposed to mean a career. Rutherford and Stanton, along with other women of their generations, would have to struggle against the belief that the life of a single woman was void of meaning, although their strategies for providing that meaning would be very different.

Rutherford and Stanton, then, received similar educations and faced similar restrictions as they tried to live independent lives in the early-twentieth-century South. By 1905, they had both settled permanently in Athens. Rutherford had only left the town of her birth briefly, to work as a teacher in Atlanta. Stanton, on the other hand, had come to visit her sister Willie in 1902 and fallen for the small-town charm, "what I do not find in Atlanta, a thoroughly congenial atmosphere," and inexpensive living of the small university town. Yet despite being trained to assume dependent positions within southern society, neither Rutherford nor Stanton ever married. Both women, then, occupied similar places as single white women in the Athens community of the time. Both sought, whether consciously or not, to endow this space with meaning. Between 1900 and 1930, each reached the peak of her career, Rutherford as a historian, writer, and UDC organizer and Stanton as a painter. Struggling to come to terms with the instability of their identities as southern white women, Rutherford and Stanton often used conceptions of race to articulate their notions of self and region. Their differing responses, perhaps extreme, reveal the ways white southern racism could both empower and constrain southern white women and in either case considerably narrow the range of options available to them in the early twentieth century.[15]

As historian general of the United Daughters of the Confederacy, Mildred Rutherford found a voice as an exponent of the "Lost Cause" and an audience for her many books, pamphlets, and articles on southern history and literature and the South in general. For her that "Cause"—the South's ability to preserve and even recreate its distinctive society and culture—was anything but lost. How would the South, then, know its "true" past amid the shame and renunciation of defeat, reconstruction, and reconciliation? Here Rutherford envisioned an important role for southern white women: "I am here tonight, Daughters, yes, Daughters of Confederate heroes, to plead with you, to urge you to a more aggressive and progressive campaign in collecting this [southern] history."[16] As the collectors of southern history and the keepers of southern culture, southern women were vital to ensuring that remaking did not ever again become reconstructing. Yet Rutherford did not see this task as any challenge to the traditional role of the southern lady. "Now you say, 'What can we do?' What can we do? Anything in the world we wish to do. If there is a power that is placed in any hands, it is the power that is placed in the Southern woman in her home!"[17]

Southern white women would simply do collectively what they had been accomplishing individually all along. From reproducing the family they would join hands to reproduce the region. Far from challenging southern gender relations, white women would help reconstruct the entire fabric of antebellum social relations by promoting the ideology of white supremacy. And they would begin creating the "old South remade" by giving their region and themselves a proper history. Rutherford had no doubts about their abilities, a power "great enough to direct legislative bodies and that, too, without demanding the ballot!"[18]

Yet Mildred Rutherford did not just ask other white women, other "daughters," to collect southern history. She immersed herself in this seemingly daunting task; for her it was a logical extension of the elite white woman's role as the keeper of family history. Rutherford's ability to construct a more public role for herself as a promoter of southern culture, however, depended on her accepting limits, on her knowing not to step outside gendered boundaries. In order to develop a role for white women that expanded rather than overturned her region's conservative ideology of womanhood, Rutherford accepted the futility of direct public challenges to white male power. She also embraced white supremacy and, with it, southern racism.[19]

In speeches, pamphlets, and issues of her journal, the *Mildred Rutherford*

Historical Circle, Rutherford expressed a belief in white supremacy extreme even for the Deep South in the early twentieth century. History, for Rutherford, was "getting the truth," and the central truth of southern history was white supremacy.[20] She excused the racial violence perpetrated by the southern white man in the speech she gave before the UDC convention on November 14, 1912: "He was compelled to establish the political supremacy of the white man in the South! So, too, the Ku Klux Klan was a necessity at that time and there can be no reproach to the men of the South for resorting to the expedient."[21] In a speech she gave at a later UDC Convention in 1914, Rutherford again used the need to establish white supremacy as an excuse for the Klan's violence: "The Ku Klux Klan was an absolute necessity in the South at this time. This Order was not composed of the 'riff raff' as has been represented in history, but the very flower of Southern manhood. The chivalry of the South demanded protection for the women and children of the South."[22] Though Rutherford never openly embraced lynching as did the more infamous Rebecca Felton, she tapped the resonance of this widespread, violent practice by invoking its predominate justification, the protection of white womanhood. For these spectacles of violence in the name of white women functioned as the terrorist arm of the ideology of white supremacy, an ideology that Rutherford promoted in all of her speeches and writings. Though too much of a "lady" to promote violence directly, she had no difficulty excusing men's participation in activities that furthered her goals. And lynching affirmed in blood a white unity that Rutherford promoted in her own work.[23]

Rutherford's representations of white women and African Americans, then, took place in a society in which the meanings of gender and race were violently intertwined. Just as she excused racial violence because it furthered white unity, however, she never challenged the ideology of white womanhood that devalued her own position as a single white woman. The "lady" was integral to the unified, ordered white world of her southern past. Thus Rutherford never issued a direct public challenge to white male power. She would not abandon "the power that is placed in the Southern woman in her home" for an "unladylike" attempt to exercise political power by demanding the vote. In an article in the *Athens Banner* called "What Would Our Grandmothers Have Done If Faced with the Problems of the Present Days?" she stated that "the history of the women of the South since Jamestown was opposed to woman suffrage" and that "the ballot is politics and women should stay out of politics."[24] She participated in antisuffrage activities and gave a speech in 1915 to the Anti-Suffrage League in Macon entitled "With the Influence She Possesses, Why Should a Woman Want to Vote?" That same year she spoke before the Georgia House of Representatives, declaring that in "the glare of public life" the woman has become "an unsexed mongrel, shorn of her true power and vainly beating against the air in dissatisfaction with herself." The "woman politician" was not an "object of adoration . . . nor has suffrage brought improvement to the homes."[25] The southern lady already possessed a more important strength; she just needed to realize where her advantage lay: "Politics are not refining, not uplifting, and Southern men would save their women from practical politics. But some are tired of the pedestal that privileges confer, not content with laws already favorable to them, but long for the limelight, for hustings, for things unfeminine."[26] And the "influence women already possessed," the privileges that conferred the pedestal, was based in the white woman's race.

Thus, for Mildred Rutherford racial violence and the ideology of white supremacy both functioned to preserve the foundation of southern society, white unity. Her opposition to suffrage was less a denouncement of independent women than a measure of her support for a static vision of the southern society and culture. Rutherford represented an "Old South" in which order and happiness reigned. In a speech given in Dallas in 1916, she quoted Henry Grady: "The civilization of the Old South has never been surpassed, and perhaps will never again be equaled by any people or nation upon the globe."[27] The "Old South remade," then, must not relinquish, for any goal, the states' rights for which the men of the Old South fought and died. In a speech entitled "Georgia's Great Men," Rutherford declared, "early take a stand, young men, against the peril that is threatening us." She continued: "If we today yield our states rights, whether for National prohibition or for National Woman Suffrage or for any other cause . . . while our negro population is so great, yes greater in Georgia today than in all of the New England States and Northern states combined, we will have a Reconstruction Period worse than that which followed the War Between the States."[28] To avoid a "second Reconstruction," the place of women, as well as that of African Americans, must remain unchanged.[29]

Rutherford saw no place in her "Old South remade" for the "New Negro." She most often represented her vision of the past as her model for the future by celebrating the "happy darkies of old." In many other speeches, Rutherford stressed the positive influences of slavery on the slaves and the exhausting responsibility of slaveholders: "Under the institution of slavery the negro was the free man and the slaveholder was the slave."[30] Before, she insisted, "Africans" were "savage," "without thought of clothes," "sometimes cannibals," and men "bowing down to fetishes." Under slavery, however, "they were the happiest set of people on the face of the globe—free from care or thought of food, clothes, home, or religious privileges."[31] According to Rutherford, "no higher compliment was ever paid the institution of slavery than by the North, which was willing to make the negro its social and political equal after one hundred years of civilization under Southern Christianizing influence."[32]

White southerners, she implied, were less generous in assessing their own influence. The Civil War, Rutherford knew, despite her speech to the contrary, had settled the issue of states' rights. How, then, would the South avoid this racial peril? On what foundation would the white supremacist state stand now that the political realm could no longer be depended on to ensure the racial hierarchy?[33] Mildred Rutherford's speeches and writings suggested a broader, more secure base for white supremacy in the "old South remade." Southern history and culture must be consciously preserved for this purpose, and women's position as the keepers of that history would move the base of white supremacy out of politics and into the family. Deepened by a past, strong in its base in the white southern home, the ideology of white supremacy would permeate all aspects of southern life.

White unity based on a distinctive southern history, however, required that the meanings of both womanhood and blackness remain the same. Paradoxically, though she never challenged directly the ideology of the "lady," Rutherford in fact lived an independent life and enjoyed real power and prestige within southern society. She wrote twenty-nine books and pamphlets, besides compiling the bimonthly issues of the *Mildred Rutherford Historical Circle*, which she published for over three years. Her books, like *American Authors* and *The South in History and Literature*, were used in colleges and schools throughout the region. And as historian general of the UDC she often spoke to large crowds in cities across the country. Rutherford, however, consciously cultivated a self-effacing attitude. In true form she publicly declined five invitations to speak at Confederate Memorial Day celebrations on April 26, 1914, declaring that as long as a single Confederate veteran survived to make an address, she would not take the podium. Yet despite her earlier comments, when the day of celebration came, Rutherford spoke at the University Chapel in Athens.[34]

Mildred Rutherford, then, constructed a strong public role for herself and was still considered a southern lady. Indeed, a large gap existed between her rhetoric and her life. Her speeches, delivered to large crowds but insisting that the lady's place was in the home, provided only the most visible example. Equally incongruous was her close social and business relationship with her niece, Lamar Rutherford Libscomb. As a member of the Equal Suffrage Party of Georgia and the editor and owner of a newspaper, Libscomb was among the foremost of Georgia's "New Women." [35]

For Rutherford, acceptance of the ideology of southern white womanhood provided a cover for her delicate questioning of the strength of southern men. She wisely realized that she could influence southern men not by confronting them directly but by subtly interrogating their "manliness." In a speech given in New Orleans at the 1912 UDC convention, Rutherford suggested that, in distinct contrast to the actions of men, after the war "those women of the Confederacy showed of what stuff they were made. They put their loving arms about those husbands and sons and they said, 'We are not conquered, we are just overpowered. . . .'" These women then began to erect monuments to the Confederate soldiers, but the men did not help them: "The men said, 'We cannot help you, for we are under oath of allegiance.' The women said, 'We are under no oath' and the work went on. . . . They did not know Southern women." With almost imperceptible condescension, she excused the men while celebrating the women: "It was very hard for our Southern men unused to manual labor of any kind to try to adjust themselves to the new order of things in the South. It really was easier for the women than for the men, and some men never did get adjusted, and some women have never been reconstructed." If "it was harder to live after the war than it was to face the bullets on the battlefield," the women, in Rutherford's mind, showed the greater courage and strength. Thus, instead of challenging the meaning of womanhood, Rutherford attempted to impose her female standard of commitment on southern white men.[36]

Yet if "unreconstructed women" could not or would not challenge southern gender ideology, then where did they find their strength? The answer lay within that other southern orthodoxy, the ideology of race. The doctrine of white supremacy was subtly contradictory: if whites were overwhelmingly superior to blacks, an ideology of gender that made white women inferior became highly unstable. As white southerners became increasingly obsessed with race as the organizing factor in southern society and culture, gender could no longer function as it had in the antebellum South. The "power of the southern woman in her home," then, was not as much about gender as about race. Rutherford did not find her autonomy upon the "lady's" pedestal. Her strength was supported by a pedestal not of dependence but of power, her place as a white woman in a society in which blackness was the overwhelming signifier of weakness. After Rutherford's speech in Savannah in November

1914, the *Athens Herald* quoted a "well known and popular man of Athens": "If she were a man she would be president of the United States . . . she is the greatest woman in the state."[37]

But she did not need to be a man. By promoting white supremacy and the superiority of the white race, Rutherford narrowed the distance between white men and women and gained access to white male power. When she died in 1928, loyal readers and fellow UDC members throughout the country mourned the loss of this great lady, an unlikely but clear example of the new autonomous southern woman.

Lucy M. Stanton, on the other hand, seemed much more aware of the contradictions of southern womanhood, the problematic nature of founding a female autonomy in a "home" in which women were dependent: "No harm comes to a good girl from contact with men in coeducational colleges or from living and working in ateliers in Paris and like experiences. There she is on her metal. . . . It is when in the shelter of her family, off her guard, and listening perhaps to their advice and entreaty that she comes to harm. There perchance she sells her birthright for peace; there she lays down her ideals for others of their choosing."[38] For Stanton, the sheltered life of the southern lady did not always provide security: "protection" sometimes failed. Could southern women, then, trust in an identity as a "lady," a class and race position defined and defended by men? A woman could be destroyed by her family as easily as by the larger world. How could she depend, as Rutherford suggested, on "the power that is placed in the Southern woman in her home"?

Although war disrupted Rutherford's happy childhood, the economic, racial, and political turbulence of the late nineteenth-century South only added to the more personal pain of Stanton's young life. Stanton's family offered her little security as a child. In 1888, when Lucy was thirteen, her invalid mother finally died, causing her father to sell her childhood home and send her beloved African-American nurse Chloe away. Her father later had an emotional and financial breakdown. Stanton's experience, then, suggested that the home was not secure, that "protection" could be a sham, and that the men on whom a "lady" depended could fail. She experienced life as a southern lady differently than Rutherford, as confined by the desire of men rather than as empowered by the place of women in the family: "What our intellectual men want are women with minds, high ideals of courage and honor and truth—wise women. What these men think they want are women with, as they express it, a freshness of charm. This freshness of charm is really ignorance of life and no thoughtful man should want an ignorant woman. No strongly womanly woman can be sullied by contact with life."[39] Stanton did

Lucy M. Stanton.
Lucy M. Stanton Papers, Hargrett Rare Book and
Manuscript Library, University of Georgia Libraries.

not believe that "ignorance of life" could ever be empowering. If for Rutherford the home provided access to an important role in southern society as a
"lady," for Stanton this space meant restriction, being cut off from the very
world in which women could find their own strength.[40]

Yet Lucy Stanton was also determined to find her place in the South. While
Rutherford represented her visions of an "old South remade" through her
histories, Stanton created her vision of a new South in her paintings. Rutherford might not have realized how much these histories revealed about herself,
but Stanton wrote in her diary about the creation of identity through art: "At
no point of his work does the artist so reveal himself as he does at this point
when he chooses the elements for his picture. . . . A painting is the thought
of the painter applied to nature . . . the painter employs . . . synthesis, con-
structing out of those elements he has selected a new whole, which is his very
own."[41] In her paintings, Stanton tested other identities for her region and
her self. There, she created a new whole. And her representations were dif-

Lucy M. Stanton, *Linton Ingrahm, Ex-slave.*
Watercolor on ivory, 1925. Museum of the
American China Trade, Milton, Massachusetts.

ferent from the vision of white supremacy Rutherford described. In a region
obsessed with race, then, Stanton's paintings of African Americans provided
an alternative picture of southern culture.

In 1925, Lucy M. Stanton had temporarily moved her studio to Boston to
study and seek the commissions that had vanished in the economically de-
pressed South. There she met and befriended an older black man who was the
owner of a profitable Boston business. He often visited Stanton in her studio,
where he enjoyed discussing with a fellow Georgia native both the southern
past and its rapidly changing present. In her studio on Beacon Hill, Stanton painted his portrait, *Linton Ingrahm, Ex-slave.* Ingrahm seemed serene—
he was at ease in Stanton's presence—and yet slightly amused; he understood the irony of having his portrait painted by a southern white woman.
Sitting in a Chippendale chair, he wore a gold watch and a ring and a light
suit strangely reminiscent of the kind worn by plantation owners. He appeared, perhaps, more southern than his former masters; he was a gentleman

Lucy M. Stanton, *Uncle George.* Watercolor on ivory,
1916. Lucy M. Stanton Collection, Special Collections,
Robert W. Woodruff Library, Emory University.

and carried the responsibility of his success comfortably, though not lightly.
Stanton's portrait depicted a secure, successful man.[42]

Yet significantly, this scene did not take place in the South, for Stanton and
Ingrahm's relationship went beyond the conventions of traditional southern
social roles. Having left the Old South before the war, Ingrahm knew that a
successful African-American businessman would also have difficulty, in the
1920s, living in most communities in the self-proclaimed New South. He
certainly would not be invited to call at white southerners' houses, though he
comfortably visited the studio that also served as Stanton's home. By portray-
ing Ingrahm in the convention of the southern gentleman, Stanton provided
another version of southern social relations. In Stanton's vision of the South,
a southern woman could also be a successful artist and activist. Why, then,
could not an African-American man be a southern gentleman?

Earlier, in 1916, the possibilities for change in the nature of southern race relations had seemed grim. Stanton spent the winter of 1915–16 in Athens in her sister Willie Forbes's home. There she painted a portrait entitled *Uncle George*, the image of the black man who remained in the South and who could never be a gentleman. Although about the same age as Linton Ingrahm and an ex-slave as well, George had none of Ingrahm's comfortable self-confidence. He also lacked, at least in this painting, a last name. Uneasy in the Forbes's living room, which temporarily served as Stanton's studio, he preferred to sit far from the window in the dark corner by the stove. The painting reflected its shadowy setting, the dark figure posed on a dark background. "Uncle" George bore the pain of a man who had been slave, then free, then "Uncle" again. Yet Stanton's painting presented more than a stereotypical picture of the black man as victim. Though slumped in his chair and looking down, George did not relax but continued to push upward against the image that constrained him. Stanton brilliantly captured the tension of George's struggle to retain his dignity. A dab of turquoise paint, seemingly out of place on his lapel, provided the only bright spot. The intensity of the purple background, however, threatened to overwhelm this crack in George's mask, just as southern racism often crushed African Americans' hopes for freedom.[43]

Lucy Stanton never found a southern Linton Ingrahm. In 1920, when she began painting her *Southern Historical Series*, the best representation of the place of blacks in southern society that Stanton could provide were idealized portraits of African-American men and women workers. *Working on the Street* was part of this series of pictures of the southern black community, a set of five paintings called the *Little Murals*. Stanton's answer, then, to the racial unrest and the reemergence of the Klan in the early 1920s was to celebrate rather than to challenge the place southern conservatives allowed blacks to hold in postbellum southern society. This image, though hardly progressive, was a part of the attack southern liberals and conservatives made on the radical racism that violently inscribed black exclusion on the very bodies of the African Americans being lynched and raped in this period. Significantly, Stanton could not paint a South in which racial equality even seemed possible.[44]

Lucy M. Stanton, then, was much less sure about the South's triumphant white supremacy, less convinced that radical racists like Rutherford had solved the meaning of race. While Rutherford remembered and to a great extent created a past of southern exceptionalism founded in racial hierarchy, Stanton recalled a childhood of loss, uprootedness, and pain. For Stanton, unlike Rutherford, had no direct experience of the "mythical" good life of the Old South. Instead, she grew to adulthood during the chaotic decades of the

Lucy M. Stanton, *Working on the Street.*
Watercolor on ivory, 1921. Lucy M. Stanton Collection, Special Collections,
Robert W. Woodruff Library, Emory University.

Lucy M. Stanton, *Chloe.* Watercolor on ivory, 1925.
Lucy M. Stanton Collection, Special Collections,
Robert W. Woodruff Library, Emory University.

late nineteenth-century South. The events of her childhood only reenforced the profound identity crisis of southern society in general.

Stanton's sense of the instability of racial categories, then, began in her childhood. Like many white southerners, she was raised by an African-American woman. However, Stanton's attachment to her nurse Chloe ran much deeper than the typical southern white child's attachment to his or her mammy. Complications with the birth of a second daughter left her mother an invalid. From the age of seventeen months, Stanton spent little time with her mother. Frances Megee Stanton died when Lucy was only thirteen. It was Chloe who guided little Lucy to adulthood. Yet Chloe was much more than a nurse to Stanton. In the later years of her life, Stanton told her nephew that Chloe had inspired her to become an artist. She remembered that Chloe's African-American lullabies and fables had first fired her childhood imagination. Her parents had noticed her creative abilities when, at age four, sitting in the creek bed with Chloe, she made little clay animal-people to act out Chloe's stories. It was Chloe's picture, not her mother's, that Lucy Stanton carried with her throughout her life, in 1925 painting a portrait from that photograph. Stanton never sold that painting of Chloe—it was part of her estate when she died. And she never painted a portrait of Frances.[45]

Because she felt her native region was the inspiration for her art, Stanton was determined, despite the obstacles, to make a place for herself there as an artist. Although she studied and worked in Paris, New York, and Boston, Lucy Stanton always returned to her little studio in Athens. Thus, though she was also exposed to the profound changes in European and northeastern American culture in this period, Stanton sought to shape her own life within the context of southern society generally and the small university town of Athens, Georgia, specifically. Like Rutherford, she celebrated southern women, though her heroines were not Confederate ladies and southern historians. In the African-American milkwoman, the Appalachian farmer's wife, the elderly white teacher, Stanton found her "new South." Unlike Rutherford, who hesitated to confront directly the image of the southern lady and sought more autonomy instead through her racial position, Stanton was willing to contend directly with the meaning of gender in the South.[46]

To live independently as a female artist in the South, then, Stanton attempted to reconstruct the meaning of southern womanhood. The problem was not that art was a more publicly visible career than history, Rutherford's work. Both women were well known within Athens, although Stanton's greatest successes lay outside the region, in the Northeast and Europe, while Rutherford was extremely popular throughout the South. Instead, Stanton's difficulties lay in her refusal to camouflage her independent life in an unquestioning public support for the status quo. Through her activism as well as her career, she pushed against the gendered boundaries of southern life, and unlike Rutherford, she made these challenges explicit. Perhaps most significantly, she founded a suffrage club in Athens in 1906 and often hosted meetings of the organization in her studio. That same year she joined the University Club, a local and mostly male organization for arts and letters, and produced and acted in a play on the steps of the University of Georgia chapel. She also wrote the local newspaper, demanding "A Museum for Athens. Why Not?" Utilizing an inheritance from a wealthy woman she had met in art school in Paris, Stanton financed the first traveling art exhibits to the University of Georgia. Before 1910 she and four other local women artists founded the Athens Art Association to support local artists and generally encourage interest in the arts. In the 1920s, she began teaching courses on the history of art and architecture to local university professors. In 1928 she helped found the Georgia Peace Society, which often met at her home, in the interest of avoiding a second world war. Stanton, then, did not find her power "in the home." "Ignorance of life," she felt, was not becoming. Art and the woman artist belonged in the larger world.[47]

In 1910 she noted the artist's inability to reconcile family and career. In her diary she expressed her own loneliness and that of other women painters she knew well: "The artist is often a complete type. Therefore he lives a lonely life—often dies in poverty, desolation, having no children to carry forward his personality. His ideals and the highest life never quite fit—these."[48] Yet as her own choice of masculine pronouns suggested, Stanton could not easily conceptualize the artist as female, even in her own diary. Perhaps the challenge of reconciling southern womanhood with life as an artist was more difficult than she had imagined. Being an artist allowed Stanton to live as a white women in the South while rejecting the conservative ideology of the "lady." Her career, however, prevented that challenge from becoming a model for others. The pursuit of art, in the South as in the North, seemed to demand the avoidance of marriage and family. Rutherford, on the other hand, provided a model for women's activism that, because the collecting and writing of southern history could literally take place within the home, was available for single and married women alike. In fact, for many Athenians, Stanton's reconstruction of southern womanhood did not seem like a threat at all. If Stanton was in demand as a colorful addition to any social gathering, she was also dismissed as eccentric. As an artist, her difference was tolerated; as a model of independent womanhood in her own lifetime, she was erased.[49]

In a 1917 self-portrait painted in Athens and entitled *The White Blouse,* Stanton attempted to present the contradictions of her identity as a southern female artist. In a soft, silky shirt, her hair neatly arranged, she seemed the perfect lady taking her afternoon tea. Yet, instead of a cup she held a paintbrush, the instrument not of leisure but of work. Her gaze appeared concentrated, determined, and yet exhausted—the effort required to project this image tired her. Suggesting that this unified identity was indeed a fleeting one, Stanton wrote on the back of the painting, "April 1917, Sunday 29th, self-portrait, forty-one years, eleven months."[50]

Although by the time Stanton painted this self-portrait, other, more powerful white southerners had already reconstructed the region, Stanton was not always content with their solutions. The "Lost Cause," white supremacy, and racial violence, she had found, did not define a clear role for a white female artist. The power of a white identity, still confined by the "helpmate" character of the "lady," did not provide the autonomy and community support she desired to pursue her career. Perhaps most importantly, Stanton was unsure about these southerners' white supremacy, their answers for the question of race.[51]

Lucy M. Stanton, *The White Blouse.* Watercolor
on ivory, 1917. Lucy M. Stanton Collection,
Special Collections, Robert W. Woodruff Library,
Emory University.

Stanton never accepted white supremacy as the foundation for her "New South." Perhaps her own difficulties living in a small southern town made her more sensitive to racial injustice. Certainly she never forgot her relationship with Chloe and how this African-American woman had encouraged her creativity. But Stanton never got involved in the budding interracial cooperation movement in Atlanta, at least not in a way that left records, although some of her closest friends participated in the Commission on Interracial Cooperation and its related organizations. Perhaps the difficulties she encountered in her attempts to work for peace and suffrage discouraged her. Without doubt much information was lost with the disappearance of many of her journals. She did, however, become friends with an African-American woman who lived behind her house, painting portraits of her and her family in 1921 and 1926. She was finishing a portrait of another friend she called *Aunt Lou*, a tough, wise, old black woman, when she died in 1931.[52]

Yet perhaps Stanton's attempts to challenge directly the gender restrictions of southern society were more successful in the long run than she understood. A younger generation of women artists in Athens remembered the support and encouragement of Stanton and the other founders of the Athens Art Association. In an article mourning her death, the *Atlanta Constitution* paid her what perhaps she would have felt was the highest compliment: "Miss Stanton was . . . a true representative of the modern woman, with all of the best qualities of the woman of a former day. Her interest in life was unexcelled. It has been said of her that few persons could accommodate themselves to the society of persons of so many different viewpoints, [and] yet with them all she was admired and loved."[53] She had managed, despite her own doubts and the racist ideology of her day, to be a woman both "southern" and "new," a wise woman at work in her community.

In the first three decades of the twentieth century, both Mildred Rutherford and Lucy Stanton attempted, one perhaps more consciously than the other, to redraw the lines of gender difference in the South. Yet while Stanton saw her place in southern society in terms of the restrictions of her gender, Rutherford saw her position in terms of the advantages of her race. Southern white women like Rutherford were able to use their understanding of race, informed by the ideology of white supremacy, to narrow the gender differences between white men and women. Rutherford believed that white women in a white supremacist society already had access to power through their racial identities. As Lucy Stanton found, however, challenging these gender differences head-on proved much more difficult. An alternative southern womanhood threatened the very structures of white supremacist society in which women like Rutherford had found their strength.

Thus, the success of Rutherford's feminine brand of white supremacy gave Stanton's southern feminism little space in which to mature and gain support. If elite white women could and did win the autonomy they desired through racism, they had much less need for a politics based on their common gender identities. Certainly, playing to the racial hysteria of the white South was an effective strategy for gaining more autonomy. Yet the victories of women like Rutherford were ambiguous at best, for white women made their choices within the context of the South's pervasive racial violence. Their racial politics strengthened white supremacy by rooting hate in the white family and expanding the base of this ideology from a more traditional foundation in politics and the law. Transgression of racial boundaries became not just breaking the law, a serious-enough offense for an African-American southerner, but also violating the family and its symbol, the southern "lady." Paradoxically, the success of strategies like Rutherford's empowered white southern women while leaving the image of the vulnerable "lady" intact to justify the violence. Lynching, after all, was necessary to "protect" the honor of southern womanhood. Yet the need for "protection" circumscribed the increased autonomy, especially of nonelite white women, that had helped instigate the cycle of violence in the first place. "Protection" emphasized that white women were not like white men. Unfortunately, by the time southern white women realized the contradictory nature of their own racial and gender identities, many African Americans had died and white (male) supremacy was firmly entrenched. Lucy Stanton, no doubt, would have found little satisfaction in having been right.

Notes

1. Mildred Lewis Rutherford, "The South in the Building of a Nation," in *Four Addresses* (Birmingham: The Mildred Rutherford Historical Circle, 1916), 3; Margaret Anne Womack, "Mildred Lewis Rutherford, Exponent of Southern Culture" (M.A. thesis, University of Georgia, 1946), 73–81, 86, 146. Other biographies of Rutherford are Virginia Clare, *Thunder and Stars* (Atlanta: Oglethorpe University Press, 1941); and Hazelle Beard Tuthill, "Mildred Lewis Rutherford" (M.A. thesis, University of South Carolina, 1929). I have taken my description of Rutherford's physical appearance from the picture on page 175 of *Four Addresses.* See also Fred Arthur Bailey, "Mildred Lewis Rutherford and the Patrician Cult of the New South," *Georgia Historical Quarterly* 78 (forthcoming).

2. Rutherford, *Four Addresses,* 14.

3. Ibid., 11. See also Rutherford, *Four Addresses; What the South May Claim and Where the South Leads* (Athens, Ga.: McGregor Company, 1916), 2; and the Mildred R. Rutherford Collection, Special Collections, University of Georgia, Athens (hereafter MLR Collection). The term "exponent of southern culture" is from the title of the Womack thesis.

4. Sources on Stanton include Grace Elizabeth Hale, "Painting the South: Class, Gender, and Race in the Life and Work of Lucy M. Stanton" (M.A. thesis, University of Georgia, 1991); W. Stanton Forbes, *Lucy M. Stanton, Artist* (Atlanta: Special Collections Department, Robert W. Woodruff Library, Emory University, 1975); the Lucy M. Stanton Collection, Special Collections, University of Georgia, Athens (hereafter LMS Collection, UGA), especially the diaries; and the Lucy M. Stanton Collection, Special Collections Department, Robert W. Woodruff Library, Emory University, Atlanta (hereafter LMS Collection, EU), especially the paintings. For Stanton's suffrage activities and paintings of African Americans, see Forbes, *Lucy M. Stanton,* 28–29, 40–42, 77–78. For Stanton's conversations about suffrage with young women, see interview with Susan Barrow Tate, October 9, 1990, Athens, Ga., in author's possession. I have taken my description of Stanton's appearance from a self-portrait she painted about this time. See Lucy M. Stanton, *Self-Portrait, the Silver*

Goblet (watercolor on ivory, 1912–15, National Portrait Gallery, Smithsonian Institute, Washington, D.C.).

5. Lucy M. Stanton Diary, 1910, LMS Collection, UGA. Many of the entries in Stanton's diaries are undated except for the year.

6. Ibid.

7. For Stanton's activities, see Forbes, *Lucy M. Stanton*, 1–19, 71–81; and newspaper clippings in the Georgia Peace Society and Athens Artists Vertical Files, Georgia Collection, University of Georgia. For her paintings, see LMS Collection, EU. See also Oral History Transcripts, LMS Collection, UGA; Interviews with Francis Forbes Heyn, New Orleans, November 2, 1990; and Paul Hodgeson, Athens, Georgia, October 25, 1990. Francis Forbes Heyn is Stanton's niece, the daughter of her sister Willie Stanton Forbes. Paul Hodgeson's mother, Mary McCullough Hodgeson, was one of Stanton's closest friends in Athens. The transcripts of these interviews are in the author's possession.

8. Womack, "Mildred Lewis Rutherford," 9; Forbes, *Lucy M. Stanton*, 74. I have developed the concept of a "doubled" class system more fully in Hale, "The Color of Class," in "Painting the South," 19–44. See also Numan V. Bartley, "Uptown and County Seat," chapter 5 in *The Creation of Modern Georgia* (Athens: University of Georgia Press, 1983), 103–26.

9. For Rutherford's family history, see genealogical notes, MLR Collection; Mrs. William Tate, "Mildred L. Rutherford: Defender of the Confederacy," *Athens Daily News*, July 16, 1968; and Womack, "Mildred Lewis Rutherford," 1–19, 144. For Stanton's family history, see genealogical notes and Oral History Transcripts, LMS Collection, UGA; Forbes, *Lucy M. Stanton*, 4–13; Julia Collier Harris, "Genius of Lucy May Stanton Recognized Here and in Europe," *Atlanta Constitution*, March 23, 1931; and LMS obituaries in *Atlanta Constitution*, March 20, 1931 and *Athens Banner Herald*, March 20, 1931.

10. For the importance of gender conventions in antebellum society, see Steven M. Stowe, *Intimacy and Power in the Old South: Ritual in the Lives of the Planters* (Baltimore: Johns Hopkins University Press, 1987), xvii–xviii, 50–121. See also Anne Firor Scott, *The Southern Lady: From Pedestal to Politics, 1830–1930* (Chicago: University of Chicago Press, 1970) 4–21 (quotes), 105–231; and Jean E. Friedman, *The Enclosed Garden: Women and Community in the Evangelical South, 1830–1900* (Chapel Hill: University of North Carolina Press, 1985), ix–xvi, 3–53.

On southern women in general in the antebellum and the postwar period, see Virginia Bernhard, Betty Brandon, Elizabeth Fox-Genovese, and Theda Purdue, eds., *Southern Women: Histories and Identities* (Columbia: University of Missouri Press, 1992); Catherine Clinton and Nina Silber, *Divided Houses: Gender and the Civil War* (New York: Oxford University Press, 1992); and "The Diversity of Southern Gender and Race: Women in Georgia and the South," special issue of the *Georgia Historical Quarterly* 76 (Summer 1992).

Little work has been done on the education of women in the South in the postwar period. See Friedman, *Enclosed Garden*, 99–102. For the antebellum period, see Catherine Clinton, *The Plantation Mistress: Women's World in the Old South* (New York: Pantheon, 1982), 105–10, 123–25; Elizabeth Fox-Genovese, *Within the Plantation Household: Black and White Women of the Old South* (Chapel Hill: University of North Carolina Press, 1988), 45–48, 110–12; Stowe, *Intimacy and Power*, 170–73, 177, 185–99; and Christie Anne Farnham, *The Education of the Southern Belle: Higher Education and Student Socialization in the Antebellum South* (New York: New York University Press, 1994). Many female academies, seminaries, and colleges, including the schools attended by Rutherford and Stanton, combined all levels of training, in effect housing primary, secondary, and higher education in one institution. This trend seems to have continued longer in the South than in the North. For the history of the higher education of women, see Barbara Miller Solomon, *In the Company of Educated Women* (New Haven: Yale University Press, 1985); and Helen Lefkowitz Horowitz, *Alma Mater: Design and Experience in the Women's Colleges from Their Nineteenth-Century Beginnings to the 1930s* (New York: Knopf, 1984), though both of these works focus mainly on schools in the Northeast.

11. Rutherford's uncle, Thomas R. R. Cobb, opened the Lucy Cobb Institute in Athens, Ga., in January, 1859. Rutherford attended from 1859 to 1868. See the Lucy Cobb Papers, Special Collections, University of Georgia; Phyllis Barrow, "The Lucy Cobb Institute" (Ph.D. diss., University of Georgia, 1951); and Womack, "Mildred Lewis Rutherford," 11–30.

Stanton's father, William Lewis Stanton, founded the Southern Baptist College for Women in College Park, a suburb of Atlanta, in 1894. After he went bankrupt, his second wife's family merged their academy, the Southern Female College in La Grange, with Southern Baptist for the 1895–96 school year. The academy remained in College Park and later became known as Cox College. Stanton attended Southern Female College from 1888 to 1894 and Southern Baptist College from 1894 to 1896. See Cox College Papers, Special Collections, University of Georgia. For Stanton's attendance, see Cox College catalogues, 1888–1896; Forbes, *Lucy M. Stanton*, 74–75; and William Stanton, Los Angeles, California, to Lucy Stanton, Athens, March 9, 1904, LMS Collection, UGA.

12. Letter to the editor entitled "Female Education in Athens," *Athens Southern Banner*, August 24, 1854. Rutherford's mother, Laura Cobb Rutherford, wrote this letter, which prompted her brother T. R. R. Cobb to found the Lucy Cobb Institute. Interestingly, because the letter was published anonymously, Cobb did not know his sister had written it. See Barrow, "Lucy Cobb Institute," 6–10; Womack, "Rutherford," 11–14; and the Lucy Cobb Papers, Special Collections, University of Georgia.

13. "Female Education in Athens."

14. Ibid.

15. Womack, "Mildred Lewis Rutherford," 17. Stanton wrote about the decision to live in a small town in America: "To diminish the cost of living and at the same time secure leisure for work, they [American artists] have reduced living to the most

simple form; they have built small studio homes, surrounded them by flowers and trees, and have succeeded in combining that certain elegance with the simplicity of which Americans delight abroad." Lucy M. Stanton Diary, 1910, LMS Collection, UGA. See also Lucy M. Stanton, Paris, France, to Mrs. Chapel Quillain Stanton, Los Angeles, Summer 1905, LMS Collection, UGA.

16. Rutherford, *Four Addresses*, 4.

17. Ibid.

18. Ibid. On Rutherford's quest to "right the wrongs of southern history," see for example *What the South May Claim*, 15; and *Four Addresses*, 3; this theme runs throughout her work. On the origins of the UDC, see *Where the South Leads and Where Georgia Leads* (Athens, Ga.: McGregor Company, 1917) 1–2. For other references to the UDC, see C. Vann Woodward, *Origins of the New South, 1877–1913* (Baton Rouge: Louisiana State University Press, 1951), 156–57; and Bartley, *Modern Georgia*, 105–7, 121–23. For the "greatness" of southern (white) women, see *Where the South Leads*, 1, 24, 28–30; *What the South May Claim*, 5, 7, 23–24; and *Four Addresses*, 37–39. For southern woman as the keepers of culture and kinship, see Nancy Press, "Private Faces, Public Lives: The Women of the Downtown Group of Charleston, South Carolina," in Holly F. Matthews, ed., *Women in the South: An Anthropological Perspective* (Athens: University of Georgia Press, 1989), 95–109.

19. For Rutherford's activities, see Womack, "Mildred Lewis Rutherford," 17–103; see also her twenty-nine published books and speeches, most of which are housed in the Georgia Collection, University of Georgia. For her thoughts on the "Lost Cause," see *What the South May Claim*, 15. General information on the "Lost Cause" can be found in Gaines M. Foster, *Ghosts of the Confederacy: Defeat, the Lost Cause, and the Emergence of the New South* (New York: Oxford University Press, 1987). See also Woodward, *Origins of the New South*, 155–57; and Bartley, *Modern Georgia*, 97, 105–8, 116, 126, 145–47, 212. For additional information on the UDC, see Angie Parrott, " 'Love Makes Memory Eternal': The United Daughters of the Confederacy in Richmond, Virginia, 1897–1920," in Edward L. Ayers and John C. Willis, eds., *The Edge of the South: Life in Nineteenth-Century Virginia* (Charlottesville: University Press of Virginia, 1991) 219–38.

20. Rutherford, *Four Addresses*, 6.

21. Ibid., 11.

22. Ibid., 39.

23. For a classification of southern racisms in this period as conservative, liberal, and radical, see Joel Williamson, *A Rage for Order: Black-White Relations in the American South since Emancipation* (New York: Oxford University Press, 1986), 70–116. For lynching, see Jacqueline Dowd Hall, *Revolt against Chivalry: Jessie Daniel Ames and the Women's Campaign against Lynching* (New York: Columbia University Press, 1979), 129–57; and Williamson, *Rage for Order*, 117–51. For Rebecca Latimer Felton, see Williamson, *Rage for Order*, 90–95, 183–84, 235.

24. *Athens Banner*, July 26, 1913.

25. *Athens Daily Herald*, August 7, 1915.

26. *Athens Daily Herald*, June 23, 1914. See also *Athens Daily Herald*, April 1, 1915; and Womack, "Mildred Lewis Rutherford," 102.

27. Rutherford, *The Civilization of the Old South: What Made It: What Betrayed It: What Has Replaced It* (Athens, Ga.: McGregor Company, n.d.), 5.

28. Mildred Lewis Rutherford, *Georgia: The Empire State* (Athens, Ga.: McGregor Company, 1914), 14.

29. The Civil Rights movement, often called the second Reconstruction, forced the enactment of Rutherford's worst fears. See Jack Bloom, *Race and Class in the Civil Rights Movement* (Bloomington: Indiana University Press, 1987).

30. Rutherford, *Four Addresses*, 34.

31. Ibid., 61, 62.

32. Mildred Lewis Rutherford, *Facts and Figures vs. Myths and Misrepresentations: Henry Wirz and the Andersonville Prison* (Athens: by the author, 1921), 19. See also John David Smith, "An Old Creed for the New South: Southern Historians and the Revival of the Proslavery Argument, 1890–1920," *Southern Studies* 18 (Spring 1979): 75–87.

33. Williamson, 3–43, 70–116. On southern racisms, see also George M. Frederickson, *The Black Image in the White Mind: The Debate on Afro-American Destiny, 1817–1914* (Middletown, Ct.: Wesleyan University Press, 1971), 198–282.

34. Mildred Lewis Rutherford, *American Authors* (Atlanta: Franklin Printing and Publishing Company, 1894) and *The South in History and Literature* (Atlanta: Franklin Printing and Publishing Company, 1907). For Rutherford's UDC activities, see the UDC files, MLR Collection: *Athens Daily Herald*, January 26, 1914; and Womack, "Mildred Lewis Rutherford," 96.

35. Lamar Rutherford Libscomb and Mildred Rutherford co-owned the *Lakemont (Georgia) Mountain Star*, and Rutherford served as its business manager; see Womack, "Mildred Lewis Rutherford," 131–32. See also MLR Collection, box 3, misc. scrapbook, for undated clipping describing Libscomb as a "New Woman" and for additional clippings from the *Mountain Star*. See also Emily C. McDougald, President, Equal Suffrage Party of Georgia, Atlanta, to Lamar Libscomb, Athens, February 5, 1920, MLR Collection.

36. All quotes are from Rutherford, *Four Addresses*, 37, 37–8, 40, 45.

37. *Athens Daily Herald*, November 16, 1914. I have greatly benefited from Mary Poovey's analysis of the ideological function of gender in nineteenth-century England in forming my own conceptions of the ideological workings of race in the late nineteenth- and early twentieth-century South. See Poovey, *Uneven Developments: The Ideological Work of Gender in Mid-Victorian England* (Chicago: University of Chicago Press, 1988), 1–23.

38. Lucy M. Stanton Diary, 1910, LMS Collection, UGA.

39. Ibid., May 11, 1913.

40. See Forbes, *Lucy M. Stanton*, 1–10. Forbes recounts how years later Stanton traded her own paintings to relatives for the furnishings from her childhood home, which she collected to furnish her Athens studio (10). See also Willie Stanton Forbes

and W. Stanton Forbes, Oral History Transcripts, compiled in 1958; and Francis
Louisa Megee Stanton obituary, *[illegible] Baptist,* June 21, 1888, newspaper clipping;
both in LMS Collection, UGA.

41. Lucy M. Stanton Diary, 1915, LMS Collection, UGA.

42. Forbes, *Lucy M. Stanton,* 58–60; and Lucy M. Stanton, *Linton Ingrahm, Ex-
Slave* (watercolor on ivory, 1925, Museum of the American China Trade, Milton,
Mass.). For the difficulties southern artists faced earning a living in their region, see
Amy Kirschke, "The Southern States Art League: A Regionalist Artists' Organiza-
tion, 1922–1950," *Southern Quarterly* 25 (Winter 1987): 1–23.

43. Forbes, *Lucy M. Stanton* 40–42. Lucy M. Stanton, *Uncle George* (watercolor on
ivory, 1916, LMS Collection, EU).

44. Lucy M. Stanton, *Working on the Street* (watercolor on ivory, 1921, LMS Collection, EU). See also the other four *Little Murals: Negroes Resting, Shovelling, Loading
Cotton,* and *Aunt Liza's House* (all watercolor on ivory, LMS Collection, EU). See
Williamson, *Rage for Order,* 70–116, for southern racism. For lynching and rape statistics, see Jacquelyn Dowd Hall, "'The Mind That Burns in Each Body': Women,
Rape, and Racial Violence," in Ann Snitow, Christine Stansell, and Sharon Thompson, eds., *Powers of Desire: the Politics of Sexuality* (New York: Monthly Review Press,
1983), 328–49; and Hall, *Revolt,* 129–57.

45. Forbes, *Lucy M. Stanton,* 1–19; Oral History Transcripts, LMS Collection,
UGA; and Francis Forbes Heyn interview (n. 7 above); Lucy M. Stanton, *Chloe*
(watercolor on ivory, 1925, LMS Collection, EU). I am not trying to perpetuate
Eugene D. Genovese's overly romantic view of the mammy here, and I realize, as
Deborah Gray White has pointed out, that Chloe's feelings for Lucy may have been
much more ambivalent. In Stanton's life, however, what matters is her understanding
of that relationship. See Eugene D. Genovese, *Roll, Jordan, Roll: The World the Slaves
Made* (New York: Vintage Books, 1976), 352–61; and Deborah Gray White, *Ar'n't
I a Woman?: Female Slaves in the Plantation South* (New York: W. W. Norton, 1985),
46–61.

46. Forbes, *Lucy M. Stanton,* 74–81; and Francis Forbes Heyn interview.

47. Forbes, *Lucy M. Stanton,* 74–81. See also interview with Susan Barrow Tate
(n. 4 above). Tate remembers visiting Stanton as a teenager. Over tea, Stanton would
lecture her and a friend, who was sitting for a portrait, on the importance of women's
suffrage and the activities of the local club. See also interview with Frances Forbes
Heyn. Heyn, Stanton's niece, remembered that her aunt worked for suffrage and
that the Athens club had a membership of about ten. I have found no mention of
the group's activities in the existing copies of the local *Athens Banner Herald.* See
also the Georgia Peace Society and Athens Artists Vertical Files, Georgia Collection,
University of Georgia.

48. Lucy M. Stanton Diary, 1910, LMS Collection, UGA.

49. For the Athens community's attitude toward Stanton, see Francis Forbes
Heyn interview, Paul Hodgeson interview, and Susan Barrow Tate interview. For
the place of female artists in American society, see April Masten, "Work, Genius,

and the Professionalization of the 'Lady Artist': American Painters and Sculptors in the Nineteenth Century," (unpublished paper, Rutgers University, 1992, in author's possession).

50. Lucy M. Stanton, *The White Blouse* (watercolor on ivory, 1917, LMS Collection, EU).

51. See Williamson, *Rage for Order*, 233–47; see also Stanton's eight paintings of African Americans in LMS Collection, EU; and five paintings of African Americans located elsewhere and documented in LMS Collection, EU.

52. Lucy M. Stanton, *Aunt Lou* (watercolor on ivory, 1931), reproduced in Forbes, *Lucy M. Stanton*, plate 6.

53. James B. Nevin, "Lucy M. Stanton," *Atlanta Georgian* 22, March 1931. This article was also printed in the *Atlanta Constitution*, March 22, 1931, and in the *Athens Banner Herald*, March 22, 1931. For Stanton's influence on younger artists, see Jean Flanigan, interview with the author, Athens, Georgia, October 29, 1990.

The Universal Negro Improvement Association in Georgia

Southern Strongholds of Garveyism

Mary Gambrell Rolinson

The Universal Negro Improvement Association (UNIA) held its first convention parade in Harlem on August 3, 1920. A division banner from Georgia flew among those representing northeastern states and African, Latin American, and British Commonwealth countries. Thousands marched that day from the UNIA headquarters at West 135th Street, up Lenox Avenue to 145th Street, down Seventh Avenue, and back to its point of origin.[1] At the time the UNIA had existed in the United States for just over three years; nevertheless its charismatic Jamaican leader, Marcus Garvey, had caught the attention of black people in the Deep South like C. L. Holum of Baxley who reported on the conditions of black Georgians at the 1920 Harlem convention.[2]

The Garvey movement exploded in the South just after World War I, and by 1926 the former Confederate states contained at least four hundred UNIA divisions and chapters.[3] Georgia alone hosted at least thirty-four local units ranging from the urban centers of Atlanta and Savannah to tiny outposts like Haylow and Ty Ty.[4] Garvey's weekly newspaper, the *Negro World*, enjoyed wide circulation in Georgia in the early 1920s, even well beyond UNIA members.

Garvey's doctrine of economic uplift, race pride, and Africa for the Africans is well known for spurring organization of the alienated masses in urban areas such as New York, Detroit, and Los Angeles. In Georgia, however, its popularity was most apparent in rural areas. Out of Georgia's divisions, only four host towns had populations over ten thousand. Most of the remaining thirty were located in communities of fewer than three thousand residents.[5] In fact, the southernmost third of the state, the region farthest away from the urban areas of Atlanta, Macon, and Augusta, contained all but two of Georgia's UNIA divisions.

The scholarship on Garveyism has thus far focused on the large urban divisions in the North and Midwest, about which there exists extensive documentation. The few attempts to address the movement in the South have more often than not raised more questions than answers.

Tony Martin, the most prolific Garvey scholar, has acknowledged the broad extent of organization by Garveyites in the South but has devoted most of his work to validating Garvey's black nationalist ideology and defending the UNIA leader against pervasive charges of buffoonery and charlatanism.[6] Judith Stein's 1986 study, on the other hand, focused on the realized and incipient urban black middle classes, which hoped to prosper as a result of the UNIA's efforts toward economic independence. She dismisses the southern divisions as mere social clubs for small numbers, suggesting that members had no grasp of the movement's broad goals. Her claim that Garvey misread the politics of the region contradicts the fact that the UNIA managed to organize in over four hundred locations throughout the South. The Klan, in Stein's view, successfully manipulated Garvey to improve its own public relations.[7]

Other scholars' neglect of the southern wing of the UNIA is understandable for several reasons. The more populous single divisions in the urban North, Midwest, and West made headlines in their cities. These divisions kept extensive records and pursued programs exclusively for improvement of the local black community. The members of these large divisions joined Garvey's UNIA Legions or the auxilary Black Cross Nurses. Historians have been able to study these substantial individual groups without feeling compelled to probe into the activities and sentiments of the smaller, widely scattered UNIA divisions of the South. This omission from the scholarship on the Garvey movement needs to be corrected. Although its divisions were smaller in size individually, southern states such as Georgia contributed faithful, generous, and active support to the overall movement. By concentrating on the UNIA's universal goals, these branches provided Garvey, throughout his legal and financial difficulties, with financial stability and moral support for his mission to redeem Africa. In return Garvey gave inspiration to latent black consciousness in isolated rural communities. His

Georgia communities with UNIA divisions, 1926.

message forcefully dispelled the myth of Negro inferiority and offered instead an economic explanation for racism to blacks in Georgia and throughout the South.

From the elusive sources on Garveyism in Georgia several themes emerge. UNIA members were older men, usually farmers, with families and financial obligations such as home mortgages or crop liens. These Georgia Garveyites showed extraordinary loyalty to their leader despite his myriad legal problems with the U.S. government, conflicts with black integrationist leaders, and neglect or criticism by both the black and white press. The *Negro World*, nevertheless, kept his rural southern followers informed about the UNIA's worldwide black concerns, and Garvey himself came to Georgia to strengthen his southern base by negotiating with the Ku Klux Klan. The appeal of the UNIA in Georgia during the 1920s is obvious, though its residual effect is difficult to pinpoint.

The young Jamaican based his movement on the goal of creating a black-ruled nation in Africa which could provide a vanguard against oppression for blacks all over the globe. He considered white racism against black people a product of economic disparity, and believed that internationally the white race hated the "darker races" because the latter had no economically strong and independent governments to defend them against the forces of twentieth-century imperialism.[8] On a more local level Garvey emphasized the dearth of black-owned businesses and the lack of commercial achievement by African Americans. Through his promotion of race dignity and prosperity, Garvey attracted a significant following. By 1924, the height of its popularity, the UNIA included at least one million members in the United States, and perhaps one million more elsewhere in the world.

The 1926 UNIA division card files, the only extant indication of specific Georgia followers, contain the names of division presidents and secretaries.[9] From a review of twenty-three Georgia UNIA leaders in the 1920 census records, a clear composite emerges (see table on following pages). Garvey's local UNIA organizers were for the most part married, middle-aged or older tenant farmers. All but two were listed as "black" rather than "mulatto." Eighteen of the twenty-three could read and write, and all but three identified themselves as at least second-generation native Georgians.[10]

Garvey's remarkable penetration of rural Georgia and his popularity with sharecroppers reflects the enormous appeal his program had to people caught in the most notorious economic trap in American agriculture. No doubt many younger Garvey sympathizers moved North to escape debt peonage. The older men, however, particularly those with families who could not move easily, sought to build an economic foundation and race dignity where they lived. Garvey's ideas were not new, but he expressed them eloquently in speeches delivered at the UNIA's large northern meeting rooms, known as "Liberty Halls," and transcribed them in the *Negro World* for his supporters worldwide. In voicing the concerns of black people and UNIA members throughout the world, Garvey was fully aware that southern sharecroppers formed a substantial part of his following.

The UNIA provided support for transient blacks as well as for those who were immobilized by permanent ties to farms and family or by financial obligations to creditors or landlords. Its founder stated often that neither governments nor individuals should hinder the migration of black people, and he encouraged movement when it meant better opportunity for prosperity. Garvey's avowed militance, however, never allowed him to encourage running out of fear. Critics accused him of doing just that with his back-to-Africa program. Garvey insisted that Africa was not an escape but rather

County	Division	Name	Age[a]	Literate	Job	Home Sta
Bacon	Alma, P[b]	Levi Vaughan (M)[c]	53	Yes	Lumber mill inspector on wages	owns
Baker	Baker Co., P	William H. Wright	59	Yes	Tenant farmer	rents
Baker	Baker Co., S[d]	Seaborn B. Presley	56	Yes	Tenant farmer	rents
Chatham	Pooler, P	Abraham J. Edwards	50	Yes	Wage farm worker	owns
Colquitt	Moultrie, P	Porter Dublin	45	Yes	Tenant farmer	rents
Echols	Haylow, P	Enoch J. Roberts (Single)[e]	73	Yes	Farm laborer	owns
Glynn	Brunswick, P	Simon Benjamin	51	Yes	Meat market owner	owns
Liberty	Limerick, P	M. S. Graham	63	Yes	Tenant farmer	owns
Liberty	Limerick, S	F. S. Lambright	62	Yes	Tenant farmer	owns
Pierce	Patterson, P	Henry W. Deal	68	Yes	Unknown	mortga,
Pierce	Patterson, S	Cain J. Jenkins	52	Yes	Tenant farmer	owns
Turner	Coverdale, P	Murray K. Kellebrew	36	No	Tenant farmer	rents
Ware	Waycross, S	Byrd Killens	44	Yes	Wage farm laborer	rents
Wayne	Jesup, P	J. B. Badger	76	No	Unknown	rents
Wayne	Jesup, S	Joe H. Spencer	55	Yes	Wage worker/tie chopper	mortga,
Webster	Kinsborough, P	James E. Jackson	75	No	Farm laborer	unknov
Webster	Kinsborough, S	Jim A. Hardwick	49	Yes	Wage worker/carpenter	owns
Worth	Powellton, P	Isaiah G. Gates	45	Yes	Tenant farmer	rents
Worth	Powellton, S	Willie Johnson (M)[c]	35	Yes	Wage farm laborer	unknov
Worth	Shingler, S	Lonzie Smith	36	Yes	Tenant farmer	rents
Worth	Oakfield, P	James Evans	66	No	Tenant farmer	rents
Worth	Oakfield, S	Albert Evans	41	No	Tenant farmer	rents
Worth	Charity Grove, S	Richmond Britt	41	No	Wage farm laborer	rents

All data derived from U.S. Census, 1920.

[a] The ages indicated here are calculated by adding six to the ages indicated in the 1920 census.

[b] President

[c] Only two of the men listed here, Levi Vaughan and Willie Johnson, were labeled "mulatto" rather than "black" by the cen takers, who made such judgments on their own, without asking.

[d] Secretary

[e] Enoch Roberts is the only single man on the list. All the rest were married and most had several children.

the black man's natural environment, and that once the united Negroes had freed Africa from control by imperialist white nations, a prosperous African nation could act against the oppression of blacks throughout the world.

Although Garvey did not actively encourage southern blacks to migrate North, the Great Migration between 1910 and 1930 undoubtedly had a profound impact on the spread of Garveyism into rural Georgia. The UNIA served as an important support group for southern blacks (and also West Indian blacks) who migrated to industrial centers in the North. These newcomers apparently wrote home about the organization and perhaps encouraged family members to organize local divisions or subscribe to Garvey's *Negro World.*[11]

Family connections provided an opportunity for the spread of Garveyism just as the circulation of the *Negro World* did. The paper began to reach small communities in the Deep South, even those without UNIA divisions, as early as October 1920.[12] As editor of the paper, Garvey courted support in rural Georgia by covering issues pertinent to tenant farmers. He reminded farmers of their power by emphasizing the white landowners' panic at the migration and resulting labor crisis in southern agriculture. At the same time he regularly featured pieces on the Klan and lynching, two subjects that dramatized black powerlessness.

Garvey's message reached more than *Negro World* subscribers because most UNIA division meeting agendas included a reading of his weekly speeches, which always appeared on the paper's front page. Through the practice of passing on Garvey's message directly, a wide array of blacks—urban, rural, literate, and illiterate—had a chance to judge the movement based on the leader's own words. Considering that the UNIA leader never visited the parts of the state where the majority of his support existed, the paper clearly played a significant part in furthering Garveyism through rural Georgia.

Garvey did, however, make three national speaking tours which included appearances in southern cities. These visits also must have enhanced the UNIA's popularity; even Garvey's bitterest enemies attested to his unmatched oratorical skills. Garvey realized that southern *Negro World* readers, division members, and contributors needed the reassurance that their leader did not presume to discuss southern issues such as lynching authoritatively from a position of safety in the North.[13]

Garvey's first visit to the South took place during a thirty-eight state tour in 1916 and 1917 to assess black conditions and to solicit responses to his ideas before launching his movement in Harlem.[14] On July 13 and 14, 1922,

Garvey spoke at public meetings in New Orleans as part of a second tour through the Deep South in the spring and summer of that year.

The rhetoric Garvey used in the South often condemned black people for their lack of accomplishment and race pride. This approach appealed to many people both black and white. In November 1922, Garvey made a divisive speech at the North Carolina State Fair in Raleigh in which he attempted to jolt southern blacks into action. He told the audience that he thanked the white man for beating and lynching race consciousness into black people.[15] Negroes in the South, he added, had never produced or organized anything; thus he had had to ride on a white man's railroad to get to North Carolina. If he had had to depend on blacks to get him there, he continued, it would have taken six weeks.

Supporters of the National Association for the Advancement of Colored People criticized Garvey for months after these statements. The *Messenger*, an NAACP–influenced socialist newspaper, called him everything from "A Supreme Negro Jamaican Jackass" to a "monumental monkey" and "the white man's good nigger."[16] Despite the negative reaction by rival editors to Garvey's harsh judgment on blacks and his tolerance for the Klan, his popularity grew dramatically in the South for years afterwards. Later he returned to Raleigh specifically to promote one of his many black-owned-and-operated commercial ventures, the Black Cross Navigation and Trading Company. His economic message, endorsement of race pride, and African Redemption plan remained the focus of southern supporters.

In the fall of 1923 when Garvey again visited the South, he had just completed a three-month jail term. A New York federal court had found him guilty of using the mail fraudulently to raise money and sell stock in the Black Star Steamship Line, which Garvey had developed as an opportunity for black investors and as a commercial link among the countries of the black diaspora. In moving through Alabama and Georgia, he was pleased to discover that his conviction and imprisonment for mail fraud had neither hurt his popularity nor weakened financial support for his mission. After speaking engagements in Birmingham, Tuskegee, and Atlanta, the UNIA leader concluded that southern blacks had great courage in the midst of racist hostility and were "anxiously awaiting the day of Africa's redemption."[17]

Amy Jacques Garvey accompanied her husband on his 1923 tour, and her impressions of the southern visits, which appeared in the *Negro World*, demonstrated characteristic candor. She described the positive reaction to her husband's address in Birmingham, especially from fourteen black ministers who were in town for a "colored ministers conference." According to Mrs. Garvey, the enthusiastic ministers shouted "Amen" throughout her husband's discussion of the UNIA's aims. She regretted, however, that not all curious onlookers were so moved.

Amy Garvey contrasted the Birmingham appearance to Garvey's arrival at a local UNIA meeting at the Bethel Baptist Church in Atlanta where some "dirty Negroes" had attended only to see "the man just out of jail."[18] There Garvey's separatist doctrine met some strong negative reactions, reflecting in part the strength of the NAACP and other integrationist organizations in the Georgia capital. Blacks in Atlanta had organized an NAACP branch in 1916. At the NAACP's annual convention in 1919, Atlanta president A. D. Williams reported that his branch included twenty-six hundred members and urged all delegates to vote to hold its next convention in Atlanta. He succeeded in his campaign and in 1920 the NAACP held its first conference ever in a former Confederate state.

Throughout Georgia, as throughout the South, opposition to Garvey and the UNIA coincided with the existence in the community of the rival NAACP. An Arkansas delegate at the 1924 UNIA Convention reported that in attempting to organize, the people of his area, "mostly farmers," were forced to wage a hard-fought struggle against preachers and professional men. He noted that the UNIA local had received the "sympathetic consideration of the town authorities so much so that when members of another Negro organization had sought to prevent them from meeting in the town, complaining that the aims and objects of the organization were not satisfactory, the mayor not only gave them permission, but recommended the work as being very good for the race."[19] This "other Negro organization," composed of middle-class blacks, had no desire to go back to Africa but rather sought to promote social and political equality in the United States.

This basic ideological difference split Georgia's black populace along much the same lines, and there, as in Arkansas, the UNIA and NAACP became natural enemies. Their animosity was intensified as the two groups competed for members. The speed with which Garvey's movement spread in the South alarmed the NAACP because it threatened the steady growth that the integrationist organization had enjoyed for almost ten years.

The older organization's fear proved valid: it experienced a sharp decline in membership during the height of the Garvey movement. In 1919, before the UNIA had held its first annual convention, which drew 25,000 blacks, the NAACP counted 91,000 members on its rolls.[20] The NAACP continued to grow until 1924, when it saw its first net loss in membership, probably linked to the fact that the UNIA convention that year passed a resolution against dual membership in the UNIA and NAACP. But even earlier, between 1920 and 1923, the NAACP lost two hundred branches, most of which were in

the South.[21] By 1928, the UNIA had begun to weaken because of faction-
alism and Garvey's deportation, but by that time NAACP membership had
dropped to 23,500.[22]

In an interview on August 20, 1920, Chandler Owen, coeditor of the *Messenger*, stated that Garvey's skill in raising money was "killing the subscription
and contribution market of the Negroes." He went on to state: "As long as
he gets the vast sums he does, no other Negro movement can prosper."[23]
As Owen became aware of the damage Garvey's popularity could inflict on
rival black organizations, he and others struggled in vain as they watched the
UNIA continue to grow until 1927.

In major cities like New York, both the UNIA and the NAACP could maintain large membership rolls. Competition in these places remained fierce,
but large numbers of potential recruits always remained available. On the
other hand, close-knit black communities scattered over the state of Georgia
provided little room for both the NAACP and the UNIA. Small rural communities did not support large numbers of middle-class blacks, if any at all,
and the possibility of integration on any level seemed remote. Therefore, if
black farmers decided to follow Garvey and if the whites in the community
approved, the NAACP had few prospects. The same logic worked in reverse.
If black farmers wanted to join the NAACP and if the local whites supported
the NAACP program (a highly unlikely combination), the UNIA would not
succeed. The black farmers may have split between the organizations and in
some cases supported both, but ultimately the predisposition of local whites
seemed to determine which organization would have been most successful.
Judging from discussions at NAACP conventions, the integrationist organization was most unwelcome in many areas in Georgia.

This dynamic helps explain why the UNIA prospered in rural areas in
south Georgia where the NAACP had not organized and did not have white
support. For instance, the NAACP had active branches in Augusta, Milledgeville and several other large Georgia towns where the UNIA never organized.[24] The UNIA, by the same token, was strong in areas that the NAACP
regarded as the most racially troubled. In an address to the 1919 NAACP
conference, H. A. Hunt of Fort Valley described Worth County as one of
the worst counties in south Georgia for tenant farmers. He explained that
landlords there frequently took a tenant's whole crop and called the account
"even." Hunt observed that "there would be difficulty lining up our people
in the rural population" to correct these ills. At the same meeting, a Dublin
minister described Worth County as an area notorious for whites locking up
and even lynching farmers who tried to leave the land.[25] Yet in 1926, Worth
County was the most extensively UNIA organized county in the state. Charity

Grove, Sylvester, Shingler, Oakfield, and Powellton, all in Worth County, had active UNIA divisions. The Garveyite solution obviously made sense to many black Georgia farmers, and they proved their support by joining. The NAACP, on the other hand, never made any inroads into Worth County.

In an address by an elderly Atlanta school teacher and fieldworker for the NAACP, the 1919 conference heard reports of glaring inequalities in teachers' pay in Georgia. Cora Finley used Bacon County as the most revealing example. "White teachers were paid an average of $52.30 and colored teachers $18.50" per month. Once again, by 1926 the UNIA had a division in Alma, the county seat, while the NAACP's closest branch was in Brunswick, nearly a hundred miles away.[26]

During his travels Garvey confronted much controversy and misinterpretation, much of which stemmed from his tolerance of the Klan. In appealing to such a diverse coalition of blacks from cities, rural areas, and foreign countries, the UNIA leader had to adjust his rhetoric in order to succeed. His followers understood his discrepancies, or at least tolerated them, while his black and white opponents regarded him as an unscrupulous opportunist. Garvey received harsh criticism from his regular detractors in the black press for modifying his tone and altering his message according to circumstances, but his Georgia supporters never seemed to waver as a result of his rhetorical ambiguities or contradictions.

White Georgians, especially in the early years of the movement, did not take Garvey seriously because his followers came from a traditionally powerless sector of the black population. In September 1920, because the Jamaica-born Garvey was a British subject, the British consul-general requested that the consul's office in Savannah submit a report on UNIA activity in Georgia. The consul there reported inaccurately that, according to a local black newspaper editor (presumably Sol C. Johnson of the *Savannah Tribune*) and a black bank manager, no UNIA branches existed in the state. The misinformed consul added that the organization was simply a money-making scheme that posed no radical threat. In his opinion, southern Negroes would be hard to organize for protest because they were basically lazy, simple, and in a happy state of ignorance.[27] What he did not realize was that not only were there dozens of UNIA divisions in the state, but that C. L. Holum, leader of the thriving Baxley division only ninety miles away, had attended the UNIA convention in Harlem that year and reported to the central administration on local conditions in Georgia.[28]

White leaders in other southern states spoke out against Garvey because the UNIA leader encouraged blacks to distrust their white representatives. The editor of the *Natchez Mississippi Democrat* charged: "The work of such charlatans as Marcus Garvey among illiterate Negroes is building up a low prejudice against whites in all sections of the country. Ignorant Negroes of the South are now pouring thousands of dollars into Garvey's coffers every year, on the belief that he is going to establish a home and a government for them somewhere in Africa."[29] Garvey vehemently denied such charges, insisting that he did not intend to cause discord between races but that "the entire Negro race must be emancipated from industrial bondage, peonage, and serfdom."[30] Goals such as these appealed to tenant farmers as much as they frightened landowners already concerned about the loss of their labor supply to increasing northward migration. Yet despite some harsh accusations, Marcus Garvey did not draw a uniformly negative reaction from whites, and surprisingly, no evidence exists that any white group, not even the Ku Klux Klan, formally opposed him.

In fact, during his 1922 tour through the South the UNIA leader visited Atlanta and held a highly controversial meeting with the acting imperial wizard of the Ku Klux Klan, Edward Young Clarke. According to Garvey's own account of the meeting in the *Negro World,* he and Clarke found many issues upon which they agreed. Garvey applauded Clarke's honesty about his racist attitudes, stating that the imperial wizard only stood up for what all white men believed whether they admitted so openly or not. Clarke, on the other hand, approved of Garvey's African colonization plans and his disdain for miscegenation.[31] Garvey used this meeting to demonstrate that he could not be intimidated and to open further avenues for local UNIA organization in the South. He gambled judiciously that his supporters in Georgia would not censure his action. Although his southern supporters did not waver, this questionable encounter with so notorious a figure rallied, without exception, all rival black organization leaders and editors against him.

Before 1921, NAACP leaders such as W. E. B. Du Bois and William Pickens, its field secretary from 1920 to 1938, had mixed praise with their criticisms of Garvey. But after the upstart leader's 1922 Atlanta summit with Edward Young Clarke, many sought to discredit him. The hastily formed "Friends of Negro Freedom" launched the "Garvey Must Go" campaign. Four prominent NAACP sympathizers started the anti-Garvey movement with a four-week lecture series in New York, in which the central themes were Garvey's "alliance with the Klan" and his "robbery of ignorant Negroes."[32]

While Du Bois did not associate himself with the organized "Garvey Must Go" campaign, he waged his own long-running personal attack on the UNIA leader. Du Bois researched and described Garvey's activities in many issues of *The Crisis,* the official organ of the NAACP, which he edited. In response, Garvey editorialized against Du Bois and the other "race haters" in the

Negro World. In a revealing racial insult, Garvey once dismissed the NAACP founder as a "confused mulatto."[33]

Robert Abbott, the Savannah-born editor of the *Chicago Defender* and an enthusiastic promoter of black migration north, published continuous criticism of Garvey after his Klan summit and eventually signed a letter to the U.S. attorney general requesting a speedy prosecution of Garvey on mail fraud charges. The UNIA leader responded by calling the *Defender* a "miscegenationist light-colored weekly paper."[34] Even the *Savannah Tribune*, under editor Sol C. Johnson, which usually ignored UNIA activity altogether, found space to condemn Garvey. When A. Philip Randolph, coeditor of the *Messenger*, received a human hand in the mail with a threatening message, the report attributed the atrocity to Garvey.[35]

The scandals of 1922 and the subsequent mass attack on Garvey did not subdue him. He jumped into another fray in 1922 when Congressman Leonidas C. Dyer of Missouri proposed an antilynching bill in the U.S. House of Representatives. The NAACP vigorously supported it, believing that such legislation would ameliorate the lynching problem by placing harsh penalties on anyone convicted of what would then be a federal crime. After initially supporting the bill, Garvey and the UNIA came out against it on the grounds that southern state governments would not enforce the measure even if it became law.[36] Garvey insisted that American blacks should not be tricked into voting for politicians, such as the white integrationist Dyer, who supported the bill for political reasons alone.

By opposing the bill, Garvey provided his critics with more fuel for the campaign against him. His rejection of the bill severely jeopardized what had become the NAACP's pet cause and a filibuster by southern Democrats eventually killed the bill in the Senate. The NAACP and Dyer were furious with Garvey, and when his downfall came, the Missouri congressman declared that the Jamaican had received his just reward for his many betrayals of the Negro race.

Opposition to the Klan and support for anti-lynching legislation were major priorities for the NAACP. Blacks in rural Georgia understood and supported both issues all too well, and yet the NAACP was far less successful in organizing in Klan strongholds than was the UNIA. Garvey and the UNIA also concentrated on the problems of white racism and lynching, but sought more pragmatic economic rather than legal solutions. Garvey saw the latter as unrealistic. He bluntly told black people that the Klan was the only group of whites who honestly admitted their hatred for the Negro race and reminded them that southern law enforcement officers often led or at least condoned racist vigilantism.[37] At the 1922 UNIA convention in

Harlem, a female delegate from Jesup, Georgia, reiterated that laws could not prevent lynching in the South. She explained that in Georgia, the so-called "lynching state," Negroes were lynched for "the fun of it," and perpetrators would respond only to force.[38] The UNIA leader's frankness notwithstanding, Georgia followers continued to support Garvey after his meeting with the imperial wizard and his criticism of the Dyer anti-lynching bill, realizing, as he did, that the integrationist impulse to employ legal solutions carried little weight in Klan strongholds where the NAACP could not even safely or openly organize.

In a 1923 address at the Liberty Hall in Harlem, Rev. J. W. Slappey, a Baptist minister from Charleston, South Carolina, called Garvey's stand on the Ku Klux Klan "heaven sent."[39] At the UNIA convention the next year, the Klan issue was discussed at length. Members from different regions of the country held different views on what the association's official position towards the Klan should be. Southern members indicated an unwillingness to make any strong condemnation of the Klan at all, choosing instead to focus on creating an independent African nation as the best solution. William Sherrill, the UNIA's Leader of American Negroes, suggested a policy of "neutral opportunism." This course of action eventually became official policy after the convention adopted a resolution to that effect.[40] This and other similar endorsements of Garvey's interaction with the Klan indicate the despair felt by southern blacks in the early 1920s. Clearly, hope for improving race relations or increasing black political power had disappeared for many. The hope for an independent African nation with Garvey as leader seemed more realistic than social equality and peaceful race relations to many frustrated black Georgians.

Garvey never promised to improve race relations or help blacks gain political influence in the United States. In the first place, he did not believe black people could achieve equality in a "white man's country." In the second, he felt that blacks needed to improve their economic conditions and develop race pride before they could accomplish any other goals. Although at times filled with despair, Garvey's message included uplifting encouragement. The UNIA's promotion of race consciousness gave the movement an important psychological component. Garvey often used black churches, the center of social and religious life, to give his organization's efforts a spiritual dimension.

The UNIA's constitution required each local division or chapter to appoint a chaplain.[41] Several divisional reports published in the *Negro World* indicate that black ministers played a role in organizing the UNIA in Georgia. The spiritual character of local meetings grew naturally out of circumstances. With many division meetings being led by ministers and being held in churches, hymns and prayers became integral parts of UNIA gatherings in the state. On some occasions, speakers for the organization gained permission to recruit new members from the congregations of cooperative pastors.

UNIA divisions from all over the South sent brief descriptions of their meeting agendas to the editor of the *Negro World*. A typical report in the "News and Views of UNIA Divisions" section of the paper included the following information: the name of a church where the meeting took place, the name of a minister who was president of the division, the prayers and hymns performed, the fact that Marcus Garvey's address from the first page of the *Negro World* was read, the topics covered, and the featured speaker. The featured speakers were the highlights of local meetings, and their addresses usually reinforced or glorified Garvey's mission, reported to the group about Africa, or reviewed the UNIA's "aims and objects."

The specific content of these talks provides clues as to what aspects of Garvey's philosophy inspired black Georgians. The most obvious characteristic of southern Garveyism is the unquestioning devotion to the organization's founder and leader. An especially revealing headline in the *Negro World* during Marcus Garvey's trial stated: "Greatest Negro Movement in the World Now on Trial." Just as the *Negro World* editor expressed in this title, Georgians perceived no separation between the UNIA leader and the movement itself. This perception contrasted sharply with that of the larger urban divisions in which local leaders encouraged the pursuit of local aims.

Garvey's followers in Georgia often compared the leader's experiences to those of Biblical heroes. Belle Beatty from Preston saw Garvey as the Moses of black people, preparing to lead them into their native land of Africa.[42] The *Negro World*'s "People's Forum" section contained letters that referred to Garvey in the most affectionate terms. R. E. Knighton, a nonmember from Dawson, claimed that he "never had much to talk about but ever since I have been reading the *Negro World* I have something to talk about and never get tired of talking about that wonderful leader, Marcus Garvey."[43]

This type of praise for Garvey appeared in every issue of the *Negro World*. Even as the leader's financial and legal troubles mounted, his Georgia followers continued to support him with contributions and to praise him in letters to the *Negro World*. After Garvey was convicted of using the mail to mislead potential Black Star Line stock purchasers about the financial condition of the company, the Baxley division held a protest meeting at the First Missionary African Baptist Church. Two hundred people signed a petition to the United States government and contributed to a collection for the Marcus Garvey Defense Fund.[44] Even the white press, which usually ignored

Garvey, noted the resentment of his conviction by blacks. The *Atlanta Constitution* reported that the Associated Press had received scores of telegrams from "nearly every state" protesting the leader's conviction and pleading with the white press to "turn on the searchlight of justice" in order "to reverse this frame-up."[45] Letters and contributions from other parts of Georgia also poured into the central UNIA office after Garvey's conviction.

Of all the funds the UNIA advertised in the *Negro World*, the leader's personal "Defense Fund" drew the most financial support from Georgians. The paper listed the name and hometown of each donor and the amount of each gift. Some Georgia contributors donated up to ten dollars, but the vast majority of the hundreds of donations listed each week were nickels and dimes. Contributions to the Marcus Garvey Defense Fund came from many towns without UNIA divisions during 1923, the year of the leader's conviction, revealing sympathy with the Garvey movement well beyond the UNIA membership.[46] Garvey's personal popularity among rural people who never heard his voice or saw him face-to-face suggests the power of his ideas and the diligence of his supporters in Georgia. Through the *Negro World* and UNIA organizers, the concept of black nationalism and race consciousness permeated the state.

Garvey gained popularity by expounding his plan to make real the nineteenth-century black religious myth of the return to Africa from the "captivity." Southern blacks responded enthusiastically to Garvey's ideas for the "redemption of Africa."[47] Two themes dominated most of the correspondence from Georgia that appeared in the *Negro World:* praise for Garvey and belief in the cause of "freeing the Motherland." From the beginning, Garvey had fueled his movement with the concept of African redemption and sought to make it the single most important focal point of UNIA activity. Whereas divisions in large urban areas developed local objectives to augment and sometimes supplant this most basic of Garvey's goals, the smaller, rural divisions such as those in Georgia remained firmly committed to the liberation of "the Motherland." Garvey preached that the other races would not view blacks as anything other than slaves or serfs as long as blacks in Africa remained under the control of white colonizers and creditors. Tenant farmers and unskilled laborers in the South could readily identify with Africans' dilemma and many seemed to take satisfaction in contributing to the relief of other black men and women whose exploitation paralleled their own. In a sense, they found the subjugation of African blacks even more deplorable than their own, since it occurred in the motherland rather than in "a white man's country."[48]

A man of action, Garvey proposed as the first step toward freeing Africa

Georgia communities without UNIA divisions from which letters
and contributions were sent, 1923–24.

and setting up a black government the repatriation of African Americans
to the motherland. Six African countries had UNIA divisions, including
Liberia, where Garvey proposed to resettle willing American blacks beginning in the fall of 1924. Garvey formally launched his "Let's Put it Over"
African colonization plan in February 1924, although his plans for Liberian
resettlement had been in preliminary stages since 1920.[49]

Before the plan became formalized in 1924, Garvey had included a provision in the UNIA constitution for an "African Redemption Fund" to be
made up of voluntary five-dollar donations from each loyal member "to create a working capital for the organization and to advance the cause for the
building up of Africa."[50] As the *Negro World* began to promote the "Let's
Put it Over" campaign in 1924, Garvey began to solicit contributions for the
"Colonization Fund." He earmarked the money to be spent for the purchase

of five hundred square miles of land along the Cavalla River (along Liberia's southern border), for planning and construction costs, and for transportation to the new colony. He described these plans in detail in the *Negro World*, and Georgia UNIA supporters became excited about the prospects. Their enthusiasm shows clearly in frequent and generous donations to the cause.

The repatriation plan seemed attractive and workable, and Georgia UNIA supporters wanted to help make it a success. Thus when the UNIA requested that each division contribute to the project, the Georgia divisions responded conscientiously. Their contributions paid for engineering, medical, and agricultural experts to study the area set aside for colonization and to have it prepared when the first five hundred African-American emigrants arrived in the fall of 1924. Individual contributions of up to fifteen dollars came from tiny communities such as Pooler, just outside of Savannah, and from larger towns such as Waycross.[51]

Financial support for Garvey's back-to-Africa plan came both from UNIA members and supporters who had no desire to emigrate themselves and from those who dreamed of actually moving to the "Motherland." In a letter to the *Negro World*, Lee Knighton of Dawson, Georgia, thanked God for Marcus Garvey having made her dream of living in Africa possible.[52] Living in Liberia under a black, independent government appealed to the prospective emigrants whether or not they knew the long history of conflict between the descendents of African-American emigrants from the early nineteenth century and the Susu and Ghebo peoples of Liberia.[53] If enthusiasm for the plan and financial support offer any indication, problems between the Americo-Liberian elites who monopolized Liberian government positions and the indigenous working class did not seem insurmountable to Garvey's aims in the eyes of rural Georgia supporters.

The NAACP leaders were quick to reject Garvey's plan for colonization. The UNIA's rival organization demanded social and political equality in the United States, which black Americans and their ancestors had helped to build. In a feature article on his "Eight Weeks in Dixie," Floyd J. Calvin told *Messenger* readers that white mob violence had encouraged blacks to leave the South. He implied that Garvey had misdirected blacks towards an unsuitable escape. In Calvin's view the UNIA misled "the most ignorant and uninformed . . . to blindly want to go to Africa—anywhere to get away from down there!"[54]

Much to Garvey's dismay, and no doubt to his critics' glee, the cause of African redemption received a fatal blow just days before he was to finalize his land transaction with the Liberian government. The Firestone Rubber Company of Akron, Ohio acquired the land, as the result of a much larger

offer than Garvey could pay. Under pressure from his country's many creditors, President C. D. B. King of Liberia thus reneged on his agreement with
the UNIA and destroyed Garvey's expensive plans.[55]

Garvey's failure to accomplish this popular and costly goal damaged morale
within the UNIA administration but had no discernible effect on his popularity or mission with the southern black masses. His Georgia followers continued to send him money and supportive letters throughout the months
after the Liberian debacle. But such support from well-wishers could not
save the Garvey movement from its inevitable undoing. Administrative power
struggles in New York caused large numbers of urban Garveyites to split
from the movement. The rural divisions in Georgia knew little of the details
of charges against their leader because they had few sources of information
beyond the biased *Negro World* or, in some cases, relatives in northern cities.
The political machinations of the large divisions, in fact, had never held
much importance for isolated rural communities. The division lists for Georgia indicate the continuing strength of the UNIA's southern wing, especially
in rural areas, as late as 1927.

Garvey's vision for bettering the conditions of his race at home and abroad
appealed to black Georgians. The UNIA's small southern divisions remained
more consistently focused on their leader's international objectives than did
their larger urban counterparts elsewhere in the country, perhaps because,
unlike Los Angeles or New York members, Garveyites in Georgia and across
the South saw few avenues for immediately improving local conditions. Garvey's disputes with leaders of large urban divisions, his conviction for mail
fraud, and his reimprisonment (ironically, at the Atlanta Federal Penitentiary) on February 8, 1925, did not diminish the impact of the UNIA in the
state of Georgia. The *Negro World* effectively inspired continued support for
the leader and the recovery of Africa for black people through conscientious
and regular attention to southern issues.

The UNIA fragmented during Garvey's two-year imprisonment, despite
his efforts from his new Georgia base to keep its quarreling administration together. On November 26, 1927, President Calvin Coolidge commuted
Garvey's sentence and deported him to Jamaica where he reestablished the
UNIA in Kingston, while his Harlem central division continued its own
program, including the publication of the *Negro World*. The former Harlem
resident was at even more of a disadvantage in trying to coordinate UNIA
activity in the United States from Jamaica, yet he managed rather well under
the circumstances. He began a new publication called *Black Man* which he
issued periodically until his death in 1940.[56]

Even though Garvey had lost too many struggles against people and institutions more powerful than he, his Georgia supporters did not allow his movement to die. The Atlanta and Savannah divisions of the UNIA appeared in a list of functioning divisions published in the April 1935 issue of *Black Man*. Contributions and letters from Georgians continued throughout the 1930s. The deterioration of the UNIA's infrastructure, however, would have forced rural Georgia divisions to become more autonomous and perhaps to focus on local improvements for the first time. With these adjustments, their activities under UNIA auspices become almost impossible to track.

It is worth mentioning, however, that major figures in later black separatist movements had strong ties to rural Georgia where UNIA sentiment flourished. Elijah Muhammad, noted leader of the Black Muslims, grew up the son of a rural preacher and sharecropper in the tiny community of Deepstep in Washington County. He lived and worked in Macon in the early 1920s, the height of the Garvey movement, before moving with his wife and two children to Detroit.[57] Malcolm X's father, a minister and native of Reynolds, in Taylor County, Georgia, preached the UNIA gospel throughout his life. His perceived agitation caused him to flee Omaha, Nebraska for Lansing, Michigan where, according to Malcolm, a white mob eventually murdered him for his militance in 1931.[58]

Long after his fall from power, Marcus Garvey's appeal and his message left an impression on African Americans, especially those living in the South. Although the African Redemption plan had become remote, Garvey's encouragement of separatism and economic improvement resonated in the black community. The white establishment responded positively to the seemingly benign separatist ideology, and consequently the UNIA penetrated communities where the NAACP could not. Garvey provided a vision for isolated, rural people. He did not give black Georgians anything tangible; by contrast they gave him financial support. The UNIA's stability during its heyday depended on the faithfulness of its southern followers like those in Georgia.

Georgia Garveyites were not ignorant or illiterate, as many people at the time charged and even some recent scholars have implied. Many worked, as the census describes, on their "own account" as tenant farmers—independent workers and thinkers who were nonetheless economically trapped by an abusive and seemingly inescapable system. They sought direction and dignity, and Garvey attended to these needs. Through his conflicts with the integrationist leaders of the day, all very well documented for *Negro World* readers, the UNIA leader created an alternative path for rural black Georgians to follow.

Since World War II, integrationists have succeeded in using legal channels to improve conditions and expand opportunities for African Americans. Historically, however, separatism has flourished in environments of racial strife and disillusionment. Rural black Georgians had two unattractive options in the 1920s: to stay put and continue to face the political, social, and economic inequities of the Jim Crow South, or to join relatives and acquaintances as they faced the same struggles in northern ghettoes. Strongholds of Garveyism formed among poor Georgians in areas where people best understood this dilemma. UNIA organizations in Georgia, despite the bleak racial landscape that nourished them, laid a foundation for productive protest and agitation in subsequent decades. And even though such later efforts proved more successful in achieving civil rights and economic opportunity for southern blacks, the separatism endorsed by the generation that grew up reading the *Negro World* continues to have considerable appeal for many African Americans.

Notes

1. Robert A. Hill, ed., *The Universal Negro Improvement Association and Marcus Garvey Papers*, 7 vols. (Berkeley: University of California Press, 1983–1990), 2:492–93 (notes) (hereafter cited as Hill, *UNIA Papers*).

2. Ibid., 563.

3. The primary unit of the UNIA was the "division," but when a locality requested a charter for a second division, this unit was designated a "chapter." At least seven members were required for a division to receive a charter. See UNIA Constitution, article I, sections 4 and 5, in Lenwood Davis and Janet Sims, eds., *Marcus Garvey: An Annotated Bibliography* (Westport, Conn.: Greenwood Press, 1980), 9.

4. In 1926, Georgia divisions of the UNIA included Adel, Alma, Atlanta, Baker County, Baxley, Brunswick, Camilla, Center Hill, Charity Grove, Clyatville, Columbus, Coverdale, Damascus, Decatur, Fitzgerald, Gardi, Haylow, Howell, Jesup, Kimbrough, Limerick, Moultrie, Oakfield, Patterson, Pelham, Pooler, Powellton (Worth County), Ray City, Savannah, Shingler, Sylvester, Ty Ty, and Waycross (2).

5. U.S. Bureau of the Census, *Fourteenth Census of the United States, 1920: Population Composition and Characteristics of Population by State* (Washington, D.C.: Government Printing Office, 1924), 2:222–24.

6. Martin has produced volumes on Garvey and the UNIA, the most comprehensive of which is *Race First: The Ideological and Organizational Struggles of Marcus Garvey and the Universal Negro Improvement Association* (Westport, Conn.: Greenwood Press, 1976).

7. Judith Stein, *The World of Marcus Garvey: Race and Class in Modern Society* (Baton Rouge: Louisiana State University Press, 1986), 153–60.

8. Emory J. Tolbert, *The Universal Negro Improvement Association and Black Los*

Angeles: Ideology and Community in the American Garvey Movement (Los Angeles: UCLA Center for Afro-American Studies, 1980). Tolbert provides an excellent overview of the Garvey movement in his introduction.

9. Universal Negro Improvement Association, Central Division Files (New York), Schomburg Collection, New York Public Library.

10. All of the data on Georgia's UNIA officers comes from the U.S. Census, *Population Schedule, 1920,* Georgia (microfilm).

11. Clarence Walker stresses that the UNIA was overwhelmingly West Indian, and argues that Garvey's infatuation with the trappings of European culture should exclude Garvey from being considered a black nationalist. He acknowledges neither the southern wing of the movement nor the migrants from the South who joined West Indians in urban UNIA chapters in great numbers. Clarence E. Walker, "The Virtuoso Illusionist: Marcus Garvey," in Clarence E. Walker, *Deromanticizing Black History: Critical Essays and Reappraisals* (Knoxville: University of Tennessee Press, 1991).

As William Cohen acknowledges in his essay, "The Great Migration as a Lever for Social Change," a "safe" level of agitation among blacks began in the inter-war years in Mississippi. He notes that a "surprising number [of black Mississippians who did not migrate] quietly joined the UNIA"; see Alferdteen Harrison, ed., *Black Exodus: The Great Migration from the American South* (Jackson: University Press of Mississippi, 1991), 95–97.

The Garvey movement receives no attention in Joe William Trotter, Jr., ed., *The Great Migration in Historical Perspective: New Dimensions of Race, Class, and Gender* (Bloomington: Indiana University Press, 1991). However, Trotter encourages the historiographical trend toward explaining the migration in terms of the roles blacks played in "shaping their own experience" through kinship, friendship, and communal networks rather than in terms of external economic, racial, or class analyses. If applied to the popularity and rapid spread of the Garvey movement in the South, this method reveals a strong, preexisting tendency toward black nationalist ideology in the region.

12. Hill, *UNIA Papers*, 2:51.

13. Martin, *Race First*, 347.

14. Hill, *UNIA Papers*, 1:cxiii.

15. *New York Age*, November 11, 1922, pp. 1–2.

16. *Messenger*, January 1923, 561.

17. *Negro World*, November 17, 1923, p. 5.

18. Ibid., November 24, 1923, p. 2.

19. Ibid., August 16, 1924, p. 2.

20. Charles F. Kellogg, *NAACP: The History of the National Association for the Advancement of Colored People* (Baltimore: Johns Hopkins University Press, 1967), 137.

21. Stein, *The World of Marcus Garvey*, 162.

22. Wilson Record, *Race and Radicalism: The NAACP and the Communist Party in Conflict* (Ithaca: Cornell University Press, 1964), 44.

23. Hill, *UNIA Papers*, 2:609.

24. Other NAACP locations included Albany, Americus, Atlanta, Brunswick, Columbus, Cordele, Dublin, Macon, Rome, and Valdosta. See *Papers of the NAACP, Part I: 1909–1950* (Frederick, Md.: University Publications of America, Inc., 1982, microfilm), reel 8, group I, series B, box 3, file 0962.

25. Ibid., box 2, file 0574.

26. Ibid., file 0588.

27. Hill, *UNIA Papers,* 3:35–36.

28. Ibid., 2:563.

29. *Negro World,* June 21, 1924, p. 4.

30. Amy Jacques Garvey, ed., *Philosophy and Opinions of Marcus Garvey or Africa for the Africans* (London: Frank Cass, 1923, 1925, reprint, 1967), 1:73.

31. Hill, *UNIA Papers,* 4:707–14.

32. Ibid., 814, 932–33. The four men were Pickens, A. Phillip Randolph and Chandler Owen, both coeditors of the *Messenger,* and Robert W. Bagnall, director of NAACP branches.

33. *Negro World,* August 8, 1923, p. 1. This issue contains the best explanation I have seen of Garvey's opinion of Du Bois, his feelings on color differences among blacks, and his reasons for the rift between the UNIA and NAACP.

34. Amy Jacques Garvey, *Philosophy and Opinions,* 2:240.

35. *Savannah Tribune,* September 14, 1922.

36. *Negro World,* January 12, 1924, p. 3.

37. Ibid., October 27, 1923, p. 1. For full accounts of the Dyer bill and the movement from which it emerged, see Donald Lee Grant, *The Anti-Lynching Movement, 1883–1932* (San Francisco: R & E Research Associates, 1975); and Robert L. Zangrando, *The NAACP Crusade against Lynching, 1909–1950* (Philadelphia: Temple University Press, 1980).

38. Hill, *UNIA Papers,* 4:917.

39. *Negro World,* October 27, 1923, p. 3.

40. Ibid., August 16, 1924, p. 3.

41. Randall K. Burkett, *Black Redemption: Churchmen Speak for the Garvey Movement* (Philadelphia: Temple University Press, 1978), 10.

42. *Negro World,* July 19, 1924, p. 14.

43. Ibid., June 21, 1924, p. 14.

44. Ibid., August 4, 1923, p. 7.

45. *Atlanta Constitution,* July 17, 1923, p. 5.

46. From issues of the *Negro World,* 1923–24, I have compiled a sample list of donors from Georgia communities that show no record of containing a UNIA division. Those communities are: Cotton, Crescent, Cuthbert, Darien, Dawson, Fort Benning, Franklin, Glenwood, Guillard, Lumber City, Macon, Meigs, Ocilla, Preston, Stockton, Thomaston, Willacoochee.

47. St. Clair Drake, *The Redemption of Africa and Black Religion* (Chicago: Third World Press, 1970).

48. Throughout his writings and speeches, Garvey consistently juxtaposed "the

Motherland" (Africa) with "the white man's country" (the United States). These usages were so common that admiring *Negro World* readers often used them in their correspondence to the editor. See for example, *Negro World*, June 21, 1924, p. 14.

49. Theodore Vincent, *Black Power and the Garvey Movement* (Berkeley: Ramparts Press, 1971), 178–85.

50. UNIA Constitution, article XV, in Davis and Sims, eds., *Marcus Garvey Bibliography*, 169–70.

51. *Negro World*, June 14, 1924, p. 10.

52. Ibid., June 21, 1924, p. 14.

53. Vincent, *Black Power and the Garvey Movement*, 178.

54. *Messenger*, January 1923, 577.

55. Vincent, *Black Power and the Garvey Movement*, 183.

56. *Blackman* was the title of the Kingston publication Garvey began shortly after his deportation from the U.S. Later the name was changed to *Black Man* and its last editions were published irregularly between 1935 and 1939 from London where Garvey spent the last years of his life.

57. Elijah Muhammad, *Message to the Black Man in America* (Chicago: Muhammad Mosque No. 2, 1965), 24–25.

58. Malcolm X and Alex Haley, *The Autobiography of Malcolm X* (New York: Ballantine Books, 1964), 1–10.

The Popular Front Alternative

Clark H. Foreman and the
Southern Conference for Human Welfare,
1938–1948

Randall L. Patton

The American South has long posed a dilemma to American liberal reformers. Twice in the twentieth century, American reformers have focused on the former Confederacy, with a different agenda each time. During the 1950s and 1960s, reformers attacked segregation directly, and American liberals came to view the "race problem" as the region's primary social ill. Earlier, however, during the 1930s and 1940s, many liberal reformers, including a majority of those within the South itself, acted on the belief that poverty was the "central problem" of the region. Those liberals who came together in the Southern Conference for Human Welfare (SCHW) in 1938 promoted mass organization, labor unionization, and economic reform as the best antidote to the South's unique problems. Poor whites and poor blacks, the South's real majority, could overcome racism only through economic cooperation, according to this view. The SCHW eventually fell victim to internal disputes and the "red scare" of the late 1940s.[1]

Throughout the SCHW's brief ten-year history, no one was more closely identified with, nor more important to, the organization than Clark Howell Foreman of Georgia. Born in Atlanta, Georgia, in 1902, Foreman was the grandson of Evan Howell, founder of the *Atlanta Constitution*, and thus a member of one of the state's elite families. He graduated from the University of Georgia in 1921, then went on to Harvard for a year. Foreman met

Alabama native Virginia Durr while they were both attending school in the North, he at Harvard, she at Wellesley. As strangers in a strange land, these young, privileged southern "colonials" attended Saturday night dances sponsored by a "Southern Club," which helped them maintain a sense of their own regional distinctiveness. As the dances began, Durr recalled, "the band would play 'Dixie' and we would all stand and cheer."[2]

His parents then gave Foreman a thousand dollars to finance a trip to Europe. Foreman's mother gave him a copy of H. G. Wells's *Outline of History* as he left, and the young Georgian read it on the voyage. So impressed was he with the book that he embarked on a campaign to arrange an audience with Wells. Foreman was particularly struck by Wells's vision of the future and "the kind of society that should be," and he sought the great author's advice on what to do with his own future. Wells eventually gave the persistent young man a fifteen-minute interview, in which he advised Foreman to learn German and French and attend the London School of Economics.[3]

Foreman decided to take Wells's advice, but had difficulty convincing his parents of the wisdom of this particular course of action. After all, Foreman later recalled, "the only reason I could give was because H. G. Wells recommended it." Unconvinced by that argument, Foreman's father initially opposed the idea, but eventually relented and agreed to "loan" his son the money to attend the London school. Foreman's experiences in London broadened his horizons and gave him a fresh perspective on his home region. He formed new ideas about economics and society and acquired an international perspective that, in retrospect, appears remarkably similar to the "world-systems" model of sociologist Immanuel Wallerstein. Commenting on the world economic crisis of the early 1930s, Foreman argued that "the withdrawal of such a large part of the world economy as the Russians represented made the old theories of capitalist economy out of date." Presaging Wallerstein, Foreman contended that socialism "wasn't going to work because of the fact that the United States and the rest of the world didn't go into it." In other words, in a world capitalist economy, withdrawal from the system by underdeveloped areas was not feasible.[4]

Like many other southern "liberals," Clark Foreman was first attracted to the cause of reform in his native region by the "race question." After reviewing a book on southern race relations, Foreman decided to return home. "Here I was from Atlanta," he recalled, "learning about what was happening here in my own home town that I had never heard of before." Foreman returned to Atlanta and sought out Will Alexander and the Commission on Interracial Cooperation.[5]

The commission acted quickly and pragmatically. "It was just a question of getting the roads paved and getting the facilities evenly distributed." Foreman, as secretary of the committee for Georgia, negotiated with white and black community leaders, promoting the idea of equal treatment of blacks within the bounds of segregation. "What we were trying to do was to get the people to working together." The commission worked at the grass roots level, attempting to build mutual trust between whites and blacks through practical problem-solving.[6]

Spurred by his work on the Interracial Commission, Foreman left Atlanta to pursue his Ph.D. at Columbia. He eventually published a dissertation dealing with "The Environmental Factors in Negro Elementary Education." Foreman's continued interest in the problems of blacks, along with his experience on the Commission on Interracial Cooperation, led Will Alexander to recommend him for a position with the federal government after the election of Franklin Roosevelt in 1932. Harold Ickes, the incoming Secretary of the Interior, had solicited from Alexander a list of names to be considered for a new post at the department: special adviser on the economic status of Negroes. Foreman was high on Alexander's list, and Ickes hired him. Foreman acted as a watchdog and troubleshooter in matters concerning blacks, particularly with regard to housing and federal employment. He fought for increased appropriations and more consideration of "Negro" problems.[7] Foreman's New Deal experiences further broadened his view of the South and its problems. Foreman eventually held several other positions in government. By 1938 he had become a sort of roving adviser to the executive branch on southern affairs. In 1938, Foreman coordinated the National Emergency Council's efforts to prepare the *Report on the Economic Conditions of the South.*[8]

The NEC report clearly presented the South as an underdeveloped, colonial appendage of the North. "Lacking capital of its own the South has been forced to borrow from outside financiers, who have reaped a rich harvest in the form of interest and dividends," its authors concluded. The National Emergency Council cited the region's dependence on "foreign" capital as a major source of economic problems. Absentee ownership, discriminatory freight rates which acted as an internal tariff, lack of access to capital—its report listed virtually every economic grievance that many in the South had complained of since the Civil War. "Penalized for being rural, and handicapped in its efforts to industrialize," the Emergency Council concluded, "the economic life of the South has been squeezed to the point where the purchasing power of the people does not provide an adequate market for its own industries nor an attractive market for those of the rest of the country."[9] President Roosevelt's signature and introduction gave the strongest endorsement yet at the national level to the idea that the South's problems were colonial in nature.

The NEC report was among the most significant factors in the creation of the Southern Conference for Human Welfare. President Roosevelt encouraged New Deal southerners like Foreman to hold such a conference of regional progressives to promote the New Deal in the South and aid the president in his efforts to purge the Democratic party of "reactionary" southern elements. The SCHW brought together a wide array of people on the "left" in a popular front to oppose "reactionary" elements in the South. The conference was not, however, merely the southern analogue to national liberal groups such as the Union for Democratic Action (though it was that as well). The Southern Conference existed precisely because southerners and many national liberals thought that the South had different problems, unique problems that required unique solutions. Many southerners perceived their region as a "poor relation" in an affluent nation, a "nation within a nation" in many respects, with a different culture and a dependent economy.[10]

Southern liberal nationalists came together in 1938 to form the Southern Conference for Human Welfare. Representatives of organized labor, middle-class reformers, black leaders, political liberals, and even a few bold members of the South's native industrial bourgeoisie attended the conference's initial convention that year. Delegates weathered a controversy over segregation and approved a broad-ranging reform program aimed at promoting "industrial and political democracy" in the South and developing the region's resources. Many, if not a majority, of those in attendance were interested in ending the South's grinding poverty through vigorous government action at both the state and federal levels. They also wanted to enfranchise and organize the southern masses, black and white, as a logical constituency for such a program of industrial development linked with social justice.

Among the most intriguing attendants at the initial Southern Conference were a few southern industrialists and business leaders, led by Donald Comer. These "uptown" leaders shared an interest with other reformers in breaking down the South's isolation from the nation's mainstream and developing the region's native industries. After that, the interests of the business elite diverged dramatically from the goals of organized labor and other segments of the SCHW. Donald Comer's experience illustrates the difficulties in holding together such a broad coalition.

Comer, the son of former Alabama governor Braxton Bragg Comer, was the chairman of the board of Avondale Mills, a cotton textile manufacturing company based in Alabama. Under Donald Comer's leadership, Avondale Mills had pioneered among southern corporations in establishing a profit-sharing program for its employees in 1938. Although he prided himself on maintaining excellent relations with his more than seven thousand workers, Comer was not interested in promoting real power for southern workers; he was a paternalist who sought better relations between management and labor while preserving management's privileges.[11] He was among the twenty industry executives who devised the first textile industry code under the National Recovery Administration in 1933. His NRA experience helped bring Comer in close contact with Franklin Roosevelt, and the Alabama industrialist became an ardent New Dealer in the 1930s.

As a member of the South's nascent industrial bourgeoisie, Comer was committed to promoting industrial progress in the South. He was quite willing to enlist the support of workers and humanitarian liberals by advocating government regulation of working conditions and wages. What Comer and other bourgeois leaders could not tolerate was real power for southern workers. During NRA hearings on the textile code in 1933, Comer had clearly expressed his aversion to organized labor. "I am impressed with the fact that the more nearly we can settle these points in Washington . . . the less need there will be for union labor organization in the plants themselves," Comer wrote to a colleague.[12]

The South's small industrial bourgeoisie developed a limited program for "national" economic development for the South. They appealed to southern workers for support, promising government regulation of working conditions in return. Comer and other members of this class feared the encroachments of the CIO and were unwilling to accept the real power for workers that the CIO represented. Comer attended the first three SCHW meetings, but after that his interest waned. As the conference moved deeper into an alliance with the CIO and became more politically active after 1944, Comer and other southern industrialists quickly abandoned the organization.

The coalition that the SCHW brought together in its initial meeting appeared impressive, drawn from a wide cross section of the South. However, the superficial agreement of the participants on the need for regional economic development masked deep divisions. In particular, the antipathy of the region's business leaders to organized labor made it difficult to hold this organization together. Nonetheless, the SCHW's initial meeting was widely hailed in liberal circles as a great success.

The initial meeting of the organization was held in November 1938. The ostensible purpose pursued by SCHW organizers was to answer the NEC report and promote the idea that the South was not the bastion of reaction many believed it to be. In the wake of the unsuccessful purge campaign of 1938, FDR considered the SCHW a viable long-term tool for building a liberal Democratic coalition in the South. With the president's blessing, southern liberals of various stripes gathered in the heart of Dixie, Birmingham, Alabama, to defy national stereotypes and present alternatives to Bourbon leadership in the region.[13]

In a brief period from 1944 to early 1947, the Southern Conference for Human Welfare acted as a liaison between the Congress of Industrial Organizations and sympathetic middle-class liberals in the South. Due to the efforts and vision of Clark Foreman, above all others, the SCHW almost became the flagship organization of a southern economic and political renaissance. The CIO heightened its participation in the conference at the latter's 1942 convention, held in Nashville. Of the approximately 500 delegates in attendance, 160 represented organized labor and 112 of these were CIO members.

Among the CIO contingent were Lucy Randolph Mason and Paul R. Christopher. Mason, a descendant of George Mason of Virginia, had spent virtually her entire adult life working for reform with the YWCA and the National Consumers' League. In 1937, she went to work as the southern publicity director for John L. Lewis's new CIO. Paul Christopher grew up in a mill village in South Carolina and worked his way up the ranks in the old United Textile Workers and then the CIO's Textile Workers' Union of America. During the CIO's "Operation Dixie" (1946–53), Christopher served as director of the CIO's organizing committee for Tennessee. Both Mason and Christopher won election to the SCHW's executive board; the latter also agreed to serve as national vice president of the organization.[14]

Lucy Mason exemplified the CIO's view of southern race relations in the 1930s and 1940s. She defined the race problem as a "class" problem. CIO partisans generally believed that race should be dealt with as a symptom rather than as the disease itself. As Mason argued, employers consciously exploited the race issue to push down wages for whites and blacks. "The basic issue [in organizing southern workers] was economic—the right of workers to organize and to challenge the supreme control of industrial conditions by powerful business interests," she said. "The race issue was *interwoven* because it is *integrally a part of* economic issues in the South" (Mason's emphasis). Unless black and white workers were organized together, employers could continue to use the same fear tactics. If civil rights for blacks came at the expense of white workers, or if white economic gains continued to come at the expense of blacks, the result would only be greater division and bitterness.[15]

The Southern Conference early on established the poll tax as its primary reform target in the South. Conference spokespersons estimated that in 1938 the poll tax disfranchised between five and eleven million poor white and black voters. Georgia's poll tax was a product of the Reconstruction era in the South. Both the "radical Republican" state constitution of 1868 and the "Bourbon" constitution of 1877 authorized the legislature to implement a cumulative poll tax as a requirement for voting, and it was put into effect in the 1880s.[16]

The conference's anti-poll-tax efforts have been criticized by some as too moderate to produce real reform but provocative enough to produce vituperative retaliation from southern reactionaries. Most of these critics emphasize the efforts of SCHW leaders to keep the issue from being identified as a racial one, implying that the conference could have better spent its time and efforts in directly attacking segregation. "The impact of the poll tax on Southern politics was clearly exaggerated, given reformers' own recognition that poll tax repeal would not enfranchise many blacks," wrote Morton Sosna in 1977. "Southern liberals," he argued, "channeled too much energy into what at best would have been a symbolic victory."[17]

From a narrow perspective focused exclusively on race, Sosna's criticism carries some weight. Clark Foreman and other conference leaders would not have understood it in the atmosphere of the late 1930s and 1940s, however. Foreman would have opposed any such effort to divorce the campaign against the poll tax from its ultimate goal: to make possible the great coalition of working-class whites and blacks, led by middle-class intellectuals of the SCHW. The anti-poll-tax movement only made sense to SCHW members in these terms. Certainly, many conference leaders made a point of mentioning the then-current "Progressive" argument advanced by C. Vann Woodward that the poll tax and other disfranchisement measures were aimed less at blacks than poor whites. Certainly Foreman and others attempted to appeal to whites with such arguments; that was pragmatic politics. The larger point was that they were trying to reconstruct the fragile, perhaps mythical coalition of whites and blacks from the Populist Era that, according to Woodward, had precipitated disfranchisement. The basis of that potential coalition in the 1940s, as it had been in the 1890s, was economic. It was pointless to try to moralize to working-class whites about the evils of white supremacy. Segregation could be ended peacefully and constructively only as black and white workers came to an understanding that they needed one another in the union hall.[18]

Southern Conference leaders viewed the poll tax as one of the chief impediments to the formation of the labor-liberal coalition. In February 1939, the SCHW's executive board established a civil rights committee whose main task was to study the poll tax issue. Chaired by Maury Maverick of Texas, the committee issued a report in September of that year calling for an all-out campaign against the poll tax. In 1940, the SCHW and the CIO joined forces to create the National Committee to Abolish the Poll Tax. Almost every year between 1940 and 1948 the Southern Conference and the Committee Against the Poll Tax helped to introduce anti-poll-tax bills in Congress. Through all the lobbying and publicity work on the poll tax issue, SCHW's most tireless campaigner was Virginia Foster Durr, Foreman's friend from their college days at Harvard and Wellesley.[19]

Virginia Foster was born in Birmingham, Alabama in 1903. Her father's family, once substantial planters and slaveholders, came from Union Springs, "in the heart of the black belt." Growing up around her grandparents' plantation, she came to know race relations in the South from the perspective of the white paternalist. Even in the 1910s and 1920s, there were old slave cabins in the backyard, occupied by people whose parents and grandparents had been Foster family slaves.[20]

Virginia married lawyer Clifford Durr in 1926, and in 1933 they moved to Washington where he took a job with the Reconstruction Finance Corporation. Durr held several government jobs during the 1930s and 1940s and became a devoted Roosevelt liberal, as did his wife. In 1938, Virginia Durr became one of the founding members of the SCHW and in 1940 became vice-chairman of the Southern Conference's offspring, the National Committee to Abolish the Poll Tax.[21] Durr used her considerable charm to lobby congressmen to support the Conference's position on the poll tax and in so doing made extensive contacts with national liberal leaders and politicians during the 1940s.[22]

For Durr, the poll tax was not an exclusively racial issue. Though she would later be intimately involved in the Civil Rights movement, during the 1940s Durr followed a different path toward social justice for her region. The National Committee to Abolish the Poll Tax formed a crucial part of the Roosevelt New Deal coalition. The poll tax disfranchised precisely those voters in the South who would be most likely to vote for pro–New Deal candidates: poor whites and blacks. Durr consciously opposed the "oligarchy" which controlled southern politics: the planters and the northern-controlled corporate interests, known in her native Alabama as the "Big Mules." Durr and the SCHW chose the poll tax issue because it had the best chance to attract a broad coalition of white and black supporters. It was opposed by almost all southerners in Congress (Claude Pepper and Estes Kefauver being notable exceptions). The poll tax, for Durr, represented yet another example of "the exploitation of human beings by other human beings." [23]

Foreman and Durr acted in unison on the race issue within the SCHW. Foreman always insisted that the conference hold integrated public meetings, and the organization did officially oppose legal segregation in the South. As Foreman recalled, the SCHW did not make fighting segregation a high priority because "we didn't want to make that the chief issue." Foreman contended that the SCHW was more concerned with "the whole economic picture."[24]

The poll tax fight dominated conference energies through World War II. Near the end of the war, SCHW leaders broadened their efforts to reform the South. The election of Clark H. Foreman as president of the conference in 1944 marked the organization's alliance with organized labor and its intensified participation in partisan politics.

Foreman joined with Lucy Mason in 1944 to advocate an alliance between the Southern Conference and the CIO. In November of that year, Foreman and James A. Dombrowski, executive secretary of SCHW, prepared an analysis of southern political conditions for Philip Murray and other top CIO leaders. "There is good ground for maintaining that the South can become, in a very short time, the most liberal region in the Nation," they advised Murray. The reactionary South was the one with which most of the nation was familiar, Foreman and Dombrowski argued, but there was "another South composed of the great mass of small farmers, the sharecroppers, the industrial workers, white and colored." This "other South," they estimated, made up about 80 percent of the southern population but was disorganized and disfranchised. The two men advocated an expansion of the Southern Conference's activities with increased CIO support in order to "organize the unorganized" in the South and create a grand coalition for social justice and development. With almost two million CIO members already in the South, as well as "a fairly large group of the most progressive ministers, editors, educators, and writers" in the country, there was a solid liberal base from which to begin. Foreman clearly wanted CIO financial and moral support in helping the conference "take the lead in mobilizing the liberal South."[25]

In July 1943, the CIO had created its own Political Action Committee, which represented a dramatic departure from the long-standing policy of the American Federation of Labor toward politics and political action. Further distancing itself from its former parent organization, the CIO advocated positive government action to establish social justice.[26] The balance of the CIO's strength centered in the North, where local and state branches of the PAC were established rather quickly. The South presented more of a challenge as conservative politicians and community leaders exploited working-class fears of "outsiders" and tried to use the very existence of the CIO PAC as evidence of the organization's intent to subvert traditional southern values. The southern branches of most CIO unions were in their embryonic stages as well, and taking on the added burden of political action might have destroyed them in their infancy. Yet conservative southern legislators were among labor's chief opponents.

In a move timed to coincide with SCHW's own request for increased CIO cooperation, Lucy Randolph Mason wrote Philip Murray suggesting that this political "gap" be filled by the Southern Conference. She outlined a plan of action which she thought might succeed in "liberating" the South from its reactionary shackles. Southern "progressives outside the labor movement and inside the CIO" wanted "to see a coordinated, widespread movement in the South" composed of all elements of southern progressivism. The implication of Mason's memorandum became clear: neither the CIO nor the South's middle-class liberals had enough strength on their own to produce any meaningful change in the region, but together they might succeed. "More than any organization in the United States," Mason wrote, "the CIO holds a key to the situation and has the power to influence the South in the right direction." She advocated a virtual alliance of the CIO and the SCHW. The conference "supplies the best instrument for promoting such a movement," while the CIO could provide the "largest financial contribution" and the mass base for a "people's movement." The Southern Conference could, in effect, serve as the CIO's "Southern PAC."[27]

Murray responded favorably to the requests of Foreman, Dombrowski, and Mason, agreeing that the conference had strong potential to promote unionization in the South. Murray believed the CIO's executive board endorsed the Southern Conference as "the natural and appropriate spearhead of the liberal forces of the South." The CIO would henceforth "give all positive and constructive support to the Southern Conference."[28]

The Southern Conference already served as the southern branch of the National Citizens Political Action Committee, which had been formed in 1944 to promote liberal support for Franklin Roosevelt's fourth-term presidential bid and then made permanent. Clark Foreman served as executive secretary of the liberal organization.[29] It is significant that Southern Conference leaders such as Foreman did not merely disband the SCHW or merge it with the NCPAC. Foreman, Mason, Christopher, and others obviously felt that the South was different enough to justify the existence of a separate liberal organization. The conference provided a forum for militant voices in the South, voices advocating sweeping political changes. The alliance between the conference and the CIO, brief though it proved to be, represented for Foreman the best chance to organize the southern masses in their own interests.[30]

The SCHW's program of "industrial and political democracy" was attractive to the CIO, and the two organizations' goals meshed for a time. Conference membership grew to over ten thousand by the end of 1946, and it put together a budget in excess of $200,000 in that year as well, thanks mainly to contributions from CIO member unions. State conferences were set up in several states. A Washington committee lobbied Congress, and a New York committee solicited donations in the North in order to, as Dombrowski put it, "reclaim for the southern people a tiny percentage of the wealth drained from them to the financial center of the nation." The Conference even began regular publication of the *Southern Patriot,* a newsletter which publicized SCHW activities and causes.[31]

Some conference members were uncomfortable with the increasing emphasis on economics and labor at the expense of tackling racial problems head-on. Lillian Smith, the noted Georgia author of *Strange Fruit,* a controversial novel on interracial romance, had enthusiastically joined the conference in 1940 and hailed it as "a symbol of a changing South, a good South," for refusing to hold segregated meetings. By 1945, however, Smith had grown concerned over the SCHW's emphasis on material concerns as well as its "suspect" position regarding communism. Smith wrote to conference executive board members in May 1945, cautioning them not to overemphasize economics: "It is so easy to forget that a man's self-esteem, his dignity, his feelings about himself, his thoughts and his freedom to express those thoughts are what give him his human stature." SCHW members should keep in mind "that human beings are our end, that their creative growth is our end. The ballot, the job, the wages, the housing are simply means to this end." In a telling letter to SCHW administrator James Dombrowski, Smith also complained that among the organization's membership as of 1942, there were no "public health workers, psychiatrists, physicians, child welfare workers, penologists, juvenile judges" and "few educators, few lawyers, few industrialists, few social scientists," who could bring to the conference's work "techniques, points of view, scientific knowledge, [and] objectivity."[32]

Thus, Smith criticized the organization for not being democratic and at the same time urged that more attention be paid to "experts." The conference remained throughout its brief history dependent on middle-class professional reformers, but at least in theory, and in its alliance with the CIO, it aspired to be a mass organization. This was apparently not good enough for Smith. Her version of democracy revolved around discovering "scientific" truth as disseminated by professionals, and then crafting policies to bring the benefits of "expert opinions" to the masses. Though the delineation is not clear (Foreman was a social scientist himself), the Southern Conference's leadership was at least nominally interested in participation by the "masses." Smith, though, like many mainstream liberals, seemed increasingly afraid of "the people," as Christopher Lasch has recently argued.[33]

The CIO-SCHW alliance began to unravel in mid-1946, as the more progressive wing of the labor movement launched "Operation Dixie," a massive organizing drive aimed at southern workers. Ironically, this was precisely the kind of mass organizing campaign the SCHW had long sought to implement. SCHW leaders hailed the April 1946 opening of the CIO's Southern Organizing Committee as the first step toward building the mass-based coalition the two organizations had promoted since 1944. The Southern Conference helped sponsor a "Help Organize the South" rally in New York City as the drive opened to show solidarity with the CIO.[34]

The leaders of the CIO's "Operation Dixie" publicly rejected the Southern Conference that same month. CIO President Murray had selected Van Bittner, an associate from the Steelworkers Union, to head Operation Dixie. In his speech announcing the drive, Bittner rejected the aid of all outside organizations. He specifically mentioned the Southern Conference and added caustically, "any other organization living off the CIO."[35]

Foreman and other SCHW leaders were shocked. Foreman wrote Philip Murray asking for an explanation of Bittner's attack on the conference. Murray intervened on behalf of the conference, urging Bittner to make amends for the insult. Communicating through SCHW board member Paul Christopher, Bittner conveyed his apologies to Foreman and the conference, saying his remarks "were in no way intended as a reflection on the Southern Conference," but that "the tenor of the campaign must be entirely organizational."[36]

The flap over Bittner's remarks was symbolic of the tension that was developing among elements of the old Popular Front in the wake of the emerging cold war between the United States and the Soviet Union. The charge of "communist" subversion was leveled at many formerly respectable groups. The Southern Conference was certainly not immune to such charges, and in the wake of Truman's campaign to "scare the hell" out of the American people, the political waters became even more treacherous. The communist issue was at the heart of the growing rift between the CIO and the SCHW.[37] The SCHW had never barred members of the Communist party from membership; it had in fact always accepted a wide array of members from various positions on the "left." Until 1945, this expansive policy of inclusion caused the organization only minor problems. After 1945, those problems escalated and finally proved fatal.

Frank McCallister of the Southern Workers' Defense League, a socialist organization, had campaigned vigorously during the SCHW's first years to purge it of its "red humors." He used guilt-by-association, innuendo, and questionable witnesses to accuse top conference officials of being Communist party members or "dupes."[38] The early debate about communist influence in the SCHW came to a head after the conference's third convention in 1942. By that time, conference liberals Frank Porter Graham and Clark Foreman had maneuvered suspected communists out of leadership positions, but that was not enough for McCallister. He wrote to Foreman, then executive secretary of the conference, to protest the continued presence of communists within the SCHW. Foreman responded by asserting the Popular Front nature of the conference, insisting that all the South's "progressive" elements had to band together to defeat fascism abroad and reaction at home. Paul Christopher and Lucy Mason wrote supporting letters to McCallister, making the CIO's position clear: the Popular Front was worth preserving.[39]

World War II had made it easy to paper over the communist issue. But in the war's aftermath, the conflict flared again with greater intensity, with the unintentional complicity of the Truman administration with national conservatives in the "red-baiting" trend. Within the CIO, the communist issue threatened to destroy the progressive wing of the labor movement. Philip Murray, who had struggled to remain neutral in the growing controversy, moved closer and closer to open hostility to his "left-wing" union brothers.

The national CIO's shift away from the Popular Front undoubtedly was motivated in large part by political expediency. The CIO had allied itself with the Democratic party during the 1930s and 1940s in order to enhance labor's bargaining power, but the postwar conservative reaction threatened to engulf organized labor. The CIO's success had been due in large part to government support. Somewhere along the line, it had become an appendage of the Democratic party and could not afford actively to oppose a Democratic administration.

Clark Foreman had another explanation, perhaps influenced by his own bitterness at the CIO's abandonment of the SCHW. Foreman believed that Murray was motivated by his Catholicism and was convinced that Murray's "father confessor told him if he wanted to get to heaven he better straighten out the CIO first." The influential Association of Catholic Trade Unions was vehemently anticommunist, as was the Church, and Foreman thought Murray caved in to their pressure.[40]

Certainly Foreman could have handled the communist issue more skillfully. Foreman was simply not concerned with trying to root out suspected "reds." To him, this was a false issue. Many anticommunist liberals must have agreed with the CIO's Alabama director, James Carey, who, in a meeting with Eleanor Roosevelt in early 1945, complained that Foreman "couldn't recognize a communist." Mrs. Roosevelt, concerned about the future of the

SCHW, passed along Carey's concern to Foreman, who responded, "It is possible that I may not be able to 'recognize a communist,' but it is also possible that others recognize communists even where they don't in fact exist," a pointed reference to the intensified "red-baiting."[41] Whatever the reasons, CIO support for the Southern Conference dwindled. In 1945, CIO unions had contributed over $28,000 to the conference. In 1946, that figure fell to less than $20,000. The CIO national office ended all its contributions to the SCHW after April 1946. In the second half of 1946, revenues fell off by at least half.[42] In the midst of all this, the conference was struck both from within and from without.

The internal conflict that hit the conference was at least in large measure a clash of personalities between Foreman and Dombrowski. President Foreman favored moving the conference full-scale into national politics, while Executive Secretary Dombrowski urged a slower and more cautious approach. The two were of different types: Dombrowski the idealist and Foreman the pragmatist. Foreman contended that Dombrowski was not energetic enough in transforming the SCHW into a mass organization.

Tensions had also developed between the national office and the Washington office and were exacerbated by the increasingly dire financial straits of the organization. In a November 1946 board meeting in New Orleans, Foreman moved to reorganize the conference in the absence of many of Dombrowski's allies. Foreman wanted to create a separate education fund to continue the SCHW's educational and propagandizing activities. This ploy was designed to preserve tax-exempt status for at least a portion of the SCHW and move Dombrowski out of SCHW by making him head of the new SCEF. Foreman favorite Branson Price, an energetic North Carolina woman, would then move up to executive secretary of the conference, where she would more aggressively carry out the SCHW's political program, according to Foreman.[43]

The entire process hurt feelings and bruised egos all around. Dombrowski called on supporters on the conference board to rally to his defense. At a special meeting of the SCHW board in January 1947, the conference's directors voted to restore the status quo ante, though the Foreman position eventually won out. The whole affair served to reduce the conference's already flagging morale.[44]

A more serious blow to the Southern Conference came from outside forces, mainly focused on the communist question. Just before the New Orleans convention of November 1946, the Americanism Committee of the New Orleans Young Men's Business Club released the results of its "investigation" of the conference, which it had carried out with assistance from the House Un-American Activities Committee. Its report cited SCHW support for "the repeal of the poll tax, the passing of the FEPC bill, better living conditions for the working man, civil liberties" and other liberal causes as evidence of communist subversion.[45]

The Business Club report was only the opening salvo. Criticism from newspapers across the South followed. The most scathing came from a fellow "southern liberal," Ralph McGill. McGill's columns in the *Atlanta Constitution* were so vehement in their accusations that Foreman threatened to sue the editor, which forced McGill to retract some of his wildest accusations. HUAC added its voice to the chorus in June 1947 when it condemned the SCHW as a communist-front organization. All this contributed to the deterioration of CIO-SCHW relations.[46]

Lucy Mason of the CIO also criticized Foreman for placing too much emphasis on the New York and Washington committees of the SCHW. According to Mason, Foreman devoted too much attention to raising support for southern reform in the North. She maintained that conference would never "grow and become greatly effective . . . unless its roots are in Southern soil." "Not the finest superstructure in Washington and the North can be of permanent value unless its [SCHW's] foundations are in the everyday people down in the Southern states. It is these people I keep thinking about and want to take along with us." [47]

Foreman clashed with Mason and the Georgia committee of SCHW in 1946 and early 1947 over this issue of local versus national control. In the Georgia Democratic gubernatorial primary of 1946, Eugene Talmadge, Georgia's veteran racist reactionary, opposed James V. Carmichael, a moderate with the endorsement of outgoing Governor Ellis Arnall. Arnall had led the fight against discriminatory freight rates during the mid 1940s and had helped abolish the poll tax in Georgia. When in 1945, the Supreme Court declared the "white primary" unconstitutional, Arnall resisted demands from white supremacists such as Talmadge that he subvert the Court's decision by such measures as removing party primaries from state control. The SCHW, who had just awarded Arnall its Thomas Jefferson Award for his stance, had little trouble choosing sides in the 1946 contest: Carmichael, as Arnall's candidate, received the organization's support.[48]

Foreman and Mason differed as to the proper role for the Georgia committee in this election. Foreman believed that it was not vigorous or open enough in its support for Carmichael. The committee's excessive caution had in effect helped Talmadge, Foreman argued. Mason and other members of the Georgia committee preferred to work quietly behind the scenes, reasoning that any open endorsement of Carmichael by SCHW would hurt more than help. The SCHW was antisegregation, and public actions on behalf of Carmichael would have given even more ammunition to the racist Talmadge forces. The dispute revolved around the local-national split. Foreman wanted the state committees to respond more directly to national direction, while Mason believed that the membership of each state committee should determine its own course of action, taking into account local conditions. By the end of 1947, Foreman had decided to withhold funds from the Georgia committee, and the committee disbanded.[49]

Although Paul Christopher and Lucy Mason remained on the conference's executive board, only Mason regularly attended meetings. Christopher declined to aid the conference in setting up a SCHW committee for Tennessee in May 1946, telling Foreman that he could not get involved "for reasons I prefer not to cite here [in a letter]." His reasons were very likely pressure from above. When the CIO's list of "approved organizations," those eligible to receive contributions from CIO member unions, appeared in March 1947, the Southern Conference was not on it. In December 1947, Paul Christopher and Lucy Mason resigned from the Southern Conference's executive board, in Christopher's case most likely under pressure from Bittner. He had remained on the board for eight months after the conference's removal from the approved list. He wrote Foreman that he regretted the move, but he "had no alternative."[50]

The CIO launched a purge of its own in 1947, beginning the process of expelling "left-wing" or "communist-dominated" member unions. In the process, any momentum Operation Dixie may have had was lost. Additionally, some of the unions eventually expelled by the CIO were particularly popular among black workers in the South. Indeed, the "left-wing" unions had recruited blacks more aggressively in the 1930s and 1940s. The "communist-dominated" unions such as the Food, Tobacco, and Agricultural Workers (a key union in Virginia and North Carolina, the South's tobacco region) certainly could be disruptive and difficult, but expelling the troublesome unions led to more problems. As the CIO leadership later admitted, it took a decade for the organization to recover; by then, the political landscape had changed dramatically.[51] With CIO support and any hope for a mass base gone, Foreman and the rapidly expiring Southern Conference latched onto Henry Wallace's third party as their last chance. President Harry Truman successfully "isolated [Wallace] in the public mind with the communists." What was left of the conference went down in flames with Wallace in 1948. The Popular Front approach had failed, as had the conference's attempt to gather the progressive forces of the South together to promote a program of "political and industrial democracy."[52]

Foreman and the Southern Conference had advocated a broad alliance to combat the South's basic problem: poverty. Their program was based on empowering the southern masses, on giving the South's poor, black and white, a voice in their own future. The alliance with the CIO had been crucial. Once that link was broken, the SCHW had had it, as its leaders knew. Clark Foreman always defended the Popular Front strategy of inclusion followed by SCHW and insisted that "much greater damage is done to an organization by exclusion for beliefs than by allowing membership to those who differ." Twenty years after the fact, Foreman summed up the significance of the CIO-SCHW schism: "Many organizations and people surrendered their principles and their interests because they were told that unless they did so they would be helping the Russians," according to Foreman. "Presumably this is what happened to Philip Murray and much of the CIO." The CIO's shift from an "endorsement of us [SCHW] in 1944 to Van Bittner's slap in the face of 1946 represents more than the fatal stab to us," the SCHW's leader argued, "it was a sign of a collapse on the part of Murray which was extremely harmful to the CIO, to the labor movement generally, and to our country."[53]

Without the SCHW, the CIO's Operation Dixie became merely an organizing drive, one which met only limited success at that. The CIO lost much of its radical potential for reordering southern and American priorities as it accepted a supporting role in the Democratic party's cold war liberal coalition. Middle-class liberals became increasingly isolated as lonely voices of protest, cut off from mass organizations. Organized labor was hamstrung in the South after the passage of the Taft-Hartley Act. The debate over the South's future was increasingly dominated by the race question. Working-class whites were increasingly alienated from a national liberalism which offered them little other than a chance to compete for a limited number of decent jobs in a broader labor market.

A cold-war, liberal Democratic Congress did direct more federal dollars to the South after World War II, continuing the New Deal trend. Defense spending, crop allotment payments, and federal welfare programs pumped capital into the South, combining with southern boosterism to promote the rise of the "Sunbelt South." Yet poverty and race relations remained a regional problem. In the absence of strong mass labor organizations or pressure groups such as the SCHW, federal aid was generally managed by local elites. As James C. Cobb has demonstrated, southern economic elites used federal aid for their own purposes, promoting the continuation of dependence and paternalism. As was often the case in "Third World" societies, the United States chose "to channel assistance to those at the bottom . . . through those at the top." As a result, Cobb concludes, "when economic reform proceeds under safeguards against the redistribution of wealth or power, civil and political rights will prove difficult to extend and dangerous to exercise."[54]

As Lillian Smith had argued, a purely materialist approach could not solve the South's, or the nation's, social problems. Foreman and the SCHW fiercely maintained, however, that poverty and the use of race to maintain a regional, low-wage labor market were important factors in the diagnosis and treatment of the South's social ills. The purely moral and spiritual appeal of the mainstream Civil Rights movement, divorced from the broader economic context, presented its own difficulties.

Notes

1. The standard account of the SCHW is Thomas Krueger, *And Promises to Keep: The Southern Conference for Human Welfare, 1938–1948* (Nashville: Vanderbilt University Press, 1967). A more recent insightful interpretation of the Conference may be found in Linda Reed, *Simple Decency and Common Sense: The Southern Conference Movement, 1938–1963* (Bloomington: Indiana University Press, 1991). For an examination of the SCHW's role in southern politics, see Numan V. Bartley, "The Southern Conference and the Shaping of Postwar Southern Politics," in Winfred B. Moore et al., eds., *Developing Dixie: Modernization in a Traditional Society* (Westport, Conn.: Greenwood Press, 1988), 179–97.

2. Virginia Durr, *Outside the Magic Circle: The Autobiography of Virginia Foster Durr*, Hollinger F. Barnard, ed. (Tuscaloosa: University of Alabama Press, 1985), 53–54.

3. Interview with Clark H. Foreman, November, 1974, Southern Oral History Program, Southern Historical Collection, University of North Carolina Libraries, Chapel Hill.

4. Clark Foreman, "The End of Internationalism," *New Republic* 75 (August 9, 1933): 332–35.

5. Foreman interview transcript, 7.

6. Ibid., 8–9.

7. Ibid., 15–18.

8. Ibid., 19.

9. National Emergency Council, *Report on the Economic Conditions of the South* (Washington, D.C., 1938), 58–60, 63–64. For a comprehensive account of the South's isolated, low-wage labor market, see Gavin Wright, *Old South, New South: Revolutions in the Southern Economy since the Civil War* (New York: Basic Books, 1986), chaps. 6 and 7.

10. For an intriguing discussion of the nature and origins of "nationalist" sentiments, see Ernest Gellner, *Nations and Nationalism* (Ithaca, N.Y.: Cornell University Press, 1983).

11. Donald Comer, "The Job of Management," *University of Alabama Business News* 18, no. 10 (June 1948), Clipping File, Birmingham Public Library, Birmingham, Ala.

12. Quoted in James A. Hodges, *New Deal Labor Policy and the Southern Cotton Textile Industry, 1933–1941* (Knoxville: University of Tennessee Press, 1986), 49–50.

13. Clark Foreman, "The Decade of Hope," *Phylon* 12 (1951): 137–40.

14. Krueger, *And Promises to Keep*, 97–98.

15. Lucy Randolph Mason to Frank Dorsey, July 16, 1943, *Operation Dixie: The CIO Organizing Committee Papers, 1946–1953* (New York, 1980, microfilm edition), Series 5: Section 1. Hereinafter cited as *CIO Papers*, followed by series and section numbers; "Minutes of Regional Conference of CIO Regional Directors," *CIO Papers*, Series 5:2.

16. Numan V. Bartley, *The Creation of Modern Georgia*, 2d ed. (Athens: University of Georgia Press, 1990), 80–81.

17. Morton Sosna, *In Search of the Silent South: Southern Liberals and the Race Issue* (New York: Columbia University Press, 1977), 103.

18. This was the rationale behind most CIO efforts in the region. See Lucy Randolph Mason, *To Win These Rights: A Personal Story of the CIO in the South* (New York: Harper and Row, 1952).

19. "The Poll Tax," SCHW Publications, box 43, and Minutes, SCHW Executive Board Meeting, March 21, 1940, box 42, Carl and Anne Braden Papers, State Historical Society of Wisconsin, Madison; Sosna, *In Search of the Silent South*, 102–4.

20. Durr, *Outside the Magic Circle*, 5–9.

21. Ibid., 93–97, 116–20.

22. Ibid., 152–60.

23. Virginia Durr to Claude Pepper, December 2, 1942, box 5, Clifford and Virginia Durr Papers, State Historical Society of Wisconsin, Madison.

24. Foreman interview, 55.

25. Clark Foreman and James Dombrowski, "Memo of the CIO Executive Board," November 13, 1944, box 14, Records of the Southern Conference for Human Welfare, Tuskegee University Archives, Tuskegee, Alabama (hereafter cited as SCHW-Tuskegee). On Dombrowski's role in the SCHW, see Frank T. Adams, *James A. Dombrowski: An American Heretic, 1897–1983* (Knoxville: University of Tennessee Press, 1992), chapters 8–10.

26. James C. Foster, *The Union Politic: The CIO Political Action Committee* (Columbia: University of Missouri Press, 1975), 102–3, 205–6.

27. Lucy Mason to Philip Murray, October 30, 1944, *CIO Papers*, Series 5:1.

28. Philip Murray to Lucy Mason, November 1, 1944, *CIO Papers*, Series 5:1; CIO memorandum quoted in Krueger, *And Promises to Keep*, 125–26.

29. Foreman interview, 72–73.

30. Ibid., 54–56.

31. James Dombrowski, "Southern Conference for Human Welfare," *Common Ground* 6 (Summer 1946): 14–25; Foreman interview, 75–76; Mary Price Adamson interview, Southern Oral History Program, Southern Historical Collection, University of North Carolina, Chapel Hill, 40–42.

32. Lillian Smith to SCHW Board Members, May 18, 1945, *CIO Papers*, Series

244   RANDALL L. PATTON

3:566, and Smith to Dombrowski, May 7, 1945, box 15, Lillian Smith Papers, Hargrett Rare Book and Manuscript Library, University of Georgia Libraries, Athens, Ga.

33. Christopher Lasch, *The True and Only Heaven: Progress and Its Critics* (New York: W. W. Norton, 1991), especially chap. 10, "The Politics of the Civilized Minority," 412–75.

34. Krueger, *And Promises to Keep*, 139.

35. *New York Times*, April 18, 1946, p. 4.

36. Clark Foreman to Paul Christopher, April 22, 1946, and Christopher to Foreman, May 3, 1946, *CIO Papers*, Series 3:566.

37. Mary S. McAuliffe, *Crisis on the Left: Cold War Politics and American Liberalism, 1947–1959* (Amherst: University of Massachusetts Press, 1978), 13.

38. Ibid., 66–67.

39. Frank McCallister to Clark Foreman, May 4, 1942, and Foreman to McCallister, May 12, 1942, *CIO Papers*, Series 3:566; and Kenneth Douty, "Research Study Prepared on the Southern Conference for Human Welfare," box 42, Southern Conference for Human Welfare Papers, Robert W. Woodruff Library, Atlanta University (hereafter cited as SCHW-AU). This study, funded by the Ford Foundation's Fund for the Republic and written by former conference member and Textile Workers Union of America official Douty, found no evidence of direct Communist influence on the SCHW.

40. Foreman interview, 56.

41. Clark Foreman to Eleanor Roosevelt, March 26, 1945, box 42, SCHW-AU.

42. Krueger, *And Promises to Keep*, 142–44.

43. "Minutes of the Meeting of the Board of Representatives," November 28, 1946, box 37, SCHW-AU; Foreman interview, 1974.

44. "Minutes of the Meeting of the Board of Representatives," January 5, 1947, box 37, SCHW-AU.

45. *Action: Official Publication of the Young Men's Business Club of New Orleans*, November 13, 1946, found in box 35, SCHW-AU.

46. *Atlanta Constitution*, November 19 and 26, 1946, and September 2 and 15, 1947; *Report of the Special Committee on Un-American Activities: Report on Southern Conference for Human Welfare*, 80th Cong., 1st Sess., June 16, 1947.

47. Lucy Mason to James Dombrowski, April 18, 1945, box 34, SCHW-Tuskeegee.

48. Randall L. Patton, "A Southern Liberal and the Politics of Anti-Colonialism: The Governorship of Ellis Arnall," *Georgia Historical Quarterly* 74 (Winter 1990): 599–621.

49. John P. Salmond, *Miss Lucy of the CIO: The Life and Times of Lucy Randolph Mason, 1882–1959* (Athens: University of Georgia Press, 1988), 162–65.

50. Paul Christopher to Clark Foreman, December 1, 1947, *CIO Papers*, Series 3:566.

51. An excellent introduction to the complex interaction of race and organized

labor may be found in Robert Korstad and Nelson Lichtenstein, "Opportunities Lost and Found: Labor, Radicals, and the Early Civil Rights Movement," *Journal of American History* 75 (December 1988): 787–811.

52. Memorandum for the President, November 19, 1947, box 21, Papers of Clark M. Clifford, Harry S. Truman Library, Independence, Mo., from notes of Numan V. Bartley.

53. Clark Foreman to Thomas Krueger, December 16, 1967, box 14, SCHW-AU.

54. James C. Cobb, "'Somebody Done Nailed Us on the Cross': Federal Farm and Welfare Policy and the Civil Rights Movement in the Mississippi Delta," *Journal of American History* 77 (December 1990): 934–36.

Race, Religion, and Agricultural Reform

The Communal Vision
of Koinonia Farm

Andrew S. Chancey

When Martin England and Clarence Jordan bought four hundred acres of land in rural Sumter County, Georgia, in 1942, they intended to offer an alternative to the southern tenant farmers and sharecroppers who were so rapidly deserting the rural South for the opportunities of city life, north and south. Many, trapped by the cycle of poverty to which the tenantry system bound them, were unable to move. England and Jordan intended for their new farm to provide a means of introducing these marginalized farm workers to scientific and practical agriculture, thereby alleviating the displacement of this labor force and the problems it created. By teaching farmers how to make the land more productive and by helping them break their credit dependency, England and Jordan hoped to eradicate an exploitative and abusive system not that far removed from slavery.

The agenda of these two agrarian visionaries included more than a challenge to the South's economic system, however. Both England and Jordan recognized other problems in southern society, a society that perpetuated the bifurcation of blacks and whites and that found support and reinforcement through the institutions of southern white Protestantism. These men believed that with the establishment of Koinonia Farm in November 1942, they could begin restructuring the society of which they were a part.

Despite the growth of urban and industrial pockets throughout the South, the region remained largely rural and agricultural, and farm tenancy and sharecropping expanded throughout the 1920s and 1930s. In Georgia, just as in other states, the crumbling plantation system, the precariousness of tenancy, and the poor condition of the land complicated the lives of owner and worker alike, and then the Great Depression only worsened the situation. The sharecropper and tenant farmer, in Anthony P. Dunbar's view, became "symbols of the starving South and were unavoidable examples of America's failure to provide a livelihood to all its people."[1]

Both Martin England and Clarence Jordan were southerners, both had grown up in the racially divided society of the early twentieth century, and both were products of the region's predominant white Protestant evangelicalism. At first a challenge to society, this religious tradition soon became a supporter of slavery and then a bulwark of the equally oppressive social mores of the Jim Crow era. Religion and culture were so intertwined that both reflected the region's basic conservatism and wariness of change. Southern religion emphasized personal salvation at the expense of social reform.[2] Out of this prevailing religious tradition, England and Jordan emerged to confront both the religious and the cultural status quo of their time.

Both men came from solid Baptist backgrounds. Martin England, a South Carolina native, graduated in 1924 from Furman University, attended Southern Baptist Theological Seminary, and taught at Yancey Institute and Mars Hill College, both in North Carolina, before completing a divinity degree at Crozer Theological Seminary. After graduating from Crozer, England, along with his wife Mabel, served from 1933 to 1939 in upper Burma with the American Baptist Foreign Mission Society. Even before going to Burma, England had dreamed of setting up some kind of institution wherein members could learn from, depend upon, and care for each other. Home on furlough in 1941, England was again seeking ways to implement his ideas when he met Clarence Jordan, and they collaborated in creating Koinonia Farm. England stayed at Koinonia for less than two years. In the fall of 1944, the mission board asked him to return to Burma, and he readily returned with his family to his first calling.[3]

Jordan, on the other hand, was to stay for the rest of his life. Born to a privileged family in Talbot County, Georgia, in 1912, Clarence Leonard Jordan recognized early the unending cycle which kept sharecroppers, black and white, tied to the land.[4] Jordan decided that he would become a farmer himself and help end the cycle by teaching other farmers how to produce more and accumulate enough to gain independence. Jordan enrolled in the College of Agriculture at the University of Georgia in 1929, studied scientific farming, and graduated in 1933. During his senior year, however, Jordan's

Mabel and Martin England, 1940.
Clarence L. Jordan Papers, Hargrett Rare Book and
Manuscript Library, University of Georgia Libraries.

life took a very different turn when the young student decided to become a minister and to respond in a strictly Christian manner to what he perceived as injustice in the South. He attended the Southern Baptist Theological Seminary, receiving a divinity degree in 1936 and a doctoral degree in New Testament Greek in 1939. Among his student jobs were positions teaching at all-black Simmons University and as superintendent of inner-city missions in Louisville.

Thus, both England and Jordan were deeply immersed in the white Protestant evangelical tradition. Both revered the Bible as the divinely inspired word of God and therefore steeped themselves in biblical teaching.[5] These studies shaped the discontent that would set the two men on a path so divergent from that of the rest of their culture. Rather than accept the prevailing biblical interpretations, particularly of race relations, they realized how southern society had twisted scripture for its own purposes. They had learned that Jesus taught sharing and caring for the needy, yet they saw around them a system that kept the poor in perpetual debt. Most relevant to their respective pilgrimages was the discrepancy between the biblical teaching that all humans are equal as children of God and the segregated society which regarded African Americans as inferior. From their scriptural encounters, both England and Jordan formed their own social ethic that differed markedly from the one their tradition propounded.

England and Jordan envisaged the creation of a communal group that would exist outside of church structures but would be based on the New Testament church described in Acts 2 and 4, where members combined their resources and shared all things in common. The Greek word expressing this concept provided the name for this future community. *Koinonia* (pronounced "coin-oh-NEE-a"), translated "fellowship," describes the relationship between persons sharing common beliefs, possessions, and needs. All members, regardless of race or sex, would share equally, drawing from pooled resources according to individual need. In an effort to break the cycle of poverty that drove so many rural farmers to the city, Koinonia Farm would make land available on which these farmers could be taught scientific agricultural methods to improve their output and foster independence.

The most radical aspect of Koinonia, however, was the advocacy of equal relations among the races. Koinonians saw themselves working, living, and eating alongside their Christian sisters and brothers, regardless of race. Described on a promotional brochure as an "agricultural missionary enterprise," the farm was to be more than either a training school or a community of common sharing; it was to be "a demonstration plot for the Kingdom of God."[6] It was to redress economic and racial oppression through a structure

based on equality and justice. Through the promotion of innovative economic principles, the advancement of scientific farming techniques, and the
advocacy of racial equality, England and Jordan directly challenged southern
social and religious mores.

The idea of separating from society was, of course, not new with England
and Jordan. Communalism has found particularly fertile ground in America,
from the arrival of the Puritans to a variety of forms to the present day.[7]
Established mostly, though not exclusively, out of religious motivations, such
communities attract members who "feel they must separate themselves, to
whatever degree is possible, from such things as war, racial inequality, opportunism in personal and group conduct, and possession of private property,"
according to former Koinonian Claud Nelson, Jr., a student of the history of
communal movements.[8]

Nor was the social ethic developed by Koinonia's founders unique or original. Indeed, each of them had developed his own ethic independently of the
other. Conditions in the South had prompted other southern whites sensitive
to issues of justice to develop similar ethics. Among these were Appalachian
natives Myles Horton and Don West, who together attempted to counter the
poverty-stricken conditions in mountainous Grundy County, Tennessee, by
establishing Highlander Folk School, which had as its stated goal to educate
"rural and industrial leaders for a new social order." [9]

An organization formed in direct response to the farm tenancy situation
was the Southern Tenant Farmers' Union, founded in Arkansas in 1934.[10]
Howard Kester, one of its leaders, raised money for the STFU and helped
establish Providence Farm in Mississippi, a cooperative for displaced farmers. In this farm, Kester believed, the Kingdom of God was being established,
and he expressed his hope that "the rural life of America may be lifted to a
new high through our community ideal," which someday would "be reckoned
as one of the really important adventures in faith on the part of a disinherited
group." [11] Kester's language is similar to that used a few years later by Martin
England and Clarence Jordan in seeking to implement those same ideals.

Even before meeting England or learning of his interests, Jordan was moving forward with his plans. He wrote the federal Department of Agriculture,
requesting a wealth of pamphlets and information. His commitment was such
that in July 1941 he turned down an invitation to teach at Bessie Tift College,
a Baptist college for white women in Forsyth, Georgia, saying that "the pleading voice of twelve million Negroes who are under the yoke of oppression,"
and above all "the commanding voice of Christ, saying, 'Go!'" compelled
him to decline the attractive offer.[12]

In the midst of making these plans, Jordan stumbled upon Martin England, who was also living in Kentucky and also searching for a means of implementing his own ideas. England had spent his furlough from Burma first at the University of Florida, where he audited courses on agriculture needed for his work in Burma, and then at an experimental farmers' cooperative in Wakefield, Kentucky. Jordan first encountered England through a newsletter published by a mutual friend in which England wrote, "If the barriers that divide [persons], and cause wars, race conflict, economic competition, class struggles, labor disputes are ever to be broken down, they must be broken down in small groups of people living side by side, who plan consciously and deliberately to find a way wherein they can all contribute to the Kingdom . . . accepting the principle of the obligation of the Christian to produce all he can and to share all above his own needs." [13] Jordan identified so readily with these sentiments that he arranged to meet England. That they met for the first time at a Fellowship of Reconciliation meeting in Louisville in the fall of 1941 must have further confirmed the closeness of their thinking.

After that initial meeting, Jordan and England began making plans to put their ideas into practice. Over the next few months, they discussed their thoughts with each other and with anyone who would listen. Even though both realized the difficulties inherent in such an endeavor, they tended to let their fantasies of its possibilities run unchecked. Beyond its scientific approach to agriculture, they saw the farm as offering theological training for black preachers, a "seminary in the cotton patch" for ministers who could carry the rural reconstruction work to other parts of the country and to war-stricken areas of the globe. Locally, the farm could become a hub from which workers went into other parts of the county to do mission work. Whatever specific form the project took, England wrote in July 1942, above all it would operate on the faith that "the Christian religion can reconcile differences and break down barriers between people of different race, class, and economic opportunity." [14]

In that summer those ideals took on tangible form with the establishment of Koinonia Farm, Inc. England and Jordan printed a brochure explaining the venture and began recruiting support for it. With their first contribution of fifty dollars, they began looking for an optimal location for the farm. After careful study, they decided that the east Alabama counties of Chambers or Barbour represented the most typical rural, poor, and predominantly black farming areas in the Deep South. They traveled to the area in October, only to have the deal fall through on the farm they had intended to purchase. Disappointed, they decided to visit Jordan's family home in Talbotton, Georgia, before returning to Kentucky.

Jordan's brother Frank, a federal farm appraiser, knew of some farm land for sale in Sumter County, about fifty miles south of Talbotton. The four-hundred-acre farm, nine miles south of Americus, had about one hundred acres for cultivation, about one hundred in forest, and about two hundred in pasture, plus a garden plot knee-deep in Bermuda grass. On the property were a tenant shack, a dilapidated farmhouse, and an old sheet-metal barn and tool shed. In spite of the run-down conditions of the farm, England and Jordan knew immediately that this was the land they wanted for their experiment.[15]

Even though England and Jordan originally believed that the Alabama counties were most representative of the dismal plight of the South, they probably could have done no better than their final selection of land in Sumter County, Georgia. Located about halfway between Columbus and Albany in the southwestern part of the state, Sumter adjoins both Macon County, one of two counties on which Arthur F. Raper based his classic portrait of the black belt, and Terrell County, later labeled "Terrible Terrell" for its strong resistance to change during the Civil Rights movement.[16] Further, Sumter County was the site of the Confederacy's most infamous prisoner-of-war camp, Andersonville.

According to federal census records from 1940, of the county's population of 24,502, 61 percent were black; in the county seat, Americus, slightly more than half (4,855) of its 9,281 residents were black. Over the next decade, the county's population decreased to 24,208, while that of Americus grew to 11,389. This change only partly reflects the dramatic decline in rural farm residents. In 1940, 13,347 people (9,349 of them black) lived on farms in Sumter County; by 1950, the total had dropped by almost half to 6,817, nearly two-thirds (4,116) of whom were black.[17] The carry-over of depression conditions and federal agricultural restrictions, the creation of nonagricultural jobs because of the war, and the decline of profitability in farming combined to drive Sumter County farmers off the land. The transition from the traditional agricultural foundation indicated by fewer farms, the prominent vestiges of the Confederacy made visible by Andersonville, and the preponderance of blacks made Sumter County typical of the black belt and thus fulfilled the criteria that England and Jordan sought in a locale for their experiment.

With the decision on the Sumter County site made and its purchase assured, England and Jordan intensified their efforts to publicize Koinonia. They prepared a promotional brochure that reflected their emphasis on religious training, thus creating an appeal as a mission endeavor. Had they emphasized the communal nature of their intentions, they would have been misunderstood; had they emphasized the interracial aspect of the work, they would have subjected themselves to controversy and a lack of support.[18]

Much work faced England and Jordan upon their arrival in November 1942, and the two preachers-turned-farmers provided quite a spectacle for their neighbors. Even though both had agricultural training, neither had much practical experience. Jordan later enjoyed making fun of their efforts by saying that they would climb to their rooftop every morning to see what the neighboring farmer was doing, planting when he planted and plowing when he plowed. They also planted a garden, hitching each other to the plow to lay off the rows. Their efforts were fruitful, however, because the house was repaired enough for the England family to join them in December. (Jordan's wife and children moved to Koinonia in April 1943.) Further, they had surplus meat from butchering a sow and extra milk and butter, enough to share with their black and white neighbors and thereby help build good relations with them.[19]

Neighborly sharing did not circumvent all the local hostility, however. Koinonia became an immediate target for white residents averse to any perceived threat to the area's way of life. Within the first few weeks after England and Jordan arrived, they hired an African-American laborer. He moved into the old tenant shack but lived under no worse conditions than his two coworkers in the dilapidated farm house. The three knew they were violating the dictates of local custom by eating their meals together, but as England explained later, too much work remained to be done to make separate preparation of meals practical, and dividing the three men, who worked side by side all day, just did not make sense. Most importantly, in spite of some ambivalence on the black man's part, England and Jordan knew that segregating themselves at meals violated the founding principles of Koinonia.

When news spread of the new neighbors' eating arrangement, local tempers flared. One evening a carload of men arrived at the farm to investigate. Upon confirming the reports, they announced they were from the Ku Klux Klan and did not allow the sun to set on anybody who ate with "niggers." Jordan did not respond immediately to the intimidation, giving himself long enough to think through his reply. Suddenly, he smiled broadly, shook the spokesman's hand vigorously, and said he was a Baptist preacher with seminary training who had read about persons who had power over the sun but had never anticipated meeting one.[20] The leader, stunned, said he was the son of a Baptist preacher and then talked more friendly with Jordan as the sun sank beyond the horizon. While humor defused the immediate hostility, it did not reduce the continued threat posed by local discomfort at Koinonia's presence.[21] England and Jordan might have been capable of challenging Jim Crowism within the region, but they were reminded repeatedly that the changes they advocated would come slowly. Nevertheless, the example they

Clarence Jordan at Koinonia.
Clarence L. Jordan Papers, Hargrett Rare Book and
Manuscript Library, University of Georgia Libraries.

set at Koinonia Farm served as a model of what they envisioned for the rest of southern society.

A major investment that first year developed into one of the most successful enterprises and a substantial means of support for Koinonia's early years. Jordan's diary indicates that the first one hundred chickens arrived on February 15, 1943. Two hundred more arrived in March and five hundred in April. That summer Jordan wrote that Koinonia had gone in "rather heavy for chickens" because of "the extreme scarcity of poultry and eggs in this section, and because [he] majored in poultry in college, and because the farmers here sorely need something besides cotton and peanuts to turn to." [22]

Although Jordan did not introduce poultry to Sumter County, he did help reverse the trend of having to import eggs to that part of the state and also helped establish one of the earliest commercial flocks in the area. Koinonia's poultry business was successful enough to interest neighbors in raising chickens themselves. Koinonia established an egg marketing cooperative to which approximately six farmers brought their eggs to be cleaned, graded, candled, and packed. Koinonia's poultry enterprise was featured (in January 1951) in *Progressive Farmer,* which reported that it earned for its eggs a six-cent premium above current market prices because of their high quality. By 1954 the number of eggs produced in the county, according to federal Department of Agriculture records, reached 500,664 dozen, in contrast to the 118,400 dozen reported in 1949 and the 218,701 dozen in 1944. [23]

Besides beginning a poultry business, Koinonia grew 12.5 tons of peanuts, 500 bushels of corn, 20 tons of hay, 2100 bushels of oats, and 500 bushels of wheat that first year. In addition, Jordan developed a mobile peanut harvester that helped offset the labor shortage of the war years. At some point in those first years, Koinonia established a "cow library" from which a local family, usually black, whose milk cow had gone dry could check out one with a fresh supply. Profit from these early enterprises and continued contributions allowed the farm to pay for new equipment and construction, half of the land, and most of the livestock by the end of the first year. [24]

When the England and Jordan families joined the men at Koinonia, Jordan insisted that the *koinonia* practiced by the early church be implemented on the farm. All property and all income would be held jointly, and all decisions, financial and otherwise, would be made by the total membership. The two families lived as one large family, maintaining separate residences but sharing meals and living off a common purse. After the Englands left Koinonia in 1944 to prepare to return to Burma, several volunteers lived at the farm temporarily, participating in the common life but not pledging to become members of the Koinonia community. Koinonia distinguished between members, who committed their lives to the group for an extended time, and volunteers and workers, who participated in communal life to varying degrees but who did not want to become actual members of Koinonia. Not until 1946 did the first person, a white man, arrive to begin the membership process.

In the meantime, however, several area black individuals or families lived and worked at Koinonia. The black man whose presence brought the visit from the Ku Klux Klan was an employee who stayed only a short time. Another black man, Denis Alman, was hired within Koinonia's first year as a farm laborer, then chose to give up his pay, gained access to the communally owned car, and began the membership process. Minutes from a meeting held in 1962, reflecting on Koinonia's early history, indicate that "things then broke apart rather quickly and [Alman] left within a few months."[25] In December 1943 and January 1944 two black families, both named Johnson and both Sumter County natives, moved to the farm. Uninterested in communal life, they maintained essentially a sharecropper relationship with Koinonia.[26]

All of these individuals lived at Koinonia, but other local African Americans worked on the farm as needed. Word quickly spread that Koinonia paid a higher daily wage and treated laborers more fairly than other area farmers. Koinonians hoped to attract some of these people to their membership, but most, while grateful for the better conditions at Koinonia, were afraid to move to the farm out of fear of repercussions from local whites. They did, however, eat some meals with the Englands and Jordans, particularly at noon. The earlier intimidation had failed to force Koinonia's leaders to curtail this practice, which continued to enrage white Sumter countians.

These unconventional associations with African Americans further exacerbated local hostilities against the work of Koinonia, keeping many from working there and almost all from living there. Had England and Jordan limited their efforts strictly to their own farming operation, their threat might have seemed less obvious. Paying higher wages was already an affront to local economic practice, but the Koinonians involved themselves in other ways in the attempt to improve living conditions for local African Americans.

During the war years, for example, England and Jordan obtained extra gasoline ration stamps which they used to pay for the fuel needed to transport black children to school, since county school buses did not service the black school system. When school officials complained, the ration board refused to stop issuing the extra stamps. E. L. Bridges, the county school superintendent, was so upset by the situation that he wrote Jordan's father, who was old and ill, that Jordan was endangering his family by violating local custom. When Jordan discovered what Bridges had done, he confronted him, stating that he knew he was supposed to love his enemies, but that if Bridges ever bothered the senior Jordan again, he would have to ask Jesus to excuse him for about fifteen minutes while he "beat the hell" out of him. Jordan was committed to nonviolence, but he was well aware that he was human.[27]

Koinonians' willingness to transport black school children was just one activity that riled the local community and the superintendent. D. B. Nicholson, state Baptist student work director and mentor of Jordan, visited Americus in 1944 and found tensions running high as a result of Koinonia's work. The county school board had called in R. L. Cousins, the director of black education in Georgia, because it was unable to keep black teachers in the county. Superintendent Bridges claimed that Jordan's program was ruining the work among blacks and hoped that Cousins could help mediate the situation and encourage black teachers to keep their jobs. Nicholson's inquiries revealed, however, that neighboring counties paid their black teachers more and conducted longer school years and that Sumter County teachers could often make more money working as domestics. Nicholson believed that the board of education was just "in the mood to lay all of the blame on Clarence." [28]

The superintendent also complained about a letter Florence Jordan had written to her daughter's teacher, requesting her not to require the daughter's participation in a school play that advocated the buying of war bonds. The child was not to participate because, the Jordans believed, Jesus' teachings were contrary to war.

Bridges told Nicholson that Jordan had so divided the county by eating with blacks that it was "fairly boiling with resentment." [29] The superintendent seemed to have had a personal vendetta against the Jordans, more so than against the Englands. Clarence Jordan had grown up just fifty miles from Sumter County and, as a fellow Georgian, could not be dismissed as easily as an outside agitator.

Nicholson revealed also that the opposition to Koinonia was not limited to Sumter County, stating that he had been told to "put a soft peddle" [*sic*] on his efforts to help Jordan because they were hurting the state Baptist student program. J. Maurice Trimmer, pastor of Macon's First Baptist Church and chairman of the Georgia Baptist Convention committee that oversaw student work, had received complaints from pastors about Jordan's work. Nicholson believed that most Georgia Baptist pastors were "in sympathy with the thing Clarence [was] trying to do" but felt that he was going too fast. "If Clarence could be prevailed upon to go slow enough so that his friends could go along with him," wrote Nicholson, "it is probable that he could do a great deal more in the long run." [30] Even in the face of the growing resentment, however, Koinonians kept trying to improve the quality of life for whomever they could. They participated in neighborly sharing with other white farmers, exchanging equipment and sharing pasture as needed, but focused most of their attention on the needs of local blacks.

Opposition appeared to diminish for a time after 1944. The *Atlanta Constitution* featured the farm in an article in May 1945, praising the "unique project of practical Christianity" that brought "productivity to wasting land and hope to oppressed, struggling souls." The article gave Jordan a public forum in which to explain that the farm focused on "co-operation rather than competition" and was to the rural community what the settlement house was to the city slum. He was able to describe what he believed was wrong with contemporary white society and to elaborate on the changes he hoped Koinonia Farm was facilitating. A similar article ran in the *Charlotte News* that same month when Jordan spoke in the area. This journalistic attention served to clarify misconceptions about Koinonia and to spread its reputation through the secular press.[31]

A small but steady stream of people came to Koinonia in the next few years as a result of this kind of publicity and Jordan's speaking tours. Floridian Harry Atkinson lived at the farm off and on from the summer of 1944 until he and his new wife Allene moved there in May 1948 to become members. Students from Auburn University visited the farm. One of them, Henry Dunn, lived at Koinonia as a member from September 1946 until June 1947. The other, Howard Johnson, moved there not long afterwards with his wife, Marion. One of the first women to join Koinonia, other than Florence Jordan and Mabel England, was Willie Pugh, who became a member in July 1947. These new members were all white people from outside the state, although all were southerners. Most of them were Baptists who had heard Jordan speak on their college campuses or at national conferences. His reputation as a Bible teacher spread, and he was able to speak often and spark interest in Koinonia.[32] Response from local whites continued to be limited to resentment.

Koinonia grew over the next few years, both in size and in number. Land purchases increased the size of the farm, eventually, to nearly fifteen hundred acres. New members continued to arrive also. The Conrad Browne family came in 1949 and stayed until Browne took a position at Highlander Folk School in 1963. Four single people joined in 1950, a couple and a family of five joined in 1952, and a family of four and a family of five plus several singles came in 1953. Short-term visitors came and went regularly. The Christmas newsletter from 1953 indicates that nineteen adults and twenty-two children formed the population at Koinonia at that time.[33] All were white, as Koinonia had failed after a decade to attract its first African American as a full member. Increasingly after 1949, the people Koinonia attracted were from outside the South, in part because Clarence Jordan gained more engagements in other parts of the country as his reputation as a speaker spread and in part because his message of racial equality was less and less welcome within the region.

The growth of the late 1940s and early 1950s required the development of operating procedures not needed when the group consisted of one or two families. Koinonia had to adopt more structure. All incoming residents deposited their money and their possessions into common holdings. This practice became more complicated when, for example, people arrived with life insurance policies and premiums to pay. The preparation of meals, the provision for worship, the division of work, and the farm's continuing growth demanded greater coordination and management. The increased number of residents made decision-making by consensus almost impossible. Still, Koinonians were committed to communal life and strove to work out how best to facilitate it. They elected officers, divided and rotated work assignments, and absorbed the growth as best they could. They borrowed money to build more housing and to expand the farm enterprises both to provide more jobs and to support themselves. By selling crops, livestock, and eggs, the farm remained solvent. Koinonia also developed a three-staged system of membership, through which a person joined as a novice and then became a provisional member before becoming, upon mutual agreement, a full member.[34]

The growth of Koinonia also required explicit articulation of the precepts upon which it operated. In the Christmas newsletter of 1953, Jordan reported that the community as a body geared its work toward the furtherance of the Kingdom of God and tried to live by the spirit of the life of Christ, casting out violence, hatred, and the "social, political, and economic ills that separate" persons. Koinonians soon learned to summarize their beliefs succinctly in four segments: they should hold all material goods in common; distribution of resources should be according to need; God had no favorite children, as all were equal regardless of color, class, or creed; and finally, as children of God they were increasingly partakers of God's nature of redemptive love, thereby requiring them to live lives free of violence, hatred, and revenge.[35] By living according to these precepts, Koinonians saw themselves as providing a model on which the rest of society could be based.

That model, however, continued to provoke hostility from Sumter County whites. Koinonia's membership was completely white, mainly because few local blacks showed any interest in becoming actual members, but the farm's population included black workers and their families. Joseph "Bo" Johnson, son of the Johnson family which moved to Koinonia in December 1943, had stayed at the farm as an employee after his father died and later had begun the membership process, although he left Koinonia before becoming a full member. For persons outside Koinonia, the distinction between membership and employment was a moot point.

The interracial arrangement there kept local suspicions high, and an incident in 1947 or 1948 brought the sheriff in to investigate. On this occasion Willie Pugh, a white female member, drove to a distant field to replace Bo Johnson, the black novice, for a night shift on the tractor, as Koinonians were working around the clock to prepare their fields for planting. A neighboring farmer saw a white woman and a black man together in the dark and evidently reported the situation to the authorities. When Pugh came in from the field the next morning, she discovered something of an uproar. The sheriff had made an early morning visit to Koinonia to investigate, and a friendly neighbor appeared to quiz Pugh until he was satisfied that the encounter was merely a change of shifts. Both Johnson and Pugh were victims of vicious gossip as the news spread quickly through the county and beyond. A few days later a reporter from out of town, having heard of the episode, visited Koinonia to pursue the story, and Koinonians made arrangements for Johnson to travel out of state until the tensions subsided. Pugh did not realize until much later that the allegations against her were serious, and that she had unwittingly put Johnson into a life-threatening situation. In the end, nothing drastic happened because of this incident, but Koinonians were reminded once again about the extreme sentiments against them.[36]

Local hostility was such that, in 1948, a local church took formal action against Koinonia. Most Koinonia members and short-term volunteers attended Rehobeth Baptist Church, about four miles from the farm, and the Jordans had been members there since arriving in the county. Since so many Koinonians were Southern Baptist, they wanted to maintain their denominational ties. They held interracial worship services and Bible classes on the farm but also attended the all-white Rehobeth. All of the blacks with whom Koinonians had contact were from the area and were involved in their own churches. Koinonians recognized the conflict in their advocating racial equality yet attending an all-white church, but they hoped that they could make inroads with their white neighbors by being faithful church members. Indeed, Koinonians held leadership positions in the church, Clarence Jordan had preached or taught Sunday School there on occasion, and Harry and Allene Atkinson were married there, with the full participation of the women's decorating committee.[37] By 1948, however, the members of Rehobeth had had enough of the Koinonians and requested that they withdraw their membership. When the Koinonians refused, the congregation removed them from their leadership positions within the church but allowed them to remain as members.

By the spring of 1950, however, the relationship had deteriorated enough to provoke an open confrontation. When Koinonians took a visitor to church with them, members of the congregation mistook the visitor, an Indian Hindu agricultural student, for a black man and accused Koinonians of trying to integrate the church. After a series of meetings, the pastor wrote Jordan that the church would hold a business meeting on Sunday, August 13, 1950, in which fellowship would be withdrawn from the Koinonians and their names stricken from the church roll. Even though Jordan was already scheduled to preach that day at Dexter Avenue Baptist Church in Montgomery, Alabama, where Martin Luther King, Jr., was later the pastor, the church held the meeting without him and carried through its intentions.[38]

In the next newsletter, Jordan wrote that while the break with the church grieved the Koinonians, it also showed them the effect their message of racial equality was having on their fellow whites. "We are now whole-heartedly committed to complete brotherhood across all barriers with no other commitments to compromise our witness," he wrote, indicating his position that membership in an all-white church had conflicted with Koinonia's interracial stance.[39]

The expulsion from Rehobeth Baptist Church helped spread Koinonia's reputation in religious and interracial circles, and the farm attracted visitors from all over the country. Koinonia organized work camps in 1951 and 1952 that brought in small groups to help with the farm's building projects, which were needed to absorb the growth, and to conduct Bible schools for the neighborhood children, most of whom were black. The reputation spread locally also, and some people willingly looked to Koinonia for aid. Because of its open door and eagerness to help people in need, local alcoholics learned they could find acceptance and a place to stay at the farm.[40]

A dozen years of work yielded only marginal progress in alleviating the county's problems. Koinonians claimed to have been involved in a campaign to get the area roads paved and to get telephone service extended to that part of the county, thereby benefiting blacks and whites alike.[41] Several neighbors enjoyed success as poultry farmers, and neighborhood children had recreational opportunities through boys' and girls' clubs. Moreover, many local African Americans had learned they had sympathetic and supportive white friends at Koinonia Farm. Even so, Koinonians had failed to attract their first full member who was black, and race relations in the county remained largely unchanged.

Jordan wrote in the Christmas newsletter of 1954 that Koinonians believed the world's misery would continue until people responded to "the call of Jesus to lay down their swords, and even their portfolios, long enough to receive a new mind and a new heart and raise their vision from their own personal and national gain to a kingdom of love in which all [people's] self-ishness and littleness and all their superficial differences of skin and tongue and [home]land shall be swallowed up in the overwhelming seas of God's love." [42] As long as the misery, local and global, continued, Koinonians intended to confront it, challenge it, and respond to it in what they perceived to be a Christian manner. Whatever progress they achieved, however, came slowly.

Nevertheless, Koinonia's growing public presence posed Sumter County's most visible threat to the bifurcated society and to the remnants of the Old South and ultimately made the farm the target of violence and persecution with the rise of massive resistance to the *Brown* decision of 1954. England and Jordan knew from the beginning that their dream would meet opposition. Indeed, less than a year into the project, they had already encountered enough friction for Jordan to write that "while there has been some thunder, the lightening hasn't struck." [43] In 1942 they could only imagine any future success of the vision they had for establishing a Christian communal farm. They, like other malcontents in various pockets across the South, recognized injustices affirmed by the existing, racially divided system in southern society and responded by challenging the system that perpetuated them. More than a half-century later, Koinonia continues in that quest.

Notes

1. Anthony P. Dunbar, *Against the Grain: Southern Radicals and Prophets, 1929–1959* (Charlottesville: University Press of Virginia, 1981), 184. See also Numan V. Bartley, *The Creation of Modern Georgia* (Athens: University of Georgia Press, 1983), 172.

2. For differing interpretations of the geographic and chronological origins of the white Protestant evangelical tradition, see John B. Boles, *The Great Revival, 1787–1805: The Origins of the Southern Evangelical Mind* (Lexington: University Press of Kentucky, 1972); and Rhys Isaac, *The Transformation of Virginia, 1740–1790* (Chapel Hill: University of North Carolina Press, 1982). See also Donald G. Mathews, *Religion in the Old South* (Chicago: University of Chicago Press, 1977), chaps. 2, 4; Samuel S. Hill, Jr., ed., *Religion and the Solid South* (Nashville: Abingdon Press, 1972), 22.

3. "Koinonia Farm," promotional brochure, Clarence L. Jordan Manuscript Collection number 2341, box 4, folder 9, Special Collections, University of Georgia Libraries, Athens, Ga. The Jordan papers comprise three collections, numbered 756,

2340, and 2341 (hereinafter cited as CLJ, followed by the collection number, then box number, then folder number if available). George Stoll to Martin England, September 30, 1932, CLJ 756:1:6.

4. Much of the general information about Jordan, unless otherwise noted, comes from Dallas Lee, *The Cotton Patch Evidence: The Story of Clarence Jordan and the Koinonia Farm Experiment* (New York: Harper and Row, 1971).

5. Jordan continued his study of the Greek New Testament after receiving his doctorate. During the 1950s and 1960s, he completed and published his own translations of most of the New Testament into southern vernacular English, using the South as the settings for the books.

6. "Koinonia Farm," promotional brochure, CLJ 2341:4:9. The phrase "a demonstration plot for the Kingdom of God" was rather common in descriptions Koinonians gave of their objectives.

7. Two recent volumes demonstrate the extensiveness of the communal tradition in this country. See Philip N. Dare, *American Communes to 1860: An Annotated Bibliography* (New York: Garland Publishing, Inc., 1990); and Timothy Miller, *American Communes, 1860–1960: A Bibliography* (New York: Garland Publishing, Inc., 1990).

8. Claud Nelson, Jr., "Community: The Bond No Bomb Can Shatter," *Motive*, February 1957, 26, in Clarence Jordan Collection, Southern Baptist Theological Seminary Library, Louisville, Ky. (hereinafter cited as SBTS).

9. Quoted in John M. Glen, *Highlander: No Ordinary School, 1932–1962* (Lexington: University Press of Kentucky, 1988), 2. See also Aimee Isgrig Horton, *The Highlander Folk School: A History of Its Major Programs, 1932–1961* (Brooklyn: Carlson Publishing, Inc., 1989); and Myles Horton, with Judith Kohl and Herbert Kohl, *The Long Haul: An Autobiography* (New York: Doubleday, 1991).

10. For information on the STFU, see Dunbar, *Against the Grain*, and Donald H. Grubbs, *Cry from the Cotton: The Southern Tenant Farmers' Union and the New Deal* (Chapel Hill: University of North Carolina Press, 1971).

11. Howard Kester to James Myers, March 10, 1936, quoted in Dunbar, *Against the Grain*, 117. See also Robert F. Martin, *Howard Kester and the Struggle for Social Justice in the South, 1904–77* (Charlottesville: University Press of Virginia, 1991); and Will D. Campbell, *Providence* (Atlanta: Longstreet Press, 1992).

12. Clarence Jordan to United States Department of Agriculture, August 1, 1941; Clarence Jordan to C. L. McGinty, July 11, 1941, CLJ 756:1:13.

13. Text for letter comes from Lee, *Cotton Patch Evidence*, 28. Other information about the meeting of the two men comes from Lee, 27–30, and from Martin England, classroom lecture, Southern Baptist Theological Seminary, October 29, 1976, cassette 1485, SBTS.

14. Martin England to Dr. Howard, May 17, 1942, CLJ 756:2:2; Martin England to Mack Goss, July 15, 1942, CLJ 2340:1.

15. Aubrey J. Hudson to Clarence Jordan, August 13, 1942, CLJ 756:2:3; Lee, *Cotton Patch Evidence*, 31–34; Newsletter, December 1942 (most Koinonia newsletters are available bound in the Hargrett Library of the University of Georgia Libraries);

Clarence Jordan to Howard Johnson, December 17, 1942, CLJ 756:2:3; Florence Jordan, classroom lecture, April 28, 1977, Southern Baptist Theological Seminary, cassette 1404, SBTS; John Pennington, "Compassion Led to Farm, Jordan Says," *Atlanta Journal*, April 17, 1957.

16. Arthur F. Raper, *Preface to Peasantry: A Tale of Two Black Belt Counties* (Chapel Hill: University of North Carolina Press, 1936).

17. United States Bureau of the Census, Sixteenth Census, 1940, Population, vol. 2, part 2, table 21, p. 223; table 27, p. 306; table 30, p. 358; Seventeenth Census, 1950, Population, vol. 2, part 11, table 33, p. 58; table 42, p. 123; table 49, p. 192.

18. Horace Montgomery, "Georgia's Koinonia: A Heritage of Communitarian Ideals and Ordeals," *Americana-Austriaca: Beiträge zur Amerikakunde* 3 (1974): 158.

19. Lee, *Cotton Patch Evidence*, 36; Martin England, classroom lecture, October 29, 1976, cassette 1485, SBTS; Newsletter, December 1942.

20. See Joshua, 10.

21. Lee, *Cotton Patch Evidence*, 37–38; Martin England, classroom lecture, October 29, 1976, cassette 1485, SBTS.

22. Diary 1943, CLJ 756:18:3; Clarence Jordan to Arthur Steilberg, n.d. [summer 1943], fragment, CLJ 2340:1.

23. "Sumter County Farm Statistics, 1900–1966," published by the United States Department of Agriculture, Statistical Reporting Service, CLJ 756:26:5; S. R. Winters, "Parson-Poultryman," *Progressive Farmer* (January 1951), CLJ 756:29:13.

24. "Koinonia Farm Second Anniversary," pamphlet, CLJ 756:31:1; Lee, *Cotton Patch Evidence*, 43–44; Clarence Jordan to Henry ——, December 22, 1943, CLJ 756:2:6.

25. "Notes on Meeting at Koinonia Farm," February 10–12, 1962, CLJ 756:19:1.

26. Diary 1943, CLJ 756:18:3; "Koinonia Farm Second Anniversary," CLJ 756: 31:1.

27. P. D. East, "East Side," *Petal Paper*, May 14, 1959, Koinonia Farm Scrapbook, microfilm, CLJ 2340:21; Lee, *Cotton Patch Evidence*, 43.

28. D. B. Nicholson to J. W. Jordan, July 31, 1944, CLJ 756:2:7.

29. Ibid.

30. Ibid.

31. Tina Ransom, "Farm Grows Prosperous on Science, Christianity," clipping labeled *Atlanta Constitution*, hand dated May 19, 1945(?); Dick Young, "Unique Georgia Farm Blends Christianity and Agriculture," *Charlotte News*, May 4, 1945, CLJ 756:28:10.

32. Lee, *Cotton Patch Evidence*, 48–50; minutes, January 20, 1949, CLJ 2341:4:16.

33. Newsletters, January 12, 1951; 1952; Christmas 1953.

34. Lee, *Cotton Patch Evidence*, 41–42; minutes, January 16, 30, 1948; January 14, 1949, CLJ 2341:4:16.

35. Newsletter, Christmas 1953; "The Story of Koinonia Farm," pamphlet, January 1957, CLJ 756:19:1; Clarence Jordan, "Christian Community in the South," *Journal of Religious Thought* 14 (Autumn–Winter 1956–1957): 29, 30. This is the first

source for the publication of these principles, but Koinonians had formulated them as early as 1949, according to Conrad Browne. Conrad and Ora Browne, "Reminiscences on Their Koinonia Experience," September 7, 1989, cassette CJ58F, Koinonia Partners Library, Americus, Ga.

36. Willie Pugh Ballard, telephone interview with author, June 20, 1992. Johnson left Koinonia about 1951, never having become a full member, ostensibly because his wife, Emma, did not want to become a member. Newsletters, Summer 1976; June 1988; September 1989; Joseph "Bo" Johnson, interview with author, April 5, 1990, Koinonia Village, Americus, Ga.

37. Clarence Jordan to Florence Jordan, December 7, 1942, letters read by Lenny Jordan, cassette CJ57C, Koinonia Partners Library, Americus, Ga.; Diary 1943, CLJ 756:18:3; Clarence Jordan to Arthur Steilberg, n.d. [summer 1943], fragment, CLJ 2340:1; Harry and Allene Atkinson, "Our Koinonia Experience," in Kay N. Weiner, ed., *Koinonia Remembered: The First Fifty Years* (Americus, Ga.: A Koinonia Publication, 1992), 19.

38. A full account of this episode may be found in the document "Relationship with Community Churches," CLJ 2340:31, and Lee, *Cotton Patch Evidence*, 74–81.

39. Newsletter, January 12, 1951.

40. *The Christian Century* 67 (September 6, 1950): 1053; 67 (October 11, 1950): 1204; Newsletters, 1952; Christmas 1953; Claud Nelson, Jr., to Hans Hermann Arnold, February 2, 1955, CLJ 2340:1.

41. "What is 'Koinonia?'" *Americus Times-Recorder*, August 8, 1956, Koinonia Farm Scrapbook, microfilm, CLJ 2340:21.

42. Newsletter, December 1954.

43. Clarence Jordan to Arthur Steilberg, n.d. [summer 1943], fragment, CLJ 2340:1.

"The Best People in Town Won't Talk"

The Moore's Ford Lynching
of 1946 and Its Cover-Up

Wallace H. Warren

Between 1880 and 1930, mobs lynched more than 3,900 victims in the South. After 1930, lynchings continued to occur at least once a year through 1952.[1] This essay is an account of one of the last lynchings in the South: that of Roger and Dorothy Malcom and George and Mae Murray Dorsey at Moore's Ford in Walton County, Georgia, in 1946. All of the victims were black. According to the (until recently) only known eyewitness, all the assailants were white.

The lynching forms part of the memory and the relation between blacks and whites in Walton County. Whites forget all too easily what they have done to blacks. Anita B. Sams, the "official historian" of Walton County, wrote in *Wayfarers in Walton*, "Time has obscured much which should be between these covers."[2] Not just time has obscured Sams's account; a selective memory has, too. She fails even to mention the lynchings in 1946, just as she fails to mention almost anything that happened to African Americans in the two centuries that they have lived and worked in Walton County.

The events that surrounded the deaths of Roger and Dorothy Malcom and George and Mae Murray Dorsey are a prism through which is refracted the economy, the society, and the polity of Georgia at the end of World War II, not just as they were, but as they were becoming. That summer of 1946, the state of Georgia was undergoing massive change in all aspects of its citizens' lives. For blacks, the change created new possibilities. For whites, it created new fears.

The new urban, industrial forces transforming Georgia failed to prevent the murders or, once the deed was done, to provide a climate that was conducive to the punishment of the murderers. Most of the rural whites in Walton County had no sympathy for the victims at all. Conversely, the white middle-class residents of Monroe, the seat of Walton County, all expressed horror at the murder. Horror, though, is where their reaction ended. They refused to cooperate with authorities in the investigation. They also balked at helping the families of the victims or extending comfort across the color line, at least in an organized way. Blacks in Walton County had little choice but to suffer the lynching in silent, bitter resignation.

The lynching at Moore's Ford was one of the few in the South that ever received much attention outside the region. Ellis G. Arnall, the governor of Georgia, sent in the Georgia Bureau of Investigation (GBI) in an attempt to convict those who conspired in the murders. Large protests against the incident were organized in several northern cities. The lynching received considerable attention in the national press, both black and white. Finally, President Harry S. Truman was moved to order the Federal Bureau of Investigation to assist in the investigation.

It was the outside attention that turned Walton County into a hotbed of seething tensions. Perhaps this is one reason why by 1946 lynchings were becoming rare in the South. Communities that suffered them were no longer able to handle them on a strictly local basis. Still, as in other cases, the FBI could not convict the guilty parties. To this day, at least some of the white murderers of the two black couples likely roam free in Walton County—and are likely admired as upstanding citizens.

The summer of 1946 was a tense one in Georgia. Over the previous three decades the profitability of cotton had collapsed. This economic and social catastrophe had destroyed the plantation belt's power and enfeebled the traditional paternalistic orientation of Georgia society. As the primacy of the plantation belt was crumbling, a new elite was rising in the South that put more pressure on the traditional order. After the traumas of the Great Depression, World War II had enriched southern cities and spurred the rise of new industries. By the end of the war, a new, white middle class had attached itself to the now thriving towns and burgeoning cities of the South.[3]

In 1946, the system of Jim Crow was coming under more strident challenge from within and without. Inside the South, black military veterans who had returned from service in World War II were no longer willing to submit to white domination. White intransigence at the black veterans' demands provoked violent racial incidents in many parts of the South. Outside the South,

Harry S. Truman appointed several commissions whose purpose was to investigate the special problems that African Americans suffered, including discrimination and lack of access to higher education.[4]

In the first year after World War II, though, most of Truman's initiatives on civil rights barely chipped the massive edifice of white supremacy that whites had erected in the South. Another branch of the federal government, the judiciary, contested the system at its very core. In 1944, in *Smith v. Allwright*, the Supreme Court declared white primary elections unconstitutional. Two years later, the U.S. District Court in Atlanta applied the high court's ruling to Georgia. Governor Arnall refused to endorse the court's decision, but did not stand in the way of its implementation. For the first time since Reconstruction, blacks organized to vote in cities and towns across Georgia. By the summer of 1946, 100,000 African American Georgians had registered to vote.[5]

Of all the new developments that portended change in Georgia, the Supreme Court's striking down of the white primary probably most riled whites. By declaring disfranchisement, a cornerstone of white supremacy, to be unconstitutional, the Supreme Court was undermining the legitimacy of the entire institution of Jim Crow.

Almost as a gift, the court decisions and blacks' vigorous response to them fell into the lap of Eugene Talmadge. That summer of 1946 Talmadge, three times governor of Georgia, was running for the statehouse once again. Talmadge had built his career on voicing the fears and the anger of rural whites. In this, his final campaign, he did it more vitriolically than ever. "I was raised among niggers and I understand them," Talmadge said in one speech. "I want to see them treated fairly and I want them to have justice in the courts. But I want to deal with the nigger this way; he must come to my back door, take off his hat, and say, 'Yes, sir.'"[6] Many of Talmadge's critics accused him of creating racial tensions in Georgia in 1946. Exacerbate them Talmadge did, but create them he did not; Talmadge was only tapping into already existing white fears and resentments.

Since its founding in the late nineteenth century, the system of Jim Crow had rested ultimately on naked coercion; as such, it had never rested easily. After World War II, the system had become especially vulnerable—to the withering of the prestige and prosperity of the plantation belt, which had always served as Jim Crow's primary protector and enforcer; to the Truman administration's new interest in civil rights; to a new unwillingness on the part of blacks to tolerate its indignities; and finally, to federal court decisions that allowed blacks to vote in the white primary.

These developments had their effect on Walton County, Georgia. The county lies about halfway between Atlanta and Athens, where it straddles Georgia's old plantation belt and its upcountry district. Walton County had been carved out of a region of beautiful, fertile hills that rolled gently to the southeast and more sharply to the northwest. Monroe, the county seat, was a prosperous marketing and cotton-mill town. In 1940, its population was 4,168. Already by 1946 the white middle-class leaders of Monroe—those Numan V. Bartley has labeled the "county planter-merchant-banker-lawyer-doctor elite"—were looking outward to the rest of the world for their economic sustenance and future. Recently founded institutions such as the Rotary Club tied Monroe's elite to their peers elsewhere while loosening the ties to their own community.[7]

The results of the 1946 Democratic primary made evident the county seat's new outward orientation. Most voters in Monroe turned away from the raving, reactionary politics of Eugene Talmadge. Instead they cast their ballots for James V. Carmichael, a business progressive who preached the new southern gospel of better schools, more highways, and the recruitment of new businesses to the state. Monroe residents cast 1,253 votes for Carmichael and 635 for Talmadge.[8]

Nevertheless, the progressivism of Monroe's upper-middle-class whites had its limits—strict limits. One of the town's most admired citizens was Clifford M. Walker, Georgia's governor from 1923 through 1927. Like Carmichael, Walker had campaigned for more highways and better schools. Unlike Carmichael, Walker had won the enthusiastic support of the Ku Klux Klan in his bid for the state's highest office. By 1946 the white elites of Monroe were not still enamored of the Klan. When Clifford Walker had served as governor, most elite whites in Georgia had believed in paternalism, the rigid control of the massive numbers of poor whites and blacks in their communities, as the best way to protect their own prosperity. By 1946, the conditions that had made paternalism necessary and feasible were disappearing. Cotton was not as important as it once was, and federal wage laws and other regulations had made untenable the tight cocoon in which the management of textile mills had wrapped their employees.[9]

Thus, many of the white elite of Monroe opposed the excesses of Eugene Talmadge's rhetoric against African Americans. They also opposed subordinating all other issues to the defense of white supremacy. But they still favored the continuation of white supremacy, as long as it did not cost them too much.

If the white elites of Monroe welcomed change of a certain kind, the whites who lived in the outlying areas of the county did not want it at all. In 1946 the farmers of Walton County still raised cotton in prodigious quantities. The year before, the county had led the state in the yield of cotton per acre and was surpassed only by Burke County in total production. Walton's farmers had produced 26,500 bales on 26,300 acres; they could always make money on bale-an-acre lint. But even if the county's farmers were enjoying fat times in 1946, they were slow to mechanize; the region was still too hilly to make the primitive machinery of that time practical. Tractors had not tilled the county's fields long, and mechanical pickers would not arrive until the early 1960s. Thus, to grow and pick their crops, landowners depended on a large, cheap, compliant labor force: blacks. Rural whites in Walton County were wedded by need to the old system of Jim Crow: their crops depended on it.[10]

County lagged behind town in other ways. In Monroe, indoor plumbing and electric lights had graced the homes of its residents since the turn of the century. Conversely, electricity did not reach the farms of the county until the 1930s, when the Rural Electrification Administration first lit up much of Georgia's countryside. Gravel and dirt roads impeded county residents' commerce with town, isolating them within their rural communities. The result was a difference between town and country that both town and country people were aware of. Country people keenly felt the condescension of townspeople toward their country ways. Thus, in the 1946 election for governor, the rural whites of Walton County nursed resentment at blacks, who threatened to upset the balance of labor and other social customs in the countryside. At the same time, they felt little affection for the sometimes smug, sometimes disdainful townspeople. The country people were Eugene Talmadge's constituency. Carmichael may have carried Monroe in the governor's race, but in the outlying areas the rural population gave Talmadge enough support to carry the entire county by seventy-eight votes.[11]

Few African Americans voted in the rural sections of Walton County. As in most of the rest of the South, most black men and many black women there served one economic purpose: to work the cotton fields. In 1940, of 1,663 black male workers in the county, 1,277 were either farmers or farm laborers. Out of 745 women workers, 234 worked on farms; another 418 worked as household domestics. Farm labor was arduous work and paid little. In 1949 median income for black families in Walton County was $482. For all families, including white families, it was $1,458.[12]

As in other parts of the South, African Americans were starting actively to try to improve their plight in 1946. The Walton County Civic League registered hundreds of blacks to vote in Walton County that year. The Civic League was led by Dan Young, a young black funeral home operator who had been educated at Morehouse College. In the governor's election, 433 blacks voted in Monroe, an indication of some grudging acquiescence to black aspirations on the part of whites in town. In the rural areas, only sixty blacks voted—whites in the country were not about to allow large numbers of blacks to put on a mantle of white folk's status.[13]

One of Walton County's more prosperous farming areas lay in Blasingame militia district, in the southeastern part of the county. In the heart of Blasingame, about six miles southeast of Monroe, Hestertown Road angles off from Pannell Road at Union Chapel Church. From there it dips into swamps and climbs hills until it empties out onto Fair Play Road, just over the Morgan County line. The road winds through the holdings of families who have lived in Walton County since its incorporation in 1819 and who live there today. Driving from Union Chapel Church, one passes houses belonging to the Adcock, then the Hester, and finally the Peters families. Composing the rambling community of Hestertown, the members of these three extended families and most others in the area used to earn their living from two- or three-horse farms. They enjoyed reputations "for raising wonderful stands of cotton" and also "for oppressing their Negroes even more than usual." [14]

The white farmers of Hestertown had had a difficult time holding on to their labor. The white population in Blasingame had remained reasonably steady between 1930 and 1940, falling from 747 to 742. Blacks, though, had moved out at a high rate; their population had plummeted from 577 to 389. Whites tried to hold blacks in Blasingame by keeping them in perpetual debt. It is no wonder that no blacks dared vote in the district in 1946 and that Talmadge carried the area by a margin of 119 to 14.[15]

Roger Malcom was one of the black residents of Hestertown. Twenty-seven years of age, Malcom was known as "a good boy"—as amenable black men were called then—and enjoyed "a good reputation in the community among both white and colored," according to the *Atlanta Daily World.* Malcom's grandmother later recalled that Roger had grown up a responsible child; he earned good marks in school, enjoyed Sunday school, and liked to sing hymns. Nevertheless, trouble had recently brewed between Malcom and his landlord's son, Barnette Hester, Jr. Sometime in July 1946, Hester's brother Weldon had tried to run down Malcom's wife Dorothy in a car, or so the gossip went. Although Malcom still lived in a tenant shack owned by the Hesters, he no longer worked for the family.[16]

The incident between Weldon Hester and Dorothy Malcom may have been tied to the rumor that Barnette, Jr. (or Barney) had made advances on Dorothy. Whether or not the rumors were true, Roger probably believed them. On Sunday, July 14, 1946, after drinking much of the afternoon, Roger came home and angrily confronted Dorothy about them. He may have become abusive. Whatever the reason, Dorothy fled to the Hesters' house to

appeal to Barney for aid. Roger followed her there. When Barney came up
shortly afterward, he and Roger fell into an ugly dispute that turned into a
fight. In the ensuing struggle, Roger stabbed Barney. His wound was serious,
and he was rushed to the hospital. Malcom fled home.[17]

In fighting Hester, Malcom had violated a primal code of white southern
honor: whites could beat blacks for any infraction, but blacks could not attack whites. It was a hoary custom that blacks violated at their own peril. In
the summer of 1946, amid the social and economic flux, whites were especially ready to smash any effort by blacks to step outside their assigned roles.
Malcom probably knew he had gotten himself in serious trouble.

And the trouble came quickly. As night fell that Sunday, news of the fight
raced from house to house in Hestertown. A gang of ten or so white men
gathered and went to Malcom's house. There they beat him and bound him
in ropes. Lilly Malcom, an elderly white lady who had known Roger since
he was a child (but no relation), either witnessed the violence or heard of
it. Fearing what the gang of Hester's neighbors was going to do next, Lilly
telephoned the sheriff's office in Monroe to save Roger from further harm.
By the time Sheriff E. S. Gordon arrived in Hestertown, Malcom was lying
on the ground, tied up, already beaten and bloody. Gordon took him back
to Monroe and locked him up. He merely dispersed Malcom's assailants.[18]
By his own reasoning, Gordon probably felt he was doing right and defusing
the situation, but by charging Roger Malcom and not charging any of his
assailants, Gordon showed that the white man's justice prevailed in Walton
County.

The trouble was not over for Malcom. On Monday night, July 15, a second attempt on his life occurred when a crowd of whites assembled outside
the jail and demanded Malcom's release into their hands. Sheriff Gordon
refused to release him, in part, said one resident of Monroe, because "too
many young kids [were] around." Thomas W. Johnson heard rumors that
a Hester from Atlanta (perhaps Barney's brother Weldon, reputed to be a
member of the Ku Klux Klan) led the mob. Johnson, an Atlanta attorney
later retained by the National Association for the Advancement of Colored
People to investigate the lynching, said that everyone in Hestertown just assumed that Malcom would be killed; the only question was when. Malcom's
relatives were so sure he was going to die that sometime after Monday night
they drove into Monroe to pick up his remains.[19]

As Malcom languished in the Walton County Jail, the Democratic primary campaign was drawing to a rancorous close in Georgia. Speaking to
his supporters in Monroe, Eugene Talmadge promised to restore the white
primary and to keep blacks from voting as long as he held office. He also

advised "good" blacks to stay away from the polls. Privately, Talmadge also met with Barnette Hester, Sr., the day after the stabbing, or so the whispers went. Talmadge's appeal touched the real, personal concerns of whites in Walton County. On election day, July 17, hundreds of blacks refused to heed Talmadge's advice and turned out at the polls. Their action angered many whites. One courthouse lounger later linked election day to the mass murders to come: "The sight of that long line of niggers waiting to vote put the finishing touches to it." Another added, "This thing's [lynching] got to be done to keep Mister Nigger in his place. Since the state said he could vote, there ain't been any holding him. . . . Gene told us what was happening, and what he was going to do about it. I'm sure proud he was elected." [20]

On Friday, July 19, news of Barney Hester's stabbing first appeared in the *Walton Tribune*. Like most small-town newspapers in the South, the *Tribune* devoted itself mainly to neighborly accounts of the daily goings-on of the white middle and upper classes of Monroe and the rural communities of Walton County. Not surprisingly, the *Tribune* ran a onesided account of Hester and Malcom's altercation. The newspaper reported that Malcom was drunk and beating his wife when Hester, "splendid citizen of Blasingame district," walked up and "remonstrated with him [Roger], whereupon the negro pulled out his knife and stabbed him." Hester's white neighbors in Union Chapel and in Ebenezer hoped for his recovery in their own columns. The paper made no mention at all of the attempted lynching on Sunday night or of the mob that gathered outside the jail the next evening. News of Hester's injury appeared alongside reports of Talmadge's victory in the Democratic primary on July 17. "Now comes the calm after the storm," predicted the *Tribune.* [21]

Within days of Talmadge's election, cotton and corn were "laid by" in Walton County. Plowing was done, and for several weeks farmers' chores would be light. Whites began to gather at the icehouse in Monroe and at other places in the county to talk over the reign of terror that seemed to be rising in Walton: a black man stabbing a white man and not dying for it, and other black men and women voting.[22] The tone of the account of the stabbing in the *Tribune* probably convinced many that an injustice had been done and that it needed to be crushed. A plan to punish Roger Malcom came out of these gatherings.

While whites were meeting around Walton County, Roger Malcom's wife Dorothy moved just across the Apalachee River to Oconee County to live with her brother George Dorsey and his wife Mae Murray Dorsey. During the war, George had served for five years as a private first class in the Army Air Corps. He saw action in the Pacific and for his valor had won the Good

Conduct Medal, the Bronze Star, the Army Defense Award, and several campaign stars. Dorsey's record did not impress his white neighbors, though; they thought he was "biggety." Dorsey was share-cropping for J. Loy Harrison and had used his army discharge bonus to keep clear of debt. Dorsey had raised "a fine crop of cotton," in George Andrews's words, and his wife grew flowers outside their cabin. Thomas W. Johnson, the NAACP investigator, had heard rumors that Harrison had picked a fight with Dorsey in an effort to run him off and keep the proceeds of the cotton crop to himself. But Dorsey did not scare easily; he boasted that he had survived far worse in the Pacific than any punishment his landlord could mete out.[23]

Even though there was bad blood between Dorsey and Harrison, the veteran, his wife, and his sister were trying to persuade Harrison to pay Roger Malcom's bail and to let Malcom work it out on Harrison's farm. Harrison looked every bit the white southern landlord. Forty-two years of age, he weighed 275 pounds and usually wore khakis, the uniform for white farmers in the area. Later, the out-of-town newspapers would call Harrison "a prosperous farmer." Locally, he was better known as a bootlegger. Art Shields, a reporter for the *Daily Worker*, described Harrison as "red-jowled, broad shouldered and big bellied." For whatever reason, Harrison decided to go to Monroe to take custody of Malcom. On Thursday, July 25, he drove there to pick Malcom up. Dorothy, George, and Mae Murray rode with him. Harrison was also going to carry Dorsey's mother, but at the last minute she stayed home to do some ironing for a white patron. The white farmer, his three tenants, and Dorsey's dog Spot departed for Monroe in Harrison's Pontiac early in the afternoon.[24]

Harrison and his party arrived in Monroe around 2:00 P.M. It took ten minutes for deputy sheriffs Ray Flannegan and Louis Howard to complete the paperwork to release Roger Malcom on bail of $600. Howard, the jailor, was also a distant relative by marriage to Barney Hester. Instead of releasing Malcom immediately, the lawmen kept him for another three hours. Meanwhile, Harrison was having work done on his car while Dorothy Malcom and the Dorseys went shopping. About 5:10 P.M., Harrison secured Roger's release, and the five departed for Oconee County. On the way to Monroe, Harrison had driven down the Atlanta-to-Athens highway, but when returning home he took another route down unpaved back roads that led eventually to Moore's Ford Road. Moore's Ford was a desolate, unpaved lane that crossed the Apalachee River to Harrison's farm.[25]

Harrison was the only passenger to survive that trip from Monroe. Later, many of that afternoon's events that he recounted would appear questionable to investigators. Nevertheless, for years Harrison's was the only version of what happened.

As Harrison and his passengers coasted down the hill to the bridge that crossed the Apalachee River, they stopped for a Ford that was blocking the road on the far side. Armed white men poured out of both sides of the parked car. A Chevrolet then nudged Harrison's car from behind. One of the Chevrolet's occupants got out, put a shotgun to Harrison's head, and commanded, "All of you put 'em up." Someone else said, "There's the man we want." A few of the gunmen pulled Dorsey and Malcom out of the car and bound their hands with ropes. Dorothy and Mae Murray begged the men not to execute their husbands. When one of the women called a man by name the leader of the mob shouted "Hold everything," and ordered the men to "get those damned women, too." The women put up a desperate struggle; autopsies would show that both had broken arms. The band dragged the two men and the two women up a sandy side road. During this time, yet another man, stationed on the far side of the bridge, covered Harrison with a shotgun. Next, in Harrison's words, "I could see the men line 'em up. I could see the Negroes four abreast. I could see the back of the men's hands. I heard the leader of the group say 'one, two, three' and then 'boom.' He did that three times. There were three volleys." [26]

Roger Malcom was twenty-seven years old. Dorothy Malcom was twenty, George Dorsey twenty-seven, and Mae Murray Dorsey thirty. All lay dead at the foot of an oak tree, crumpled in a bloody, confused heap, almost unrecognizable, the victims of white rage. Only Roger and George were guilty of any affronts to the sensibilities of white people; Dorothy and Mae Murray were murdered for recognizing their assassins. Eleven days after the stabbing of Barney Hester, whites in Walton County had gotten the revenge they wanted. "They took my boy away from me like a dog. . . . They killed him like a dog," Roger's grandmother Dora Rae Malcom later cried in Chicago, where she had fled after Malcom's fight with Barney Hester.[27]

After the shooting, Harrison said, the mob let him leave the scene. Turning his car around, Harrison drove about two miles to the nearest store and called the sheriff's office. "Mr. Howard, they just hijacked me and killed my niggers," *Time* magazine reported him as saying. Two hours later, Coroner W. T. Brown convened a six-man jury at the scene of the killings. Those present included Lewis E. Howard and C. J. Sorrells, both deputy sheriffs. Sheriff Gordon did not attend because of illness, he explained later. Harrison, the only known witness, testified. The jury returned a verdict by then hackneyed in the long annals of lynchings in the South: "Death at the hands of unknown parties." The scene at Moore's Ford quickly became like that of a carnival, as dozens of bystanders toured the site and picked up souvenirs. Back in Monroe, night police chief Lewis Malcom cleared black residents off the streets.[28]

The *Walton Tribune* appeared the next day, Friday, July 26. Since the murders of the Dorseys and the Malcoms had happened after its deadline, the paper made no mention of them. However, readers who followed the news in Ebenezer, a community close to Hestertown, found an uplifting thought in Mrs. Mann Knight's correspondence from that neighborhood. Knight noted that the summer revival had recently concluded at Ebenezer Baptist Church. "If everyone . . . would always have the brotherly love and devotion, and feel the nearness of Christ during the summer revivals, what a glorious world this would be," she wrote.[29]

In 1905, sociologist James E. Cutler defined lynching as "an illegal and summary execution at the hands of a mob, or a number of persons, who have in some degree the public opinion of the community behind them." The murders of the Malcoms and the Dorseys fall well within Cutler's definition. So do the hangings, shootings, burnings, and torchings of thousands of other blacks who died at the hands of white mobs in the nineteenth and twentieth centuries. Southern lynchings of the late nineteenth and early twentieth century were staged, public affairs that thousands of observers sometimes attended. The last great public lynching in the South occurred in 1934 in Marianna, Florida, when thousands of whites watched the ten-hour torture and murder of Claude Neal, a black man accused of murdering a white woman.[30]

The sadism of Neal's killers turned many southern whites against lynching. Another factor that changed white minds was the crusade of Jessie Daniel Ames and her Women's Campaign Against Lynching. Lynchings still occurred, but by the 1930s they happened less frequently and were generally more furtive affairs, like the killing of the Dorseys and the Malcoms. Two infamous lynchings of the 1950s, those of Emmett Till and of Mack Charles Parker in Mississippi, also fit this pattern.[31]

Lynching had become common in the late nineteenth century in the wreckage of slavery. Whites wanted to reimpose control over blacks, and blacks no longer enjoyed the protection of being property. Lynchings were intended to convey bloody messages to the living as much as they were meant to punish the dead. As messages, they worked well. Anne Moody, who was a teenager in Mississippi when Emmett Till was murdered, has written, "Before Emmett Till's murder I had known the fear of hunger, hell, and the Devil. But now there was a new fear known to me—the fear of being killed just because I was black. . . . I didn't know what one had to do or not do as a Negro not to be killed. Probably just being a Negro period was enough."[32]

Arthur F. Raper, a sociologist whose *The Tragedy of Lynching* is one of the early systematic studies of the practice, observed that lynchings occurred again and again in the same counties. That was true in Walton County, Georgia. In 1898 a mob there murdered Samuel Chandler for an unknown offense. Thirteen years later a mob shot Thomas Allen for rape and, not yet satisfied, went to the jail and hung Foser Watts, a black prisoner. In 1939, Sheriff Gordon averted a lynching in Monroe with the help of fifty state troopers. J. D. Vaughn, a black farm laborer, was convicted of attacking a white woman and condemned to death. Meanwhile, fifteen hundred angry young white men milled around outside the courthouse, demanding Vaughn's release— into their hands. The state police had to lob canisters of tear gas to disperse the mob. Sheriff Gordon called members of the mob "irresponsible rowdies who didn't really mean to lynch anybody." The next day police advised the black reporters of the *Atlanta Daily World* to leave town for their own safety.[33]

The large crowd at the trial of J. D. Vaughn indicates that as late as 1939 many whites in Walton County were elated by the prospect of a lynching. Seven years later, after the deaths of the Malcoms and the Dorseys, the feelings were considerably more mixed. Some whites still had no doubt that the actions taken at Moore's Ford were justified. As J. P. Adair told one reporter, "You got to understand that niggers is the most brutish people they is. They're African savages, and you got to keep them down. . . . They don't think the same way as humans. They all lie and steal and when they get drunk all they want is a white woman. You got to keep them down."[34] The sentiments of Adair, a white farmer, were shared by an alarming number of his fellow citizens.

In contrast to the mixed local reaction, the national press showed only outrage at the incident. The *New York Times* attributed the killing of the Malcoms and the Dorseys to "the bigoted hatred of neighbors led by 'bigoted' white men." *Time* magazine declared that Eugene Talmadge's campaign "ripped the thin gauze of decency from the body of his state" and revealed "the running sores beneath it," because of "the hatred of white men for their Negro neighbors." *Newsweek* said Barney Hester's "neighbors" lynched Roger Malcom while "gloating over the Talmadge triumph."[35]

Much of the national press treated the incident at Moore's Ford as another example of the aberration of the South in a freedom-loving nation that had just crushed fascism in the name of democracy. There was a clear implication that the South had to climb on board the American Century. Again and again, newspapers and magazines attributed the incident to the hatred of white folks for black folks, and nothing more. They did not analyze the complexities of a system that had set white people on top of black people for three centuries. One of the few national organs that differed from this line was the *Nation*, which argued that the lynching was the outcome not just of individual iniquity but of an oppressive system as well.[36]

The reactions of journalists did not constitute the only outside responses to the lynching. Governor Ellis Arnall loudly denounced the crime, called the Georgia Bureau of Investigation into the case, and offered a reward of $10,000 to anyone who aided in the conviction of the murderers. Arnall was a moderate who had greatly opened the Georgia political process, but except for silently acquiescing to blacks' effort to vote, he had not challenged segregation. His reaction to the lynching of the Dorseys and the Malcoms showed his decency, if not his understanding. It contrasted starkly with Eugene Talmadge's reaction. Asked about it while on vacation in Colorado, the "sage of Sugar Creek" responded: "Things like that are to be regretted." He then raised the alarm of "giving equal rights to" blacks who had achieved only an "artificial civilization."[37]

Other organizations joined the state of Georgia in offering rewards to capture the murderers of the Dorseys and the Malcoms. They included the NAACP, the Congress of Industrial Organizations, the American Civil Liberties Union, and the Mariners Union. The incident also had repercussions in Congress: Senator William Knowland of California denounced the crime in the *Congressional Record*. Rising to the South's defense, Senator Richard B. Russell of Georgia retorted that "brutal crimes" happened elsewhere, too. In the White House, President Harry S. Truman agreed to order the FBI to investigate "this and any other crimes of oppression."[38]

Because it was the closest town to the murder site, national attention focused quickly on Monroe, much to the chagrin of its white middle-class citizens. Most Monroe residents truly abhorred the crime; indeed, the First Baptist, First Christian, and First Methodist churches (spiritual homes for the elite) all passed resolutions "condemning" the crime and supporting the investigation by the FBI and GBI. Tom O'Connor, a reporter for the New York newspaper *PM*, reported hearing over and over again, "I'm ashamed to be a Georgian."[39]

Nevertheless, as much as Monroe's leaders lamented the killings, what most saddened many was the pillorying that the town took in the national press. Local disclaimers soon became a pattern: to denounce "the recent horrible slayings" and then get on to the real business, which was to state that residents of Monroe did not participate in the lynching, that it had happened barely fifty feet within the county line, that outsiders actually committed the murders, that the national press was blaming the entire county for the acts of a tiny band, and so on. There was little willingness to see the killings as the product of an oppressive system, rather as than just a random crime.

Ernest Camp, the editor of the *Walton Tribune*, chastised an Atlanta newsboy for shouting that a white mob had murdered four blacks in Monroe, instead of in the county. Camp did not consider that the mob itself carried most of the blame for Monroe's notoriety. The *Tribune* whined that the national press "hammered a defenseless people." Judge Henry H. West of the Walton County Superior Court denounced "the nationwide unfair publicity given to Monroe, Walton County, and the people of this county." Bernard Butts, the cashier of Farmers' Bank in Monroe, complained about "the wholesale condemnation of the community for something in which we had no part and which we know nothing about. No one from Monroe was in the mob, and we don't feel we should be condemned by people outside the state for what the mob did." [40]

How Butts knew nothing about the incident and at the same time knew that no one from Monroe took part in it he did not explain. His remark revealed the contempt that townspeople felt for country people—the implication was that the residents of Monroe were too sane or civilized to murder four black farm laborers, while the residents of the county were not.

The sympathy of Monroe's whites only went so far. When they discussed the murders, they usually denounced only the crime itself; never did they express sorrow for the victims themselves or their survivors. White citizens of the town never made any public effort to aid relatives of the Malcoms or the Dorseys or to pay funeral expenses. Even if they did not lynch blacks themselves, southern whites had long ago hardened themselves to black suffering at white hands. [41]

If whites in Monroe felt unfairly accused, blacks had more complicated reactions. The most accomodationist remarks came from the Reverend O. M. Collins, pastor of the Tabernacle Baptist Church in Monroe, where Mae Murray Dorsey was buried. Collins said all whites should not be held responsible for the crime—a fair statement that probably helped to relieve tensions in itself. He went on to say that he had seen "no evidence that there has been serious racial friction here." Whether Collins believed that or not, it was patently untrue. [42]

The reactions of other blacks to the incident were far less forgiving. On a visit to Monroe, Ollie Harrington of the NAACP turned down the mud alley that led from South Broad Street (the main street in Monroe) past a mule stable to the tiny black business district to interview blacks in a Jim Crow res-

taurant. One black veteran said, "They're exterminating us. They're killing
negro vets, and we don't have nothing to fight back with but our bare hands.
In Italy and Germany we knew which way they were coming, but here . . . ,"
and he stopped. A white landlord reported that one of his tenants had told
him, "Mister Will, we get a lot of mean niggers around here, and they ain't
going to let this thing rest." [43]

Blacks and whites did share one emotion: fear. The belief ran rampant that
those who cooperated with the authorities put their own lives and the lives
of their families in danger. Walter White, the secretary of the NAACP, wired
U.S. Attorney General Tom Clark about "threats" that were made against
anyone suspected of providing any information to the investigators, "particularly Negroes." Dan M. Young, the black funeral director who had headed
the Walton County Civic League, the organization that had registered blacks
to vote, reported frequently on the investigation to Walter White's brother-
in-law in Atlanta. However, Young feared that he would meet a violent end
himself if his name were somehow attached to any information about the incident. Young's funeral home did handle the bodies of the Malcoms and the
Dorseys. [44]

Whites felt the same fear as blacks did. A white businessman who lived in
Monroe and was a member of the Democratic committee confided to a reporter from New York's *Amsterdam News:* "It's not that I'm scared for myself,
but I have a family, and that mob has gone so far it will stop at nothing." F. A.
Caldwell, the editor of the *Walton News*, complained, "A mob who'd kill four
niggers like that, they'd burn you out. If I knew anything, I wouldn't tell nobody nothing, not for $10,000 or all the money in the world." The *New York
Times* later snidely denounced "the cowardly human nature that declined to
name the guilty . . . from fear of reprisal or self-recrimination." But the *Times*
failed to appreciate that residents of Monroe lived in a face-to-face society
and felt they risked real danger by talking to the investigators. Of course, not
talking did nothing for the Dorseys and the Malcoms either; thus, the refusal
to cooperate made the entire community complicit in a cover-up. [45]

Fear and lack of cooperation soon stymied the investigation by the FBI and
the GBI. Early on, Maj. William E. Spence, director of the GBI, announced
that "the mystery is being unraveled," yet the search for the killers quickly
ground to a halt. Sheriff Gordon and his deputies proved less cooperative
than anyone, and for good reason. The courthouse had no record of the $600
in bail money that had been assessed having been collected or even recorded.
The amount of the bond was unusually small anyway for the seriousness of
the crime with which Roger Malcom was charged. Thomas W. Johnson, the
NAACP investigator, reported to Walter White that the sheriff's office was

"covering up." Sheriff Gordon said that he had expected no violence before the lynching, even though Gordon had averted Malcom's death the day he stabbed Hester and Gordon himself had faced a mob's demands to turn Malcom over to it the day afterward. To Gordon, everything seemed "quiet and peaceful."[46]

Even more incriminating evidence concerned Deputy Sheriff Lewis Howard. Johnnie Burdette, a black man from Monroe, told NAACP officials that on the afternoon of the lynching he was indulging in a "petting party" with his girlfriend at Moore's Ford. Burdette and his girlfriend were interrupted when Deputy Sheriff Howard drove up with another man who brandished a weapon at Burdette. But Howard interceded, saying, "Don't shoot that nigger," and then said, "Johnnie, go on ahead up the road and stop all niggers coming down this road." Later, witnesses saw the deputy again down at Moore's Ford only half an hour after the shootings—before Harrison had reported them. When Burdette refused to testify, Eugene Martin, Walter White's brother-in-law in Atlanta, agreed that if Burdette did not get money "to get out of the South . . . his life would not be worth a tinker's dam if the crackers thought that he would tell his story." Deputy Howard later became so edgy during the investigation that he threatened to smash a photographer's camera if he did not stop taking pictures of him.[47]

Even more questions arose over J. Loy Harrison's story. One landlord found it "unthinkable" that a landowner would take another landowner's tenant out of jail to work without first consulting with the original landowner. At the same time, it was highly unusual for a white man to stand bond for a black man who had attacked his landlord's son, especially when the son's recovery was still problematic. Russ J. Cowens of the *Detroit Chronicle* reported that blacks in Monroe believed that Harrison brought along Mae Murray Dorsey and Dorothy Malcom so they could testify to his version of events, implying that the whole scene was staged. Harrison's plan went awry when one of the women called out a mob member's name.[48]

Harrison resolutely denied knowing a single member, which seemed unlikely given that he had lived just over a mile from the Walton County line all of his life. When a reporter observed to Sheriff Gordon and his deputies that "Mr. Harrison must have mighty few acquaintances in these parts," Gordon just "smiled broadly." Authorities finally arrested Lester Little, a beer tavern employee, as the leader of the mob, but Harrison insisted that the actual leader was about twenty pounds heavier than Little. One agent remarked that it "looked like [Harrison's identification] . . . came mighty fast." Major Spence of the GBI responded more angrily: "Till my dying day, I will always believe that he [Little] was the boss of this gang. Harrison is either scared of being killed himself, or he's lying in his teeth, or both." Harrison complained of the agents' suspicion. "They think I had something to do with it," he said. "Why, I'm mad as anybody, the way they killed my niggers. I need all the nigger hands I can get. If I knew anything, I'd sure tell it." [49]

Without the cooperation of citizens and officials, even the involvement of the FBI and the GBI could not produce any results. More than twenty FBI agents questioned twenty-five hundred people around Monroe. Since local authorities were not cooperating, in December 1946 U.S. Attorney General John Cowert raised the lynching before a federal grand jury in nearby Athens, Georgia, in hopes of winning some indictments under federal civil rights statutes. That jury consisted of thirteen farmers, two coal dealers, a clerk, a barber, a laundry manager, a ginner, and a retiree. Twenty-one members were white; two were black. Cowert subpoenaed one hundred witnesses but failed to produce an indictment. Judge T. Hoyt Davis dismissed the jury and the case came to an end. Justice was never meted out to the killers of Roger and Dorothy Malcom and George and Mae Murray Dorsey. Major Spence of the GBI summed up the problem: "Even the best people won't talk about this; they have an idea who it is." [50]

Walton County residents did indeed have an idea of who made up the mob, but no one was willing to talk. The incident that set off the lynching of the Dorseys and the Malcoms was a private quarrel that the code of Jim Crow turned into a public incident. If a white man had stabbed Barney Hester, whites would have looked at their fight more judiciously. Nor would a gang of white men have beaten and tied up Hester's attacker. But Roger Malcom was black. Thus was set in motion the chain of events that ended in the death of Malcom, his wife, her brother, and her sister-in-law.

The lynching of the Dorseys and the Malcoms indicates that, in all its trauma, change was sweeping Georgia in 1946, as paternalism collapsed and a more individualistic society emerged. Rural whites found their own way of life vanishing. Upper-middle-class whites eagerly looked forward to the prosperity that they expected the new organization of society to bring. Lost in the change were African Americans, for whom these changes promised little. Monroe's upper middle-class whites were horrified by the lynchings of the Dorseys and the Malcoms, yet they were not moved to push for justice for the killers or to help the victims' families. The murders at Moore's Ford were typical of the late lynchings in the United States—clandestine affairs that did not quite meet the approval of the community. They were also typical in that the killers were never punished for their crime.

"Just bury them quick," J. Loy Harrison had said about the Malcoms and the Dorseys. "Go ahead and bury them. That's the best thing to do." [51] It was a feeling that many whites in Walton County shared. But the memory of this brutal mass murder comes back again and again. In 1992, Clinton Adams, a white man who lived in Florida, confessed that he had witnessed the murders of the Dorseys and the Malcoms from above Moore's Ford when he was a ten-year-old child. Loy Harrison took part in the shooting, Adams stated, along with three other white farmers whom he named—all neighbors of Adams and not residents of Hestertown, all now dead.[52]

Adams seems sincere, but the central part of his account—the murders and Harrison's part in them—cannot be verified. Still, Adams's statement has once again reawakened some of the bitterness that followed the lynching at Moore's Ford. An egregious wrong was done in 1946, not just to the Malcoms and the Dorseys, but to all African Americans who lived in Walton County, who had to live with the fear that the lynching set off. Today, whites in Walton County are still divided on the incident. Some deride the raising again of a murder that took place forty-seven years ago. For others, Adams's confession has provided an opportunity for introspection on the darker aspects of Jim Crow. The Walton County chapter of the NAACP has proposed the placement of a memorial to the Malcoms and the Dorseys, perhaps to sit next to the Confederate soldier on the courthouse square in Monroe. That proposal has angered many—but not all—whites.

The murders of the Dorseys and the Malcoms and the aftermath heightened the discord and distrust between blacks and whites in Walton County for years to come. Although the GBI and FBI failed to convict the murderers, they likely applied enough pressure to avert some future incidents: prospective lynchers might well have been reluctant to face federal, state, and local law enforcement agencies. Yet the murderers in Walton County remained free and unscathed, a troubling portent for those who cared about human rights in the South. The lynching at Moore's Ford and its cover-up showed that whites would violently defy the law, or protect those who did, in order to maintain the supremacy of their race. In the decades to come, the Civil Rights movement had to face the full, sometimes bloody, force of that intransigence.

Notes

1. W. Fitzhugh Brundage, *Lynching in the New South: Georgia and Virginia, 1880–1930* (Urbana: University of Illinois Press, 1993), 8.

2. Anita B. Sams, *Wayfarers in Walton: A History of Walton County, Georgia, 1818–1967* (Monroe: General Charitable Foundation of Monroe, Georgia, 1967), viii.

3. Numan V. Bartley, *The Creation of Modern Georgia* (Athens: University of Geor-

gia Press, 1983), chap. 8. See also Allison Davis, Burleigh B. Gardner, and Mary R. Gardner, *Deep South: A Social Anthropological Study of Caste and Class,* directed and with an introduction by W. Lloyd Warner (Chicago: University of Chicago Press, 1941), part 2; John Dollard, *Caste and Class in a Southern Town,* 3d ed. (New York: Doubleday Anchor Books, 1969), chaps. 6–8; Gerald David Jaynes, *Branches without Roots: Genesis of the Black Working Class in the American South, 1862–1882* (New York: Oxford University Press, 1986); Jay R. Mandle, *The Roots of Black Poverty: The Southern Plantation Economy after the Civil War* (Durham: Duke University Press, 1978); Roger L. Ransom and Richard Sutch, *One Kind of Freedom: The Economic Consequences of Emancipation* (New York: Cambridge University Press, 1977); Joel Williamson, *The Crucible of Race: Black-White Relations in the American South since Emancipation* (New York: Oxford University Press, 1984).

4. John Hope Franklin and Alfred A. Moss, Jr., *From Slavery to Freedom: A History of Negro Americans,* 6th ed. (New York: Alfred A. Knopf, 1988), 411–12.

5. Manning Marable, *Race, Reform, and Rebellion: The Second Reconstruction in Black America, 1945–1982* (Jackson: University Press of Mississippi, 1984), 18; David R. Goldfield, *Black, White, and Southern: Race Relations and Southern Culture, 1940 to the Present* (Baton Rouge: Louisiana State University Press, 1990), 33–34; Bartley, *Creation of Modern Georgia,* 186–87.

6. William Anderson, *The Wild Man from Sugar Creek: The Political Career of Eugene Talmadge* (Baton Rouge: Louisiana State University Press, 1975), 219; Talmadge is quoted on 230.

7. U.S. Bureau of the Census, *Sixteenth Census of the United States: 1940,* vol. 2; *Characteristics of the Population* (Washington: U.S. Government Printing Office, 1943), 360; Sams, *Wayfarers,* 275–81.

8. "How Walton County Voted in the Primaries," *Walton Tribune,* July 19, 1946, p. 1; H. William Fitelson, "The Murders at Monroe," *New Republic,* September 2, 1946, p. 259.

9. George B. Tindall, *The Emergence of the New South, 1913–1945* (Baton Rouge: Louisiana State University Press, 1967), 194.

10. "Georgia Cotton Counties Led by Walton in 1945," *Walton Tribune,* August 30, 1946, p. 1; Sams, *Wayfarers,* 366–67; author's conversations with farmers from Blasingame.

11. Sams, *Wayfarers,* 253; author's conversations with Blasingame farmers; "How Walton County Voted," 1; Fitelson, "Murders at Monroe," 259.

12. *Sixteenth Census,* 281; U.S. Bureau of the Census, *U.S. Census of the Population: 1950,* vol. 2; *Characteristics of the Population,* part 11, *Georgia* (Washington: U.S. Government Printing Office, 1952), 159–61.

13. "Will Stay in Georgia, Citizens Tell Chronicle Editor," *Detroit Chronicle,* August 10, 1946, News Clippings File, Division of Social Science Research, Carver Research Foundation, Tuskegee Institute, Tuskegee, Alabama (Tuskegee: Division of Behavioral Research, 1971) microfilm, 233F342 (hereafter TINCF); "Georgia Pri-

mary Occurs Next Wednesday," *Walton Tribune*, July 5, 1946, p. 1; "Talmadge Wins," *Walton Tribune*, July 19, 1946, p. 1.

14. Sams, *Wayfarers*, 49, 284; Tom O'Connor, "Portrait of a Lynch Town: 'Best People,'" undated, typed copy of an article in the newspaper *PM* (New York), in Papers of the National Association for the Advancement of Colored People, part 7, "The Anti-Lynching Campaign," series A, microfilm, 4, 28F618.

15. O'Connor, "Portrait of a Lynch Town," 4, 28F618; U.S. Bureau of the Census, *Fifteenth Census of the United States: 1930*, vol. 3; *Population*, part 1, *Alabama–Missouri* (Washington: U.S. Government Printing Office, 1932), 352; *Sixteenth Census*, 352; "How Walton County Voted," 1.

16. Thomas W. Johnson to Walter White, July 28, 1946, NAACP Anti-Lynching Campaign (hereafter ALC), series A, 2–3, 28F343–44; Rose Vaughn, "'He Did Not Deserve It!' Says Lynch Victim Kin," *Chicago Defender*, August 17, 1946, TINCF, 233F393.

17. Thomas W. Johnson to Walter White, July 28, 1946, 2–3; "B. H. Hester, Jr., Stabbed by Negro Sunday Afternoon," *Walton Tribune*, July 19, 1946, p. 1; Joel W. Smith, "Lynching Bee Staged at Monroe," *Atlanta Daily World*, July 27, 1946, pp. 1, 4.

18. Smith, "Lynching Bee Staged," 1, 4; "Governor Arnall Acts to Apprehend and Convict Mob," *Atlanta Daily World*, July 28, 1946, pp. 1, 4; "White Woman Prevented First Attempt on Monroe Lynch Victim," *Pittsburgh Courier*, August 31, 1946, p. 4.

19. Fitelson, "Murders at Monroe," 259; Frank McAllister to William White, August 28, 1946, NAACP ALC, series A, 28F376; Art Shields, "Still No Arrests in Georgia as Talmadge Reign Nears," *Daily Worker*, August 9, 1946, TINCF, 233F342.

20. Ollie Harrington, TM, NAACP ALC, series A, 28F578; "Arnall Finds Georgia Lynchings Hot Potato," *Chicago Defender*, August 24, 1946, TINCF, 233F341; Tarleton Collier, "Blood of Lynched Negroes Stains Georgia Pines," *Louisville Courier-Journal*, July 28, 1946, TINCF, 233F335.

21. "B. H. Hester, Jr. Stabbed," 1; Mrs. Mann Knight, "Ebenezer News," and Hester Adcock, "Union Chapel," *Walton Tribune*, July 19, 1946, pp. 2, 3, 6B.

22. "FBI Arrests Two in Lynching Case," *New York Times*, January 5, 1947, p. 20.

23. Associated Press, "Georgia Mob of 20 Men Massacres 2 Negroes, Wives: One Man Was Ex-GI," *New York Times*, July 27, 1946, pp. 1, 32; I. P. Reynolds, "Lynch Victims Laid to Rest on Georgia 'Black Sunday,'" *Atlanta Daily World*, July 30, 1946, p. 1; Cordell W. M'Vickers, "$10,000 Reward by Arnall Spurs Statewide Manhunt," *Baltimore Afro-American*, August 3, 1946, TINCF, 233F370; Shields, "Still No Arrests"; George H. Andrews, "*World* Reporters Revisit Lynch Scene," *Atlanta Daily World*, August 4, 1946, p. 1; Thomas W. Johnson to William White, July 28, 1946, 1; Shields, "Georgia Victims Buried as Kin Stay in Hiding," *Daily Worker*, July 30, 1946, TINCF, 233F336.

24. Andrews, "*World* Reporters Revisit," pp. 1, 8; "Georgia: The Best People Won't Talk,'" *Time*, August 5, 1946, 25; Shields, "Georgia Victims Buried."

25. "Four Negroes Ambushed, Slain Near Monroe," *Atlanta Journal,* July 26, 1946, pp. 1, 14; Andrews, "*World* Reporters Revisit," 1, 8; "Racial: Men with Guns," *Newsweek,* August 5, 1946, 24; Fitelson, "Murders at Monroe," 259; Thomas W. Johnson to William White, July 28, 1946, 4.

26. "Farmer Describes Slaughter of Four," *New York Times,* July 27, 1946, p. 32; Tom O'Connor, "Lynch Law Back in Georgia—4 Murdered," *PM,* July 28, 1946, typed copy of article in NAACP ALC, series A, 28F591; "Georgia: 'The Best People Won't Talk,'" 25.

27. Vaughn, "'He Did Not Deserve It!'"

28. "CRC Asks Arrests of Three in Georgia Massacre," *Atlanta Daily World,* August 25, 1946, p. 1; "Reward for Lynchers Hiked near $30,000 by CIO, MU," *Walton Tribune,* August 2, 1946, p. 5; "Four Negroes Ambushed," 1, 14; "Georgia: 'Best People Won't Talk,'" 25; Tom O'Connor, "Leader and Five of Mob Are Known," *PM,* July 30, 1946, typed copy of article in NAACP ALC, series A, 3, 28F602; "Monroe Police Chief Deplores Tragedy: Denies Routing Negroes," *Pittsburgh Courier,* August 3, 1946; Vaughn, "He Did Not Deserve It!"

29. Mrs. Mann Knight, "Ebenezer News," *Walton Tribune,* July 26, 1946, p. 6B.

30. James E. Cutler, *Lynch Law: An Investigation into the History of Lynching in the United States* (New York: Longman, Green, and Co., 1905), 276, quoted in Jacquelyn Dowd Hall, *Revolt Against Chivalry: Jessie Daniel Ames and the Women's Campaign Against Lynching* (New York: Columbia University Press, 1979), 139; James R. McGovern, *Anatomy of a Lynching: The Killing of Claude Neal* (Baton Rouge: Louisiana State University Press, 1982).

31. On Jessie Daniel Ames, see Hall, *Revolt Against Chivalry.* On Emmett Till, see Stephen J. Whitfield, *A Death in the Delta: The Story of Emmett Till* (New York: Free Press, 1988). On Mack Charles Parker, see Howard Smead, *Blood Justice: The Lynching of Mack Charles Parker* (New York: Oxford University Press, 1986).

32. Anne Moody, *Coming of Age in Mississippi* (New York: Dial Press, 1968; reprint, New York: Dell Publishing Co., 1976), 125–26. The best summaries of the literature on the context of lynching are in W. Fitzhugh Brundage, "Mob Violence, North and South, 1865–1940," (review essay), *Georgia Historical Quarterly* 75 (Winter 1991): 748–70; and Brundage, *Lynching in the New South,* 8–16. See also Grace Elizabeth Hale, "Conjuring White Unity: Southern Lynching and the Violence of Modernity, 1900–1950," paper presented at Southern Historical Association meeting, Orlando, Fla., November 1993.

33. National Association for the Advancement of Colored People, *Thirty Years of Lynching in the United States, 1889–1918,* ed. William Loren Katz, with an introduction by Roy Wilkins, "The American Negro: His History and Literature" (New York: National Association for the Advancement of Colored People, 1919; reprint, New York: Arno Press, 1968), 19, 58; "Patrol Disperses Crowd in Monroe," *Atlanta Constitution,* May 23, 1939, Association of Southern Women for the Prevention of Lynching Papers, Woodruff Library, Atlanta University Center, Atlanta, Georgia, microfilm,

3F51; "Troopers Prevent Lynching; Man Sentenced to Die," *Atlanta Daily World,* May 30, 1939, ibid.

34. J. P. Adair, quoted in O'Connor, "Portrait of a Lynch Town," 3.

35. "White Supremacy in Georgia," *New York Times,* July 28, 1946, sec. 4, p. 8; "Georgia: 'The Best People Won't Talk,' " 25; "Racial: Men with Guns," 24.

36. "The Shape of Things," *Nation,* August 3, 1946, p. 270.

37. "Reward for Lynchers Hiked Near $30,000 by CIO, MU," 1; Associated Press, "Georgia Mob of 20 Men," 32.

38. "Reward for Lynchers Hiked Near $30,000 by CIO, MU"; "Reward Hiked to $32,000 Thursday," *Atlanta Daily World,* August 2, 1946, p. 1; "Lynchings Declared 'Blot on Whole U.S.,' " *New York Times,* July 28, 1946, p. 12; "Truman Orders Lynchers Found: Voices Horror at Georgia Crime," *New York Times,* July 31, 1946, pp. 1, 48.

39. "Monroe Churches Denounce Killing of Negroes," *Walton News,* July 31, 1946, p. 1; O'Connor, "Lynch Law Back," 5.

40. Mrs. G. E. Osburn, "Monroe Citizen Speaks Out," letter to the editor, *Atlanta Journal* July 31, 1946, p. 10; Ernest Camp, "Tenting on the Old Campground," *Walton Tribune,* August 2, 1946, p. 1; "Local Lynchings Are Denounced by Press of Nation," *Walton Tribune,* August 9, 1946, p. 2; "Judge Henry H. West Scores Newspapers for Unfairness and Distortion," *Walton News,* August 16, 1946, p. 1; "Western Writer Speaks of Walton Folks," *Walton Times,* August 16, 1946, p. 5.

41. John Dollard made this observation about whites in Mississippi; *Caste and Class,* p. 49.

42. "Colored Pastor Gives Views on Race Relations," no paper, n.d., TINCF, 233F240.

43. "Mob Victims' Funeral Held Up for Two Hours," *Pittsburgh Courier,* August 1, 1946, p. 4; Collier, "Blood of Lynched Negroes."

44. William White to Attorney General Tom Clark, telegram, August 12, 1946, NAACP ALC, series A, 2, 28F406; Eugene Martin to William White, August 8, 1946, NAACP ALC, series A, 1, 28F398.

45. "Monroe, Georgia Typical of South's Cruel Jim Crow," *Amsterdam News,* August 24, 1946, TINCF, 233F353; "The Silent Indictment," *New York Times,* December 21, 1946, p. 18.

46. "Arrest of Loy Harrison as Accessory in Lynchings Urged by Prominent Southerner," *Black Dispatch* (Oklahoma City), August 17, 1946, TINCF, 233F382; Thomas W. Johnson to William White, July 28, 1946, 2.

47. Eugene Martin to William White, August 8, 1946, TINCF, 233F382; Thomas W. Johnson to William White, July 28, 1946, 2.

48. "Arrest of Loy Harrison as Accessory"; Russ J. Cowans, "Georgia Folk Point Finger at Harrison in Lynching of Four," *Detroit Chronicle,* August 10, 1946, TINCF, 233F365; Thomas W. Johnson to William White, July 28, 1946, 5; "Mob Victims' Funeral Held Up," 4; Jan Edmund Boyick, "Talmadge Hate Campaign Responsible

for Georgia 'Mass Murders,' " *Pittsburgh Courier,* August 3, 1946; O'Connor, "Frightened Kin Avoid Lynch Victims' Funeral," *PM,* July 29, 1946, typed copy of article in NAACP ALC, series A, 28F594.

49. "Arrest of Loy Harrison as Accessory"; Cowans, "Georgia Folk Point Finger"; Thomas W. Johnson to William White, July 28, 1946, 5; "Mob Victims' Funeral Held Up," 4; Boyick, "Talmadge Hate Campaign"; O'Connor, "Reward Hiked," 1; "Lynchings Declared 'Blot.' " 12; "Truman Orders," 1, 48.

50. Madison Jones to William White, memorandum, December 7, 1946, NAACP ALC, series A, 28F652; "Inquiry Is Opened in Georgia Lynching," *New York Times,* December 3, 1946, p. 25; "Georgia Inquiry on Lynching Ends," *New York Times,* December 20, 1946, p. 3; "The Shape of Things," *Nation,* August 3, 1946, p. 220.

51. Shields, "Georgia Victims Buried."

52. Hyde Post, Andy Miller, and Peter Scott, "Murder at Moore's Ford," *Atlanta Constitution,* May 31, 1992, pp. A1, A8–10.

Contributors

Jonathan M. Bryant, assistant professor of history at the University of Baltimore, completed his Ph.D. in 1993 under the direction of William McFeely. His essay is an excerpt from his dissertation, "'A County Where Plenty Should Abound': Race, Law, and Markets in Greene County, Georgia, 1850–1885."

Andrew S. Chancey is a doctoral student in history at the University of Florida. He earned his M.A. in 1990 under the direction of Numan Bartley. His essay is drawn from his thesis, "Restructuring Southern Society: The Radical Vision of Koinonia Farm."

Russell Duncan, assistant professor of history at John Carroll University, completed his Ph.D. in 1989 under the direction of Emory Thomas. His essay is drawn from his book *Entrepreneur for Equality: Governor Rufus Bullock, Commerce, and Race in Post–Civil War Georgia* (Georgia, 1994), which is based on his dissertation.

Glenn T. Eskew, an instructor of history at Georgia State University, completed his Ph.D. in 1993 under the direction of Numan Bartley. His essay is based on a seminar paper written for William McFeely in 1990.

Grace Elizabeth Hale is a doctoral student in history at Rutgers University. She completed her M.A. at Georgia in 1991 under the direction of Jean Friedman. Her essay is an outgrowth of her thesis, "Painting the South: Class, Gender, and Race in the Life and Work of Lucy M. Stanton," which began as a seminar paper for Lester Stephens.

John C. Inscoe is associate professor of history at the University of Georgia and editor of the *Georgia Historical Quarterly*.

Randall L. Patton, assistant professor of history at Kennesaw State College, completed his Ph.D. in 1990 under the direction of Numan Bartley. His essay is excerpted from his dissertation, "Southern Liberals and the Emergence of a 'New South,' 1938–1950."

Mary Gambrell Rolinson is a Ph.D. candidate in history at Georgia State University.

She completed her M.A. degree in 1989 under the direction of Numan Bartley. Her essay is drawn from her thesis, "Universal Negro Improvement Associations in the Southern United States: Strongholds of Garveyism."

Mark R. Schultz is a doctoral student in history at the University of Chicago. He earned his M.A. at the University of Georgia in 1989 under the direction of William McFeely. His essay is an extension of the first chapter of his thesis, "A More Satisfying Life on the Farm: Benjamin Hubert and the Log Cabin Community."

Jennifer Lund Smith, a doctoral student at the University of Georgia, teaches history at North Georgia College. She completed her M.A. degree in 1989 under the direction of Emory Thomas. Her essay comes from her thesis of the same title.

Daniel W. Stowell earned a Ph.D. in history at the University of Florida. He completed his M.A. in 1989 under the direction of Jean Friedman. His essay is drawn from his thesis, "The Failure of Religious Reconstruction: The Methodist Episcopal Church in Georgia, 1865–1871."

Wallace H. Warren lives in White County, Georgia, and is working on his M.A. degree under the direction of Numan Bartley. His essay is an expanded version of a seminar paper written under the direction of Lester Stephens in 1990.

Index